Authentication

Authentication

From Passwords to Public Keys

Richard E. Smith

Addison-Wesley

Boston • San Francisco • New York • Toronto • Montreal
London • Munich • Paris • Madrid
Capetown • Sydney • Tokyo • Singapore • Mexico City

Many of the designations used by manufacturers and sellers to distinguish their products are claimed as trademarks. Where those designations appear in this book, and Addison-Wesley, Inc. was aware of a trademark claim, the designations have been printed with initial capital letters or in all capitals.

The author and publisher have taken care in the preparation of this book, but make no expressed or implied warranty of any kind and assume no responsibility for errors or omissions. No liability is assumed for incidental or consequential damages in connection with or arising out of the use of the information or programs contained herein.

The publisher offers discounts on this book when ordered in quantity for special sales. For more information, please contact:

    Pearson Education Corporate Sales Division
    One Lake Street
    Upper Saddle River, NJ 07458
    (800) 382-3419
    corpsales@pearsontechgroup.com

Visit AW on the Web: www.aw.com/cseng/

Library of Congress Cataloging-in-Publication Data

Smith, Richard E., 1952–
    Authentication: from passwords to public keys / Richard E. Smith.
        p. cm.
    Includes bibliographical references and index.
    ISBN 0-201-61599-1 (pbk.).
    1. Computer security. 2. Authentication. I. Title.
QA76.9.A25 S65 2001
005.8–dc21

                                  2001046001

Copyright © 2002 by Addison-Wesley   11-02-01

ISBN 0-201-61599-1
Text printed on recycled paper
1 2 3 4 5 6 7 8 9 10—CRS—0504030201
First printing, October 2001

Dedicated to the memory of
Fred Atwood
1927–2001

as a tribute from one of many
whose personal triumphs owe so much to
Fred's relentless encouragement

CONTENTS

CHAPTER 4
DESIGN PATTERNS

CHAPTER 5
LOCAL AUTHENTICATION

CHAPTER 6
PICKING PINS AND PASSWORDS

CHAPTER 7
BIOMETRICS

CHAPTER 8
AUTHENTICATION BY ADDRESS

CHAPTER 9
AUTHENTICATION TOKENS

CHAPTER 10
CHALLENGE RESPONSE PASSWORDS

CHAPTER 11
INDIRECT AUTHENTICATION

CHAPTER 12
KERBEROS AND WINDOWS 2000

CHAPTER 13
PUBLIC KEYS AND
OFF-LINE AUTHENTICATION

CHAPTER 15
PRIVATE KEY SECURITY

PREFACE

*... upon receiving on her ninety-second birthday the first
copy of* Why Buildings Stand Up, *[my mother-in-law]
said matter-of-factly, "This is nice, but I'd be much more
interested in reading why they fall down."*

— Mario G. Salvadori, *Why Buildings Fall Down*

WHAT THIS BOOK IS ABOUT

Although we're all inspired by engineering triumphs, we often learn
the most from engineering failures. This observation was behind the
book *Why Buildings Fall Down* by Levy and Salvadori, and it's the
driving force behind this book, too. Not only do failures have important lessons to teach, but they have a special power to capture one's
interest unlike a dry recitation of technical criteria or even the
breathless evocation of some techno-utopian ideal.

This book looks at the problem of *authentication*: how computers
can confidently associate an identity with a person. Most computers
use passwords to do this, but even password systems can pose subtle and difficult problems for users, administrators, and developers.
Once we decide to use something fancier than a list of passwords
stored in a server, we face a broad range of choices and their associated risks. In this book we explore those choices by looking at situations in which different techniques fail and by examining ways to
strengthen them. Often it becomes a game of ping-pong in which the
new defense falls to a new attack, which inspires an even newer
defense, and so on.

Individual security measures don't work in a vacuum: they work
in an interconnected web with other measures. This book takes a
high-level, architectural view of that web instead of diving into the
details. Discussions cover physical and procedural requirements for
security as well as technical requirements. Moreover, our technical
discussions will bring up only as much detail as needed to clarify
the security issues. Readers can find the exact order of bits for a

particular protocol elsewhere. Here we focus on why the bits need to be there and what they need to convey. We look at what could happen, or may have happened, if we omit that part of the protocol.

I've tried to include real world examples of every important concept and mechanism. Such examples take abstract concepts and make them concrete. Every example here has a published source or comes from my own experiences assisting others with computer security. In the latter case, names must often be changed to protect the privacy of people and enterprises. When not threatened with retribution, people can be quite honest about how they handle passwords and about unauthorized shortcuts they might employ. Names have been changed or omitted to protect both the innocent and the guilty.

Who This Book Is For

This book is written for people who want to understand both the *how* and *why* of computer authentication. Such people may be designers, developers, administrators, planners, or managers. Authentication is often their first line of defense against attack. The book's principal focus is on existing, off-the-shelf solutions. But in order to understand what we can buy, we often need enough design detail to guide an independent developer to achieve the same security results.

The book assumes a general familiarity with computer systems and the Internet as people typically use them today. It does not require specific knowledge about operating systems, networking protocols, or computer security. The book explains new technical concepts before discussing their implications, and uses plain English, graphical diagrams, and examples to make the important points. Some people learn by reading, others by seeing, and still others by doing. The book tries to accommodate the first two groups directly and, at least, entertain the third with stories of disaster.

It isn't practical to purge mathematical notation entirely from a book like this, even though some readers confront it like a poorly understood second language. Since there are a few places where a little simple algebra goes a long way, the book doesn't try to avoid algebraic notation entirely, but strives to make it straightforward.

ACKNOWLEDGMENTS

Late in 1996 I was finishing up *Internet Cryptography* and describing its status in a hallway discussion with Sandy Miezwa, then a sales executive at Secure Computing Corporation. Being in the throes of trying to meet end-of-year sales targets, she impatiently snapped, "You should have written about authentication. Nobody understands it!" Her comment struck me like that of Salvadori's mother-in-law.

This book benefited from the patient encouragement of my editor, Karen Gettman, of Addison-Wesley. Thanks also to other members of the team: Katie Noyes, John Fuller, Elizabeth Ryan, Chrysta Meadowbrooke, and Emily Frey.

Thanks also to vendors who provided me with extra help, equipment, and materials, including Secure Computing Corporation, RSA Security, American Biometrics Corporation, Cross Match Corporation, Informer Systems, Ltd., and Datakey Corporation.

I would like to thank the people, both the anonymous and the acknowledged, who reviewed this book in its various stages of production. These reviewers have often provided a lot of important technical input as well as showing me how to make things better: Fred Baker of Cisco Systems, Joseph Balsama, Theodore Sedgwick Barassi of Certco, Douglas Barnes of Securify, Bob Bosen of Secure Computing, Bob Bruen, Andrew Brown of Crossbar Security, William Bulley of Merit Network, Steve Koehler of Secure Computing, Phillip Koenig of Electric Kahuna Systems, Brian A. LaMacchia of Microsoft, Marcus Leech of Nortel Networks, David Mitton, Clifford Neuman of the University of Southern California's Information Sciences Institute (USC ISI), Ed Norris, Greg Rose of Qualcomm Australia, John Sellens of Certainty Solutions Canada, Brian Tung of USC ISI, and David Weisman of Lydon, LLP.

Although these people have provided valuable input to this book, I'm the one with the last word. The mistakes are mine, not theirs, and this book does not necessarily reflect what any of them might say on the same topics.

Beyond the reviewers, I've talked to numerous people about technical details contained in this book, often through e-mail. These people have taken the time to answer my questions, supply me with technical fine points, lend me equipment, or, at least, lend me books that I still need to return: Ross Anderson, Maris Bergmanis, Jan Bibee, Anne Chenette, Fernando J. Corbató, Ron Cuffe, Al Dowd, John Gall, Nathan Gilbert, Brian Huss, Georage Jelatis, Colleen Kulhanek, Tim Leonard, Brian Loe, Richard Mills, Roger Needham, Jeff Pomeroy, Fred Roeper, Shirley A. Smith, Tom Van Vleck, Bill Wood, and Jianxin Yan.

I also acknowledge the valuable comments of participants in the security mailing lists I've been following over the past few years, including the Cryptography list moderated by Perry Metzger, the Firewall Wizards list moderated by Marcus Ranum, the Robust Open Source list moderated by Peter Neumann, and the IETF IPSEC mailing list.

I'd also like to thank my colleagues at Secure Computing Corporation for all their inspiration and help. It's terrific to work at a real center of excellence in its field. I can't do justice to everyone there who has helped me out with the book in one way or another, though I've tried to list the particularly guilty ones elsewhere.

I must also thank my bosses for giving me the flexibility I needed to work on this book while holding down a demanding job. Over the years, these have included Dr. Dick O'Brien, Cornelia Murphy, Dr. John Hoffman, a couple of vice presidents: Chris Filo and Carr Biggerstaff, and their boss, our CEO John McNulty. Thanks to all for making Secure Computing a fun place to work again.

I also thank my extended family, friends, and neighbors for putting up with the self-centered obsession that goes with writing a book. Thank you to Team TFNR of the Great American Ski Challenge for a terrific five-year run at ski racing. It made Minnesota winters fun instead of bearable.

I'd also say "thanks" to my wife and kids, but that just doesn't convey what my family has meant to me during the writing process. They've been at Ground Zero of my obsession to get things right, and I've growled at them countless times when they interrupted me while writing a tricky paragraph or trying to align widgets in a diagram. But I don't think I could have finished this book without their comings and goings, and the sense of "home" that emerged from creaking doors, clattering dishes, papers brought home from school, and wandering pets.

CHAPTER 1

THE AUTHENTICATION LANDSCAPE

Open, Sesame!

— Scheherazade (attr.), *Ali Baba and the Forty Thieves*

IN THIS CHAPTER

This chapter provides an overview of *authentication*, the problem of verifying identities, and the major issues in making it work.

- Elements of authentication systems
- Early developments in password authentication
- Attacks via cleverness, theft, and trickery
- Authentication factors: passwords, tokens, biometrics
- Judging attack prevalence
- Summary of the chapter's attacks and defenses

1.1 A VERY OLD STORY

For centuries, people have relied on guards, spoken passwords, and hard-to-forge seals to prove their identity to other people and to verify important messages. Unattended authentication by mechanical devices is also quite old: key-operated locks date back to the ancient Egyptians. Practical mechanisms did their job with as little human interaction as possible.

Unattended authentication is essential with today's computer-based systems. It may be a cliché to call the Internet the "information superhighway," but here it captures truth: we can't afford to post a policeman at every cloverleaf or on the countless

1

interconnected streets and driveways. We must depend on mechanized protection.

The notion of an unattended, password-controlled lock appeared centuries ago in *Ali Baba and the Forty Thieves*, the Mideastern folk tale. In the well-known story, the narrator Scheherazade told of a great treasure hidden in a cave behind a stone. The password "Open, Sesame" caused the stone to move out of the way. Guards in cities of that era also used passwords to allow citizens through the city gates. But the thieves' cave didn't need a human guard to recognize faces, voices, or styles of dress. Instead, there was an unexplained and probably magical device that mechanically responded to the spoken words. Most importantly, the mechanism didn't discriminate between different people speaking the words. It responded to the words themselves, just like modern combination locks or password-protected workstations, which admit anyone knowing the secret.

see Note 1.

The point of Scheherazade's tale is that magic (or mechanism) always follows its own logic, independent of people's wishes or intentions. The same thing plagues us today with computer-based authentication systems. We have a wealth of technical alternatives, each following its own logic and falling to its own distinctive weaknesses. But if we understand the logic and the weaknesses of a given method, we stand a better chance of bending technology to fulfill our real needs.

The passwords and other authentication mechanisms used with computers today cover a broad range of techniques and technologies. Web site designers, e-commerce planners, and other system developers must choose from numerous products and make numerous configuration decisions within each product. Systems like Windows NT and Windows 2000 by themselves incorporate several password alternatives to provide interoperability with other products. Some organizations need the extra security of smart cards or authentication tokens like Safeword or SecurID. A major motivation behind the "public key infrastructure" (or PKI) is to someday revolutionize, strengthen, and simplify individual authentication. But, as with any evolving technology, it's hard to predict how much of its promise it will ultimately achieve.

TABLE 1.1: *Examples of the Five Elements in an Authentication System*

Authentication Element	Cave of the 40 Thieves	Password Login	Teller Machine	Web Server to Client
Person, principal, entity	Anyone who knew the password	Authorized user	Owner of a bank account	Web site owner
Distinguishing characteristic, token, authenticator	The password "Open, Sesame"	Secret password	ATM card and PIN	Public key within a certificate
Proprietor, system owner, administrator	The forty thieves	Enterprise owning the system	Bank	Certificate authority
Authentication mechanism	Magical device that responds to the words	Password validation software	Card validation software	Certificate validation software
Access control mechanism	Mechanism to roll the stone from in front of the cave	Login process, access controls	Allows banking transactions	Browser marks the page "secure"

1.2 ELEMENTS OF AN AUTHENTICATION SYSTEM

Regardless of whether an authentication system is computer based or not, there are several elements usually present, and certain things usually take place. First of all, we have a particular *person* or group of people to be authenticated. Next, we need a *distinguishing characteristic* that differentiates that particular person or group from others. Third, there is a *proprietor* who is responsible for the system being used and relies on mechanized authentication to distinguish authorized users from other people. Fourth, we need an *authentication mechanism* to verify the presence of the distinguishing characteristic. Fifth, we grant some privilege when the authentication succeeds by using an *access control mechanism*, and the same mechanism denies the privilege if authentication fails. Table 1.1 gives examples of these elements.

For example, the person of interest to the thieves' cave might be Ali Baba, his brother, or whichever thief wanted the door to open. The distinguishing characteristic was knowledge of the password, "Open, Sesame." The cave's proprietors were obviously the gang of the Forty Thieves. There was some unexplained authentication

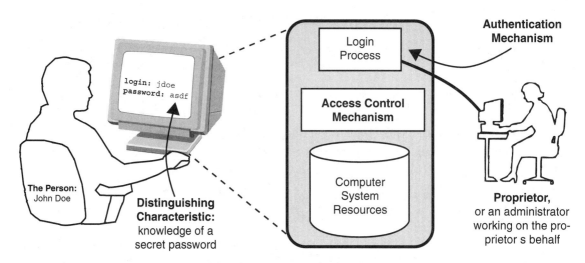

FIGURE 1.1: *Five elements of authentication.* These elements are: the person, the distinguishing characteristic, the proprietor, the authentication mechanism, and the access control mechanism.

device in the cave to identify the correct password and to ignore incorrect ones or, presumably, general conversation (the story did not say what would happen if a thief mentioned the password in a conversation near the cave door; probably the stone would have rolled out of the way). The access control mechanism moved the stone which granted access to the cave.

A genuine example is, of course, the password-controlled login operation we encounter in most computing environments. The person of interest is an individual allowed to use the computer. The system usually assigns the person a symbolic name or user identification code which we will call the *user name.* For example, John Doe is an authorized user of the system in Figure 1.1, and the proprietor has assigned him the user name "jdoe." The distinguishing characteristic for John Doe is his secret password, "asdf." The process should be familiar: John gets the computer's attention and the computer's login process prompts him for a user name and a password. The process contains an authentication procedure that compares the typed-in password against the password established by or for John Doe; the procedure succeeds if the two match. The access control mechanism allows John to proceed with using the system, and the system uses John's user name whenever it makes access control decisions on protected resources.

When looking at computer security problems, we always need to distinguish what we want to do from what we really do. The former question, "what we want," is usually spoken of as *security objectives*. The gang of the Forty Thieves, for example, had the objective of protecting their loot from theft. They relied on a *security mechanism*, the cave's door, to do this. In a computing system, the proprietor has the objective of granting access only to authorized users. In Figure 1.1, the proprietor relies on the operating system, and its password controlled login, to achieve this objective.

As a practical matter, there's always a gap between what we want and what really happens. A lock lets anyone in, as long as they have a copy of the right key. The lock does not keep the wrong people out unless we can prevent the wrong people from having a key. That can be hard to do, especially if the people we lock out really want to get past that door. Moreover, we can't always afford to put separate locks on everything. Often there's just a big lock on the outer door, and we have to trust the people we've allowed inside.

Computer systems usually provide authentication and access control as clearly separate things. While it sometimes makes sense in the mechanical world to distinguish between the bolt that holds the door shut and the lock that controls the bolt, such things are often built into a single mechanism. On computers, the authentication process establishes the correct user name to use, and access control happens separately. Computer systems generally control access by comparing the person's user name with the access rules tied to a particular file or other resource. If the rules grant access by the person with that user name, then the person gets to use the resource.

The Forty Thieves intended their cave to grant access only to members of the band, but the mechanism couldn't prevent others from using the password. This problem infects both authentication and access control. In authentication, we can identify the people we want to allow to use a system, but the mechanisms aren't perfect. There's always a way for an unauthorized person to masquerade as a legitimate user.

We have a similar problem in access control: we want to authorize certain people to use the system, and we implement those desires by setting up the access control system to allow this. In an ideal security engineering world, we grant access using the principle of "least privilege," in which people have just as many permissions and privileges as they need: no more, no less. But in the real world, the access control system can't give people exactly the privileges they need: we must either give them too many or omit a few that they really need. In a practical world we usually extend a measure of trust to authorized users so that they have the tools to get their work done, even though this technically gives them permission to do things they shouldn't be doing.

Access control can be very complex, even without trying to achieve least privilege. Modern computing systems provide a broad range of access control policies and mechanisms. Even the access control mechanisms provided by relatively common systems like Unix, Windows NT, or Windows 2000 allow users and administrators to establish very complicated sets of rules for granting or denying the use of various computer resources. However, many organizations take the relatively simple approach of tying access control and authentication together, so that authenticated users have only a few broad access restrictions.

Although the problem of authenticating people poses a real challenge to computer systems, they aren't the only entities we need to authenticate. We also need to authenticate unattended computer systems like Web servers, especially when we ask them to perform an expensive service. Unlike user authentication, there isn't really a person standing at the server for us to authenticate. Instead, we want to ensure that we speak to the right piece of equipment under the control of the right people or enterprise. We don't want to order boots from a computer claiming to be "L. L. Bean" unless we will receive the boots. When we authenticate L. L. Bean's server, we need confidence that its distinguishing characteristic is managed and controlled by the L. L. Bean enterprise. Usually, the browser warns its operator if it can't authenticate the site, and leaves the access control decision to the operator ("Should I still order boots, even though this site doesn't really seem to be L. L. Bean? I don't think so!"). In a sense, the process turns the automatic authentication function upside-down, but the underlying concepts are still the same.

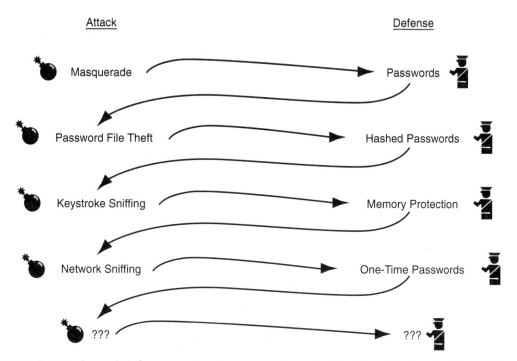

FIGURE 1.2: *Attacks and defenses evolve in response to each other.* As attacks develop, defenses develop in response. Newer attacks evolve to circumvent the new defenses. The examples shown here tell only the beginning of the story.

REVISED ATTACKS AND REVISED DEFENSES

Today's authentication systems evolved from decades of attacks, many of them successful. Starting with password systems in the early days of timesharing, authentication systems have been under constant attack. The earliest attacks were from members of the local user community protesting against the notion of authentication and access control. Early success at stealing password files led to a defensive measure called *password hashing.* This led to attempts to intercept ("sniff") passwords, which in turn led to other defensive measures. Figure 1.2 illustrates the general progression of increasingly sophisticated defenses in response to increasingly sophisticated attacks. While the figure doesn't represent an accurate historical time line, it accurately captures the dynamics of an ongoing competition between proprietors and attackers. Later sections of the book describe these attacks and defenses in detail.

Several of these attacks appear in the next section on the evolution of passwords in timesharing systems. Each attack description is marked with a numbered "bomb" icon in the right margin, shown here. The attack's number begins with "A-" and is keyed to the summary of attacks at the end of the chapter. The "uniformed guard" icon in the right margin indicates the description of a defense, usually against a recently described attack. Again, the defense's number is keyed to a summary of defenses at the end of the chapter. As suggested by the figure, the bombs and guards tend to alternate throughout the book.

A-n

D-n

SECURITY STRATEGIES

An important question to ask about any defensive measure is whether or not it is truly necessary in a given situation. Although this question often hinges on technical questions (i.e., does the defense do its job in the particular situation?), it also hinges on questions of organizational policy and the motivation behind its security activities. There are three general policy rationales to justify security measures:

- **Standards of due care**

  This is a legalistic concept. Businesses are legally obligated to install well-known safety measures to protect against well-known risks. Court cases have found businesses negligent for failing to do so in other industries, although there are as yet no such precedents involving information security. However, some information security measures are so common and so well known that they are obvious candidates for representing standards of due care. Anything noted in this book as an *essential defense* should be considered a minimum standard for due care and should always be present.

  see Note 2.

- **Risk analysis**

  This approach is based on a cost/benefit trade-off. A business determines that it should install security measures (at a particular cost) by estimating the losses it might incur from likely attacks. This computation is often called *risk analysis*, and the U.S. government published a standard describing the process (the standard was withdrawn in 1995). Because of management

and budgetary inertia, enterprises rarely perform such assess-
ments until after a significant loss occurs. Occasionally, an
enterprise learns from the mistakes of its peers and installs a
defense before they themselves are attacked.   *see Note 3.*

- **Exceed industry practices**

  In this approach, a business tries to avoid attack by posing a
  slightly more challenging target than its neighbors. For example,
  most banks use conventional passwords to protect all on-line
  transactions, even for large corporate customers. A bank can
  deter certain types of fraud from large accounts by adopting
  one-time passwords. In theory, this should encourage attackers
  to turn their attention to other banks, since weaker security
  measures are easier to overcome.

  In some regions this is called the "bear chase" strategy, based
  on an old adage: when a bear chases your group of hunters, you
  yourself don't have to outrun the bear, you only have to outrun
  the slowest hunter. In practice, some companies do this after a
  peer suffers a serious loss: they install a defense against the
  same type of attack before they suffer loss themselves.

The best balance for most enterprises probably combines these
approaches. By meeting standards of due care the enterprise can
deter claims of negligence. By implementing industry practices the
enterprise avoids drawing attacks by being perceived as an easy target. By exceeding expectations, the enterprise poses an unpredictable target for potential attackers. Even if the enterprise can't afford
to do a full cost/benefit risk analysis, there are often a few obviously
risky areas where improved security pays for itself.

Today, the right authentication choices for a particular enterprise
or application depend on how people use the systems in question,
how the systems are built, and what types of attacks they expect. We
explore those choices by looking at how well different authentication
systems have worked over the years and what problems persist
today. The authentication capabilities of today's commercial systems, and the promise of tomorrow's evolving systems, all stand
upon our past successes and failures.

1.3 AUTHENTICATION IN TIMESHARING SYSTEMS

We start with a look at timesharing systems because they have a lot
in common with modern server systems and because they hold the
genesis of modern password systems. Just as cheap locks remain
popular for desks and cabinets, passwords will always play some
role in computer-based authentication. Today, they are wildly popular on Internet Web and e-commerce sites. While password security
isn't foolproof, modern systems reflect many lessons learned from
the days of timesharing systems.

In the earliest days of computers, the computer itself didn't have
to handle access control and authentication. People either worked
with the computer directly (if they could unlock the computer room
door) or they submitted computer programs to other people (computer operators) to run the programs on their behalf. This changed
in the 1960s with the advent of timesharing systems, which were
the first interactive "server" systems that provided services to lots of
different, noninterchangeable people simultaneously.

The Compatible Time Sharing System (CTSS) at the Massachusetts Institute of Technology (MIT) was arguably the first successful
timesharing system. Its designers, notably Fernando J. Corbató,
envisioned a system that handled a large and varied community
with hundreds of users. Under such circumstances, Corbató saw
the need for some degree of privacy and separation between different people's work. Moreover, computers back then were astronomi-
cally expensive by today's standards: a single second of borrowed
CPU time could cost $100, and often cost more.

To provide the modest level of security Corbató thought sufficient
for an academic environment, he proposed what seemed to him an
obvious solution. Students generally stored personal items in metal
lockers secured with combination locks: it was a simple matter to
provide a similar, memorized "lock" for timesharing users. In 1963,
the feature was added to CTSS. From then on, people had to type a
memorized "private code" in addition to the user name that told
CTSS how to find their personal files.   *see Note 4.*

Today, of course, we refer to Corbató's private code as a *password.* Figure 1.3 illustrates the basic mechanism. The computer
asks the person to type in a user name and a password. The com-

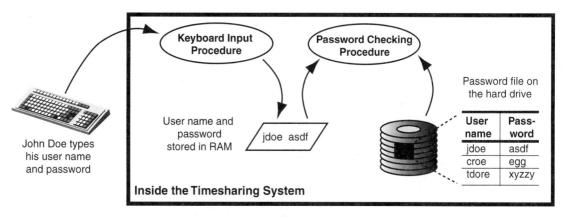

FIGURE 1.3: *Basic password checking on a timesharing system.* John Doe's user name and password are read into main memory. The user name is used to look up the password in the system's password file. The typed-in password must match the copy stored in the system password file, otherwise the procedure fails.

puter searches the system's password file for an entry matching the user name. If the password in that entry matches the password just typed, then the login succeeds.

Some early computer users, particularly among the technically sophisticated ones called "hackers," did not like the notion of user names and passwords. They might have tolerated the restrictions of locked doors or computer operators, but the password mechanism was different. It took power away from them and put the computer itself in charge. This role reversal unsettled some and outraged others.

see Note 5.

PASSWORDS UNDER ATTACK

A battle of wits ensued. Programmers who missed the absolute control they had over the computer would probe the timesharing software, and the password mechanism in particular, looking for flaws that would give them back their lost power. The programmers responsible for the timesharing system would examine their own work to try to stay one step ahead.

Sometimes the timesharing programmers did stay ahead. Across the Charles River from CTSS, at Boston University's Remote Access Computing System (RAX), a timesharing programmer was looking

```
#*rax v3 m86, sign on.
/id 10,ma319,001
*password?
●●●●●●
*sign-on at        13.19  14 dec 73
*see /news for the christmas schedule ⌐⌐⌐⌐⌐⌐
*in case of restart, use /restart  10,10,ma319001
*go
```

FIGURE 1.4: *Logging on a timesharing system.* The timesharing system printed the first line to identify itself. The user typed the line starting with a slash to identify himself. The system asked for the password and overprinted several characters in a row so that other users could not read the typed password. This is called *password blinding.* The remaining lines were typed by the RAX timesharing system after the login succeeded.

over the program that checked a typed password (Figure 1.4). The program was unusually complicated because programmers had revised it several times to allow backspacing and other line editing functions to correct password typing errors. Suddenly the programmer realized that a peculiar sequence of backspace, tab, and line delete characters would cause the program to log the person on without checking the password at all. He managed to correct the problem before anyone else found out about the problem and tried to use it.

    A-1

Other times, the hackers got the upper hand. Back at CTSS, members of the local hacking community found that the weak point in the password system was often the password file itself. The CTSS programming staff tried to build the system so that users could not retrieve the password file, since the file listed the names and passwords of all CTSS users. According to legend, a hacker would occasionally manage to extract a copy of the password file from its secluded location, print it out, and post the file on a nearby bulletin board for all to see.

    A-2

The most notorious occasion, however, was blamed on a flaw in CTSS itself. One afternoon, an administrator was editing the password file at the same time another administrator was editing the daily message, which was automatically displayed whenever a user logged in. Inside CTSS, the editor program confused the temporary file containing the daily message with the temporary file containing the passwords. Whenever someone logged in, the system automati-

cally displayed the password file to them. Naturally, the problem
emerged late on a Friday afternoon and went unnoticed until after
the administrators left for the weekend. It persisted until a thoughtful user invoked a hardware fault that crashed the computer.   *see Note 6.*

In these early days, many timesharing programmers treated bug
fixing as their principal defense against such attacks. While some
considered passwords a practical but limited security technique,
others really believed they could provide foolproof authentication,
especially given the physical arrangement of typical timesharing
systems (Figure 1.5). Any weaknesses were caused by fixable software flaws, not by fundamental weaknesses in the technique itself.
This attitude hinged on two assumptions: first, the programmers
believed they could identify and eliminate most, if not all, of the
security flaws in the system; and second, they believed the system
could reliably prevent users from reading the password file.

Security experts today would dispute both assumptions. By the
1960s, computing systems had become too complex to ever be bug-

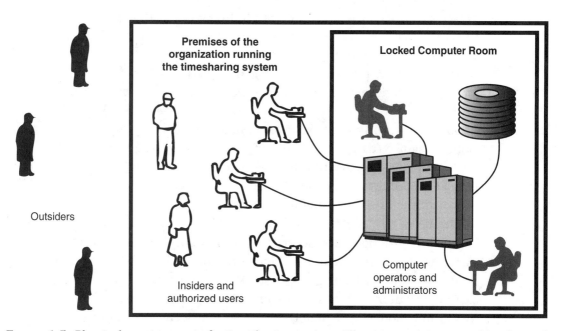

FIGURE 1.5: *Physical arrangement of a timesharing system.* All equipment connected to the earliest timesharing systems resided within the physical premises of the organization that ran the
system. The computer itself was kept inside a locked computer room, following the older tradition
of batch processing sites.

free. Large-scale software design was in its infancy; the RAX line
editing problem might not happen today because the particular
problem could be "designed out" of the password handling proce-   *D-1*
dures. The same is true for the problem underlying the switched
files on CTSS.

But these problems were replaced by other, unexpected ones. In
practice it has proven almost impossible to unconditionally protect a
file from unauthorized reading. In a classic attack, a user privileged
to see a protected file, like the password file, could be tricked into   *A-3*
running a program that secretly copied the file to an easy-to-reach
location. That style of attack was named the *Trojan horse*. If any
program on the system could read a secret file, then attackers could
usually find a way for other programs to do the same thing.

HASHED PASSWORDS

In 1967, Cambridge University started running their Titan timesharing system on a continuous basis in order to provide a reliable,
full-time computing service to the university community. Even in
1967, people knew it was essential to make back-up copies of files
to protect against disasters. But these back-up tapes posed a security dilemma, since they held copies of Titan's password file.   *see Note 7.*

One evening, Roger Needham was sharing a few pints with
another Titan developer, Mike Guy, and discussing the vulnerability
of password files stored on back-up tapes. They struck on the
notion of encrypting the passwords using a "one-way cipher" that
would disguise the passwords in an irreversible way. The procedure   *D-2*
converted a text password into an undecipherable series of bits that
attackers couldn't easily convert back into the password's text. Mike
coded up the one-way function and they installed the revised logon
mechanism.   *see Note 8.*

One-way functions are depressingly common in real life: it takes
moments to injure or break something, but it can take hours or
weeks to make it whole again, or stacks of money to replace it with a
new copy. Automobile accidents provide an extreme case: it takes a
lot of time, money, and material to build a new car, but it takes only
a moment to "total" that car in a crash. Mathematics provides similar functions: we can easily combine numbers in various ways, but

it might be difficult or impossible to figure out what numbers we started with.

The function that Guy and Needham installed in Titan is today called a *one-way hash*. Figure 1.6 shows how we use it with passwords. When John Doe logs on, he types his user name and password as usual, and they're read into RAM. Next, the system applies the one-way hash procedure to his password. Then the system extract's John's entry from the password file on the system's hard drive. The password entry contains a copy of John's password as it appears after applying the one-way hash procedure. If John typed the right password, the hashed copy should match the copy in the password file.

The one-way hash thwarts the objective of stealing the password file from the back-up tape (or from anywhere else), since attackers can't retrieve users' passwords simply by looking at the stolen password file. The technique is still used today: every modern server system stores passwords in hashed form. Password hashing has become an essential defense in any system that uses passwords.

A good one-way hash function has two properties. First, the function must compute a result (the *hash*) that depends on all of the input data. The hash result should be different, and often wildly different, whenever we make minor changes to its input. Second, there

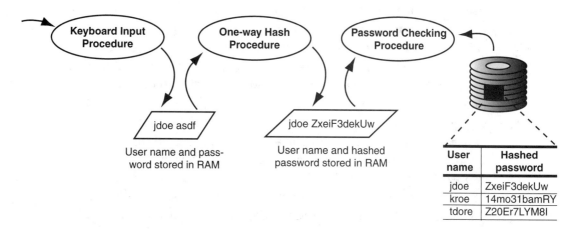

FIGURE 1.6: *Checking a hashed password.* John Doe's user name and password are read into main memory. A one-way hash procedure transforms the password into an undecipherable mass of bits. The password checking procedure compares the hashed version of the typed-in password against the hashed password stored with John's user name in the password file.

must be no practical way to convert the hash result back into the original data. Since the function accepts an arbitrarily large amount of input data and yields a fixed amount of output, it's going to be possible to generate the same output to two different hash results. Even so, there should be no easy way to find the input data that yields a particular hash result.

In fact, there should be no way to produce a particular result from a one-way hash function except by trying all possible input values until the desired hash result appears. Encryption procedures have a similar property: there should be no simple way to deduce the original plaintext data from the encrypted data unless one knows what encryption key was used (we will take a closer look at encryption in Section 5.3). However, encryption procedures are designed to be reversible, and that's why they use a key. We don't need to reverse the password hashing and, in fact, the passwords are safer that way.

A system that uses hashed passwords must perform the hash whenever someone enters a password into the system. First, the system hashes the initial password assigned to the user before storing it in the password file. Then every procedure on the system that collects a password from the user must hash it before doing anything further. The login procedure hashes the password before comparing it against the password file. The password changing procedure hashes the old password to authenticate the user before allowing the password to change, and then hashes the new password before storing it in the password file.

Many timesharing designers adopted password hashing over the next several years. Developers at MIT used the technique in the ambitious follow-on system to CTSS known as Multics, the "Multiplexed Information and Computing Service." However, the Multics experience illustrated the importance of using a good hash function. In the early 1970s, the U.S. Air Force began "Project ZARF," which probed the security of the early Multics system. The Air Force team quickly penetrated Multics file protection and stole a copy of the password file. After examining the hash function it used, they found a way to invert it. At a subsequent meeting with the Multics developers, the ZARF team presented a slip of paper to the author of the password software, and he found his password written on it. The security problems were largely cleared up in subsequent versions of Multics and, in time, it developed one of the best reputations in the community for operating system security.

see Note 9.

1.4 ATTACKING THE SECRET

Clearly, passwords will not work if people can steal them directly from the authentication system. But this isn't the only way of retrieving passwords. Attackers can also exploit the fact that most people do a bad job of creating and keeping secrets. This opens the door for guessing attacks and social engineering.

GUESSING ATTACKS

Although technically savvy attackers might go after a password file, other attackers might take a simpler approach: they exploit human nature to try to guess what passwords people use. In a typical case, the attacker develops a list of possible passwords and makes successive attempts to log on using the different passwords. We refer to this general strategy as a *trial-and-error* attack. Uninspired attackers might try every legal password in hopes of hitting the victim's password soon. Cleverer attackers construct a list of likely passwords, like the victim's name, the victim's spouse's name, the victim's kids' names, and so on.

A-4

Guessing attacks can succeed if people are careless about password selection and if trial-and-error attacks proceed without detection. The first defense against such attacks is to keep an *audit trail* of attempts to log on to the system. An audit trail is a record of significant events within the system and is a common feature in modern computing systems. Auditing in Unix is provided by the syslog facility, and both Windows NT and Windows 2000 provide similar features. All computing systems that meet U.S. government security requirements (traditionally defined by the *Trusted Computer System Evaluation Criteria*, or TCSEC) must provide an auditing mechanism. Typically, an audit system will record the date, time, user name, and specific details associated with each audited event.

D-3

see Note 10.

Unfortunately, detailed audit records can actually cause problems with password mechanisms. In most cases, a good audit mechanism will record enough information so that someone reviewing the audit later can reconstruct what happened in great detail, even to the point of understanding the types of mistakes users have made. Clearly, however, audit records about password authentication should never include the typed password, whether the password was correct or not. If a potential attacker reviewed the audit log, misspelled passwords would clearly provide strong hints as to the actual password.

Even basic audit records can unintentionally leak passwords when they record the user name. Occasionally, when people respond to a prompt to log on, they enter the password when they should enter the user name. For example, imagine what would happen in Figure 1.1 if John mistyped his user name and/or password a couple of times in a row. If he types the return or enter key too many times, he may find himself typing his user name into the password prompt and his password into a subsequent user name prompt. If the system generates an audit record of this mistake, the record will contain his password. Then an attacker can retrieve John's password by reviewing the audit log.

A-5

The typical defense against this is to treat password auditing as a special case. While the audit software normally attempts to record the user name associated with an event, we must admit that we really don't know what user name to associate with logging on until the operation has succeeded. We achieve better security if we focus on trying to detect guessing attacks instead of burying the password attempts in audit records. A typical strategy, used by systems ranging from RAX to Windows 2000, is to keep a separate count of unsuccessful password attempts for each user name. RAX would report unsuccessful password attempts to the system operator (a full-time employee, since RAX ran on a traditional IBM mainframe) and also report the number of bad password attempts each time the user successfully logged on. Windows 2000 provides a mechanism to explicitly limit password guessing: Windows will "lock out" an account and not accept any attempts to log on following an excessive number of unsuccessful attempts. The threshold is established by an administrator. Unfortunately, this lockout mechanism has a negative impact on usability as discussed in Chapter 6.

D-4

SOCIAL ENGINEERING

Some attackers don't even bother with password guessing; they simply ask for the password. This remains the biggest problem with passwords: there is no way to prevent someone's sharing secret information with someone else. Often, a clever attacker can trick someone into sharing a secret password, saving the attacker the trouble of performing a technical attack on the target system. Such trickery is usually called a *social engineering* attack.

The typical attack has been summarized best by Jerry Neal Schneider, one of the earliest computer criminals on record, who went into the computer security business after being released from jail. When interviewed in 1974, Schneider declared that he could break into any timesharing system in existence. He demonstrated this by cajoling a system operator into giving him a password. When the observer objected that Schneider hadn't "really" broken into the system, Schneider replied, "Why should I go to all the work of trying to technically penetrate a computer when it is so easy to con my way in through the timesharing service personnel?"

A-6

see Note 11.

Another story, recounted by Katie Hafner and John Markoff, described a "cheerful technician" who called up a company, claimed to be the service representative for their computer vendor, and asked if they were having performance problems. Of course, just about everyone who owns a computer is convinced that it is not working as hard as it should, so the company was happy to give the technician a login and password so he could "fix" the problem. At some point, however, a site administrator found something suspicious. He called the vendor, only to find that no such "cheerful technician" worked there.

see Note 12.

Fortunately, most modern systems resist this attack because they use password hashing. Operators, administrators, and help desk people can't possibly reveal passwords because the password file contains only the hash values, not the password text. The remaining risk is the handling of lost passwords: an attacker could claim to be a legitimate user with a lost password. Then the attacker can talk the help desk into changing a victim's password and disclosing the new one to the attacker. The only way to protect against that is by restricting the password change procedure. Some sites might simply refuse to change users' passwords remotely, but instead require

D-5

that users arrange to replace lost passwords in person. Other sites might accept remote requests to change passwords, but then deliver the new password via a different (and hopefully safer) path that should reach the legitimate user instead of an attacker.

Of course, attackers can still social engineer a password without battling the help desk. One way is to approach individual users and trick them out of their passwords. For example, the attacker could call John and make a speech of the following sort:

> Mr. Doe, my security assessment has revealed that the symmetric bi-quinary azimuth of your datasets has been corrupted. You must log off immediately to prevent damage to your differential b-tree entries. I need to log on from your precise execution context in order to verify the longitudinal redundancy of your i-nodes. Please supply me with your most recent login name and password so I can prevent the irretrievable loss of your files.

While many computer users might recognize such a speech as pure drivel, others will be chanting their password before the attacker has run out of breath. Telephone fraudsters have used similar speeches for years to trick people out of credit card numbers. The successful attacker simply needs to convince the victim that disaster is imminent and the attacker can prevent it, once the victim divulges the secret.

The best defense against such an attack is to establish a policy of never, never sharing passwords with anyone, including administrators. Otherwise, an attacker can probably trick a gullible person into *D-6* revealing a password simply by twisting the policy to make it sound like a legitimate request. Modern server systems should never require users to share their passwords with administrators. If administrators need access to something, they can generally do it from an administrative role.

A different attack yields a similar result by turning the tables. In April 1991, several Internet sites reported that their users received the following e-mail message, or variants thereof:

```
To: [ adddress list suppressed]
From: root
Subject: Security Alert


This is the system administration:
  Because of security faults, we request that you change
your password to "systest001". This change is MANDATORY
and should be done IMMEDIATLY. You can make this change
by typing "passwd" at the shell prompt. Then, follow the
directions from there on.
  Again, this change should be done IMMEDIATLY. We will
inform you when to change your password back to normal,
which should not be longer than ten minutes.


          Thank you for your cooperation,


          The system administration (root)
```
see Note 13.

The message was, again, complete nonsense. The message took advantage of the ease with which attackers can forge Internet e-mail addresses in order to trick people into changing their passwords. *A-7* Naturally, the attackers would simply wait for people to change their passwords, and somehow never get around to sending a message telling them to change their passwords back.

In a truly extreme case, an attacker might go after the victim directly and use threats or physical harm to extract a password or a similar secret. Indulging in black humor, cryptographers often refer *A-8* to this as *rubber hose cryptanalysis*, since the secret could be an encryption key as well as a computer password.

One approach to reduce the risk of such attacks, particularly when the victim and proprietor are both trying to defend against the attack, is to implement a *duress signal* in the authentication mechanism. The signal is similar to the silent alarm a teller might activate during a bank robbery. In an authentication mechanism, the victim *D-7* sends the signal via a seemingly legitimate variant of the conventional login procedure. For example, a person could have two passwords, one to indicate a legitimate login operation and a separate one to use when forced.

A duress signal, however, is only worthwhile if the victim is going to use it. Victims may be too traumatized to remember the duress signal, particularly if they've had no practice using it. Moreover, bank tellers use silent alarms when they believe it will increase their chances of survival. Few victims use a duress signal simply to protect the proprietor; they are more likely to use it if the signal will summon help but won't put them in greater danger.

In his role working with agents sent behind enemy lines during World War II, Leo Marks became very skeptical of the value of duress signals in real-world applications. In many cases, the agents appeared to have revealed all of their operating procedures to their captors, including signals for both routine and duress messages. Moreover, duress signals were rarely recognized as such, and the headquarters in Britain often interpreted them as erroneous transmissions.

see Note 14.

A victim has to know exactly how the duress signal will be handled in order to have confidence in its value. At a minimum, a computer-based duress signal should alert the system's proprietor that a member of the user population is in serious trouble. The computer system itself should also take some action to minimize damage from the attack. However, victims are unlikely to use a duress signal if it simply disables their computer account, since that would clearly announce to the attacker that a duress signal was used.

A more promising approach is for the duress signal to cause subtle but important changes in the victim's capabilities as a system user. The attackers should feel that they have gained access to the victim's resources while really being prevented from doing serious harm to the system. Some sites use a similar approach for handling remote intrusions: the attackers are diverted to a special system called a *honey pot*. To the attackers, the honey pot looks like an attractive system to attack, when in fact its resources are all a sham to divert attackers' interest away from the really important systems. The honey pot is supposed to keep the attackers connected to the system while the proprietor's investigators, and possibly law enforcement, try to track them down. This approach could also be applied to duress signals: the signal would connect the victim to a

D-8

honey pot, giving the attackers the illusion of penetrating the system without actually placing critical resources at risk.

1.5 SNIFFING ATTACKS

In password *sniffing*, the attacker tries to intercept a copy of the secret password as it travels from its owner to the authentication mechanism. Like guessing attacks, sniffing attacks start off with relatively trivial, low-tech mechanisms. But over the years, attackers have developed numerous high-tech approaches to sniffing. Risks from sniffing place a limit on all password systems: the more the password must travel around, the more opportunity attackers have to sniff it.

One type of sniffing starts right at a person's elbow: a nearby attacker can look over a person's shoulder and watch him type his password. This is called *shoulder surfing*. Modern systems either don't echo the password or they use a variant of the password blinding shown in Figure 1.4 to reduce this risk. Some systems go so far as to echo a different number of blinded characters than the actual number of characters typed. Despite these techniques, it is sometimes possible to watch the keystrokes themselves. Passwords are vulnerable to even more sniffing as they travel from the keyboard to the authentication mechanism.

A-9

D-9

SNIFFING IN SOFTWARE

Figure 1.7 shows a classic sniffing attack associated with timesharing systems, like the RAX system. When people logged in, the system copied the user name and password into a special area of RAM called the keyboard input buffer. The password checking procedure compared the data in the input buffer against the password stored on the RAX hard drive and logged the user on if the password matched. Meanwhile, however, another user on the RAX system could run a "sniffer" program that copied information out of the keyboard input buffer as people typed. The attacker watched the typed information especially closely when people logged on, since both the user name and the password would promptly show up in the input buffer.

A-10

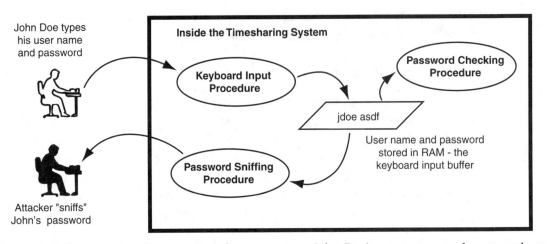

FIGURE 1.7: *Password sniffing on a timesharing system.* John Doe's user name and password are read into RAM. The attacker runs a "sniffing" program that retrieves passwords from the RAM location where the keyboard input procedure reads them in. Password hashing does not protect against this attack, since the password must always arrive from the keyboard input procedure in plaintext form.

Although the RAX system at the time did not implement any form of password hashing or encryption, such a mechanism would not have protected against this attack. The keyboard input procedure had to read the entire password into RAM without hashing it first. RAX ran on an IBM mainframe (the IBM 360 family) and the IBM computer hardware put restrictions on how data was exchanged with peripheral devices like keyboards. In particular, the keyboard input procedure was written as a "channel program" that could only read a full line of text at a time from a keyboard. Whenever a user typed a password, the channel program had to read the entire line of text containing the password directly into RAM. There was no way for the RAX software to disguise the password before it was stored in RAM in a sniffable form.

Instead, the attack was blocked by changing the RAX system to restrict use of the keyboard input buffer. The IBM mainframe *D-10* included memory protection features that RAX already used to keep user programs from accidentally writing information into other people's keyboard input buffers or from damaging other system data in RAM. The software was changed so that only the RAX system software itself was allowed to see the contents of people's keyboard input buffers. When the attacker's sniffer program attempted to read data from someone's buffer, the mainframe hardware blocked the attempt, generated a signal, and RAX aborted the sniffer program.

Modern systems can be vulnerable to the same threat and usually solve it the same way. The hardware protections provided on classic IBM mainframes are standard equipment on state-of-the-art microprocessors like the PowerPC and the Pentium. Sophisticated operating systems like Unix, Mac OS X, Windows NT, and Windows 2000 protect keyboard input buffers from sniffing.

Unfortunately, traditional desktop systems like Windows 95 or 98, and single-user Macintosh systems, rarely make use of hardware protection mechanisms. Sniffers designed for single-user systems usually save the password information in a file or transmit it across a network to another computer. Sniffer programs targeting those systems are common features in collections of hacker tools. Well-known sniffers in the Windows environment include "keycopy," "playback," and "keytrap." Sniffer software poses a very real threat in academic and educational settings where roomfuls of personal workstations are shared among many students and occasionally with administrators.

Not all sniffer problems are hacker based. In an attempt to prevent computer misuse by employees, several organizations use *keystroke monitor* software. This software works almost exactly like a sniffer except that it collects *every* keystroke. This allows managers to review employee activities and identify employees that indulge in personal or recreational activities on company time or equipment. Unfortunately, any employee that looks at the keystroke monitor logs will be able to retrieve passwords of monitored employees. This makes the logs even more sensitive than system password files, since modern password files are usually hashed. Keystroke monitoring poses a dilemma wherever passwords are used, since managers must choose between monitoring and the reliable authentication of employees.   *see Note 15.*

Just as timesharing and other forms of distributed computing brought the need for authentication and passwords, it also produced some new threats as computing became even more distributed. As connections became more widespread and systems were used for more and more important tasks, sites had to contend with sniffing threats on their communications lines. Matters got even worse with the evolution of the Internet.

In early 1994, network news broadcasts made an unprecedented announcement: All computer users on the Internet should change their passwords. The announcement was triggered by a notorious sniffing incident: a centrally located Internet service had been penetrated and an attacker had installed unattended sniffer programs to collect passwords from the user traffic passing through it. Further investigations found sniffer programs in many other Internet sites. Investigators estimated that at least 100,000 passwords were collected by the sniffers they found.

see Note 16.

The evening news recommendation reflects a major advantage of passwords—if the user thinks the password has been stolen, it is relatively easy to block the attacker from exploiting the stolen one by replacing it with a new one. This is another essential defense: every password system must have a mechanism to allow users to change their passwords easily.

D-11

TROJAN LOGIN

Another clever method for intercepting passwords is a *Trojan login* program. This is a program that tricks people into revealing their passwords. Unlike the Trojan horse program described earlier, this one doesn't need to have the victim start it up. Instead, the attacker starts up the Trojan login program on some workstations or terminals, and the program's display perfectly mimics the system's standard login program. For example, a RAX Trojan login program would print the following text, just as shown in Figure 1.4:

 A-11

```
#*rax v3 m86, sign on.
```

When someone like John Doe tries to log on by typing the appropriate command ("/id"), the Trojan login program saves a copy of his user name in a secret file. Then the program types "*Password?" on one line and the blinding characters on the next. When John types his password, the program responds by typing "*Password incorrect." Meanwhile, the program saves John's typed-in password in the file along with his user name. Finished, the program exits and logs out. If John tries again, he sees the same printout on the terminal, but this time it comes from the actual RAX login procedure. Meanwhile, the attacker has captured John's password.

Modern systems solve this problem with a *secure attention* signal. This is a special keystroke that the underlying system always recognizes as a request for special services like logging on. Whenever someone types that keystroke, the system intercepts it and runs a built-in program to find out what the person wants to do. The secure attention key provides a *trusted path* between the person operating the computer and a piece of trustworthy software on the computer. The U.S. government requires the presence of a trusted path mechanism on systems with extremely high security requirements as described in the TCSEC.

D-12

see Note 17.

User application programs, like the Trojan login program, never see the secure attention signal, so they can't perform their masquerade. Microsoft Windows NT and Windows 2000 use the keystroke control-alt-delete as a secure attention signal. Other systems, like Digital's VAX/VMS and high security versions of Unix, also provide secure attention keys.

VAN ECK SNIFFING

In 1985, a Dutch scientist named Wim van Eck described how one could eavesdrop on any video monitor using relatively simple techniques. Video monitors use a lot of energy, and the process of scanning data onto the phosphorescent screen of a video tube generates lots of stray electromagnetic signals. The signals are called *van Eck radiation* and, in theory, are visible from as far away as 1 kilometer.

see Note 18.

An attacker with the right equipment could read passwords and other secrets displayed on any nearby video screens. Win Schwartau, a well-known figure in information warfare circles, demonstrated the technique on a television show in 1991. Schwartau has suggested that a properly designed van Eck receiver would not be limited to intercepting video signals. In one theoretical scenario, a receiver could retrieve enough information from an automated teller machine (ATM) to reconstruct customers' bank cards and the corresponding personal identification number (PIN).

A-12

see Note 19.

The first defense against van Eck interception is to be sure that passwords do not appear on video displays. Most systems include this feature already, even though it has a serious impact on reliability and usability of the user interface (see Section 6.1). Additional protection could be provided by adding some shielding to video displays and other computer equipment. Unfortunately, research and engineering in this area traditionally has been discouraged in the United States by government intelligence agencies, notably the National Security Agency (NSA).

Classic passwords are not, of course, the only authentication technique available on computers. They are merely the oldest and easiest to implement. In the years since timesharing first evolved, password systems have improved dramatically and have incorporated additional security measures. Moreover, other authentication techniques have evolved to handle situations where passwords simply can't do the job.

1.6 AUTHENTICATION FACTORS

> *Things you know...*
> *Things you have...*
> *Things you are...*

> — Carlton et al., *Alternate Authentication Mechanisms*

Even before computers came along, people used a variety of distinguishing characteristics to authenticate one another. Computer systems have applied these characteristics whenever people have found a cost-effective way to implement them digitally. Today, authentication techniques are usually classified according to the distinguishing characteristic they use, and we classify the characteristics in terms of three *factors* described below and summarized in Table 1.2. Each factor relies on a different kind of distinguishing characteristic to authenticate people.   *see Note 20.*

- **Something you know: a password**

   The distinguishing characteristic is secret information that unauthorized people do not know. Before computers, this might be a spoken password or a memorized combination for a lock. In computers it might be a password, a passphrase, or a PIN.

   Developers can implement a plausible looking password mechanism cheaply and easily. A memorized secret is perfect for

TABLE 1.2: *Authentication Factors*

Factor	Benefits	Weaknesses	Examples
Something you know: password	Cheap to implement, portable	Sniffing attacks, Can't detect sniffing attacks, Passwords are either easy to guess or hard to remember, Cost of handling forgotten passwords	Password, PIN, Safe combination
Something you have: token	Hardest to abuse	Expensive, Can be lost or stolen, Risk of hardware failure, Not always portable	Token, Smart card, Secret data embedded in a file or device, Mechanical key
Something you are: biometric	Easiest to authenticate with, portable	Expensive, Replay threats, Privacy risks, Characteristic can't be changed, False rejection of legitimate users, Characteristic can be injured	Fingerprint, Eye scan, Voice recognition, Photo ID

roaming users, that is, people who connect to the system from unpredictable remote locations, since it travels with them.

Passwords are weak, however, for two reasons. First, their effectiveness depends on secrecy and it is hard to keep them secret. There are countless ways to sniff or otherwise intercept them, and there is usually no way to detect a successful sniffing attack until damage is done. Second, evolving threats on passwords have made it relatively easy for attackers to figure out the passwords that people are most likely to choose and remember. Even if they choose hard-to-guess passwords, people are more likely to forget them or be obliged to write them down in order to have them available when needed. A written password is, of course, more vulnerable to theft than a memorized one. Even well-meaning people are likely to violate password usage rules at some point, simply to ensure they can use their computer when needed. Chapters 2 and 3 discuss passwords further, and Chapter 6 explores the problem of choosing effective passwords.

• **Something you have: a token**

The distinguishing characteristic is that authorized people possess some specific item. Before computers this might be a seal with a personal insignia or a key for a lock. In computers it might be nothing more than a data file containing the distinguishing characteristic. Often, the characteristic is embedded in a device like a magnetic stripe card, a smart card, or a password calculator. In this book, such things are called *tokens*. The characteristic might even be embedded in a large piece of equipment and thus not be very portable.

Token-based authentication is the hardest technique to abuse since it relies on a unique physical object that one must have in order to log on. Unlike passwords, the owner can tell if the token has been stolen, and it's hard for the owner to share the token with others and still be able to log on. The major weaknesses are higher costs and the risk of loss or hardware failure. Portability can also be a problem. Tokens are discussed further in Chapter 9.

- **Something you are: a biometric**

  The distinguishing characteristic is some physical feature or behavior that is unique to the person being authenticated. Before computers, this might have been a personal signature, a portrait, a fingerprint, or a written description of the person's physical appearance. With computers, the person's distinguishing characteristic is measured and compared against a previously collected pattern from the authentic person. Well-known techniques use a person's voice, fingerprints, written signature, hand shape, or eye features for authentication. In this book, such things are called *biometrics*.

  Biometric authentication is usually the easiest approach for people to use for authentication. In most cases, a well-designed biometric system simply accepts a reading from the person and correctly perform the authentication. The distinguishing characteristic is obviously portable, since it's part of the owner's body.

  However, the benefits are offset by several weaknesses. Typically, the equipment is expensive to buy, install, and operate in comparison to other systems. Biometric readings face the risk of interception when used remotely; the thief might replay the reading to masquerade as its owner or use the reading to track its owner. Once the biometric reading has fallen into the wrong hands, its owner has no way to reverse the damage, since the biometric trait is usually impossible to change.

Moreover, the process is a tricky one. In practice, it can be hard to make the system sensitive enough to reject unauthorized users without occasionally rejecting authorized users. Physiological changes and injuries can also invalidate biometric readings: in one case a woman working at a high-security installation was denied entrance by the biometric device at the front door because her pregnancy had caused changes in her retinal blood vessels.

Despite their shortcomings, biometrics remain a promising technique. Biometrics are discussed further in Chapter 7.

In other words, authentication always depends on something lost, injured, or forgotten. There really is no "one best way" to authenticate people. The choice depends on the particular risks faced by a computing system and the costs (in terms of equipment, administration, and user impact) that the proprietor is willing to incur. Sites often rely on passwords because of lower costs: the implementation requires no special hardware to purchase, install, and maintain. Organizations use other techniques only when the potential loss from mishandled passwords clearly exceeds the cost of something different.

All authentication factors have their own shortcomings, and individual factors can't always provide the level of protection a site might need. In such cases, sites will use authentication mechanisms that incorporate two or three factors. Such systems are often referred to as *strong authentication* since the benefits of one factor can block the shortcomings of another. ATM cards, which always require a memorized PIN, provide a well-known example of two-factor authentication.

A common theme in all three factors is that the distinguishing characteristic is uniquely associated with the person being authenticated. This becomes a problem when operating over computer networks. Often, the authentication mechanism has nothing to go on except a collection of bits derived from the distinguishing characteristic. There is no mechanism (aside from additional authentication) to establish the provenance of the bits themselves. There is no way to tell if a biometric reading was really collected from the person at the other end or if it was sniffed and retransmitted by someone else. There is no way to tell if the password comes from the authorized person or from someone else. In short, simple authentication mechanisms often rely on keeping the distinguishing characteristic secret.

1.7 JUDGING ATTACK PREVALENCE

While it is important to be aware of the attacks that could take place against a given security technique, it is also important to understand how likely a particular attack might be. This often depends on the degree of sophistication each attack requires. Most proprietors won't be as concerned about attacks that require the resources of a national government as they are about an attack that's known by every teenaged Internet user.

This book classifies attacks into five levels of prevalence. The different levels indicate the relative knowledge and resources the attacker will need, as well as the degree to which such attacks seem to occur. Attackers faced with very attractive targets will spend significant amounts of effort on intrusions. The rest of this book uses these classifications to indicate the prevalence of attacks.

- Trivial attack

  There are books filled with trivial attacks. Anyone who knows the "trick" behind one of these attacks can perform it using conventional software already present on a typical workstation. Internet e-mail forgery is the classic example of a trivial attack. Anyone with a typical Internet e-mail package on a personal computer can configure it to generate e-mail that claims to be from someone else (for example, president@whitehouse.gov). The attack doesn't rely on special hacker tools or nonstandard software. Anyone can do it if he or she knows how.   *see Note 21.*

- Common attack

  Unlike trivial attacks, the attacker must acquire specific software tools or take similar steps that may indicate premeditation. Password sniffing is an example of a common attack: a hacker installs keystroke capture software that collects someone's password to exploit later. Viruses are another example: the author either must use a virus construction program to create the virus or must intentionally write the virus from scratch. The presence of attack software on workstations indicates the owners may be either victims or perpetrators of software-based attacks, depending on the particular software involved. Often, there are well-known security measures to apply to common attacks. Unfortunately, there are also a large and growing number of common attacks. There are tools that help attackers detect well-known vulnerabilities and it can be time consuming to try to block all of them.

- **Physical attack**

  These attacks require the attacker's physical presence at the point of attack. They may also require the manipulation of computer hardware and/or special hardware tools. The attacks may also depend on special knowledge and training. In Section 1.4 we briefly described "rubber hose" attacks, but the other physical attacks in this book are directed against equipment, not people. In Chapter 4 we discuss attacks in which the attacker opens the computer case and rewires the hard drive in order to copy its contents. Other examples include sniffing or wiretapping when the connecting wire is physically tapped. Unlike common attacks, physical attacks tend to leave physical evidence, and this tends to deter less motivated attackers.

- **Sophisticated attack**

  A sophisticated attack is an attack that requires sophisticated knowledge of security vulnerabilities. While common attacks may be performed by people with good tools and limited knowledge or skill, a sophisticated attack may require the attacker to construct a tool to implement the attack. The work of the Wily Hacker tracked by Clifford Stoll in the late 1980s is an example of a sophisticated attack: the hacker had a "bag of tricks" consisting of trivial and common attacks, and he applied multiple tricks to penetrate and exploit the systems he attacked. The attacks and exploitation took a significant effort by an individual attacker working part-time. Sites defend against sophisticated attacks by restricting their operations to reduce their vulnerability to them.   *see Note 22.*

- **Innovative attack**

  These are attacks that exploit theoretical vulnerabilities that have not been publicly demonstrated to be practical. Such attacks often bring significant resources to bear in order to breach a strong security mechanism. An innovative attack probably involves a large, well-funded team of attackers working for months or years to breach the adversary's defenses. For example, Allied cryptanalysts during World War II made an innovative attack against German cryptographic equipment by combining mathematical analysis with trial-and-error decryption attempts. Innovative attacks tend to be very expensive, but they also tend to succeed if the attacker is willing to invest the resources needed to achieve success. Nuclear command and control systems are designed to resist innovative attacks by spending enormous amounts of money on redundancy and least privilege.   *see Note 23.*

While security experts may often agree in general terms about the prevalence of various attacks, there is no widely accepted notion of attack prevalence or how to estimate it. The estimates of prevalence appearing in this book are based on attack reports and descriptions, and try to reflect the consensus of the computer security community. These estimates primarily reflect the author's qualitative opinion and are not based on any systematic measurements. As time goes on and attacks evolve, the prevalence of various attacks will no doubt change.

1.8   SUMMARY TABLES

The last section of each chapter contains two summary tables: one summarizing attacks described in the chapter, and another describing the corresponding defenses. The attack summary gives a brief name for each attack, summarizes the security problem, estimates the sophistication, and briefly describes how the attack works. Sophistication is assessed using the classification described in Section 1.7. If modern software systems routinely provide a defense against a particular attack, it is marked as "Obsolete" in the attack summary. The defense summary gives a brief name for each

defense, a list of attacks it should protect against, and a brief
description of what it does. If the chapter introduces an attack for
which it introduces no defense, the attack is noted in an additional
subsection titled **Residual Attacks**.

TABLE 1.3: *Attack Summary*

Attack	Security Problem	Prevalence	Attack Description
A-1. Keystroke confusion	Masquerade as someone else	Obsolete	A bug found in the timesharing software allowed a peculiar sequence of characters to skip password checking
A-2. Password file theft	Recover all other users' passwords	Obsolete	Weak protection of password file allowed its contents to be stolen
A-3. Trojan horse	Recover hidden information, like a password file	Common, Sophisticated, or Innovative	Attacker writes a program that gets used by the victim. Unknown to the victim, the program copies or modifies the victim's data. A virus is a well-known example
A-4. On-line password guessing	Recover a user's password	Trivial	Interactive trial-and-error attack to try to guess a user's password
A-5. Password audit review	Recover a user's password	Common	Review audit records of a user's mistakes while logging on to make guesses of the user's password
A-6. Helpful disclosure	Recover a user's password	Trivial	Attacker convinces a victim to reveal a password in support of an apparently important task
A-7. Bogus password change	Recover a user's password	Trivial	Attacker convinces victims to change their passwords to a word selected by the attacker
A-8. Rubber hose disclosure	Recover hidden information, like a user's password	Physical	Attacker uses threats or physical coercion to recover secret information from the victim
A-9. Shoulder surfing	Recover a user's password	Trivial	Attacker watches a user type his password, then uses it himself

TABLE 1.3: *Attack Summary (Continued)*

Attack	Security Problem	Prevalence	Attack Description
A-10. Key-stroke sniffing	Recover a user's pass-word	Common	Software watches keystrokes transmitted from the user to the system for typed-in user names and passwords, save for later use
A-11. Trojan login	Recover a user's pass-word	Common	Run a program that mimics the standard login program, but collects user names and pass-words when people try to log on
A-12. van Eck Radiation	Recover hidden informa-tion, like a user's password	Physical	Use a device to intercept van Eck radiation from the victim's video monitor, and retrieve any secrets the victim displays

TABLE 1.4: *Defense Summary*

Defense	Foils Attacks	Description
D-1. Good software design	A-1. Keystroke confu-sion	Design software in an organized way to reuse existing functions; keep procedures simple and comprehensible
D-2. Hashed passwords	A-2. Password file theft A-6. Helpful disclosure	Store passwords in a one-way hashed for-mat. Avoid storing or handling the password in its readable, unhashed form
D-3. Audit bad passwords	A-4. On-line password guessing	Keep an audit trail of all attempts to log on, and use the trail to detect password guess-ing attacks
D-4. Limit password guessing	A-4. On-line password guessing A-5. Password audit review	Keep track of the number of incorrect guesses someone may make of a password, and respond to excessive guesses as indicat-ing a password guessing attack

TABLE 1.4: *Defense Summary (Continued)*

Defense	Foils Attacks	Description
D-5. Password change policy	A-6. Helpful disclosure	Establish a policy to restrict the ability of the help desk to change passwords for users. Password changes must take place under safe circumstances
D-6. Password nondis-closure policy	A-6. Helpful disclosure A-7. Bogus password change	Establish a policy that nobody should dis-close a password to another person under any circumstances
D-7. Duress signal	A-8. Rubber hose dis-closure	Lets a user signal that the login process is tak-ing place under duress
D-8. Honey pot	A-8. Rubber hose dis-closure	Allows attackers to enter the system, pre-sents them with a legitimate-appearing tar-get, while restricting their access to truly valuable resources and keeping them under surveillance
D-9. Password blinding	A-9. Shoulder surfing	Do not print or display the keys typed when the user types a password
D-10. Memory protec-tion	A-10. Keystroke sniffing	Use the CPU's memory protection feature to protect the keyboard input buffer from read-ing by any software except the OS
D-11. Change pass-word	A-2. Password file theft A-9. Shoulder surfing A-10. Keystroke sniffing	The password's owner can change the pass-word to something new when there is a risk that it has been intercepted by an attacker
D-12. Secure attention	A-11. Trojan login	System assigns a special keystroke to secu-rity-related user requests like logging on

RESIDUAL ATTACKS

A-3. Trojan horse—There is no general-purpose defense against this attack. There are techniques to resist Trojan horses designed to operate in particular ways. For example, antivirus software addresses the virus problem. There are also integrity checking programs that can detect modifications to files that rarely change, like the login program.

CHAPTER 2
EVOLUTION OF REUSABLE PASSWORDS

The use of encrypted passwords appears reasonably secure in the absence of serious attention of experts in the field.

— Morris and Thompson, *Password Security: A Case History* (1979)

IN THIS CHAPTER

This chapter describes the evolution of modern password systems. Most of the examples are taken from Unix, since its password system has had a well-documented history.

- Basics of memorized secrets like passwords and safe combinations
- Base secrets, cultural secrets, and random secrets
- The Unix password mechanism and its evolution
- Attacks on hashed passwords, like dictionary attacks
- The Internet Worm and its attacks against authentication
- Guessing attacks and average attack space estimates

2.1 PASSWORDS: SOMETHING YOU KNOW

Passwords inherit many strengths and weaknesses of older security techniques. In the days before identity papers, passports, and photo IDs, guards at city gates used passwords to help distinguish outsiders from local citizens. The password identified a person as a member of a particular group of citizens, or perhaps simply as someone the guard should allow to pass the gate. Of course, passwords had shortcomings even then. A spy could bribe citizens to learn the password, and then masquerade as one of them. But these passwords didn't provide unconditional access. If a squad of soldiers in enemy regalia walked up to the gate, the trained guard would probably be doing battle with them before they could offer a password.

Passwords are usually based on random, memorized base secrets, like the one learned by Ali Baba ("Open, Sesame"). Mechanical locks based on secrets remained in the realm of fiction until the advent of combination locks for safes and padlocks. Combination locks are the most widely used mechanical devices that behave like passwords. There are several important similarities between memorized passwords and combination locks, and these similarities make it worthwhile to briefly review combination locks and how they often fail:

- Although the combination or password might be preset at the factory to some predictable value, we can reset it to a different value that outsiders can't guess. People occasionally forget to do so, and this simplifies the job for attackers.

- People have trouble remembering arbitrary digits and keystrokes, so they like to choose combinations or passwords based on personal information (birth dates, etc.) they are more likely to remember. Again, this simplifies the job for attackers.

- People also like to write down combinations and passwords, particularly if they are hard to remember.

Figure 2.1 shows the inside of a typical combination lock. The heart of the device is the wheel-pack, whose mechanical configuration establishes the combination for a particular lock. The wheel-pack contains a separate, notched wheel for each number in the combination. Each wheel has pegs, called wheel flies, that catch upon one another when someone spins the combination dial. The location of the wheel flies and notch on each wheel work together to determine a lock's combination. Quality safes allow the safe's buyer to change its combination after the safe arrives at its new home. If we can assume that all safe buyers do this, then it is unlikely that any two safes selected at random have the same combination even if they are the same make and model.

The security of the safe relies very heavily on the inability of others to guess the combination. Quality safes are built so that any combination is as likely as any other. The safe itself should provide no hints to the combination. Unfortunately, there is often a gap between theory and practice. Manufacturers have to set a safe's combination during manufacture, and not everyone changes the combination after purchase. This yields a list of "try-out combinations" based on combinations generated by the safe's manufacturing process. If a top-quality safe has three wheels, it could have a million possible combinations. If the combination wasn't changed since it was manufactured, then a safecracker can open it by working through the list of combinations used by that manufacturer. A typical try-out list will contain 100 combinations or less, which poses a tedious but surmountable obstacle for a determined safecracker.   *see Note 1.*

Similar phenomena have happened with computer passwords in the past, and will no doubt occur again. Digital Equipment Corporation, developer of the PDP and VAX lines of computer systems, used to ship systems configured to allow easy access by their field service staff: each computer always had a user name "FIELD" with the password "SERVICE." Although sites had the option of changing the password, the user ID, or both, many found it most convenient to leave the user ID and password in place, simplifying the task of maintenance personnel and attackers alike. The first rule when installing any software with password protection is to change all

FIGURE 2.1: *A typical combination lock.* The combination has been dialed in and the lock is ready to open. The three wheels making up the wheel-pack have been turned so that their notches line up with the locking bolt. The row of holes around each wheel allows the owner to change the combination by moving the wheel flies.

passwords that were shipped with the product, but the rule isn't consistently followed. A similar situation led to widespread security problems with Internet router products in the mid-1990s.   *see Note 2.*

Once people change safe combinations (or passwords for that matter) the problem isn't over. In both cases security may depend on the owner's memorizing a hard-to-guess secret. Often, people choose a well-known piece of information as their combination. Birthdays and other personal milestone dates are very popular choices for three-wheel safes, since both the date and the combination require three two-digit numbers. It is relatively simple for a locksmith or safecracker to assemble a list of relevant dates for the safe's owner and produce a comprehensive list of combinations worth trying. Phone numbers, Social Security numbers, and so on also earn a place on the list. Their ease of prediction disqualifies them as sensible combinations, but many people choose them anyway.

Passwords suffer a similar fate even though they can contain letters, digits, or even punctuation: some people use personal information instead of a random, hard-to-guess secret. Stories abound of people using their own names, family names, computer names, and other obvious words as passwords. Section 3.4 analyzes the impact of this on password attacks.

No matter how easy it might be to guess a particular combination or password, some people will still feel the need to write it down somewhere. An experienced safecracker always examines the room where the safe resides, as well as the safe itself, to see if the combination has been written down. Often it is, and the brief search saves time otherwise spent on try-out combinations. Passwords suffer a similar fate, and this is discussed further in Section 6.1.

These problems reflect fundamental shortcomings of all defenses that depend on memorized secrets. Initially, the most visible members of computer user communities tended to be technically sophisticated scientists and engineers. Developers and administrators could convince themselves that such users would memorize increasingly complicated passwords in exchange for stronger security. Unfortunately, few people seriously addressed the opposite question: what happens to system security if not everyone chooses complex passwords? We examine that problem further in Section 2.5.

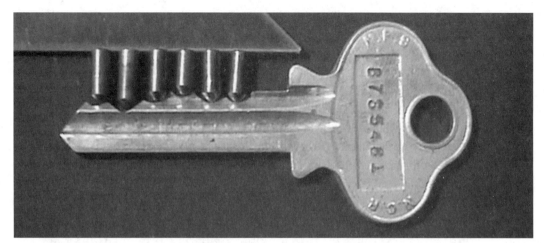

FIGURE 2.2: *Conventional keys encode a base secret.* The depth of the notches along the top of a key correspond to the length of pins within the key's lock. A locksmith can duplicate a key if the notch depths are known. The key's serial number plays a similar role to that of a user name: it associates the key with the lock but does not disclose its base secret.

2.2 AUTHENTICATION AND BASE SECRETS

All practical remote authentication depends on secrecy to prevent masquerades. If attackers can make a copy of someone's distinguishing characteristic, they can masquerade as that person. This is obvious with passwords and should be clear with biometrics, since a distant authentication mechanism won't know whether a biometric reading really comes from a live person or a retransmission. Token-based authentication generally relies on unique information embedded in each token; if attackers know this unique information (like an ATM card's account number), they can make a copy of the token.

An effective distinguishing characteristic generally contains a unique and usually secret element called the *base secret*. This is the information that an attacker must know in order to copy the victim's distinguishing characteristic and perform a masquerade. To take a noncomputer example, the keys for mechanical locks encode a base secret in the pattern of notches they carry (Figure 2.2). Although most attackers who replicate keys will make a duplicate directly from the original key, knowledgeable locksmiths can replicate any key if they know the type of key (its "blank") and the depths of its notches. So, in theory, the key simply encodes information, and the security of the key's lock can be compromised if the information itself is revealed. Some lock manufacturers sell special gauges to measure notch depths for their keys. Jerry Schneider, whose career in computer crime was noted earlier, claimed to have used calipers to measure key notches in order to reproduce keys, as part of a scam to steal equipment from the telephone company. Fortunately, few people can accurately estimate a key's notch depths simply by looking at it.

see Note 3.

Practical authentication with base secrets tends to fall into two categories: cultural authentication and random secrets. Cultural authentication relies on personal information or peculiar traits that potential victims are unlikely to share with attackers. Random secrets rely on possession of secret information that potential attackers should never be able to acquire. While many enterprises deem cultural authentication sufficient for many applications, random secrets are essential for strong, hard-to-forge authentication.

CULTURAL AUTHENTICATION

> [5] And the Gileadites took the passages of Jordan before the Ephraimites: and it was so, that when those Ephraimites which were escaped said, Let me go over; that the men of Gilead said unto him, Art thou an Ephraimite? If he said, Nay;
>
> [6] Then said they unto him, Say now Shibboleth: and he said Sibboleth: for he could not frame to pronounce it right. Then they took him, and slew him at the passages of Jordan...
>
> — The Book of Judges 12:5–6 *King James Version*

We all use cultural authentication. If a new acquaintance claims to be a friend of a friend, most of us will feel the urge to pose questions that only a friend's friend might be able to answer. A classic scene from World War II was that of American troops contending with German soldiers dressed in American uniforms: the Americans verified each others' citizenship by asking questions about baseball and the World Series. Credit card companies rely heavily on cultural authentication to verify cardholders when phoning for assistance: "Thank you, sir. Can you verify your address, please? Your Social Security number? Your mother's maiden name?"

Cultural authentication is a very familiar and widely used technique. That is its principal advantage: most people understand the process and it is based on knowledge and capabilities that are peculiar to each person. The technique blocks many potential attackers since it relies on information that can vary dramatically from one person to the next, except perhaps within groups whose members know one another well. However, the technique suffers from two shortcomings. First, the base secrets are not necessarily secrets. Second, the base secrets are often impossible to change.

Cultural authentication differentiates between members of different groups. Within the nuclear family, parents often know childrens' Social Security numbers, and extended families know each others' mothers' maiden names. The Old Testament quotation at the beginning of this section tells of the army of the Ephraimites retreating after a defeat by the Gileadites. Refugees who reached the fords of the Jordan River were required to say the password "Shibboleth" in order to pass. Unfortunately, the Ephraimite's dialect did not pronounce the first "h," and those who said it incorrectly were slain. In this case, the base secret consisted of the difference between local dialects, and the procedure depended on people's ability to pronounce words in the way of the Gileadites.

Today, cultural authentication generally relies on information that friends or family or acquaintances or personal business associates might know but the rest of the world is unlikely to know. Some cultural secrets seem almost biometric, like one's birth date or parentage. Often, however, such information is a matter of public record — your birth certificate lists your mother's maiden name, but many still treat it like a "secret" that only the particular individual would know.

Personal knowledge does provide a practical authentication strategy in some cases. While many Web sites rely on user names and passwords, sites can also use quizzes to control who uses them. For example, there is a family that has shared a large summer home for several generations. All of the information about the home—draft summer schedules, home maintenance instructions, contact information, photos of last summer, and so on—naturally resides on the family Web site. The site grants access only to family members, and it authenticates them by demanding information that other people are unlikely to know (questions like "How do we pour milk at breakfast?" or "Where did the eagle go?"). This technique may fail occasionally due to lucky guesses or trespassing by nonfamily guests. Still, the technique succeeds at its primary goal of granting access to family members while protecting the family's privacy in most cases.

The essential shortcoming of cultural authentication is that it relies on base secrets that can't be changed even if attackers learn how to exploit them. Although the biblical story from Judges goes on to say that thousands of Ephraimites died at the banks of the Jordan River, many may have been familiar with the different dialects and tricked the Gileadites into letting them pass. Likewise, a credit card company can be fooled repeatedly by determined attackers who thoroughly investigate their victims. The modern problem of identity fraud relies on the way the financial community uses cultural secrets to authenticate its customers. One is stuck with one's mother's maiden name, and it's not much easier to change one's Social Security number or driver's license number.

RANDOM SECRETS

Tokens and passwords hold a strong advantage over cultural authentication when they incorporate a *random secret* that serves as the base secret for authentication. Users can change their random secrets if the previous one is lost or stolen, or otherwise becomes vulnerable to attack. The authentication system associates a given base secret with each user name, and assumes that only the authorized person can provide the right base secret. For example, a password is a base secret that is only known by authorized people.

Magnetic stripe cards are another example. Many sites issue such cards to employees and have door locks that are unlocked with these cards. The data stream stored on a card's magnetic stripe is a base secret. The value is hidden from view, and a third party cannot duplicate that card without knowing the contents of the data stream. The only way to deduce the contents of the data stream is to capture it, either by reading the card or by intercepting the data stream as it travels from a card reader. If a card's owner loses the card or believes it has been copied, she can replace it with a new card containing a different base secret.

Account numbers often serve as random secrets. The enterprise issuing the number will use it to authenticate a legitimate account holder, since others probably don't know which number corresponds to which person. Most people encounter this process in the credit card industry. If the account owner fears that the account number has been compromised or misused, he can contact the company and receive a new, different account number. The company disables the old number, preventing any further misuse.

A practical problem with random secrets is that they must be synchronized between authentication mechanisms and their users. Unlike cultural secrets, there is no way for cooperating people to predict which random secret another might pick. Computer systems often rely on physical exchange of such secrets. For example, a new computer user at a company may receive an initial user name and password on a hand-carried piece of paper, or the account will be established in the new user's presence by a system administrator.

2.3   THE UNIX PASSWORD SYSTEM

The 1960s and 1970s saw the development of numerous timesharing systems. Section 1.3 introduced password features of two systems, CTSS and RAX, but these weren't the only examples of such systems. Password security caused problems and inspired innovations in numerous other systems, such as the Michigan Terminal System (MTS), the PDP-10 Executive (TENEX), IBM's Time Sharing Option (TSO), and numerous others.

The Unix system originated at Bell Laboratories, the research arm of the old Bell Telephone monopoly, in the late 1960s. Its multiuser capabilities, including the login process, were developed in the early 1970s. Unix began as a practical subset of Multics, a far more ambitious project that sought to implement a sophisticated, high-performance, reliable, and general-purpose timesharing utility. Unix pursued more modest goals, but it adopted several important Multics features, like the hierarchical file system, file access control on the basis of users and groups, and eventually a hashed password file.   *see Note 4.*

Another essential feature was that both Multics and Unix were written in high-level programming languages, and in both cases the source code was made available to the computing community. In the case of Multics, the availability of source code played a comparatively modest role in the system's evolution, promotion, and use, perhaps because Multics relied on very specific hardware features.   *see Note 5.*

Unix, on the other hand, relied on typical features of contemporary computer architectures, and it proved relatively simple to adapt Unix to run on different types of computing hardware. AT&T, the owner of Unix, established a reasonable licensing policy for academic Unix users, which encouraged researchers and students to study the Unix source code and port the system to even more computers. At one point, an instructor in Australia, John Lions, even published a booklet containing a specially commented copy of the Unix kernel source code with cross-references to detailed commentary. Unix source code provided the operating system community with a common language for discussing various practical aspects of operating systems, like the password facility. This made Unix password evolution a compelling candidate for public discourse, and it is probably the most thoroughly discussed and documented password system of its age.   *see Note 6.*

Originally, Unix operated in a "clubhouse" environment that did not implement passwords. As the system evolved, it adopted password authentication and stored its plaintext passwords in a text file named "/etc/passwd." Access to the file was restricted to the "root" user. Around 1973, Unix incorporated password hashing.

The hashed password file brought practical benefits beyond its security improvements. Unix developers recognized that many utilities on a multiuser computing system need to operate on user identities, so the password file was made visible, and password security relied on the fact that the password values stored in the file were hashed. Unlike CTSS and even Multics at that time, Unix adopted a relatively strong encryption algorithm to prevent attackers from reversing the hash. This strategy provided adequate security for much of the 1970s, until faster processors made the aging hash procedure too vulnerable.

see Note 7.

Each line of text in the password file represented an entry for a single user. Each entry was subdivided into a fixed number of text fields, each separated by a colon. The "classic" Unix password file format appeared in Unix Version 7 and contained the following seven fields:

```
jdoe:5YgkEo542mWvc:12:31:John Doe:/home/jdoe:/bin/csh
```

These fields provided the essential pieces of information for identifying and authenticating the user.

- **User name (jdoe)**—the textual user name associated with this entry. Not all user names were associated with people. There was also the all-powerful administrative user "root" as well as special user names associated with particular services (uucp, ftp, and so on).
- **Hashed password (5YgkEo542mWvc)**—the user's hashed password, prefixed with a "salt" value. (Figures 2.3 and 2.5 show how the salt and hash are used.)
- **User ID "UID" number (12)**—number assigned to this user name.
- **Group ID "GID" number (31)**—numeric "user group" assigned to this user.
- **GCOS field (John Doe)**—Miscellaneous field that usually carries the user's personal name. The field is named after one of the commercial operating systems used at Bell Laboratories.
- **Home directory (/home/jdoe)**—this user's personal directory.
- **Shell program (/bin/csh)**—this user's favored command program.

Figure 2.3 shows how the Unix login procedure operates. Although login is started by the system with certain privileges, its environment is the same as other programs run under Unix. In particular, other programs cannot spy on the RAM it uses, not even the RAM that exchanges data with external devices like user terminals. This

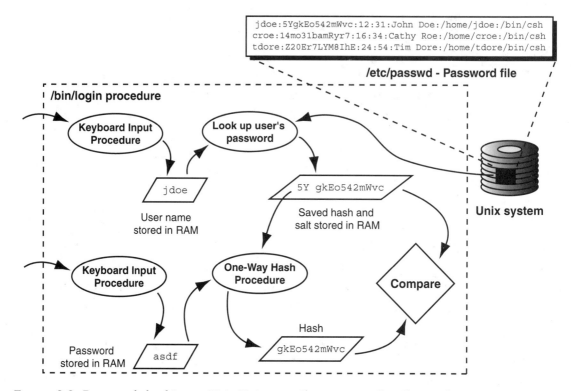

FIGURE 2.3: *Password checking on Unix.* Unix runs the program /bin/login when a person tries to log on. First, login reads the user name and extracts the appropriate entry from the password file /etc/passwd. Next, login reads in the user's password and hashes it along with "salt" from the stored password entry. If the result matches the hash stored in the password file, then the user will be logged on.

immediately blocks some of the sniffer attacks described in the previous chapter. The login operation begins by displaying a message that requests a user name. When someone types in the user name, the login process looks up that name in the password file and, if found, retrieves the password hash. Then the program requests the person to type in a password. Traditionally, Unix passwords were restricted to eight characters or less, although more recent versions allow longer passwords. The program hashes the password and compares the result with the hash stored in the password file. If they match, Unix logs the user on. If the process fails, many versions of Unix take steps to avoid making things simple for an attacker:

- If the password file does not contain an entry matching the user name, login reports "Invalid password" so that the person can't tell if the problem is with the user name or the password. This makes attacks by outsiders more difficult by denying them information about legitimate user names.

- Login always computes the hash on the typed-in password even if it failed to find the user name in the password file. This is because the hash computation often produces a recognizable delay. Attackers could use the absence of the delay to guess whether or not a user name was valid.

- Login typically gives the user three chances to type in the correct password. After the third attempt, login closes the connection to the user and quits running. If an outsider is trying to guess passwords, this introduces an extra delay into the process since he will need to reestablish his connection.

- Login makes a record whenever someone tries to log in, reporting either that the user logged on successfully, or that bad passwords were entered for that user. This gives the administrators a way to identify and track attempts to guess passwords.

While these may be "classic" features of Unix password protection, the login process of many modern Unix systems contain more or different features. Some systems have added fields to the password entries to improve password management in various ways. Most modern Unix systems also use *shadow password files* to hide the hash values from attackers. This is a response to escalating threats that we shall examine next.

2.4   ATTACKING THE UNIX PASSWORD FILE

Since the Unix login program took various steps to resist systematic password guessing, like keeping records of login attempts and introducing delays after bad guesses, attackers developed strategies that didn't involve on-line password guessing. These strategies usually concentrated on the Unix password file. The classic attack always began by extracting a copy of the password file which, after all, was readable by any logged on Unix user. Then the attacker would use various software tools to guess passwords and check the guesses against the hashed values stored in the file.

Unlike interactive guessing, this attack does not directly confront an active software security mechanism like the login program or the file protection mechanism. The attacker does not need to use the victim's resources and can do the job on any machine containing the appropriate attack software.

In the early days of the World Wide Web, search engines unintentionally aided these dictionary attacks. Some of the earliest engines, notably AltaVista, attempted to index every page on the Web by monitoring Web traffic and following links in previously indexed pages. Some early Web sites unintentionally "published" most of their readable files on the Web, including their Unix password file. Canny attackers could then simply ask the search engines to retrieve all files on the web named "/etc/passwd" and they would retrieve hundreds of password files.

The most obvious, systematic, and unsophisticated technique for attacking a file of hashed passwords is to try to generate every legal password one by one and compare each resulting hash against those in the victim's password file. If users all choose long pass-   *A-13* words, this trial-and-error attack can succeed only if either of two conditions occur. First, the attack becomes feasible if attackers find a weakness in the encryption that reduces the number of values they have to try. Second, the attack may become feasible once computing speeds improve enough.

THE M-209 HASH

When Unix first started using hashed passwords, it used a World War II–vintage encryption procedure to generate the hash (Figure 2.4). The procedure was based on the design of the M-209 cipher machine, a mechanical device previously used by the U.S. Army. Encryption procedures take two inputs: plaintext and a key, and produce a single output: the ciphertext.

The designers quickly realized that they could not simply encrypt the password in the obvious manner by treating the password as plaintext and using a secret key. To do so, they would have to embed a secret key in the login program and there was no way to reliably hide such a key from an attacker. Any attacker who recovered that key would be able to decrypt the entire password file. On the other hand, if they used the password as the key and encrypted some constant data (zeroes work fine), then they didn't need to store a secret key on the system.

The initial threat that concerned Unix developers was an off-line attack that systematically tried all possible passwords. It was relatively simple to construct such an attack on a Unix system since the necessary functions (crypt() in particular) were readily available in the Unix procedure libraries. All passwords were eight characters or less, and practical considerations restricted the password to the 95 printable ASCII characters. This yielded a trial-and-error search space containing over 10^{15} possible passwords.

Although Unix systems generally ran on "minicomputers" that were considered low-cost computer systems in the 1970s, the systems were still very expensive and not particularly common. Practical trial-and-error attacks had to be mounted from an individual computer. In the early 1970s, the fastest Unix system was hosted on the PDP-11/70 built by Digital Equipment Corporation. The crypt() *D-13* function was benchmarked on the 11/70 at approximately 1.25 milliseconds. Thus, it would have taken almost 263,000 years to perform a trial-and-error search of all possible 95 character Unix passwords.

Unfortunately, most users chose much simpler passwords. A more effective strategy was to structure the search so that shorter passwords were tried first, and longer passwords consisting of low- *A-14* ercase letters were tried before shorter passwords with other types of characters. Although it might still take eight years to try all possi-

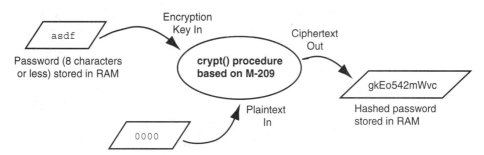

FIGURE 2.4: *Unix password hashing, first implementation.* Originally, Unix used an encryption program based on a military cipher machine from World War II to generate password hashes. Since they did not want to be able to convert the encrypted data (the hashed password) back into plaintext, they used the plaintext password as the encryption key and encrypted a constant value (a field of zeroes).

ble passwords containing eight lowercase letters, it would only take 107 hours to try all six-character passwords, and only 10 minutes to try all four-character passwords. As the computers hosting Unix improved, the problem rapidly worsened.

Another problem was that the M-209 procedure itself did not provide very strong protection against attack. Although it did withstand trivial attacks, it could not withstand stronger ones. As researchers examined the procedure and reasoned about encryption, they realized that there was a shortcut, a flaw, in the encryption procedure. Attackers didn't have to try every possible encryption key in order to "crack" its encryption and decrypt protected data. Eventually, some students even wrote a Unix package called the "Crypt Breakers Workbench" to decrypt files that had been encrypted with M-209 encryption. By then, fortunately, the Unix password procedure had been revised to use a different encryption procedure.

A-15

see Note 8.

THE DES HASH

In 1975, the National Bureau of Standards published the Data Encryption Standard (DES) and recommended it for encrypting sensitive commercial data. A software version of the DES algorithm soon found its way into Unix and became the replacement for the M-209 algorithm. Unlike the older algorithm, DES took advantage of almost two decades of progress in information theory applied to the design and analysis of encryption algorithms. In practice, a major advantage to DES for password hashing was that its Unix implementation was much slower than the older M-209 algorithm. To ensure that password encryption took as long as possible (though not so long as to infuriate users during login) the DES algorithm was iterated 25 times to generate the final password hash. This increased the time required for a trial-and-error attack, making it less practical.

To further complicate trial-and-error attacks, this improved version of crypt() modified the DES algorithm. The developers added another parameter to the procedure to include a random 12-bit value they called "salt" (Figure 2.5). This value was used to change one of the internal tables (the "E" table). This made it impractical to use conventional DES implementations to try to crack Unix password files. In particular, this prevented the use of hardware DES

D-14

implementations, particularly those based on DES-specific commercial integrated circuits.

This defensive technique of modifying a common algorithm was a success in the Unix case, but it does not always happen that way. Cryptographic algorithms are notoriously difficult to design. It requires extreme care and a deep understanding of the mathematics to modify such an algorithm without fatally weakening it. Even skilled cryptographers and mathematicians avoid such things unless the benefit clearly outweighs the risk. This appeared to be the case for Unix.

see Note 9.

The benefit of slow, nonstandard DES lasted only a few years before faster processing and more efficient encryption procedures brought back the trial-and-error attack threat. By the end of the 1980s, Unix performance had reached the point of executing the DES version of crypt() at 0.92 milliseconds. As the 1990s progressed, the power of networked desktop computers came to dominate most computing environments. This put significant amounts of computing power in the hands of potential attackers, since they could run the inefficient crypt() function on numerous workstations

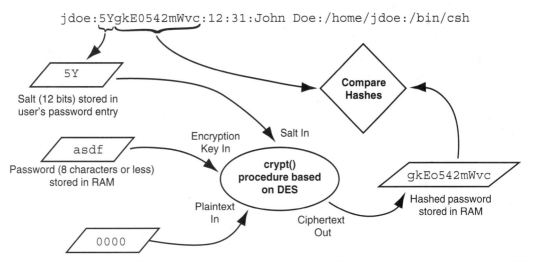

FIGURE 2.5: *Unix password hashing, second implementation.* The new technique used a modified version of the Data Encryption Standard (DES). As before, the password was used as the encryption key. The 12-bit salt value was used to permute an internal DES encryption table, rendering it incompatible with standard DES implementations, notably those built to achieve high encryption speeds.

TABLE 2.1: *Guess Rates on Passwords and Unix Hashes*   *see Note 10.*

Guess Rate per Second	Target of the Attack	Resources Used	Described by
0.23333	Login program	14 interactive guesses per minute	DOD *Guideline*
800	M-209 hash	PDP-11/70	Morris & Thompson
1092.8	DES-like hash	Sun SPARCStation	Feldmeier & Karn
3,000	DES-like hash	4 DecStation 3100s	Klein

at a time and crack passwords that much faster (Table 2.1). The real threat to hashed passwords, however, turned out to be people's password selection habits, and dictionary attacks exploited this weakness.   *see Note 11.*

2.5 DICTIONARY ATTACKS

Section 2.1 explains how safecrackers use lists of try-out combinations to try to guess a safe's combination. Attackers can use the same strategy against hashed passwords by trying a long list of candidate passwords. When applied to passwords, this technique is called the *dictionary attack*. It yields a dramatically shorter number of passwords to try out than the more systematic trial-and-error techniques described in the previous section. Section 3.4 describes how to numerically estimate the effectiveness of dictionary attacks. In general, a dictionary attack transforms an intractable computational problem into a tractable one.   *see Note 12.*

If we take the attack's name literally, it suggests that we pick up a commercial dictionary, copy the words into a long list, and test them one by one against hashed passwords. Typical commercial dictionaries might contain around 150,000 or 200,000 entries. If, like earlier examples, each attempt takes about one millisecond, then we can hash every word in the larger dictionary in only 200 seconds. If we take those 200,000 entries and permute each one in obvious ways (capitalize the first letter, all letters, obvious letter substitutions, etc.) so that we have 10 different versions of each word, then the dictionary still takes just a little over a half hour of computation time.

Password files that simply hashed the password were vulnerable to a precompiled dictionary attack (Figure 2.6). To do this, the attacker performed the dictionary computations once and stored the results in a large file. Then the attacker could iterate through the entries in a captured password file, extract each entry's hash, and search the hashed dictionary for a match. If he found a match, its offset into the dictionary file would tell him which dictionary word matched that entry. If the attacker used the 2 million word list of candidates, then the 11 bytes of hash per entry would yield a 22-megabyte dictionary file. Although disk storage was much more precious in the 1970s than today, a 22MB file was well within the realm of practicality for many Unix users.

This was another problem solved by the introduction of salt into the password process. As described earlier, the password process used salt to permute the DES encryption procedure so that faster implementations of the standard procedure could not be used to

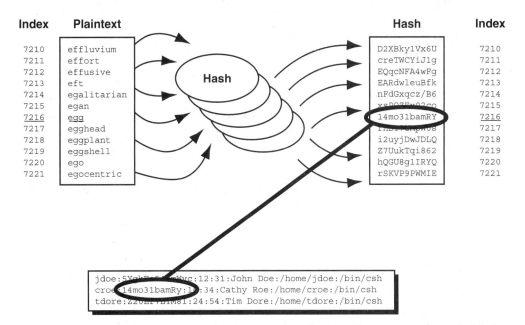

FIGURE 2.6: *Precompiled dictionary attack.* The attacker finds a dictionary of words likely to be used as passwords. This example uses the /usr/dict/words file as the dictionary (upper left). The attacker computes a hash for each word in the dictionary to create the attack file (upper right). The attacker retrieves a password file, extracts the password entries one by one, and searches the attack file for a matching hash. In this case the hash for croe matched hash index #7216 in the attack file. The matching index in the dictionary retrieves croe's password (egg).

crack Unix passwords. But the process yielded another benefit that greatly reduced the value of precompiled dictionaries: it produced variations in a given password's hash result when different salt values were used. The same password could therefore appear in any of 4,096 different ways in the password file.

D-15

Here is how the salt produced randomly different password hashes. Whenever Unix created a new password for a user, it would sample the real-time clock to collect a 12-bit salt value. This value was passed to crypt() as shown in Figure 2.5. The resulting 11 character hash value was then appended to the 2 character salt value and stored in the password entry.

The salted entries countered the threat of precompiled dictionaries. The attacker could build a dictionary of hashes with a salt value included, but the dictionary could only be used on password entries that also used that particular salt value. A determined attacker with enormous amounts of storage might have produced a dictionary containing 4,096 salted variants of each dictionary entry. The 2 million-word dictionary list would have required over 80 gigabytes. This vastly exceeded the amount of storage usually available to potential attackers at that time.

Another side effect of salting was that it also made it difficult to detect situations in which two different users had chosen the same secret password. Without salt, a particular password would always produce the same hash value. If two people coincidentally chose the same password, others could detect it by searching password files for matching hash values. The same technique would uncover whether a user was using the same password on other accounts or on different Unix systems. By introducing the salt, however, passwords were unlikely to match because their salt values were likely to differ.

2.6   THE INTERNET WORM

One of the more dramatic incidents of Internet prehistory (that is, before the World Wide Web) began at approximately 5:01:59 P.M. on November 2, 1988 when a Cornell University graduate student started a program on his Unix workstation. The program searched for addresses of nearby Unix computers and proceeded to break into them via Internet connections. Not all breakins succeeded, but when one did, the program started itself up on the new computer and started the breakin process again. This continued until over 3,000 hosts were running copies of this program. The program became known as the Internet Worm, though sometimes it is called the Morris Worm after Robert T. Morris, its author.

see Note 13.

Clearly, neither the worm's author nor the software itself were authorized to use most of the systems it infested. Yet the worm managed to penetrate roughly 5% of the Internet. The worm was successful because it automated the basic strategy often used by sophisticated humans when attacking computer systems: use multiple intrusion techniques, adapt to the target's weaknesses, and be persistent. Specifically, the worm used four intrusion techniques:

see Note 14.

- **Back door**—the worm exploited a *back door* in "sendmail," the popular e-mail server. Outsiders could connect to sendmail across the network, issue the "debug" command, and then be able to execute arbitrary commands on that host. This feature had been inserted to aid in debugging e-mail problems at a particular site, and was supposed to be removed from later versions of the server software. Unfortunately, it remained.

 A-17

- **Buffer overrun**—the worm exploited a software error in the "finger" server on many versions of Unix. The error, a *buffer overrun*, allowed the worm to insert its own procedure into the finger server. Since many systems ran the finger server in a privileged mode, the inserted procedure could then disable other defenses and let the Worm in.

A-18

- **Mutual trust attack**—the worm used the "r" commands (Section 8.6) to log on to other Unix hosts or to execute commands on them. This worked only if the two hosts, or user accounts on those hosts, had been configured to trust one another. Such trust relationships were very common in many sites, so that penetrating one host in the site provided access to most of the other hosts there.

A-19

- **Dynamic dictionary attack**—This attack tried to crack passwords via the hash and, literally, used a dictionary to reduce the search space. Specifically, the worm used the standard Unix online dictionary plus its own 433-word dictionary. Unlike the precompiled dictionary attack described in Section 2.5, this attack would extract the salt from password entries and use a

A-20

fast version of crypt() to check entries individually. This technique uncovered as many as 50% of the passwords at some sites.

It is very hard to fight a sophisticated worm like this. The attacks succeed in the first place because the worm is programmed to be persistent. Killing the worm on one computer does little good because that computer will soon be infected again. Effective solutions are disruptive, especially when users rely heavily on computer networks. The first step is to isolate vulnerable or infected machines from the network. Then the cleanup crew must kill the worm on each infected machine and patch the vulnerabilities on all vulnerable machines, whether already infected or not.   *see Note 15.*

When the Internet Worm struck, the defenders identified the back door attack relatively quickly. The problem was in the sendmail program, which has become a legendary source of Internet security problems. The "debug" feature could be turned on or off when the program was compiled from its source code. Most sites had left it on because they didn't realize it was there. Now they either had to patch the program to rename the command or they had to recompile it with the debug command disabled.

Unfortunately, the sendmail back door was not the last back door to appear. In 1992, people at some sites using Digital's VAX/VMS system discovered they didn't need to type their own password to log on: they could type any five alphanumeric characters and the system would log them on. Further investigation revealed that an attacker had replaced the login program, and the new version contained this special back door. More recently, several commercial and open-source versions of the Interbase database program were found to have a special user account and password built into their source code. People knowing that user name and password could connect to any server running an affected version of Interbase and have complete access to its databases.   *see Note 16.*

The general lesson here is zero tolerance of back doors. Built-in "secret" commands or back door passwords carry far more risk than benefit. Some people seem to think that programmers habitually   *D-16* implement back doors; the idea was even enshrined in cinema during a discussion by realistically scruffy computer experts in the 1982 movie *WarGames*. The problem with back doors is that they have the unsettling habit of popping open when it is least convenient. Most security experts find it challenging enough to design a system that meets the overt goal of preventing attacks. Attempting to add a safe, but hidden, back door would significantly increase the complexity of the system and increase the overall security risk. The safest strategy is to eliminate back doors in existing systems and to avoid products that contain them.

The "finger" vulnerability took a bit more time to detect in the Internet Worm. Once it was identified, however, sites blocked the vulnerability in one of two ways. Some sites acquired a corrected version of the finger server that correctly checked incoming data to ensure that it fit in the server's buffers. Other sites simply blocked the finger service entirely so that attackers couldn't send queries to it. This second strategy forms the basis for modern Internet firewalls. Although this approach doesn't actually address the problem of buffer overflow, it does help control the amount of risk to an Internet site. If attackers can reach fewer services, then it is less likely that they can reach one that has an internal flaw like a buffer overrun. Firewalling also reduces the risk posed by "r" commands, since the firewall can block such traffic from external and potentially hostile hosts. By blocking access by outsiders to every service except the essential ones, the site is less open to attack.

D-17

see Note 17.

Naturally, the firewalling strategy doesn't help if the site really needs to make vulnerable services available to outsiders. Internet e-mail and the World Wide Web both lose much of their appeal if such traffic isn't allowed between hosts within a site and those on the rest of the Internet. However, such services remain vulnerable to previously undetected buffer overrun attacks or other security vulnerabilities, if only because both services are such large and complex programs.

Server encapsulation is a good defense in such cases. This technique uses the system's protection mechanisms to isolate the server process from the rest of the system. The server can still reach all the files and other resources it needs, but the encapsulation prevents it from accessing other system resources. This limits the potential damage of an attack since the attacker's capabilities will be limited to what the server itself can do. Many people try to use "chroot()" to provide server encapsulation on Unix, although it is not a foolproof

D-18

approach. Better encapsulation techniques exist, but aren't usually available with standard, commercial operating systems.   *see Note 18.*

Sites attacked by the Internet Worm had little recourse for blocking the dynamic password dictionary attacks. The only quick and reliable way of closing that vulnerability would have been to immediately change all passwords to text not in any of the Worm's dictionaries. However, this probably would have caused even more chaos than the worm itself. Instead, the general solution was to encourage users to change their passwords to be longer and harder to predict.   *D-19*
Some sites experimented with versions of the login program that enforced restrictions on passwords in order to reduce the risk of dictionary attacks. Section 3.5 discusses specific mechanisms for producing more complex passwords. See Chapter 6 for a discussion of how password selection interacts with other security risks.

Another defense described earlier also addressed the problem of password attacks: the shadow password file. This ultimately eliminated a classic Unix feature: the world readable password file containing hashed passwords for every user. Instead, Unix systems kept two files, the original password file with the hash values omitted, and a "shadow" copy that contained the password hashes. The   *D-20*
original file was still readable by all users. The shadow version could only be used by privileged programs like login and by administrators when updating user information. Attackers could no longer simply fetch the file from the system. Now they had to mount a special attack to bypass the file's read protection before they could initiate a dictionary attack.

The Internet Worm was a watershed event in Unix and Internet security, but it was not the only major incident that aroused interest in 1988. Later in November an unidentified attacker penetrated two military computers via a flaw in their file transfer services. The incident led the Defense Communications Agency to temporarily disconnect the unclassified military networks from the rest of the Internet. Earlier that year, Cliff Stoll, an astronomy graduate student at Berkeley, published a paper describing his pursuit of an intruder across continents. His exploits were eventually published in the best-seller *The Cuckoo's Egg*. A major outcome of these events was the establishment of security incident response teams. The Computer Emergency Response Team (CERT) was established at Carnegie-Mellon University to track private and commercial incidents. Government and military organizations also organized response teams, notably the Computer Incident Advisory Capability (CIAC) of the U.S. Department of Energy.   *see Note 19.*

2.7 RESISTING GUESSING ATTACKS

We make guessing attacks harder when we give the attacker a larger range of possible values for a base secret. If every possible value is equally likely to occur, then a guessing attack must, on average, try half of the possibilities in order to succeed. The range of possibilities depends in part on the base secret's size. More importantly, it depends on the number of unique values the base secret really acquires in practice. We can compare the relative strength of different base secret implementations by comparing the number of guesses, on average, an attacker needs to make to guess the secret's value.

RANDOMNESS AND BIT SPACES

We can assess the strength of a secret by counting the total number of trials required by a trial-and-error attack. The number of trials reflects the randomness, or *entropy*, of a particular base secret. We measure the entropy of a base secret by counting the number of different values it can actually have. This corresponds to the number of trial and error attempts required by a hapless attacker trying to guess the base secret, if every guess is wrong except the attacker's final one.

For example, many pieces of luggage have combination locks, usually with a three-digit combination. Such locks provide a range of 1,000 different combinations. Since an attacker might have to try every possible three-digit combination to find the right one, we say its entropy is 1,000. A few more expensive pieces of luggage have four-digit combination locks, which give the attackers 10,000 alternatives to work through. Higher entropy provides the base secret with a bigger margin of safety against guessing.

Although these examples are relatively small, the entropy in practical base secrets is usually quite large. A 56-bit key used with the Data Encryption Standard (DES), for example, could be any one of over 72 quadrillion alternatives, and this is considered a smallish base secret in many applications.

This book deals with a lot of large numbers, since really strong authentication often depends on using numbers that are too large to attack through trial-and-error guessing of any kind. Instead of stumbling over large numbers like quadrillions and quintillions, we will talk about large numbers in terms of the number's *bit space*, that is, the number of binary bits in that number. Many experienced programmers are familiar with this approach since it reflects the amount of RAM required to store the number. So, instead of talking about an entropy of "16 million," we can say the entropy is "24 bits," since it takes 24 binary bits to store the number 16 million.

We can compute the number of bits required for a number by computing its logarithm, relative to the binary base 2. In this example, we compute the $\log_2$(16 million) = 23.93, and we must always round upward to account for the partial bit. This yields 24 bits. Figure 2.7 illustrates the bit space of a four-digit luggage lock: the base secret's range covers 10,000 possible values, which requires 14 bits of RAM.

BIASES IN BASE SECRETS

Strictly speaking, entropy relies on more than just the size of the base secret: it must also reflect any biases or restrictions on base secret values. Often, the biases arise from the fact that people don't really behave randomly, and their actions often fall into predictable categories. Section 2.5 amply illustrates this with dictionary attacks.

Here, we'll return to a simpler example involving smaller numbers: four-digit combination locks for luggage. Many luggage owners have a habit of choosing a date for the combination instead of choosing an arbitrary four-digit number. The right-hand side of Figure 2.7 illustrates the result: an attacker has to make far fewer guesses to find the combination.

The date bias significantly reduces the entropy of the four-digit combination lock. The bit space of this biased base secret equals the number of bits of storage needed to store any of 366 possible values. Since $\log_2(366) = 8.23$, we need nine bits of memory to represent the range of possible values. Thus, there are only nine bits of entropy if we only choose dates for combinations. This gives the four-digit lock less entropy than a three-digit lock, unless the owners usually choose dates for those combinations, too.

Passwords carry an obvious source of bias: they are usually limited to printable text. Some very early password systems would not accept passwords unless they consisted entirely of single-case letters. This seriously reduced the entropy in the resulting base secret. We compute the entropy of a four-letter password like this:

$$S = A_1 \times A_{2(1)} \times \ldots \times A_n \qquad S = 26^4$$
$$S = A^n \qquad S = 26 \times 26 \times 26 \times 26$$
$$S = 456{,}926$$

This computation illustrates the typical approach for finding the number of possible passwords (shown as **S** above), given the number of different characters allowed (shown as **A** above) and the password's allowed length in characters (shown as **n** above). So, if we allow only 26 different character values (single-case letters) and all

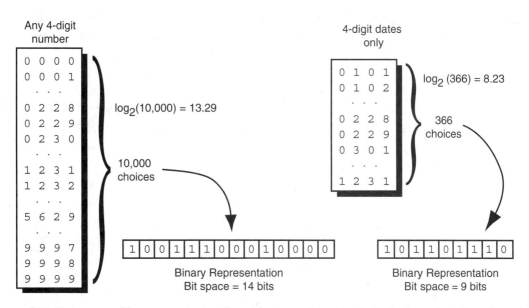

FIGURE 2.7: *Entropy and base secret size.* Consider a combination lock that can handle a four-digit base secret. The 10,000 possible combinations yield a bit space of 14 bits. We can say that the entropy is 14 bits as long as all possible combinations are equally likely. But, what if people always choose dates for their combinations? We still have a 14-bit base secret, but since the base secret takes on a smaller number of values, its entropy changes from 14 bits to only nine bits.

passwords are four letters long, we are limited to less than a half million alternatives. To find the bit space, we again compute the log base two:

$$B = \log_2(A_1 \times A_2 \times \ldots \times A_n) \qquad B = \log_2(456{,}926)$$

$$B = \log_2(A^n) \qquad\qquad\qquad B = 18.80$$

$$B = \log_2(S) \qquad\qquad\qquad B = 19 \text{ bits, rounded up}$$

This dramatically shows us how a bias can affect the range of values in a base secret. A typical computer will store a four-letter password as a sequence of four eight-bit bytes. So we have a base secret that requires a 32-bit space. Above, we've found that we only have 19 bits of entropy in that four-letter password. The remaining bits are sacrificed to make passwords easier for people to handle and remember.

In one way, our computation underestimates the number of possible passwords. Password systems are traditionally word-oriented, and will usually accept shorter words. We would get a more exact number by adding up the number of passwords of shorter lengths as well. However, the above computation is correct if the system uses *passphrases*, which are essentially passwords that permit embedded blanks. In the case above, that would yield 27 possible characters, instead of only 26. The shortcut of ignoring shorter passwords was popularized by the *Password Management Guideline* produced by the National Computer Security Center (NCSC) for the U.S. Department of Defense (DOD) in 1985.   *see Note 20.*

Biases are not necessarily a fatal flaw in base secrets. If the entropy of the base secret is large enough, its absolute size doesn't directly affect its security. Problems can arise, however, when people choose base secrets with relatively little entropy, as shown by the success of the Internet Worm's dictionary attacks. A further discussion of how biases affect the strength of base secrets appears in Section 3.4. A base secret is hard to guess if it has high entropy, even if the base secret's entropy is significantly smaller than the base secret itself. Its entropy determines its resistance to guessing attacks.

AVERAGE ATTACK SPACE

A simple way to compare different authentication techniques is to look at the number of trial-and-error attempts they impose on an attacker. For example, an attacker faced with a four-digit combination lock has 10 times as hard of a job as one faced with a three-digit lock. In order to compare how well these locks resist trial-and-error attacks and to compare their strength against the strength of others, we can estimate the number of guesses, on average, the attacker must make to find the base secret. We call this metric the *average attack space* when represented as a bit space.

Many experts like to perform such comparisons by computing the length of time required, on average, to guess the base secret's value. The problem with such estimates is that they are perishable. As time goes on, computers get faster, guessing rates increase, and the time to guess a base secret will decrease (see Section 5.3). The average attack space leaves out the time factor, allowing a comparison of the underlying mechanisms instead of comparing the computing hardware used in attacks.

Each item counted in an average attack space represents a single computational operation with a finite, somewhat predictable duration, like hashing a single password or performing a single attempt to log on. When we look for significant safety margins, like factors of a million or more, we can ignore the time difference between two fixed operations like that.

If all possible values of a base secret are equally likely to occur, then a trial-and-error attack must, on average, try half of those possible values. Thus, an average attack space reflects the need to search half of the possible base secrets, not all of them.

In practice, people's password choices are often biased in some way. If so, the average attack space should reflect the set of passwords people are *likely* to choose from. In the case of the four-digit luggage lock, we might want to represent the number of choices that reflect dates instead of counting combinations that aren't used as often.

If we decide to measure the number of likely combinations, we should also take into account the *likelihood* that people chose one of those combinations to use on their luggage. The average attack space, then, doesn't estimate how many guesses it might take to

guess a particular password or other secret. Instead, it estimates
the likelihood that we can guess *some* base secret, if we pick it randomly from a community.

To illustrate this, consider that four-digit lock again. Ideally, it
yields 10,000 possible combinations. But let's assume for a moment
that someone has made a study of peoples' luggage lock combinations and found that 50% of all luggage owners choose a calendar
date for their combination. We know that there are 366 legal combinations that represent dates (shown by **S** below) and we divide that
by 2 to reflect the need to search, on average, only half of those combination. In this example, however, we *do* need to make 366
attempts, on average, to account for the 0.5 likelihood that the
owner used a date for a combination (shown by **L** below). We compute the average attack space (shown by **V** below) as shown here:

$$V = \log_2\left(\frac{S}{2 \times L}\right) \qquad V_{\text{4-digit-lock}} = \log_2\left(\frac{366}{2 \times 0.5}\right)$$

$$V_{\text{4-digit-lock}} = \log_2(366)$$

$$V_{\text{4-digit-lock}} \approx 8.23$$

Rounding up to a full bit, we have a nine-bit average attack space. If
we are in the basement of the airport, this means we must try, on
average, approximately 512 combinations (that's 2^9) on randomly
selected bags before we're likely to guess one successfully.

As far as the average attack space estimate goes, the likelihood is
the same regardless of whether the attacker makes a series of
guesses on several bags or makes each guess on a different bag
every time. As long as bags are chosen randomly, the likelihood estimate should be accurate. The only case in which it doesn't really
work is if we're trying to guess the combinations of specific bags.
Then we face the possibility that a particular individual might have
chosen a combination that's not a date.

The average attack space lets us estimate the strength of a password system as affected by the threat of dictionary attacks and by
people's measured behavior at choosing passwords. Section 3.4
describes this in detail. We can then compare password strength
against other mechanisms such as one-time password tokens or
public keys. Although we also discuss the average attack space of

biometric devices, these figures aren't directly comparable to those of passwords, since trial-and-error attacks against biometrics are far more complex.

Although we've eliminated the time factor from our estimate of attack resistance, people often want to know how long, on average, a successful attack might take. We estimate the average attack time (called **T** below) using the rate at which individual guesses can take place. We've seen examples of Unix password guess rates in Table 2.1 at the end of Section 2.4, and we can undoubtedly perform 1,000 individual guesses per second (called **R** below). If we take the average attack space for four-letter passwords (19 bits, called **V** below), we compute the average attack time like this:

$$T = \frac{2^V}{R} \qquad T = \frac{2^{19}}{1,000}$$

$$T = \frac{524,288}{1,000}$$

$$T = 524.3 \text{ seconds}$$

Choosing an appropriate estimate for the attack rate is a black art. The right choice must estimate the amount of processing the attacker will have available either today or at some point in the future when this system is still being used. We return to this problem in Chapter 5.

2.8 SUMMARY TABLES

TABLE 2.2: *Attack Summary*

Attack	Security Problem	Prevalence	Attack Description
A-13. Off-line password search	Recover a user's password	Physical, Sophisticated	Trial-and-error attack that generates a legal password, hashes it, and compares it against the hash of the victim's password

TABLE 2.2: *Attack Summary (Continued)*

Attack	Security Problem	Prevalence	Attack Description
A-14. Structured password search	Recover a user's password	Common	Ordered trial-and-error search that tries short, lowercase passwords, then capitalized ones, then longer ones, etc.
A-15. Weak encryption procedure	Recover hidden information	Common, Sophisticated	Find or build a procedure that uses a shortcut to crack a weak encryption procedure
A-16. Precompiled dictionary attack	Recover a user's password	Common	Compute hashes for all words in a dictionary. Search the password file for hashes that match any in the dictionary list.
A-17. Back door	Bypass host security and run selected programs	Trivial	Execute "secret" command in the server that permits remote command execution
A-18. Buffer overrun	Bypass host security and run selected programs	Common, Sophisticated	Exploit a bug in an existing server to trick it into executing some downloaded code
A-19. Mutual trust attack	Masquerade as someone else	Trivial	After penetrating the first host, find another host that trusts it and allows unauthenticated access by the first host's users
A-20. Dynamic dictionary attack	Recover a user's password	Common	Trial-and-error attack that chooses a dictionary word, hashes it with the salt of the targeted victim's password, and compares the result with the victim's password hash

TABLE 2.3: *Defense Summary*

Defense	Foils Attacks	Description
D-13. Force lengthy trials	A-13. Off-line password search A-14. Structured password search	Build the system so that each attempt in a trial-and-error attack takes as long as possible
D-14. Nonstandard algorithms	A-13. Off-line password search A-14. Structured password search	Carefully modify standard algorithms so that standard products can't be used to attack the system. This can also introduce vulnerabilities
D-15. Salted password entries	A-16. Precompiled dictionary attack	Add salt (random data) to each password during hashing and save the salt value in the corresponding password entry
D-16. Eliminate back doors	A-17. Back door	Disable known back doors, and avoid products with back doors that can't be disabled
D-17. Service firewalling	A-18. Buffer overrun A-19. Mutual trust attack	Block network services so that outsiders can only reach those that are essential to provide
D-18. Server encapsulation	A-18. Buffer overrun	Run the server software in a special environment that restricts its access to the rest of the system. If an attacker penetrates the server, his access to the rest of the system is limited
D-19. Increase base secret's entropy	A-13. Off-line password search A-14. Structured password search A-20. Dynamic dictionary attack	Implement procedures to help maximize the amount of entropy in base secrets used for authentication. Examples: make the base secret larger, establish rules to discourage the choice of secrets from low entropy categories (passwords from dictionaries)
D-20. Shadow password file	A-13. Off-line password search A-14. Structured password search A-20. Dynamic dictionary attack	Store the actual password hashes in a file that is protected from reading by normal system users. Grant access only to privileged programs that need it, like login and user administration programs

RESIDUAL ATTACK

A-15. Weak encryption procedure—The solution is to replace the weak procedure with a stronger one. See Section 5.3 for a discussion of encryption strength.

CHAPTER 3

INTEGRATING PEOPLE

Inter oves locum praesta,

Et ab hoedis me sequestra

Give me a favored place among the sheep,

and separate me from the goats

— Giuseppe Verdi, *Requiem Mass, Part II (Dies Irae)*

IN THIS CHAPTER

Here is a first look at the administrative aspects of people and authentication systems, particularly with regard to password systems:

- The different roles people play in computing systems
- Enrolling users in an authentication system
- The effects of bias on the passwords people select
- Mechanisms to try to restrict password selection

3.1 ROLES PEOPLE PLAY

When we look at authentication systems, we classify people's roles according to three criteria. First, we classify them according to their relationship to the proprietor of the computing system. Next, we classify the people who have been granted access to the computing systems of interest. Third, we classify the people who have access to the information when it is outside the proprietor's control, such as when it travels over commercial communications lines. This yields the following groups of people:

- **Insiders and Outsiders**—divides the world's population into people whom the proprietor must trust to some extent and those who aren't trusted at all.

- **Users and Administrators**—divides people that actually access a computer into those who use it and those who keep it running.
- **Carriers and Crackers**—divides outsiders with access to data in transit into those who work to deliver the data between sites and those with unauthorized access as it travels between sites.

There are many ways to classify people. This particular set of criteria supports our discussion of various authentication systems without getting sidetracked into problems of access control. These criteria also reflect security policies practiced by many enterprises and organizations.

INSIDERS AND OUTSIDERS

This is the most general classification of people who could possibly have access to a particular computing system (Figure 3.1). *Insiders* are people with an established relationship with the system's proprietor. Typical insiders are employees of the proprietor's organization. Other insiders might be contractors, consultants, or other types of business partners. The essential feature shared by all insiders is that they have a direct interest in the success of the organization and therefore have good reasons to avoid injuring the organization through theft, vandalism, or spying. Moreover, the proprietor must rely on insiders to get the organization's work done, and insiders use the organization's assets when doing their jobs. So the proprietor must trust insiders with assets and, for the most part, insiders work to benefit the organization.

Outsiders are people without a similar relationship to the organization. Outsiders might be arbitrary members of the general public, occasional customers of the organization, or people actively seeking to do harm to the organization.

These relationships may be fairly clear in personal, business, and professional environments. At home, insiders are members of the family and, perhaps, a trusted household employee. In volunteer organizations, insiders are people with a history of working to the benefit of the organization's goals.

However, it's not always easy to draw the insider/outsider distinction. Schools, for example, often have to treat students as outsiders since their goals and motivations are different from those of the professional staff. Businesses may also draw an insider/outsider distinction between employees involved in a sensitive activity, like payroll, and the rest of the employees, to better protect an especially tempting target.

The insider/outsider distinction is no guarantee of safety. Surveys by the U.S. Federal Bureau of Investigation (FBI) show that insiders always account for a significant number of financial crimes; insiders accounted for as many as 60% of convictions for such crimes in the 1980s. In the annual poll of computer security incidents sponsored jointly by the FBI and the Computer Security Institute (CSI) released in 2001, 31% of the respondents reported that their own internal systems were the origin of attacks they suffered.

A-21

see Note 1.

The MIT CTSS hackers discussed in Section 1.3 were all insiders, but most observers agree that their objectives were not malicious or destructive. CTSS administrators reported in 1966 that despite some quite successful attempts by "MIT sophomores (in fact or in temperament)" to attack CTSS security, there were no earnest attempts at fraud or destruction. Though not perfectly behaved, hackers of that era shared the essential insider attitude.

see Note 2.

Insider attacks are particularly challenging, because computer-based security mechanisms can't generally protect against them directly. Effective protections must be designed into the enterprise's systems and applications. There are two design principles

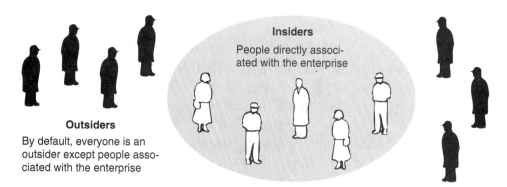

FIGURE 3.1: *Insiders and outsiders.* Insiders usually have direct physical access to a variety of enterprise resources, including computers. The enterprise grants access to individuals as part of their jobs or other roles with the enterprise. Outsiders have no such role or job and have little or no access.

that usually play a role in such protections: separation of duty and least privilege.

Separation of duty means that a process is designed so that separate steps are performed by separate people. At the end of Chapter 1 we alluded briefly to its role in reducing the risk of nuclear annihilation: no single person can set off a nuclear weapon since the arming mechanisms depend on the actions of several different people working independently. We find a much more common, if less dramatic, example in larger businesses: the accounting department usually organizes the process of making payments into two or more activities performed by separate people. For example, items requiring payment might be processed by one person, the checks are actually produced by a second person, and the canceled checks are reconciled by a third. This reduces the risk of individuals making undetected payments to themselves of company funds. Separation of duty often finds its way into computing systems at the application level: an automated purchase order system will usually enforce a requirement that different people perform different steps in the process.

D-21

Least privilege means that we only give people the permissions and privileges required to get their jobs done, no more and no less. If we look at the accounting example, this means that the person who reconciles the canceled checks does not have access to blank checks. In a computing system, it usually means that people on Project A are not granted access to the files used by Project B.

D-22

USERS AND ADMINISTRATORS

Once we've identified people as insiders and as authorized computer users, we classify them further according to their responsibilities regarding those computers (Figure 3.2). *Users* are people who rely on the computer systems to help them do useful work for the proprietor. The computer system provides the users with the tools to get that work done. Systems often use their access control mechanisms to limit what individual users may do. The system grants users permission to use the system components required to get their usual work done, and it denies access to other components, notably those that maintain the system's integrity.

Administrators are people responsible for the operation and integrity of the computer system. The system's proprietor assigns this role to the administrators, and they perform it on the proprietor's behalf. Administrators typically have unrestricted access to some or all elements of a computer system so that they can fix any problems that may arise.

In the days of centralized mainframes, this gave administrators all the access they might need to indulge in fraud or embezzlement, and such antics happened on occasion. Donn Parker described an incident from the 1960s in which an accountant started his own computer service bureau and sold his services to his former employer. The accountant set up the entire system with the express purpose of embezzling money from this one client, and used his position as administrator and proprietor of the service bureau to execute his scheme. Ultimately, the embezzler was caught, but only because he wanted to retire and could terminate the scheme only by exposing it.

A-22

see Note 3.

There are ways to address the risk of corrupt administrators. One obvious approach is separation of duty: divide up critical enterprise functions so they involve two or more computers, and assign different administrators to the different computers. If we also implement the concept of least privilege, then administrators have access only to the systems directly assigned to them. This yields a situation in

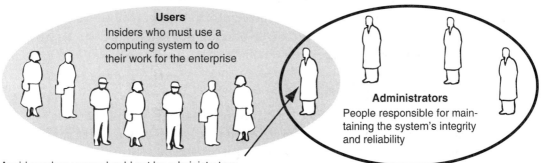

Avoid overlap: users should not be administrators

FIGURE 3.2: *User and administrator roles.* Users are people who have access to computing systems in order to do work to promote enterprise objectives. Administrators take care of computing systems. Combining the roles will produce conflicts of interest that tend to shortchange other users of the computing system.

which abuse requires collusion among two or more people, which dramatically reduces risks.

We can also reduce risks by good record keeping. Whenever the computer system performs an important step in a valuable activity, the system should note the event in an audit log. For example, when an accountant tells the system to pay the amount due to a supplier, the audit log should identify the transaction and the accountant who performed it. Later on, company auditors can look at the logs and match up individual transactions to ensure their authenticity. This reduces risk by providing accountability for people's actions. Although the situation varies with time and place, administrators are often far too busy to indulge in a profitable embezzlement and completely cover their tracks.

D-23

Users and administrators play very different roles on a computing system. Proprietors should avoid overlap between those roles as much as possible, since overlap can skew administrative priorities and generate divided loyalties. For example, an administrator who does other work for the company may be tempted to give priority to the nonadministrative work, since administration is an overhead expense while the other work might produce revenue. Managers have a hard time complaining when someone concentrates on revenue producing work instead of spending more overhead. Unfortunately, the administrator then shirks the task of maintaining the system's integrity in order to satisfy more immediate goals. For example, a combined user/administrator might be tempted to disable or bypass security controls while performing "more important" tasks, and such actions could place other computer assets at risk. The safest approach is to avoid placing such temptations in an administrator's path.

A-23

CARRIERS AND CRACKERS

Here we classify a particular group of outsiders: people who have access to an organization's private data as it travels across commercial communications circuits among that organization's sites. *Carriers* are people working for companies that provide the communications service; such a company may be a telephone company, an Internet service provider (ISP), cable company, or similar organization. Carriers are usually professional employees who have incidental access to the organization's data as it travels from one location to another.

Crackers are people who have unauthorized access to information on commercial communications circuits. Intrusions and data sniffing became a common occurrence on the Internet in its early days. This led some observers to say that sending data on the Internet was the same as publishing it in the newspaper. The reality is somewhat less grim in practice, but Internet communications remain very vulnerable. Beginning with a notorious incident in 1994, there have been regular reports of crackers installing password sniffing software in major ISP nodes.   *see Note 4.*

Traditional communications are not immune from cracker penetration either. People who penetrate the international telephone system, traditionally called *phone phreaks*, are discussed in Section 8.2. Although large-scale cracker behavior may have emerged with the phone system, earlier communications technologies were not risk free. In the days of telegraph, outsiders didn't usually try to crack into it, probably since those who knew the technology could always find a well-paying job as an insider. But this simply meant that eavesdropping and fraud had to be performed by the carrier's employees.

Examples of communications fraud date back even to the optical telegraphs of the 1830s. In one case, speculators induced the operators to insert particular patterns of transmission errors that would indicate the direction of the Paris stock market (this was, arguably, the first instance of a "covert channel" in digital communications). Naturally, the problem persists today with the Internet, where almost anyone can become an ISP. In late 1999, the Associated Press reported that a bookseller had been caught eavesdropping on competitors' e-mails: the bookseller had established an ISP catering to other booksellers and was exploiting his role as their communications carrier.   *see Note 5.*

People's roles do not predict their behavior—they only identify their *likely* behavior. Still, roles are important because they often reflect the genuine needs people may have for computer access. As such, security policy decisions and access controls will often reflect people's roles regardless of resulting security risks.

3.2   ENROLLING USERS

The first step in making an authentication system really work is to establish user names and distinguishing characteristics for the authorized users. Most proprietors have no problem assigning user names: they might be some combination of initials and names, or they might be alphanumeric identifiers assigned sequentially or randomly. The tricky problem is to establish a distinguishing characteristic for each authorized user. The proprietor wants to enroll every authorized user with a minimum of inconvenience, and to avoid granting access to any unauthorized people or attackers by mistake. If the proprietor needs to distribute passwords or other base secrets manually, then those secrets must not fall into the hands of attackers. The enrollment process always strikes a balance between safety and convenience.

In general, the enrollment process creates a *user account* for the new user. There is generally a database that contains account information associated with that user, like the user name, password, permissions, statistics on resource use, and so on. The system must restrict the use of this file to ensure that it contains only accounts authorized by the proprietor. The general user population might have restricted access to it to make changes of a personal nature, like configuration preferences. In Unix, there is a tradition of allowing the general user population to run programs that might search the account file to validate user names (see Section 2.3). Unix generally provides this service with a special copy of the file that omits sensitive information like password hashes. In general, nobody can add users or update arbitrary information in user records except for administrators who are specifically authorized to do so.

There are three general approaches for enrolling users: self authentication, enrollment in person, and assigned initial secrets. We examine the first two in this section, and we examine the assignment of initial secrets in Section 3.3. We illustrate these approaches by considering what must happen for a user named Tim to establish a user name and distinguishing characteristic.

SELF-AUTHENTICATION

Self-authentication relies on people to establish their own distinguishing characteristics for authentication. There are two general approaches to setting up user accounts for self-authentication: to establish no initial password and to establish a default initial password.

- **No initial password**

  This is arguably the simplest approach. The proprietor enrolls Tim as a new user by assigning him a user name and telling Tim the name. Tim can log on to the system whenever he wants. His account is not protected, but he has the option of creating a password for it if he wants. The approach has a long history, since it was used on Titan, the pioneering timesharing system at Cambridge University.

  The obvious problem with this approach, particularly in large-scale environments, is that it makes account misuse easy. There are always a lot of people who won't use passwords unless they're required to. Attackers only need to know a victim's user name in order to use such accounts. If Tim doesn't install a password on his account, then he's not going to know if someone has examined or manipulated his files. In an educational environment, there's the obvious problem of copying homework and of other forms of plagiarism or mischief.

  A-24

  Even worse, an attacker could steal Tim's account by installing a password that Tim doesn't know. Tim can retrieve his account from the attacker by contacting the system's proprietor or an administrator, but meanwhile Tim can't use the computer.

  A-25

  This approach is probably acceptable in a "clubhouse" atmosphere of trustworthy people, especially if the system contains little to arouse the interest of attackers. It may be acceptable in situations in which physical security protects the system from unauthorized or simply untrained users.

- **Default password**

  By establishing a default password, the proprietor makes it a little more difficult for attackers and might prevent some cases of account theft. If the attacker isn't familiar with local procedures,

  D-24

then the attacker might not know the default password. This reduces the risk of account misuse and theft.

The effectiveness of default passwords really depends on who is attacking the system. If the attackers tend to be people in the community (as it usually is with educational systems), then attackers probably know the default password already. The default password might provide sufficient protection in unsophisticated business environments where the computing system isn't managing costly resources. The primary threat in such environments is probably from outsiders who are unlikely to have learned the default password.

The most common and practical application of default passwords is with new equipment. Instead of pre-enrolling the users, the manufacturer includes built-in user names like "root" on Unix or "Administrator" on Windows servers. To provide a patina of security, these accounts may have predefined "default" passwords, described in the installation documentation. The proprietor avoids theft of these accounts by changing the associated passwords, and possibly the account names, before putting the system on-line.

The usual problem with the default password approach was described in Section 2.1: it's just too easy to leave defaults in place. If we fail to change the default passwords, then attackers have an easy path into the system. Such passwords are quite well known among people who attack systems, just as the lists of "try-out combinations" are well known among safecrackers.

A-26

In a well-designed system, the initial setup procedure should lead the installer (Tim, for example) to change every default password that was shipped with the system. The procedure could even lead him to eliminate the predefined user names and substitute his own (or those of his staff or colleagues), but this rarely happens.

Although self-authentication works poorly in situations involving shared base secrets, it has similarities with enrollment in the "public key" systems introduced in Chapter 13. In a public key system, a user like Tim can generate the secret part of the public key himself, and share the public key with a system's proprietor as part of the enrollment process. The public key serves as a distinguishing characteristic that does not depend on secrecy. However, the process isn't foolproof, and the public key enrollment process faces its own set of risks.

ENROLLMENT IN PERSON

In this approach, people must meet with the proprietor or with an administrator in person when setting up a user account. This eliminates the risks of account misuse and theft, and eliminates the need for default passwords. When Tim arrives for enrollment, he can provide his distinguishing characteristic directly to the authentication system, usually without having to share it with the administrator.

D-25

Biometric systems often use enrollment in person. Enrollment is similar to the process of receiving a picture ID card: Tim must submit himself to the appropriate equipment to collect the appropriate biometric readings. Those readings are then processed to create his distinguishing characteristic for the authentication system.

The principal security benefit is that the enrollment involves genuine, physical people instead of slips of paper or electronic data exchanges. The administrator can see Tim in person and compare him against other information that might be known about him in order to verify his identity. A really cautious administrator might even ask for identification, like a driver's license, if the company's employee badge isn't authoritative enough.

The only security risk would be if an attacker has enough drive to try to physically impersonate a legitimate employee. Many people who attack computers do so because they aren't comfortable dealing with people face to face, so this approach would discourage such attackers. On the other hand, attackers with a flair for social engineering might not mind this challenge, and such people probably pose the biggest threat.

3.3 ASSIGNING AN INITIAL SECRET

The previous cases often yield the extremes in terms of safety and convenience: self-authentication is convenient but unsafe, while enrollment in person is safe but inconvenient. The most common compromise is for the proprietor to assign initial secrets to users and then deliver those secrets to them. Proprietors may assign

D-26

either a random secret or a cultural secret. We examine those alternatives below.

RANDOM SECRET

To enroll Tim as a new user, the proprietor creates a user name and a base secret for him. Next, the proprietor delivers that information to him, taking care not to leak the secret to any potential attackers.

This approach is very popular in business settings. As a new employee, Tim fills out the forms for requesting use of the corporate systems. The information services department sends him back a user name and initial password, usually sealed in an opaque envelope marked "Personal and Confidential." The envelope should resist tampering, and Tim should report it immediately if the envelope was opened before he received it. Banks use this technique to distribute randomly generated PINs for new ATM cards.

This approach was often used in educational settings where students were given temporary accounts on a timesharing system to use for a particular class. The system administrators would generate a batch of accounts for a given class and print out slips of paper, each with a user name and password. The instructor would distribute these to students in the class. Even if accounts fell into the hands of people not in the class, the accounts would expire at the end of the session, reducing the potential for loss or abuse. However, there was rarely any individual accountability, since the instructor did not keep records of which student ended up with which user name.

While this approach is obviously popular to use with passwords, it is also the usual procedure for token-based authentication. The token contains the user's base secret, and the proprietor must deliver that particular token to the right user. Unlike a password, however, it is much more difficult for an attacker to sniff the base secret. Usually, the attacker will actually have to steal the token.

CULTURAL SECRET

In this approach, the proprietor chooses some secret information about Tim and uses it as the authentication secret. For example, the proprietor might use Tim's employee number or his mother's maiden name as his initial password. When Tim first tries to use the system, the instructions can tell him what information is used as his initial password without actually repeating the password itself.

If the proprietor is particularly concerned about masquerades, the authentication system should put restrictions on Tim's initial password. When he first logs on to the system with this password, the system should make him choose another one, since cultural secrets are too easy to uncover. In addition, the system should also establish a time limit for Tim to change the password. If he fails to log on and change the password soon, the system should block Tim's account and require him to start the enrollment process over. The risk of an attacker stealing Tim's account will increase as the account sits idle, protected only by Tim's cultural secret.

Cultural secrets are widely used for Web-based enrollment and authentication, particularly for consumer e-commerce. Before closing a sale, commercial Web sites collect the buyer's name, credit card number, expiration date, billing address, and telephone number. The basic theory is that an attacker might manage to collect part of this data, but is unlikely to collect all of it. For example, someone who steals a credit card might not have the victim's billing address, or might have the address but not the telephone number. If the thief intercepts a victim's credit card statement, the statement doesn't provide the card's expiration date or the telephone number. Moreover, unscrupulous Web merchants can't masquerade as customers, because the credit card companies insist on even more data when they themselves must authenticate a customer over the Internet or over the phone.

Web-based enrollment has also been adapted for establishing user accounts on corporate systems. Such a system uses a cultural secret about an employee for initial authentication as described earler. Instead of simply installing the base secret as an initial password, the base secret is used to protect a more sophisticated enrollment process that can install passwords and other distinguishing characteristics for a variety of systems.

CHANGING THE INITIAL PASSWORD

We usually need to change the initial password, particularly if it's a default password or based on a cultural secret. A careful system will demand a change of just about any initial password, simply on the assumption that initial passwords get handled a lot more than ones that users think up themselves. Moreover, passwords are often changed periodically for other reasons, so it's important to examine how it's usually done and the rationale behind it.

Password changing is tricky business. Usually, the password changing process reflects a worst-case security environment: shoulder surfing, van Eck sniffing, and pre-video computer terminals that record everything on printed paper. The usual process asks the user, Tim for example, to enter his current password first. If that password is correct, it prompts him to type in his new password twice. The system collects the passwords, old and new, in a way that keeps them hidden from everyone's sight, including Tim's. Here is an example, based on the Unix password changing procedure:

```
% passwd
Enter old password: old-password
Enter new password: new-password
Retype new password: new-password
Password successfully changed.
%
```

Neither the text *old-password* nor *new-password* are actually displayed. Unix systems generally disable the character display while collecting passwords. Other systems, like Windows and Macintosh, will substitute uniform x-marks or black dots for the actual characters typed. Few systems display the password being typed, although this would be a good thing to do in some situations (see Section 6.3).

The password hiding process follows an ancient tradition, dating back to the early days of timesharing, when people used printing terminals. Almost everything a user typed during a timesharing session would appear on the reams of paper typed out by the terminal. When the timesharing system requested a password (a new one or a changed one), the system would either type a "mask" of characters (Figure 1.4 in Section 1.3 gives an example of this) or it would disable the "echo" of each character a person typed. Moreover, timesharing connections usually resided in crowded terminal rooms and computer labs. Shoulder surfing was a real concern, as were discarded copies of typescripts containing a user's login procedure.

The password changing procedure asks Tim to type the new password twice because he can't see what he has typed. By typing it a second time the system reduces the risk that Tim has mistyped his password in a way he can't see. Moreover, typing it twice gives Tim a slightly better chance of remembering the password he chose. However, as discussed in Section 6.1, this still poses a real challenge to most people's memories.

3.4 ENTROPY AND USER PASSWORD SELECTION

In Section 2.7 we discussed how a bias in choosing base secrets can reduce the entropy of those base secrets. If people always use dates for a four-digit secret, then the average attack space drops from 14 bits to nine bits. Such biases often infect passwords, since people are much better at choosing and remembering words than at choosing less predictable strings of characters. Numerous studies of computer user behavior have shown that many people in any reasonably sized computer user population will choose memorable words for passwords.

If password choices are especially poor, attackers can guess them at human speeds. There is a legend about a university timesharing system in which the administrators studied user password choices and, for some reason, the most common password was found to be "raquel." When a student later complained that his account had been penetrated, the system administrator said with a straight face, "That is impossible unless, of course, your password is 'raquel'." The student's jaw dropped and he exclaimed, "How did you know?"

More recently, someone on the Internet claimed that an associate had uncovered someone's password by consulting a psychic telephone hotline. While the actual story may be fiction, it carries a grain of truth. Psychics have flourished in the past by performing very simple investigations on their targets, and by choosing targets based on information they collect. Anyone can guess a few passwords by combining personal information with shrewd guesses.   *see Note 6.*

Given proper guidance, typical computer users will choose a good password. However, this doesn't guarantee that *all* users will choose good passwords. A study by Eugene Spafford at Purdue University found that 1% of the passwords encountered during a nine-month survey consisted of only one or two characters, and 5% were four characters or less. A study at AT&T a decade earlier found 31% of the passwords were four characters or less. Password length is not the only problem. Some users choose their user name to be their password. This phenomenon is so common that such accounts are given a name: "Joe accounts." The Purdue study found that 3.9% of the accounts examined were "Joe accounts." Later studies have found similar results.

see Note 7.

Section 2.7 also introduced the average attack space as a way to compare trial-and-error attacks. An accurate estimate of the average attack space must reflect well-known biases in people's behavior. If people are likely to choose passwords from a particular set (that is, words they use), then it is more efficient for an attacker to search for passwords out of that small subset. We must capture that bias when computing the average attack space, just as we did with date combinations on luggage locks.

There are three general approaches for taking that bias into account. One approach is to examine statistical properties of languages, English in this case, and compute estimates based on the entropy of linguistic utterances. A second, more accurate, approach is to look at dictionaries used in biased attacks and compute attack times based on their assumed password spaces. A third approach is to look at experimental results from studies of biased attacks. We examine these approaches below.

STATISTICAL BIAS IN TEXT

To start with, we can try to estimate how many random, unpredictable bits might really exist in a password, given that the password is probably a word or some other textual item from the victim's native language. While this doesn't necessarily give us a way to attack passwords, it gives us a theoretical measure of how strong (or rather, how weak) passwords might be.

We start by just looking at the bias introduced by using a particular alphabet. If passwords consist of any sequence of 26 letters, then we compute the entropy by multiplying the number of letters in a word times the number of bits in a letter. If any one of the 26 alphabetic letters is equally likely, then the entropy per letter is $\log_2(26)$, or approximately 4.76 bits per letter.

Of course, not all letters are equally likely. This fact has played a well-known role in code breaking. Most people are familiar with the fact that certain letters (notably E, T, and A) are far more common in English text than other letters, and this information is widely used to break cryptogram puzzles. If we are faced with some English text, we immediately know that the text is biased toward including the more common letters. If we take into account the likelihood of individual letters, we find that the entropy of English text is really closer to 4.19 bits per letter. Even though this example refers to English text, the same phenomenon exists in all human languages.

see Note 8.

To break even more sophisticated codes, code breakers performed more sophisticated statistical analyses on text in order to detect more sophisticated patterns. For example, code breakers have analyzed the statistics for *digraphs* in text, that is, the likelihood that particular pairs of letters will occur in a particular language. Since certain digraphs never occur in some languages, like the letter Q followed by anything except a U in English, there are obvious biases toward certain digraphs. When we apply the biases found in English digraphs to our estimate of the entropy per character in an English word, the estimate drops again, yielding approximately 3.90 bits per letter.

Having computed the statistics for sequences of two letters, we can proceed to estimate the statistics for sequences of three letters (trigraphs), four letters, and so on. The pattern of worsening entropy continues as we consider arbitrarily long English text. Experiments have estimated the overall entropy of English text to lie between 1 and 1.5 bits per letter. Thus, we *dramatically* reduce the size of the average attack space when we know the passwords are English words. Although the statistical details may vary, the basic concept is undoubtedly true for other natural languages. Here is an estimate of the average attack space on 10-character passwords, assuming that 25% of the user population chooses an English word for a password:

$$V_{English} = \log_2 \frac{(2^{1.5})^n}{2 \times L} \qquad V_{English} = \log_2\left(\frac{(2^{1.5})^{10}}{2 \times 0.25}\right)$$

$$V_{English} = \log_2\left(\frac{32,768}{0.5}\right)$$

$$V_{English} = 16.0$$

If we store the password's individual characters in eight-bit bytes, we have an 80-bit base secret that only provides a 16-bit average attack space.

However, this computation is purely theoretical. While it suggests that there are 32,768 likely English words to use as 10-character passwords, it does not reflect the existence of some particular list of 32,768 words. There is no known procedure to exploit the entropy in English and generate a dictionary of candidate passwords for an attack like this. At best this example suggests that an attacker could successfully use a dictionary of 32,768 words to guess passwords with 10 letters or less.

Also, notice the effect of the 25% likelihood term. The password space size of 32,768 corresponds to 15 bits. This reflects an implied list of easy-to-guess passwords. If the likelihood had been 100%, then everyone would have chosen an easy-to-guess password. A trial-and-error attack would have to search half of that space, on average, so the average attack space would be half of the original password space, or 14 bits. If the likelihood had been 50%, we would have had to search twice as hard to find a match, since half as many users would have chosen passwords we knew how to guess. This would bring the average attack space back up to 15 bits. When we drop to a 25% likelihood, we double the attack space, which yields 16 bits.

DICTIONARY ATTACKS

Of course, we aren't limited to theoretical estimates of password strength. We can also estimate the strength of biased passwords by looking at the practical properties of dictionary attacks. In particular, we can look at dictionary sizes and at statistics regarding the success rates of dictionary attacks. Figure 3.3 shows excerpts from dictionaries that either have been or could be used in dictionary attacks.

The Internet Worm tried successfully to crack passwords by working through a whole series of word lists. First, it built a customized dictionary of words containing the user name, the person's name (both taken from the Unix password file), and five permutations of them. If those failed, it used an internal dictionary of 432 common,

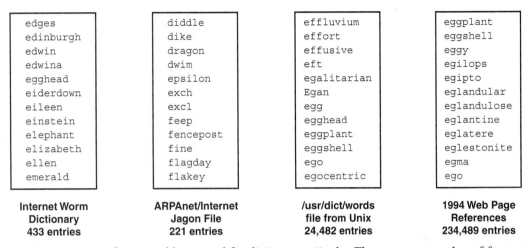

edges	diddle	effluvium	eggplant
edinburgh	dike	effort	eggshell
edwin	dragon	effusive	eggy
edwina	dwim	eft	egilops
egghead	epsilon	egalitarian	egipto
eiderdown	exch	Egan	eglandular
eileen	excl	egg	eglandulose
einstein	feep	egghead	eglantine
elephant	fencepost	eggplant	eglatere
elizabeth	fine	eggshell	eglestonite
ellen	flagday	ego	egma
emerald	flakey	egocentric	ego
Internet Worm	**ARPAnet/Internet**	**/usr/dict/words**	**1994 Web Page**
Dictionary	**Jagon File**	**file from Unix**	**References**
433 entries	**221 entries**	**24,482 entries**	**234,489 entries**

FIGURE 3.3: *Excerpts from word lists used for dictionary attacks.* These are examples of four candidate word lists for use in dictionary attacks. These are only four of dozens of potential word lists. Other candidates list words from movie trivia, various fiction genres, sports, proper names, places, and so on. Word lists also exist for different languages and cultures.   *see Note 9.*

Internet-oriented jargon words. If those failed, it used the Unix on-line dictionary of 24,474 words. The worm also checked for the "null" password. Some sites reported as many as 50% of their passwords were successfully cracked using this strategy. Adding these all up, the worm searched a password space of 24,914 passwords, yielding the following average attack space: *see Note 10.*

$$V_{\text{Worm}} = \log_2\left(\frac{S}{2 \times L}\right) \qquad V_{\text{Worm}} = \log_2\left(\frac{24,914}{2 \times 0.5}\right)$$

$$V_{\text{Worm}} = 14.6$$

This suggests that a traditional memorized password provides a 14.6 bit average attack space, regardless of the actual password sizes permitted by the system. Using the Pentium P100 guess rate noted earlier, the worm's dictionary attack runs through the entire dictionary in less than a half second.

ESTIMATING BIAS IN PASSWORD SELECTION

The "50%" likelihood figure in the previous discussion reflects the crucial property of biased passwords: users are not *forced* to choose passwords from dictionaries, but they are statistically *likely* to do so. The 50% estimate is based on anecdotal evidence from the Internet Worm incident. A more realistic model looks at experiments that measure real user behavior. The beginning of this section noted the results of a few studies, but the first truly comprehensive study was performed in 1990 by Daniel V. Klein.

see Note 11.

Klein collected encrypted password files from numerous Unix systems, courtesy of friends and colleagues in the United States and the United Kingdom. This collection yielded approximately 15,000 different user account entries, each with its own password. Klein then constructed a set of password dictionaries and a set of mechanisms to systematically permute the dictionary into likely variations. When Klein ran his tool against the password files, he quickly cracked 368 passwords (2.7% of the collection) simply by looking for Joe accounts.

Klein's password cracker used six general strategies. Like the Internet Worm, he started with permutations of the user name and user's proper name, but Klein's approach generated as many as 130 different alternatives for a given account by varying the order of letters, capitalization, and so on. Second, he used a set of dictionaries of names, places, literary titles, character names, mythological references, numbers, biblical terms, Romanized Chinese syllables, and so on. This produced approximately 60,000 words. Third, he generated as many as 17 variations of those dictionary words by replacing letters with similar looking digits, changing endings, and so on. This produced an additional million words. Fourth, Klein tried variations of uppercase and lowercase, yielding almost 2 million more words. Klein found that he could perform these first four searches in a practical amount of time, and they yielded significant success.

The last two strategies produced potential passwords by combining other items. The fifth strategy generated two-syllable Romanized Chinese passwords and tested these as passwords for individuals with Chinese-appearing names. Sixth, Klein tried word pairs, constructed from three- and four-letter words in the Unix dictionary.

Klein's strategies produced a basic dictionary of over 60,000 items. The list included names of people, places, fictional references, mythical references, specialized terms, biblical terms, words from Shakespeare, Yiddish, mnemonics, and so on. After applying the permutation strategies, he produced a password space containing

TABLE 3.1: *Percentage of Passwords Found by Systematic Searches*

Report	When	Passwords Searched	Percentage Found
Internet Worm	1988	thousands	~50%
Study by Klein	1990	15,000	24.2%
Study by Spafford	1992	13,787	20%
CERT Incident IN-98-03	1998	186,126	25.6%
Study by Yan et al.	2000	195	35%

over 3 million possibilities. After systematically searching this space, Klein managed to crack 24.2% of all passwords in his collection of accounts. This yields the following average attack space: *see Note 12.*

$$V_{\text{Klein}} = \log_2\left(\frac{3{,}321{,}261}{2 \times 0.242}\right)$$

$$V_{\text{Klein}} = 22.71$$

Klein's results suggest that the reported Internet Worm experience underestimates the average attack space of Unix passwords by about eight bits. Still, a 22- or 23-bit attack space is not a serious impediment to a reasonably well-equipped attacker, especially when attacking an encrypted password file. The guess rate of a Pentium P100 can search that average attack space in less than two minutes.

The likelihood statistic tells us an important story because it shows how often people pick easy-to-crack passwords. Table 3.1 summarizes the results of several instances in which someone subjected a collection of passwords to a dictionary attack or other systematic search. Spafford's study at Purdue took place from 1991 to 1992, and produced statistics regarding people's password choices. The study also compared passwords against a few dictionaries and simple word lists, and found 20% of the passwords in those lists. *see Note 13.*

The CERT statistic is based on a password cracking activity uncovered in 1998. The cracker had collected 186,126 user records, and had successfully guessed 47,642 of these passwords. In 2000, a team of researchers at Cambridge University performed password usage experiments designed in accordance with the experimental standards of applied psychology. While the focus of the experiment was on techniques to strengthen passwords, it also examined 195 hashed passwords chosen by students in the experiment's control group and in the general user population: 35% of their passwords were cracked. Although the worm statistics may be based on a lot of conjecture, the other statistics show that crackable passwords are indeed prevalent. If anything, the prevalence of weak passwords is increasing as more and more people use computers.

see Note 14.

3.5   RESTRICTING PASSWORD SELECTION

Since people tend to choose weak passwords, some experts believe that we can improve security by restricting the passwords people can use. There are three general strategies for making people select stronger passwords. First, some sites use password cracking programs to find weak passwords. The site runs the cracking program against encrypted password files, and if the program cracks any passwords, the administrator warns the errant user to choose a better password. Second, there are programs that automatically generate passwords for people. Whenever someone needs a new password, the system generates the password and assigns it to that person. The third approach is to check passwords proactively. When people change their passwords, the system checks each new password against various password construction rules to ensure that it is strong enough.

The latter two strategies are the type of thing often called *forcing functions* since they force people to take particular actions. Such things should be used sparingly, since people adapt them in surprising and often dangerous ways. As discussed further in Chapter 6, people in general have a very hard time memorizing random data. If a forcing function interferes with a person's ability to use an essential system, the person will find a way to circumvent the forcing function, and may adapt to it in a way that compromises system safety. It is best to restrict such mechanisms to particularly important passwords, like those with administrative privileges.

THERAPEUTIC PASSWORD CRACKING

In this approach, a site administrator uses password cracking programs to search for weak passwords in encrypted password files. The *crack* program is the classic password cracker in the Unix world: it accepts specialized dictionaries of candidate passwords, it supports distributed cracking so that several machines share the task, and it runs on several platforms besides Unix. The best-known cracker for Windows systems is *l0phtcrack*, which attacks password hashes extracted from the SAM file in the Windows NT Registry. Some programs evolved into general purpose utilities to scan for computer vulnerabilities; the SATAN program by Dan Farmer was one of the earliest programs of this type.   *see Note 15.*

When an administrator uses a cracking program, the objective is simply to identify which users have weak passwords. The administrator does not actually need the password, though a few users might find the administrator's arguments more convincing if actually presented with the cracked password. In most cases, the administrator simply needs to identify which users need additional guidance on choosing strong passwords.

Password cracking programs reflect the rather bizarre duality of security tools and attack tools. Many people who developed or promoted password cracking tools emphasized their value as devices to improve site security. However, the basic mechanism that finds weak passwords can also disclose them to attackers.

This duality can have unsavory side effects. In 1993, Randall Schwartz, a well-known expert on Unix and the Perl programming language, was working as an administrator at an Intel Corporation site in Oregon. While working there, he ran the program *crack* on his own initiative and found dozens of weak passwords. Although there was no evidence that Schwartz intended harm, he could not prove that anyone at Intel had authorized his activities. Intel management pressed charges against him under Oregon's computer crime law, and a jury found Schwartz guilty.   *see Note 16.*

AUTOMATIC PASSWORD GENERATION

An automatic password generator is a program that produces random passwords. In its simplest form, the program could simply generate a random numerical value and encode it as a sequence of printable characters. If the program uses a good random number generator, then it can produce passwords that are both relatively short and impractical to guess. Unfortunately, such passwords will also be extremely difficult to memorize.

Most password generators try to produce "pronounceable" passwords in order to make the password more memorable. Such generators can often produce passwords simply by alternating vowels and consonants. More sophisticated generators produce easier-to-remember passwords. One such approach was defined in the U.S. government standard FIPS 181.

see Note 17.

In a sense, the password generator introduces a bias into the password space. If the authentication system accepts passwords with ten single-case letters, then there are over 141 trillion legal passwords. But if we only use "pronounceable" passwords, then the password space will not contain arbitrary sequences of letters. A FIPS 181 pronounceable password generator, for example, will generate about 1.6 trillion different 10-character passwords, which yields an average attack space of over 39 bits. Unlike the human bias toward well-known words, however, this bias is rigidly enforced. Users cannot choose to use "more random" passwords any more than they can choose less random ones. They must use the automatically generated ones.

Occasionally, password generators are plagued with implementation problems. In one incident (often attributed to a version of the Multics system), the password generator program used a defective random number generator. The program was set up to produce eight-character passwords consisting of single-case letters and digits. This should have produced a password space with over 2.8 trillion possibilities (a 40-bit average attack space). Unfortunately, the random number generator always used a 15-bit starting value, so it could not possibly generate more than 32,768 different passwords (a 14-bit average attack space).

see Note 18.

The advent of high-performance off-line attacks against encrypted passwords essentially has killed pronounceable password generators. First of all, there just aren't enough short, pronounceable passwords to resist a brute force attack. The 10-character passwords generated by FIPS 181 won't withstand an attack by a well-equipped attacker. Some researchers have even developed specialized attacks to specifically target pronounceable passwords.

see Note 19.

PROACTIVE PASSWORD CHECKING

This approach attempts to prevent weak passwords by screening each password a user chooses. Whenever people try to change their passwords, the system checks the newly selected password for various properties in order to weed out vulnerable choices. This occasionally produces an "arms race" between the user community and the people responsible for password enforcement. The users keep finding shortcuts and mnemonics while the password software designers keep tightening up the constraints on acceptable passwords.

Following his survey of user password choices, Klein compiled several design recommendations for proactive password checking. He used the permutation mechanisms from his password cracker to identify important properties of hard-to-guess passwords. He argued the system should reject passwords with any of the following properties:

see Note 20.

- Shorter than six characters
- Contains the user's account name, given name, or initials
- Exactly matches a dictionary word, a word with a few letters capitalized, a reversed word, a reversed word with some letters capitalized, a word with some character substituted for a control character, a word with obvious digits substituted for letters
- Simple conjugations of dictionary words
- Single-case words (all upper or all lower)
- Does not contain a mixture of letters and digits or letters and punctuation
- Matches a pattern on the keyboard
- Contains entirely digits or looks like a state license plate number

Although many proactive password checkers are available, none try to test for all of these properties. This level of password filtering would probably be unacceptable in many environments. Without extensive training, people would not know how to construct legal passwords and would have trouble understanding why their personal choices were rejected. Under such circumstances, a user community is more likely to accept machine-generated passwords, since the draconian rules make a mockery of the concept of personal choice.

One example of a less draconian system was the Unix-oriented "Obvious Password Utility System" (OPUS) developed by Spafford at Purdue. OPUS focused on eliminating passwords that appeared in a dictionary. The system was designed to rapidly and accurately check each candidate password against the dictionary, and also check some basic permutations like capitalizations, order reversals, and simple letter substitutions as well.   *see Note 21.*

Microsoft also incorporated basic mechanisms for proactive password checking into Windows NT and Windows 2000. A local administrator can establish minimum and maximum password lengths, maximum password lifetime, and can prevent users from reusing previously expired passwords. Microsoft also provided an optional package that can force users to choose "complex" passwords by requiring that they have some of Klein's properties. In particular, the password must contain at least six characters, must contain a mixture of character types, and must not contain any part of the user's personal name or user name.   *see Note 22.*

LIMITATIONS ON PASSWORD STRENGTH

Table 3.2 summarizes the average attack spaces discussed earlier in this chapter. It is sobering to consider that DES has been broken, yet it has the largest average attack space in the table (DES is discussed in Section 5.3). However, the lesson is that *some* passwords will always be vulnerable, not that all passwords are vulnerable. Klein's research in 1990 was able to crack less than 25% of the passwords he encountered, which means that over 75% withstood his attacks.

However, Klein's statistics look slightly optimistic in comparison to more recent data. As shown earlier in Table 3.1, later studies of

TABLE 3.2: *Comparison of Average Attack Spaces*

Example	Theoretical Password Space	Biased Password Space	Average Attack Space
Random 10-letter English text	141 trillion	32 thousand	16 bits
Internet Worm password cracking	54 trillion	24 thousand	15 bits
Klein's password study	54 trillion	3 million	23 bits
FIPS 181 10-letter password generator	141 trillion	1.6 trillion	40 bits
"Broken" automatic password generator	2.8 trillion	32 thousand	16 bits
56-bit Data Encryption Standard (DES)	72 quadrillion	72 quadrillion	54 bits

password selection behavior suggest that password choices are getting weaker on average. This isn't surprising.

The user populations at the beginning of the 1990s were far different than those a decade later. That period saw explosive growth in the Internet and corresponding growth in personal computer deployment. Newer computer users were far less sophisticated than those 10 years earlier, and much less likely to exercise care with passwords than the user community that Klein surveyed.

This author's own discussions with users and administrators bear this out: people are more worried about having their computers available and usable than they are about password cracking. Problems reported at U.S. nuclear laboratories in 2000 also reflect this problem. A retired general recently placed in charge of security for the Department of Energy said that many employees used their last name or initials as their password, and some simply used the word "password." If Klein's experiment were repeated today, his cracking would probably achieve a much higher success rate.   *see Note 23.*

3.6 SUMMARY TABLES

TABLE 3.3: *Attack Summary*

Attack	Security Problem	Prevalence	Attack Description
A-21. Abuse by insider	Bypass host security and run selected programs	Common	Authorized user uses privileges to access unauthorized resources
A-22. Abuse by administrator	Bypass host security and run selected programs	Common	Administrator uses privileges to perform unauthorized activities
A-23. Divided loyalty	Bypass host security and run selected programs	Trivial	Administrator uses privileges to optimize other business duties, to the detriment of overall system operation
A-24. Account abuse	Masquerade as legitimate user	Trivial	Attacker exploits the lack of password protection on the victim's account
A-25. Account theft	Masquerade as legitimate user	Trivial	Attacker defines a new password for an account that the legitimate owner doesn't know
A-26. Default password	Masquerade as legitimate user	Trivial	Attacker uses a well-known default password to gain access to an account

TABLE 3.4: *Defense Summary*

Defense	Foils Attacks	Description
D-21. Separation of duty	A-21. Abuse by insider A-22. Abuse by administrator	Divide critical activities into two or more steps that cannot be performed by a single person
D-22. Least privilege	A-21. Abuse by insider A-22. Abuse by administrator	Restrict users' access so that they can only use the resources they really require to do their jobs, no more and no less
D-23. Log all critical events	A-21. Abuse by insider A-22. Abuse by administrator A-23. Divided loyalty	Ensure that all business application programs and systems software will write entries to the audit log whenever a critical activity takes place that identify the person performing the activity
D-24. Default passwords	A-24. Account abuse A-25. Account theft	Define a default password for all accounts to reduce the risk of outsiders stealing or abusing accounts
D-25. Enrollment in person	A-24. Account abuse A-25. Account theft A-26. Default password	Require new users to enroll in person and provide their distinguishing characteristics directly to the authentication system
D-26. Assign initial secret	A-24. Account abuse A-25. Account theft A-26. Default password	Proprietor chooses the initial secret and delivers the chosen secret to the user

CHAPTER 4
DESIGN PATTERNS

Each pattern describes a problem which occurs over and over again in our environment, and then describes the core of the solution to that problem, in such a way that you can use this solution a million times over, without ever doing it the same way twice.

— Christopher Alexander et al., *A Pattern Language*

IN THIS CHAPTER

This chapter describes architectural design patterns that often appear in the deployment of authentication systems. The patterns arise from the people involved and physical distribution of components in an authentication system.

- Physical security in authentication
- Identifying administrative requirements
- The four patterns: local, direct, indirect, and off-line
- Applying the patterns

4.1 PATTERNS IN AUTHENTICATION SYSTEMS

In the late 1960s, the architect and builder Christopher Alexander developed the notion of recurring "patterns" that produced successful solutions to common architectural design problems. Alexander's work inspired the object-oriented software community to adopt a similar notion of "design patterns" for software architecture. This chapter examines some basic design patterns that appear in authentication systems.   *see Note 1.*

In some ways, the patterns described here resemble Alexander's original architectural patterns more than object-oriented patterns. These patterns analyze problems in terms of space and people, not data and processing. Like the authentication factors (something you know, have, or are), these different patterns offer blends of strengths and weaknesses; the best choice for a particular enterprise will provide essential protections while imposing minimal administrative and operating costs. This chapter describes four patterns, starting in Section 4.4:   *see Note 2.*

- Local, which we see in laptops or single desktop systems. The entire system, including its authentication and access control mechanism, resides within a single physical security perimeter. The system proprietor and/or user maintains an up-to-date database of authentication data within that perimeter.

- Direct, which we see in older server systems on local area networks (LANs) and on timesharing systems. Many different users may share the system and use it remotely. The system's authentication and access-control mechanisms still reside inside a single physical perimeter. The proprietor maintains an up-to-date database of authentication data within each system.

- Indirect, which we see in modern network server systems, can be implemented with the RADIUS protocol, Kerberos, and Windows domain logons. The system contains several separate points of service that require access control and may reside in separate locations. Users access the system's services remotely as needed. The proprietor maintains a single, up-to-date database of authentication data for the overall system.

- Off-line, which we see in public key infrastructure systems, contains numerous autonomous components that can make accurate access control decisions even when they can't contact other systems for authoritative authentication decisions. The proprietor accepts the risk that such decisions occasionally may be made using stale access control or authentication data, and as such possibly yield incorrect results.

These patterns fall into roughly two categories: those dealing with individual, stand-alone computers and those dealing with remote access. The local pattern clearly involves an individual device. Direct and indirect authentication provide different strategies for implementing remote access. Off-line authentication provides a way of applying some administrative features of remote authentication to systems that can't always establish a remote connection.

Before we examine these four patterns, we examine two motivating factors behind pattern selection: the physical security of the computing system and administrative requirements that may influence the choice of patterns. Then come four sections that examine the deployment patterns individually. The final section discusses the selection and application of the patterns.

4.2 THE ROLE OF PHYSICAL SECURITY

Physical security is the bedrock of any computer security system. In authentication systems, physical security ensures the integrity of the decision-making mechanism and protects the base secrets. There are two separate situations with respect to physical security: protecting the software and protecting the hardware. The former case involves software running on conventional off-the-shelf computing equipment that incorporates little or no anti-tamper mechanisms. The latter case involves hardware devices used by outsiders or other potentially untrustworthy people: these devices are often built to resist tampering. The two cases converge in the problem of protecting individual workstations or laptop computers that may be subject to attack.

The essential issue is to identify the *security perimeter* of a device or system. The entire decision-making mechanism and all confidential data must reside inside that perimeter. The only people capable of reaching inside the perimeter should be administrators assigned to that task by the system's proprietor. We can rely on the authentication mechanism as long as only trustworthy people can breach its security perimeter.

PROTECTING SOFTWARE AUTHENTICATION

Modern server systems combine two strategies to protect themselves. First, the computers themselves reside inside layers of physical protection (Figure 4.1). Second, the server software running on the host computer uses protection mechanisms built into the computer's central processing unit (CPU) to protect the system's software from attack.

In the days of classical timesharing systems, the server provided all of the processing horsepower. People interacted with the systems

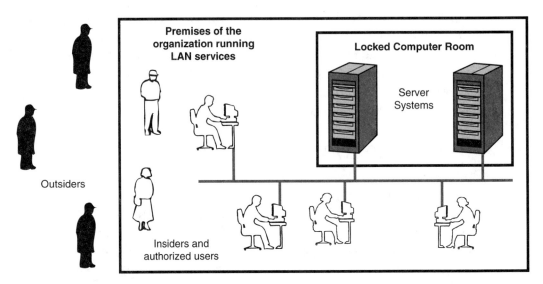

FIGURE 4.1: *Physical arrangement of a site LAN.* All of the site's workstations and servers are within the physical premises of the system's proprietor. Servers reside inside a locked computer room, since only the administrative staff needs to actually touch them. Network connections and wiring resides within the company premises.

through text-oriented terminals that served as glorified typewriters. Today's LAN systems use computing power on the desktop to do much of the work for users. Each desktop contains specialized client software that communicates with the server via a set of protocols to provide worthwhile services. Most such systems also provide special authentication protocols to ensure that the server is talking to an authorized user.

A well-designed server site provides a classic example of layered physical protection (Figure 4.1). At each layer we identify classes of people and the type of access they have. Outermost we have the distinction between insiders and outsiders introduced in Section 3.1. Within the server's community we also have the distinction between users and administrators. Insiders can pass through the first perimeter but not necessarily the second. Administrators must pass through the first perimeter before they are allowed through the second. The relationships work as follows:

- **Outsiders and Insiders**

  The classification of insiders versus outsiders reflects the basic element of physical security: insiders are allowed to freely enter the proprietor's premises and outsiders are not. Most organizations trust employees to some degree and can do so as long as they can reliably restrict access to employees only. Typically, employee workstations and communications lines receive some protection by residing inside the enterprise's premises. The enterprise uses physical security like locks, burglar alarms, guards, and so on, to ensure that outsiders stay outside except when invited in. The locked-up premises of the enterprise represent the security perimeter with respect to insiders versus outsiders.

- **Users and Administrators**

  Shared remote access systems like servers and mainframes rely on the distinction between users and administrators to maintain security. Users don't need direct, physical access to such systems, so the computers themselves are generally locked away in a machine room. Entry to the machine room is restricted to administrators. This increases our confidence in the integrity of the system. The computer room represents the security perimeter for the computing hardware and software. Not all enterprises and cultures enforce this distinction, but most recognize it as an essential defense.

The two different security perimeters reflect two different access control situations. In both cases, the perimeter serves as a filter to remove people from the population who can physically touch and manipulate the computer equipment. The outermost filter provided by the company premises prevents outsiders from accessing workstations on the corporate LAN. The innermost filter provided by the locked machine room prevents anyone except authorized administrators from tampering with the server systems. The distinction between insiders and users is enforced by the server system itself using software-based protection mechanisms. The software mechanisms usually enforce an additional distinction between users and administrators, so that administrators can make fundamental changes to the system that users cannot.

Software protection mechanisms were originally developed in the late 1950s on the Ferranti Atlas computer to support *multiprogramming*, that is, the ability to run multiple programs on a single CPU at

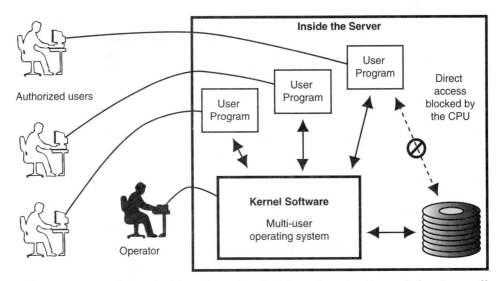

FIGURE 4.2: *Protecting software inside a computer.* CPU-based protection mechanisms allow the kernel software to control the operation of user programs and other applications. The mechanisms prevent applications from interfering with one another, or with shared resources like the hard drive and the kernel software.

roughly the same time. Most modern operating systems (OSes) support some form of multiprogramming, particularly those that support server systems. Multiprogramming generally relies on certain protection mechanisms built into the CPU that restrict what user programs may do. Thus, the protection is not really provided by software per se, but by special hardware features that enforce a security perimeter inside the computer itself.   *see Note 3.*

The CPU's protection mechanisms generally provide a *kernel mode* used by the OS or timesharing system and a restricted *user mode* for executing application programs (Figure 4.2). In addition, there is a memory protection mechanism like the one described in the discussion of password sniffing in Section 1.5. Software running in kernel mode is responsible for running the rest of the software safely and securely.   *see Note 4.*

PROTECTING WORKSTATIONS

The best protection for individual workstations is to place them in physically protected locations to prevent access by potential attackers. As noted in the previous section, most enterprises place their workstations inside their physical premises. Workstations are highly vulnerable to attack. Even if the attacker isn't motivated to steal the workstation, other risks remain, since attackers can steal sensitive data or modify critical information. The following threats persist even if the workstation's software attempts to prevent unauthorized use:

- **OS substitution attack**

  Most workstations will allow someone to boot up an operating system from a different disk, like a CD-ROM or a diskette. This capability is provided for administrative or maintenance purposes. Attackers can use it to boot an operating system that is configured with access control protections disabled. Then the attackers can read and modify files on the workstation even if its standard operating system had placed protections on the files. *A-27*

  Some workstations implement a *BIOS password* to protect against such attacks. This password is stored in the workstation's start-up configuration combined with instructions to always boot the workstation from a particular hard drive. The attackers can redirect the boot operation only if they know the password. *D-27*

  Unfortunately, the BIOS password feature is not a foolproof solution. Most systems arrive with a predefined BIOS password and many administrators fail to change it to a new and unpredictable password. As with the combination locks described in Section 2.1, the vendors' preinstalled passwords provide a fertile starting point for an interactive password guessing attack. Popular choices include "bios" or "j262" or "setup" or "cmos" in either all upper- or all lowercase, or some variant of the vendor's name. *A-28*

  see Note 5.

  The obvious defense against this guessing attack is to change the BIOS password to something unpredictable. However, this still doesn't prevent a successful attack. The BIOS password is stored in a special RAM powered by a battery. The attacker can wipe out the password in several ways. For example, if the computer is running, the attacker could install and run a program that clears the BIOS RAM. Otherwise, the attacker could zero the RAM (and the password it holds) by shutting off its power, either by physically removing the battery or by shorting it out. *D-28*

  A-29

- **I/O bus attack**

  In these attacks, the attackers take the cover off of the computer and attack at the hardware level. This generally requires extra equipment, like a different computer and the appropriate cables to cross-connect various peripheral devices. Essentially, the attackers can make complete copies of the workstation's hard drives. Given sufficiently sophisticated tools, the attackers can also modify files. This bypasses the software and BIOS entirely.

  A-30

  Physical defenses against such attacks can, at best, buy time until someone walks by and catches the intruder in the act. For example, enterprises could buy special enclosures for computers, providing a variant of the armor used on ATMs. Of course, this approach just rearranges the security problem a bit: there needs to be a way to open the armored enclosure, for example, a lock whose key also needs protection. A less expensive alternative is to place hard-to-forge seals on computer covers. This does not prevent an attack, but it may deter an attack by making it detectable.

  D-29

  D-30

  A third defense is to embed all critical functions in a single integrated circuit. While it may be possible to "reverse engineer" certain features of an integrated circuit by peeling back the layers, the manufacturer can make it an extremely expensive and tricky operation.

  D-31

The risk of I/O bus attack was a major motivating factor behind investigations of John M. Deutsch, a former U.S. Director of Central Intelligence, who had stored top secret government information on personal computers in his home. Intelligence agencies have always been obsessed with keeping their data secret, since disclosures can show adversaries how to plug their information leaks, occasionally by liquidating agents. Investigators found that Deutsch had been writing highly secret memos on the same computer that he used to surf the Internet and do on-line banking. Despite the well-known risks of Internet-based attacks, however, technical experts at the Central Intelligence Agency concluded that the greatest risk was of someone secretly breaking in and copying his hard drive. The experts doubted they could tell with confidence if such a break-in had actually occurred, since a skillful team would not leave any definite traces.

see Note 6.

Earlier we noted that the simplest and most effective strategy is to lock the workstations up in office areas where only the workstations' authorized users can reach them. Unfortunately, this is not always a practical choice. Few organizations can put all employees in private offices or even in locked offices limited to a few people. Student computing laboratories in schools offer enough physical security to deter theft but this is rarely enough to prevent trivial or common attacks by malicious students. As modern operating systems become more complex, they will render the OS substitution attack less practical. Physical protection and monitoring by trusted individuals remains the most reliable method of protecting workstations.

D-32

HARDWARE PROTECTION OF AUTHENTICATION

Hardware protection tries to enforce a security perimeter in the absence of people to guard that perimeter. ATMs provide a relatively large and familiar example. Many ATMs carry armor plating to enforce their security perimeter. People can reach a keyboard and display to type their requests, and the ATM can accept deposits and emit cash through carefully constructed ports. Specially trained guards can enter an ATM's security perimeter to add more cash and collect deposits. For the most part, however, the machine is unguarded and subject to attack by thieves.

In authentication, hardware protection generally serves two purposes. First, it protects the base secret and some portion of the authentication process from theft, modification, or other interference by blocking it from direct access by an attacker. Second, it detects attacks on itself so it can take steps to protect the base secret from disclosure.

Password tokens (covered in detail in Section 9.1) illustrate hardware protection in practical, off-the-shelf authentication devices. Figure 4.3 shows how tokens incorporate an external connection or display to interact with the device's owner or with a workstation, and that is the only path to the token's insides. Attackers who try to use the device directly must comply with its built-in capabilities and can't simply extract the base secret unless the token contains a function to do so. These devices often require an extra "unlock" step, like a memorized PIN, before they allow use of the base secret. The device considers itself under attack if someone tries to use it without

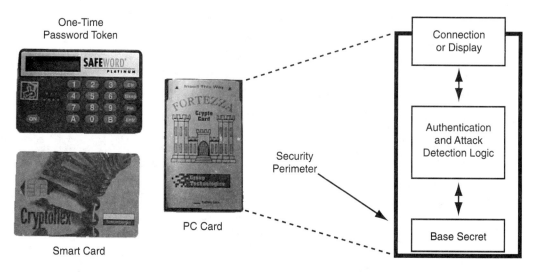

One-Time Password Token

Smart Card

PC Card

Security Perimeter

Connection or Display

Authentication and Attack Detection Logic

Base Secret

FIGURE 4.3: *Tokens protect the authentication mechanism with hardware.* Each of these devices encapsulates a base secret and uses it to perform authentication or other security procedures. Each device establishes a security perimeter to protect the base secret. Each provides some degree of protection against attacks on the security perimeter. (Cards courtesy of Secure Computing Corp. and American Biometrics Corp.)

providing the right PIN. Persistent attacks will cause some devices to erase the base secret while others simply introduce longer and longer delays into the processing.

In addition to procedural defenses, most tokens carry physical defenses. Typically, a token's circuits are encapsulated in plastic so there is no way to touch wiring connections between components. Some systems embed the authentication, attack detection, and base secret into a single integrated circuit to make hardware attacks even more difficult. Highly engineered devices might also carry tiny sensors to detect when permanent outer covers are removed, and erase the base secret if that occurs. However, such mechanisms also reduce the token's reliability, since there is a risk that the mechanism might trigger accidentally and render the device useless.

Although hardware protection provides important benefits, it is not 100% reliable. A determined attacker can whittle away at plastic encapsulation. With the right equipment, an attacker can even penetrate the insides of an integrated circuit. Some experiments have taken advantage of inadequacies in tamper-resistant designs and shown how to extract data directly from the chips themselves.

A-31

see Note 7.

In some cases, it may be possible to infer the base secret by analyzing the token's operation. Researchers have experimented with *differential power analysis* to attack base secrets stored on smart cards. This technique measures variations in the device's electrical consumption, which in turn depend on the value of the base secret. Another effective approach is to manipulate the device's clock signals or exploit other timing information. In some cases, this gives attackers enough information to make an attack practical.

A-32

see Note 8.

Fortunately, most attacks on hardware devices require a lot of expertise, not to mention time and equipment. Keep in mind the objective of any defense against a physical attack: most defenses only buy time until reinforcements arrive. In the case of an authentication token, the device must resist attack long enough for the owner to realize the device is missing and report its loss.

4.3 ADMINISTRATIVE REQUIREMENTS

Although it's often tempting to dive immediately into designing an interesting system, it's best to identify the needs before we focus on the solution. Our choice of a design pattern must meet the particular requirements of the proprietor's computing systems. This section reviews several types of requirements that we must consider before choosing a particular pattern.

The requirements we consider here are in addition to the obvious requirement of accurate authentication, that is, to consistently reject attempts by unauthorized people while not rejecting authentication attempts by authorized people. For the most part, the reliability requirements depend on the *authentication factors* used: what you know, you have, or you are (Section 1.6).

The point of this section is *not* to prescribe a set of requirements. Instead, we are looking at certain features that vary from one computing system to another. The features at hand will determine the requirements for a particular enterprise, site, and proprietor. Here is an outline of the features to be considered in this section:

- **Physical protection**—The authentication mechanism must rely on the physical plant already available, and practical extensions to it, given how the system is installed and used.
- **Efficient administration**—The mechanism should make it easy to add or revoke user credentials.

- **Ease of authentication**—The mechanism should make the user's interaction as simple and reliable as possible.
- **Point of service support**—The mechanism should efficiently support the range of systems the proprietor has that require authentication.

The following discussion considers each of these in turn.

PHYSICAL PROTECTION

For physical protection we need to consider the amount of protection that is practical to provide along with the desired robustness of the resulting system. Different architectures have different protection requirements; it is important to choose one that requires no more protection that the proprietor can really provide. Likewise, different architectures can tolerate different types of failure and still provide reliable authentication services. These trade-offs are summarized below.

- **What parts must be protected**

  There are essentially four parts of the system that might need physical protection: the desktop clients, the servers, the communications lines between them, and the authentication mechanism itself. While in some cases it might be possible to lock up the entire system, it's not always practical. Fortunately, a proprietor can often achieve a reasonable level of protection without locking all of these pieces up.

  Often, the proprietor has a distributed system and can't guarantee the safety of communications between all users and all computer systems. The proprietor might be able to physically protect all of the client and server systems, or perhaps just the server systems. It's not practical to assume that clients can be protected if there are roaming users, or if clients routinely connect from premises that are not under the proprietor's control, like home offices.

- **Interception risks**

  If the proprietor can't physically protect the communication lines that connect clients to servers, then the architecture should take interception risks into account. If ignored, interception would neutralize the benefits of biometric authentication (Section 7.7).

If interception is a risk, then the system will need to use cryptographic techniques ("crypto") to resist interception attacks. Earlier chapters introduced hashing and password encryption, which are crypto techniques. Different protection problems require different crypto techniques (for example, "secret" keys versus "public" keys), and this is often affected by the choice of a design pattern.

- **Fault tolerance**

  Many security experts believe in the "basket principle" in which you put all of your eggs in one basket and then watch that one basket very carefully. While this can provide efficient security, it also introduces a single point of failure: if the basket breaks, you can lose all of your eggs.

  If we look at this in terms of authentication architecture, then the "basket strategy" is to rely on a single device for authentication. But while we can focus our security efforts on that basket, it also poses a reliability problem: if the device fails, then we can't authenticate anyone. We can achieve higher reliability by using systems that provide distributed or back-up mechanisms for authentication.

EASE OF AUTHENTICATION

Ease of authentication is determined by *how* people authenticate themselves and *how often* they must do so. Other sections of this book cover the problem of "how," which will depend on the choice of authentication factors, and how the system handles those factors. Here we review the question of how often a person needs to authenticate. The Holy Grail of authentication is *single sign-on*, which minimizes either the number of times people must log on within a site or the number of authentication characteristics they need (usually passwords), or both. Here are three strategies for single sign-on:

- **Shared characteristics**

  This strategy tries to make things easier for users by ensuring that they can use the same distinguishing characteristic whenever a system component demands authentication. Although this approach might not reduce the number of times people must type in passwords, it makes life a little easier by reducing the number of passwords they must memorize. Here are two common techniques to implement this:

Password synchronization is a mechanism that updates passwords stored on individual systems so that every user has the same password on every separate system within the site or enterprise network. Unix provides a variant of this capability through its "Network Information Service," described in Section 8.6.

An *authentication server* also ensures that most, if not all, authentication challenges use the same characteristic by forwarding all authentication requests to a server with a single, comprehensive database. We examine such systems in Chapter 11.

- **Bundled characteristics**

  Another approach to single sign-on is to store a single person's characteristics in a crypto-protected bundle. When a software component demands a password, the bundle's software intercepts the demand, extracts the appropriate password from the bundle, and supplies it to the component. Typically, the owner must supply a password in order to decrypt the bundle and gain access to its passwords, so people exchange the problem of memorizing (or writing down) several passwords for the lesser problem of remembering the bundle's password. We examine this mechanism further in Section 6.6.

- **Proxy authentication**

  This provides the most comprehensive single sign-on solution: the system provides a mechanism by which software components can query the desktop client for authentication data associated with the workstation's operator. This is a more sophisticated technique than the bundled mechanism described above, since the authentication often uses cryptographic techniques that are much harder to attack. Modern LAN server systems provide this capability so that the user doesn't need to enter a password to open new files or to print another file.

EFFICIENT ADMINISTRATION

Aside from monitoring the system for signs of disaster, administrators have two basic tasks with respect to authentication: add new user records and revoke the obsolete ones. This is usually a relatively simple and straightforward chore, especially if it doesn't happen very often. However, a poor match between the site's service arrangements and the design pattern of its authentication system will needlessly increase the administrative burden. The essential point to consider is how the enterprise has organized computing services on its network, and whether or not its authentication decisions might need to span enterprises. This yields the following possibilities:

- **Single point of service**

  This is when the proprietor runs all services on a single host computer. This presents a relatively simple administrative problem, since everything is in one place. Once upon a time, this was the common situation, since few sites could afford to run more than one server.

- **Multiple points of service**

  This is when the proprietor has services running on several different computers. This has become the typical situation as the cost of computer hardware has dropped. Services are often installed on hosts for a variety of reasons unrelated to security or authentication, and many individuals find themselves using services on several different computers. Authentication must work reliably and transparently between the separate host computers. Ideally, the design should make this easy for the administrators and easy for the users.

- **Multiple enterprises**

  This is where people from multiple enterprises need to share computing resources among one another. This is similar to the challenge of handling multiple points of service, but it involves multiple proprietors as well. This is a real challenge to older authentication systems.

4.4 LOCAL AUTHENTICATION

This first pattern covers the simplest situations: those where people manipulate the system directly and not remotely. Obvious examples include portable or handheld devices, and extend to laptop computers and stand-alone workstations.

The essence of the local design pattern (Figure 4.4) is that the entire authentication and access control mechanism resides inside a single security perimeter. People use the computer or other protected system via an interface that straddles the security perimeter. Users don't breach the perimeter, but their inputs pass through it and the computer's outputs return through it. The authentication system works correctly only as long as attackers don't breach the physical security perimeter. Chapter 5 discusses this pattern.

Laptop computers provide a good example of the local pattern. Many laptops, like Apple's PowerBooks, support some sort of password lock: the system won't boot unless the user supplies the correct password. While the lock provides a certain amount of protection against misuse, it won't stop an attacker who gains physical possession of the laptop. A determined thief can usually pop open the laptop (breaching its physical security perimeter) and

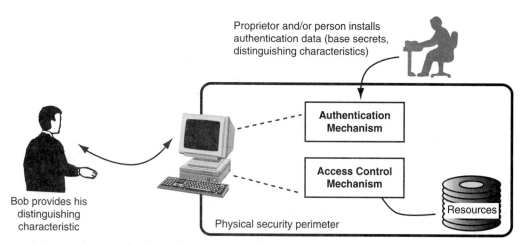

FIGURE 4.4: *Local authentication: the pattern.* In this pattern, the entire system resides within a single physical security perimeter. People enter base secrets or other distinguishing characteristics directly into the system. Data processed by the system resides entirely inside. Examples include stand-alone workstations and personal organizers like Palm-based systems.

extract data directly from the internal hard drive. In many cases, the thief doesn't even have to be handy with a screwdriver, since there are tricks to disable password locking without even opening the case.

If the system designer trusts the system's physical security perimeter, this greatly simplifies the system design and operation. Users can use easier-to-remember passwords or even PINs, since attackers would be stuck with interactive trial-and-error password guessing as the only available mode of attack. If the attackers can't breach the perimeter, they can't extract passwords stored on the system, encrypted or not. Indeed, a reliable perimeter eliminates the need for password hashing or other forms of encryption. The system could also enhance its usability by implementing biometrics for authentication. Though sniffing and replay represent a major risk to biometric systems, a reliable physical security perimeter eliminates such attacks.

In practice, of course, physical perimeters are very hard to ensure. This leads many security practitioners to use additional measures, like encryption, to provide a layered defense. For example, we can improve a laptop's security by encrypting its hard drive. This prevents the attacker from being able to extract data, assuming that the hard drive encryption uses a quality algorithm and that the encryption key is properly protected (Section 5.2). However, solutions of this pattern still rely somewhat on the security perimeter: a really determined attacker could install sniffer software to extract the hard drive's encryption key before the theft takes place. Although this requires a level of sophistication beyond most laptop thieves, the FBI has used this trick to capture memorized encryption keys in at least one criminal investigation.   *see Note 9.*

For many enterprises, the main shortcoming of local authentication is its administration. Each device represents a single point of service that must be individually administered. If two people need access to a single, secured laptop, then both need authentication credentials, such as a shared password. There is no way to revoke a user's access to a particular device other than by taking possession of the device, changing the necessary authentication credentials, and (if necessary) sharing revised credentials with the remaining users. The process gets more complex as the user population and the number of devices increases.

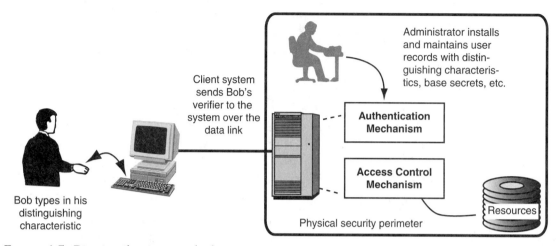

FIGURE 4.5: *Direct authentication deployment pattern.* In this pattern, people don't use the system directly. People use the system by entering identifying data into a remote client. The information is sent (often in encrypted form) to the system's database of authorized users. A positive match grants access; the authentication and access-control mechanisms reside in a single device.

4.5 DIRECT AUTHENTICATION

The direct authentication pattern yields the simplest architecture for authenticating remote users. The design works best when each proprietor provides a single point of service, or each point of service has a separate user community. Typically, the proprietor of each point of service knows ahead of time who should be allowed to use it. If the proprietor has more than one system, each system has its own unique group of users. The Unix password mechanism introduced in Chapter 2 provides direct authentication. Other examples include early, single-point LAN servers, like Microsoft's original LAN Manager and Novel Netware 3.

see Note 10.

The essence of the direct authentication pattern (Figure 4.5) is that the computing services reside in a single, physically secure location, while the points of use (clients) are not necessarily secure. This is called the "direct" pattern because the point of service makes the authentication decisions itself. The authentication mechanism, the access-control mechanisms, and the services themselves all reside in a single device. Administrators maintain a database of authorized users within each system. A change to the user database takes effect immediately, since the system refers to its user database whenever someone tries to log on. An obvious drawback to the direct pattern is that it lacks fault tolerance, since everything is centralized.

Since users don't necessarily interact with the system from a secure location, attacks can target the users' remote workstations or their communications links. This makes biometric techniques impractical by themselves: an attacker could sniff a remote biometric reading from an authorized user and later replay it in order to masquerade as that user. Similar problems apply to reusable secret passwords.

Because of sniffing and replay risks, systems built with this pattern usually require crypto protection of some sort. It may not be necessary to encrypt all traffic; encrypted passwords of some form may be sufficient to ensure proper authentication. For example, one-time password tokens use a secret key to encrypt an internal value that yields a password that works only once (Chapter 9). Other tokens use a challenge-response technique: these tokens encrypt the challenge to yield a single-use password (Chapter 10). Although such systems could use either secret-key or public-key encryption, most products of this type currently use secret-key cryptography.

Direct pattern solutions work best if a proprietor manages a single system or a group of systems with independent user populations. Otherwise, the proprietor may incur considerable administrative inconvenience, since each user may need to be entered into several different user databases. The problem worsens each time the proprietor installs another host to provide another point of service. Sun Microsystems developed the Network Information System to try to overcome this problem while retaining the traditional Unix direct authentication mechanism (Section 8.6).

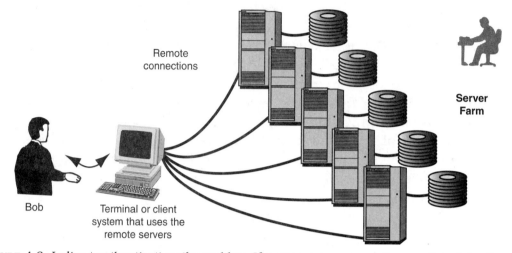

Remote
connections

Server
Farm

Bob

Terminal or client
system that uses the
remote servers

FIGURE 4.6: *Indirect authentication: the problem.* If a proprietor runs a "server farm" for the user community, then direct authentication yields a troublesome solution. If each server is an independent remote system with its own authentication mechanism, then administrators must perform every authentication maintenance task (that is, adding or revoking a user's account) individually on each server.

4.6 INDIRECT AUTHENTICATION

Indirect authentication solutions address the scalability problem posed by sites with a single population of users but multiple points of service (Figure 4.6). Even a site with only two servers will want to avoid the headache of trying to maintain consistency between two separate authentication databases.

While other design patterns combine authentication and access-control mechanisms, the indirect authentication pattern (Figure 4.7) extracts the authentication mechanism from the point of service and moves it to a separate *authentication server.* Other components provide services or control access to resources but do not make authentication decisions. Instead, they authenticate people indirectly by contacting the authentication server when someone tries to log on. Chapter 11 discusses the indirect pattern in more detail.

AUTHENTICATION PROTOCOLS

Whenever two or more computers talk to each other, we will usually find there is a predefined *protocol* that identifies the messages they exchange, what they mean, and the sequence of events. Figure 4.7

shows how Tim enters data in his client, which sends his login request to the server, which in turn sends it to the authentication server. The protocol defines how to format the data sent between the different host computers, and how to interpret the data received. If Tim's client fails to follow the protocol, then the server won't recognize his request, and won't log him in.

see Note 11.

The simplest authentication protocols are those for the "challenge response passwords" described in Chapter 10. When Tim tries to log on to a server that uses challenge response, he must exchange a series of messages in order to authenticate himself. The protocol usually works as follows:

1. Tim sends his user name to the server.
2. The server sends back a random number, the "challenge."
3. Tim then determines the correct "response" to that challenge and sends back the response to serve as his password.
4. The server verifies that Tim sent the correct response to that particular challenge and logs him in if it's correct.

To log on correctly, either Tim or his workstation software must understand the server's protocol. He needs to know what response would correspond to what challenge. This can involve any manner of secret information, although practical systems tend to use a crypto function that combines the challenge with a base secret.

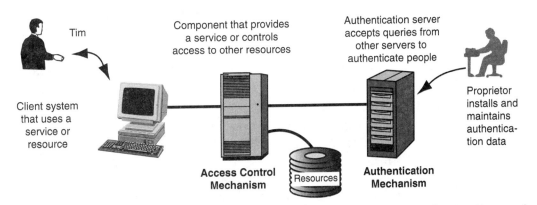

FIGURE 4.7: *Indirect authentication: the pattern.* In the indirect pattern, the authentication mechanism is located remotely from the system's other servers, which communicate with it whenever a user requests access. This use of a separate authentication server, which requires only a single update for each user, is transparent in practice.

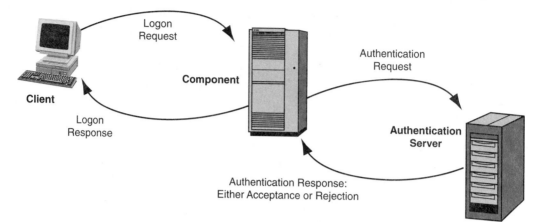

FIGURE 4.8: *Indirect authentication message traffic.* When a user directs a client to log on to a component, the client sends a "logon request" message that identifies the user and includes a verifier. The component converts this into an authentication request, forwarding both the user name and verifier to the authentication server. The server compares the user name and verifier against the user record and returns a response to the component. The component replies to the user.

INDIRECT AUTHENTICATION PROTOCOLS

Protocols for indirect authentication follow a similar pattern of message exchange, but the exchanges are more sophisticated. Many well-known systems today provide indirect authentication via specially designed protocols. The RADIUS protocol provides an open standard for implementing indirect authentication. So does the Kerberos protocol, a version of which appears in Microsoft Windows 2000, and the domain logon facility of Windows NT 4.0. Vendors of one-time password systems, like Secure Computing's SafeWord and RSA Security's SecurID, generally support RADIUS in addition to one or more proprietary protocols for indirect authentication. These protocols are described in Chapters 11 and 12.

In general, an indirect authentication protocol begins when someone tries to log on to a point of service from a remote location, perhaps a workstation. When the point of service receives the logon request, it forwards the user's name and the password, biometric reading, or other distinguishing characteristic to the authentication server. These messages often use a back-end protocol, like RADIUS or a vendor's proprietary protocol, to transfer this data. If the server validates the authentication, it sends an acceptance message back to the point of service, formatted according to the back-end protocol.

Upon receipt, the point of service accepts the user's logon attempt. If the server sends back a rejection message, the point of service rejects the request. Figure 4.8 illustrates the process.

Aside from the separation of services from authentication, the direct and indirect solution patterns share certain properties: biometrics tend to be risky, while cryptography can serve a valuable role—although it becomes slightly more important in indirect authentication. Since authentication requests are redirected to the authentication server, there is a risk that an attacker will forge an "authentication approved" message to trick the server; cryptography must be used to authenticate the back-and-forth messages between points of service and the authentication server.

Some systems that use indirect authentication can achieve a high degree of fault tolerance by supporting automatic database replication to distribute the authentication load across several geographically distributed systems. If any server goes down, authentication requests can be directed to an alternative server containing a copy of the entire authentication database. This allows an enterprise to replicate its services on multiple hosts, and its authentication mechanism on multiple authentication servers, eliminating single points of failure.

An important benefit of indirect solutions is that they scale well—geographically and in the number of hosts they support—as an enterprise's computing environment grows, while still providing rapid turnaround for adding new users or revoking expired ones. These systems display shortcomings only when the user population spans multiple enterprises. While such sharing may be technically possible, it introduces a number of administrative and security problems that usually make it impractical.

4.7   OFF-LINE AUTHENTICATION

Off-line deployment addresses the internal contradiction of truly practical, distributed authentication: a proprietor cannot trust every device that needs to perform authentication. Some applications are so large or so broadly distributed (or cut off) that they can't rely on a centralized server for real-time authentication decisions. Yet the proprietor may still want central authority over authentication.

The best-known examples of such problems occur in consumer-oriented electronic commerce. Each vendor wants to assure customers that they are indeed talking to the vendor's computer. Yet the vendors can't automatically trust their customers or their customers' computers. Similar dilemmas also confront e-mail security packages.

In a sense, the e-commerce problem is the opposite of what we do with the direct and indirect patterns. Here, the client is trying to authenticate the server instead of vice versa. The millions of clients act like numerous independent "points of service" that are trying to authenticate one out of thousands of servers. The proprietor is an independent organization (the "certificate authority") that promotes e-commerce by providing trustworthy server authentication to desktop clients.

Off-line pattern solutions (Figure 4.9) combine several design features of the other three. As with local pattern solutions, authentication can be performed on an off-line system without a real-time network connection. As with local and direct pattern solutions, the authentication mechanism resides in the same device as the access control mechanism. And, as with indirect pattern solutions, the proprietor can maintain a single, centralized list of authorized users.

Public key infrastructures implement offline solutions by using a relatively small number of preestablished public keys to validate the

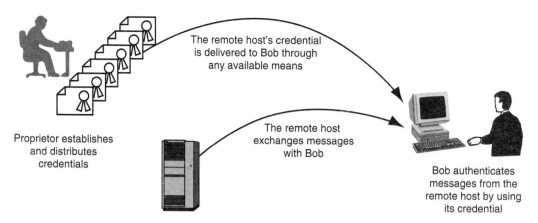

The remote host's credential is delivered to Bob through any available means

Proprietor establishes and distributes credentials

The remote host exchanges messages with Bob

Bob authenticates messages from the remote host by using its credential

FIGURE 4.9: *Off-line authentication.* Public-key certification software follows an offline authentication pattern, which recognizes authorized users, is stored in multiple locations throughout the system and is accessible offline. Adding users, however, is faster and easier than revoking them.

authentication data of individual users or other entities, like service hosts. The preestablished public keys belong to the certificate authorities, which issue public key certificates that contain authentication data for users and other entities. Authentication takes place in two steps. For example, if Bob wants to authenticate his bank's server, his workstation first acquires the bank's public key certificate and authenticates it with a preestablished public key. The second step is to use the public key within the bank's certificate as part of some other protocol, like Secure Sockets Layer (SSL), to authenticate the bank as the genuine owner of the private key, which is mathematically related to the certificate's public key. Chapter 13 introduces public key technology, and Chapter 14 explains public key certificates.

A particularly interesting security feature of off-line pattern solutions is that the proprietor does not have to create, maintain, and administer the user records with a system that's accessible on-line. The certification authority software that creates certificates can operate off-line and transfer the certificates to a public directory via removable media. Attackers can't directly penetrate the enrollment mechanism, since it's not accessible on-line.

Like direct and indirect pattern solutions, off-line authentication cannot use pure biometrics for authentication. Unlike those other solutions, it can't be implemented with secret key cryptography—it relies on public key cryptography.

Another important feature of off-line authentication is its fault tolerance. As long as an authentication device can get a copy of the appropriate certificate, it can authenticate any entity it needs to. The device can ensure its access to the necessary certificates by looking in a variety of directories, by maintaining its own local cache of certificates, or by retrieving certificates from the actual entity being authenticated. (The latter mechanism is used by SSL.) The off-line pattern can also provide fault tolerance by maintaining numerous replicated certificate directories, so that certificates can be found even in the face of widespread directory host and network failures.

The off-line, distributed nature of this pattern is, however, a double-edged sword. Proprietors can easily add people and devices to the system by issuing public key certificates from any approved certification authority. Once the certificate exists, it can be immediately recognized by all of the enterprise's hosts, a process at least as fast and reliable as indirect authentication. Unfortunately, it makes revoking a user's credentials much harder, since each certificate is self-validating.

4.8 APPLYING THE PATTERNS

It should be clear that no particular pattern is perfect for all cases. Planners and designers must make conscious trade-offs, balancing resistance to attack against ease of administration and the potential losses posed by authentication failures. Each design pattern provides a different blend of strengths and weaknesses, and choosing among them will demand, in the end, a careful assessment of the proprietor's practical needs.

Table 4.1 summarizes a few general features of the four patterns. The first row shows how much of the system must be physically protected by the proprietor to protect against widespread authentication errors. The second row indicates whether the pattern handles biometric authentication safely. The third row identifies the types of cryptographic algorithms required by solutions of each pattern. The fourth row compares the fault tolerance of the different patterns: "Low" indicates a pattern with a single point of failure.

From Table 4.1 it should be clear that the more sophisticated patterns lower the physical security demands while potentially increasing fault tolerance. These benefits are paid for with increased complexity: the indirect and off-line pattern solutions tend to be harder to install than local or direct solutions. Regarding fault toler-

TABLE 4.1: *Properties of Authentication Patterns*

Property	Local	Direct	Indirect	Offline
Parts needing protection	Whole system	Points of service only	Authentication servers only	Certification authorities only
Biometrics safe	Yes	Not by itself	Not by itself	Not by itself
Crypto used	None	Secret or public	Secret or public	Public only
Fault tolerance	Low	Low	High–Low	High

ance, the indirect solution can achieve high fault tolerance if the implementation provides a redundant authentication server. Otherwise, we again have our eggs in one basket, since the authentication server represents a single point of failure.

Table 4.2 compares the responsiveness of different solution patterns to user administration requests. "High" indicates that the request is simple to perform and that it takes effect immediately, while "Low" indicates that the request either requires multiple steps or may encounter a significant delay before taking effect. Separate rows compare responsiveness to requests for adding a new user ("Add user") or disabling an existing user "Revoke user") in systems of different sizes. The smallest system provides a single point of service, such as an individual computer or a single, centralized network server. The next larger scenario considers multiple points of service shared by a population of users. The largest scenario considers a user population that spans multiple enterprises or organizations.

The question of administrative responsiveness generally favors the indirect pattern, followed by the off-line pattern. The only problem with the indirect pattern is its uneven coverage of authentication across multiple enterprises: some systems, like Kerberos, have a way to do this, but not all solutions do. The off-line pattern provides the best approach for authenticating users across enterprises, although the pattern handles revocation poorly. The direct pattern is, of course, most efficient at handling a single remote server. Local authentication can be used with stand-alone devices, and may be the best choice in some circumstances.

TABLE 4.2: *User Administration Responsiveness of Authentication Patterns*

Administrative Services		Local	Direct	Indirect	Off-line
Single point of service	**Add user**	Medium	High	High	High
	Revoke user	Low	High	High	Medium-low
Multiple points of service	**Add user**	Low	Low	High	High
	Revoke user	Low	Low	High	Medium-low
Multiple enterprises	**Add user**	Low	Low	High-low	High
	Revoke user	Low	Low	Low	Medium-low

In practice, some systems may combine two or more patterns in a layered defense. This typically involves using the local pattern in conjunction with a remote pattern. For example, the local device accepts a PIN for authenticating its owner, and "unlocks" a client to use with direct or indirect authentication.

4.9 SUMMARY TABLES

TABLE 4.3: *Attack Summary*

Attack	Security Problem	Prevalence	Attack Description
A-27. OS substitution	Recover or modify hidden information	Physical	Boot a different OS on the workstation that ignores access restrictions instead of the OS installed on the hard disk. Use this OS to access protected files
A-28. Default password guessing	Recover a user's password	Trivial	Perform trial-and-error guessing based on a list of the passwords usually installed by the vendor during manufacture
A-29. Erase the password	Recover a device's password	Common or Physical	Either run software that erases the password memory or interrupt the power supply that maintains password memory
A-30. I/O bus	Recover hidden information	Physical	Connect the workstation's hard drive to a different system that can copy its contents for later analysis
A-31. Token hardware penetration	Recover hidden information, like a base secret	Sophisticated or Innovative	Remove encapsulation from the token module and probe its electronics to extract secret data
A-32. Non-destructive analysis	Recover hidden information, like a base secret	Innovative	Measure variations in the token's power consumption or the timing of cryptographic functions in order to deduce the base secret

TABLE 4.4: *Defense Summary*

Defense	Foils Attacks	Description
D-27. BIOS password	A-27. OS substitution	Requires a password to change the disk drive from which the workstation boots its OS
D-28. Reset vendor passwords	A-28. Default password guessing	Change the initial password installed in the system during its manufacture to a hard-to-guess password
D-29. Special computer enclosures	A-30. I/O bus	Install the computer inside a tamper-resistant enclosure so that attackers can't easily open the case and attack the peripherals
D-30. Seals	A-30. I/O bus	Makes an intrusion inside the computer's cover detectable by putting hard-to-forge seals over the case edges
D-31. Integrated circuit	A-30. I/O bus	Embed all sensitive functions in a single integrated circuit.
D-32. Lock up workstations	A-27. OS substitution A-29. Erase the password A-30. I/O bus A-31. Token hardware penetration	Install workstations in areas that limit access to a very small number of people including the people authorized to use those workstations.

RESIDUAL ATTACK

A-32. Nondestructive analysis—the principal defense against this attack is to build the cryptographic mechanism so that it defends against it. This issue is being addressed in the development of the Advanced Encryption Standard (AES) in the United States. This attack was not a consideration in earlier commercial cryptographic systems. Fortunately it requires physical access to the device holding the base secret under attack, plus a high degree of attack sophistication.

CHAPTER 5
LOCAL AUTHENTICATION

...acting on the principle that possession was nine tenths of the law...

— Aaron Sokolski, *Land Tenure and Land Taxation in America*

IN THIS CHAPTER

This chapter looks at the basics of local authentication and the fundamental techniques used for it.

- Workstation authentication and lock screens
- File and disk encryption
- Choosing and using effective encryption
- Key handling issues

5.1 LAPTOPS AND WORKSTATIONS

History often repeats itself, especially in the history of computers. Many things that befell the first large-scale computers (large in size and cost if not in computing power) also befell the "minicomputers" that evolved in the 1960s, and ultimately the personal computers of today. Each generation started out using the new computers for very specialized tasks, and initially adopted only the simplest programming tools: machine or assembly language. As the machines improved, programmers argued the relative merits of better programming tools and languages until a few pioneers managed to implement effective programming languages for the new computers. As the new systems matured, they were applied to essentially the same jobs as the computers that came before. The similarities are so striking that some observers call it a "wheel of reincarnation." *see Note 1.*

133

Patterns of sharing and access control also followed parallel evolutions. When desktop computers first appeared in offices, they were often shared. Anyone with physical access to a particular computer could do some work with it, just like researchers using the first computers in the 1950s. In the 1990s, the personal computer became an extension of the office worker's desk and file cabinet, and sharing became less common. People used the software equivalent of desk drawer locks to protect the privacy of their work in progress as well as sensitive company information.

Individual personal computers face two different threats: casual attackers and determined attackers. The casual attackers are like coworkers that might rifle through a colleague's desk uninvited—someone who takes advantage of easy access even if it violates social and ethical standards. Such people are usually deterred by relatively simple defenses. Casual attackers don't usually think of themselves as dishonest or unethical. Some people can twist the lack of defenses into an invitation: "If it was really meant to be kept secret they'd have a lock on the door, or password protect it, or something."

The earliest personal computer security mechanisms (beyond the lock on the office door) were designed to thwart casual attacks. The best known, the lock screen, grew out of a software fix for a hardware problem. Older computer screens suffered from a problem called "burn in," in which the screen's phosphor coating would wear out unevenly in response to the image it displayed. Macintosh displays that suffered from burn in, for example, would carry a faint image of the menu bar with the "apple" in the left hand corner, even if the computer and display were turned off. "Screen saver" software would detect when the computer had not been used for some period of time and then display changing patterns to prevent any single image from being burned in.

The lock screen was a security feature grafted onto the screen saver. As it was, the screen saver would essentially "take over" the computer's screen, keyboard, and mouse when it was unattended and retain control of it until the owner touched the keyboard or mouse. By adding a password, the screen saver could "lock out" anyone except the person knowing the password: this produced the lock screen mechanism.

Lock screens were soon caught up in the evolution of attacks and defenses. At first, screen savers with passwords often could be defeated by simply rebooting the computer. A few security-oriented screen savers tried to prevent this by tying themselves into the operating system so that they could retain control even if the computer was rebooted. Ultimately, the lock screen technology was built into desktop operating systems. While this prevented obvious attacks, even sophisticated lock screens remain vulnerable to fundamental attacks on personal computer hardware (see Attacks A-27, OS substitution, and A-30, I/O bus, in Section 4.2).

Determined attackers are rarely stopped by lock screens alone. A determined attacker has decided already to do something unethical or illegal, and has decided to expend personal effort on the attack. The only way to resist a determined attacker is with defenses that are too risky or costly to break down. In many cases, we can deter the attacker by making the attack visible or ensuring that it leaves a trail of evidence behind. In some cases it is enough just to detect and record the fact that the attack occurred, even if the attacker isn't identified.

More sophisticated desktop systems, notably Unix and Microsoft Windows NT or 2000, addressed the threat of more sophisticated attacks with more sophisticated access control. Unix originally had been designed as a multiuser operating system so it already incorporated the CPU-based protection mechanisms discussed in Section 4.2. Although Windows NT was designed at the outset as a personal computer operating system, the developers recognized that multiuser security features were essential to gain acceptance with major computer buyers, notably the U.S. government. These features were also incorporated into Windows 2000. *see Note 2.*

Even the Apple Macintosh system has incorporated access controls with Mac OS 9 and Mac OS X. Mac OS 9 incorporated user-based authentication and access control so that different users of a shared desktop computer could keep their files separate and, to some extent, confidential from one another. Mac OS X evolved from the Mach system, which had itself evolved from Unix and inherited Unix-like access controls. *see Note 3.*

User-based access controls, while important, are not perfect. A really motivated attacker can usually bypass these controls through a Trojan horse attack (Attack A-3 in Section 1.3). Moreover, user-based access controls on a single desktop workstation are vulnerable to the same physical attacks as lock screens.

Workstation security has achieved better results with network-based access control and with encryption. In network-based access control, the workstation's most important data resides on a server and the workstation's operator can use the data only after being authenticated. If the data resides on the workstation, then encryption is the only reliable technique to protect it, since the protection relies on knowledge of a base secret (the encryption key) and not on software defenses that attackers can bypass. The rest of this chapter examines cryptographic techniques, especially encryption and how it can provide a strong form of authentication and access control for workstation data.

5.2   WORKSTATION ENCRYPTION

Encryption is the only really strong and practical way to protect information when it is not physically controlled by its owner. We can use this technique to protect data on portable or hard-to-protect computers. As with classic encryption applied to secret messages, encryption can transform stored data into an unreadable form, called *ciphertext*, based on a *secret key*. Anyone who knows the key can retrieve the information, that is, transform it back to *plaintext*. As with any base secret, attackers can also retrieve the information if they can figure out the secret key.

In general, a good encryption mechanism will provide certain features, regardless of whether it is built into an operating system or packaged as a separate product:

- An encryption algorithm whose strength and trustworthiness has been reviewed and endorsed by the open cryptographic community. This is discussed in Section 5.3.

- A sufficiently long key length to make a brute force attack impractical. This is also discussed in Section 5.3.

- Allow secret keys to be entered as passphrases containing at least as many letters as there are bits in the secret key. This is discussed in Section 5.4.

- Must *not* have a "back door" or other "emergency data recovery" mechanism, unless that mechanism is simply an additional encryption key that the user or proprietor can change. This is also discussed in Section 5.4.

There are two strategies for applying encryption to data stored on computers: file encryption and disk encryption. File encryption works on a file-by-file basis at the discretion of the workstation's operator. Disk encryption automatically encrypts everything on a disk. Both techniques can provide good results in appropriate circumstances. Both can provide strong results, but only if they use strong encryption.

FILE ENCRYPTION

File encryption is the easiest way to provide encryption to a workstation user. Numerous applications provide file encryption either as their primary service or as an extra feature. The PKZIP program provides notoriously weak encryption that is still widely used. Pretty Good Privacy (PGP) is a very capable program for encrypting electronic mail, and many people use it to simply encrypt files. File encryption is best used to protect files that are shared across a network through file transfers or e-mail.   *see Note 4.*

Figure 5.1 shows how file encryption works. The file's owner selects the file to be encrypted and chooses a secret key, usually in the form of a password or passphrase. Others cannot read the encrypted file unless they have the secret key. To decrypt the file, the owner (or anyone else who knows the secret key) invokes the decryption program and provides the secret key. Apple's Mac OS 9 integrates this capability into the desktop: when a user opens an encrypted file, the system automatically prompts for the secret key, decrypts the file, and then opens it in the appropriate application.

File encryption does not reliably protect data from other workstation users. Figure 5.1 also suggests a potential source of trouble: the encrypted file uses different disk space from the plaintext file. The attacker can simply retrieve a plaintext copy of the file if the application does not take special steps to erase the plaintext. Early file encryption programs simply deleted the file. This strategy worked tolerably well on timesharing systems, though it would not prevent

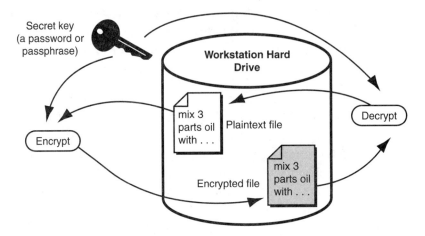

FIGURE 5.1: *Protecting workstation files with encryption.* The file's owner chooses a secret to use as a key, and then encrypts the file to hide its contents from others. The encryption function should write zeroes over the plaintext data after producing the encrypted file, so that attackers can't recover the encrypted data by searching for the original file. Anyone who knows the secret key can decrypt the data.

an administrator from retrieving the plaintext. However, many workstations have "undelete" programs to retrieve accidentally deleted files, and such a program can just as easily retrieve the "deleted" plaintext file. Experts refer to this as the *object reuse* problem, since reusing the deleted disk space allows unauthorized people to reuse the contents of the "object" (the file). *A-33*

Effective file encryption programs overwrite the plaintext file before deleting it. For most purposes, it is enough to overwrite the original data with any other data. This prevents an attacker from retrieving the deleted file, copying it to another location, and then examining its contents. *D-33*

This defense does not prevent sophisticated, laboratory-based attacks. Hard drives store data magnetically, and all data leaves a slight magnetic residue. A detailed laboratory analysis of magnetic patterns on a disk surface can retrieve data from a disk even if another layer of data has been written over it. *A-34*

Fortunately, there is a relatively simple defense against laboratory attacks: apply a three-step overwriting process to the data at least once. The process requires three binary data patterns: one random bit pattern (like 0011 0101), the complement of the pattern *D-34*

(1100 1010), and a pattern consisting of a mixture of bits from the two (like 1001 0111). Although this does not prevent all laboratory attacks, it is sufficient to make most attacks impractical.   *see Note 5.*

However, even the best file encryption program should be used only to encrypt files shared over a network. File encryption can reduce, but does not eliminate, the risk of attackers recovering information if they have physical access to the workstation. The principal risk is not even a sophisticated laboratory attack or other storage problem, though these remain. The principal risk is the attacker scavenging the sensitive data from other places on the same hard drive. Few people construct a document or other sensitive file purely from scratch. The information in the file often comes from other files, which may be earlier drafts of the same document, or perhaps databases or spreadsheets that managed the raw material. Even if attackers can't retrieve the plaintext report, they can retrieve all the raw material, assuming the owner didn't laboriously encrypt each file individually.   *A-35*

Moreover, most document production programs like FrameMaker and word processors like Microsoft Word produce temporary and back-up files that contain some or all of the document in plaintext. There is no way the file encryption program can track down all of those files and overwrite them. But a motivated attacker can retrieve deleted temporary files and scan the contents of plaintext back-up files. Attackers can even look for deleted "spool" files that carried the plaintext report to the printer. A sophisticated attacker can search sectors of the disk that were marked as bad blocks; such sectors can't be reached by most overwriting programs. File encryption is not practical for protecting data from motivated attackers with physical access to the workstation.

VOLUME ENCRYPTION

As the name implies, volume encryption converts the entire contents of a hard drive into ciphertext. This prevents attackers from recovering data by scavenging the hard drive, since *all* data on the hard drive is encrypted. Users don't have to worry about whether they failed to encrypt a critical file because everything gets encrypted automatically, even temporary and spool files. Attackers cannot recover sensitive data by scavenging the hard drive, since everything   *D-35*

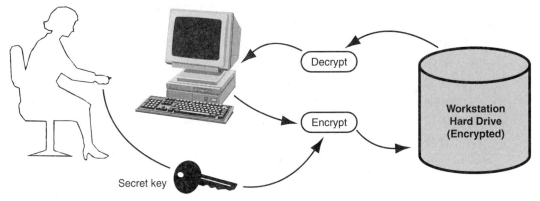

FIGURE 5.2: *Protecting a hard drive with volume encryption.* Volume encryption protects everything on the hard drive by encrypting every block of data before it is written. This is easy to use since encryption happens automatically. The user never has to decide whether a particular file needs encryption. All the user needs to do is provide the correct secret key in order to use the hard drive.

is encrypted, including scratch space, deleted files, and temporary files. The only shortcoming is that encryption requires a lot of computation, and that either increases the cost or reduces the performance of the protected computer.

As shown in Figure 5.2, the encryption generally takes place between the hard drive and the workstation's other components. Operation is almost completely transparent so that the workstation's CPU, memory, and standard, off-the-shelf software does not know that encryption takes place. The most obvious difference might be the presence of a special program that collects the secret key as a password or passphrase when the computer boots up.

Volume encryption products may be software based or hardware based. The software-based products usually install as a special device driver. Software products often reduce the computer's overall performance since encryption shares the CPU with the application programs. Hardware-based products are usually installed in the workstation either as a custom interface card or as a device connected between the hard drive and its connection to the workstation. Systems with encryption hardware generally achieve better performance by off-loading the encryption computations onto special circuitry. Some products use custom encryption circuits to provide the highest practical performance.

Volume encryption provides better security than file encryption when potential attackers may have physical access to the hard drive. As shown in Figure 5.3, this technique encrypts all data stored permanently on the computer. Potentially sensitive plaintext data resides only in RAM, except when it is typed in or displayed. Thus, plaintext data disappears when the computer is turned off, leaving only the encrypted data on the hard drive.

This is particularly appealing to laptop users, since laptops face a serious theft risk. Some thieves reportedly realize that the data on a laptop may be more valuable than the laptop itself. There was once a report of a $10,000 bounty for laptops stolen at Washington National Airport. Volume encryption prevents thieves from recovering any information from the laptop's hard drive.   *see Note 6.*

Attackers achieve nothing from an OS substitution or I/O bus attack on an encrypted volume: they can't even get started with the encrypted hard drive. The operating system will treat the encrypted volume as an unformatted disk because it won't be able to read the volume description data. Files can't be listed because the directory is encrypted. Even the disk space belonging to deleted files or bad blocks is encrypted, so scavenging fails.

A volume encryption system must be highly reliable, since certain failures will cause the loss of all of its data. Proper key handling is

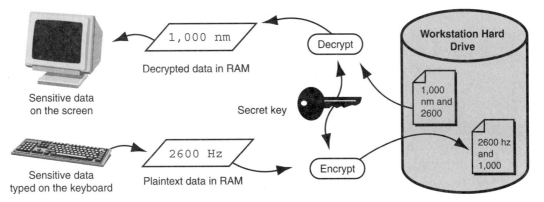

FIGURE 5.3: *How volume encryption works.* Volume encryption is installed transparently between the hard drive and the rest of the workstation, either in the device driver or in a separate interface circuit. Sensitive data still resides in the workstation's RAM in plaintext form, but it is always encrypted before it is written to the hard drive. All data read from the hard drive is automatically decrypted before it is delivered to the software inside the workstation.

crucial: there must be no misunderstanding between owner and software regarding the password or passphrase that protects the data. If the passphrase is lost, the data itself should be considered lost. There should be no way to enter a correct passphrase and have it fail to be recognized as such.

Any security mechanism that relies on secrets should provide a way to change them periodically. With volume encryption, the product should provide a mechanism that changes the secret key or passphrase. This requires that the product systematically decrypt the entire disk and then re-encrypt it with the new secret. This will be a time consuming process on a large volume, but it must be done when the volume changes ownership.

To summarize, a disk encryption product should provide the following features:

- All of the features of good encryption systems that were listed at the beginning of this section
- Bulletproof reliability, since all data is lost if *anything* goes wrong in data handling, key management, or encryption
- Allow users to rekey a volume, essentially changing the passphrase used to decrypt it

While volume encryption provides a high degree of security, it also has some properties that sometimes become shortcomings. First, it doesn't usually provide a way to distribute encrypted files. Since the encryption takes place transparently, the workstation can't read anything from the disk except for decrypted plaintext. If users need to exchange encrypted files through e-mail, they will need a separate file encryption program. A second shortcoming is that each volume can have only a single secret, and all of that volume's users must share that secret. Thus, volume encryption can't keep things private between users sharing a single volume.

In some cases, people think it's a shortcoming that volume encryption protects everything indiscriminately. This is especially true on systems that use software to perform the encryption, since it slows down overall system performance. While people may tolerate delays when the system encrypts their secret memoranda, they're less patient to wait for the system to decrypt Microsoft Office, which attackers probably already have copies of. But the only way to ensure that *all* sensitive information gets encrypted is to encrypt everything.

While volume encryption provides very strong protection against some attacks, it does not protect against every attack. Cryptanalysts have an old saying about retrieving data: "First, go after the plaintext." This means that the best attack snares the data while it is still in plaintext form, instead of trying to overcome cryptographic protections. The same holds true for attacking an encrypted volume. Practical attacks would use Trojan horse software to sneak plaintext data onto unencrypted diskettes or to transmit plaintext data to other computers via a network connection. In the late 1990s, for example, there were rumors of a Microsoft Word macro virus that would post a copy of the document it infected to the Usenet news system, essentially publishing it worldwide on the Internet. Volume encryption by itself cannot protect against such an attack.

5.3 ENCRYPTION FOR DATA PROTECTION

Section 5.2 introduced requirements for quality encryption products that, in particular, recommend the use of strong encryption with hard-to-guess secret keys. While this may sound like obvious advice, it's often harder to achieve than we might wish.

Strong encryption starts with a strong *encryption algorithm*, a computational procedure that either encrypts the plaintext data or converts encrypted data back to its plaintext. These algorithms use a secret key to control the encryption. A well-designed algorithm provides no way to decrypt some encrypted data without the correct key, except through a trial-and-error search. If the secret key is large enough, the search isn't practical.

The combination of these features—the strong algorithm and the long key—yields *computationally secure* encryption, that is, encryption that isn't practical to break. Good commercial encryption is based on computationally secure encryption. To understand what good encryption means, we will briefly examine the problem of bad encryption, the role of key length in cryptographic strength, and attack times on cryptographic keys.

Encryption algorithms tend to fall into two categories: *stream ciphers* and *block ciphers*. Most of the widely used modern algorithms are block algorithms: the old Data Encryption Standard

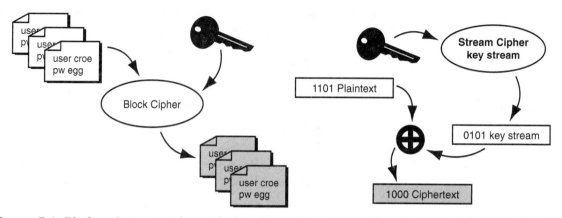

FIGURE 5.4: *Block and stream ciphers.* Block ciphers, as shown on the left, encrypt data one block at a time. Stream ciphers, as shown on the right, encrypt the data one bit at a time. The stream cipher generates a key stream that encrypts the data by performing an exclusive-or between corresponding bits of the key stream and the bits of the plaintext.

(DES), the new Advanced Encryption Standard (AES), the International Data Encryption Algorithm (IDEA), Blowfish, and the CAST algorithm (created by Carlisle Adams and Stafford Tavares).   *see Note 7.*

Stream ciphers were used in the electromechanical machines from the mid-20th century, including World War II. The best-known modern stream cipher is *Rivest Cipher #4* (RC4), which is used in most Web browsers to protect e-commerce transactions. Although there isn't anything fundamentally weak in stream ciphers, it is difficult to use them safely. Microsoft chose RC4 to encrypt secure channels for Windows NT domains and in PPTP and encountered problems trying to use RC4 safely (see Section 11.4).

Figure 5.4 illustrates the difference between block and stream ciphers. Block ciphers encrypt data in fixed-sized blocks. The cipher uses the encryption key to thoroughly scramble the plaintext block of bits to yield the ciphertext. If you change a single bit in the plaintext, it could change several bits in the ciphertext, and vice versa.

Stream ciphers encrypt a stream of data. The mechanical encryption machines would encrypt streams of letters that formed secret messages. Modern computer-based ciphers tend to encrypt streams of bits. The ciphers work in two stages. In the first stage, the algorithm takes the secret key and uses it to generate a stream of random bits. In the second stage, the algorithm encrypts the data bits by combining them one by one with the random bit stream using the exclusive-or operation. If we change a single bit in the plaintext, we will affect only that same bit in the ciphertext. This can lead to integrity weaknesses in protocols that use stream ciphers; an example appears in Section 11.4.

SHORTCUT ATTACKS ON ENCRYPTION

Strong encryption algorithms are hard to construct. While serving as a deputy director of the NSA, William Crowell told Congress that the German Enigma machine from World War II could not be broken today, even with modern computers, and that the Allies' success against the Enigma relied on German mistakes as well as the Allies' smart code breakers. The Germans had the raw materials to achieve strong encryption, but they failed to put them together correctly. Their errors opened up shortcuts the Allies could use to crack their messages.   *see Note 8.*

During the war, the Germans were largely convinced that the Enigma's code was uncrackable, and Crowell's testimony indicates that they weren't entirely unrealistic in their belief. The Enigma was broken through an unexpected coincidence: the Allies built machines to perform trial-and-error searches at unprecedented speeds, and the German coding procedures had weaknesses that made such trial-and-error searches practical. Those weaknesses introduced shortcuts into the decryption process, since not every possible encryption key needed to be considered. Although encryption technology has made incredible progress since World War II, weak encryption still shows up in commercial products.

The fatal flaw of much encryption software is best called *hubris*, an ancient Greek word for excessive pride and arrogance that leads a smart person to do something foolish. The foolish act in this case *A-36* is for software developers to invent their own encryption algorithms. It is very difficult to construct a computationally secure algorithm. Homemade algorithms, even by large and profitable corporations, deserve to be treated with suspicion. Two particularly interesting examples of this emerged in the late 1990s. First, cryptographers uncovered weaknesses in encryption algorithms used for digital mobile phones. Second, people posted software to the Internet to crack the encryption used to control the viewing of videos sold on

DVDs. Neither system used a well-known, proven algorithm. In both cases the algorithms had been home-grown and kept secret in an ultimately futile attempt to prevent attackers from cracking the encryption.

see Note 9.

The simple solution to this problem is to use a strong, well-studied cryptographic algorithm. Such procedures are well known and easy to find. The first candidate is AES, the new, "advanced" encryption algorithm endorsed by the U.S. government for encrypting sensitive information in government and commercial applications. As of this writing, the AES has not been formally adopted as a Federal Information Processing Standard (FIPS), but this is considered almost certain to happen. Despite its newness, the AES provides a combination of speed and security that recommend it to almost any application. AES uses a 128-bit key, which presents attackers with a 127-bit average attack space. As of this writing, the principal shortcoming of AES is that few products have as yet incorporated it.

 D-36

see Note 10.

In practice, of course, the available software products don't always provide the exact choice we may want, but there are alternatives that provide reasonable security. The first is Triple DES, a variant of DES that uses double-length or triple-length secret keys. Although DES is relatively slow, especially when run three times for Triple DES, its security is well respected and has stood the test of time. Indeed, the only weakness anyone has attacked successfully is its relatively short 56-bit key length. Other respected algorithms include IDEA, RC4, Blowfish, and CAST.

see Note 11.

An interesting footnote regarding DES is that it contains one well-known, though minor, shortcut. DES has a property, called *complementation*, which means that we can actually test two DES keys at a time when performing a trial-and-error attack. Each time we choose a key to try, we run the DES algorithm, and then we can test both the chosen key and its bit-by-bit inverse. So we actually need to run the algorithm only half as many times when performing a trial-and-error search. To compute the average attack space for DES, we subtract one bit as usual to account for searching half of the keys on average, and another bit to account for complementation. Thus, the average attack space for DES is 54 bits.

see Note 12.

TRIAL-AND-ERROR ATTACKS ON ENCRYPTION

Aside from the successful wartime attacks against German codes, DES provides the best-known example of breaking a modern code by trial and error. Skepticism about its 56-bit key size emerged as soon as it was introduced. Shortly after DES was announced, cryptographers Whitfield Diffie and Martin Hellman outlined the design for a machine that could crack one DES-encrypted message per day. Although they did not actually build the machine, they described how such a thing could be built for $20 million using 1975 technology. While such a machine may have been impractical for most enterprises, there were certainly a few large nations, corporations, and criminal enterprises that could afford such a thing. But at the time, nobody had actually demonstrated that it was feasible to crack a DES-encrypted message.   *see Note 13.*

The skeptics had time and progress on their side. In the 1960s, Gordon E. Moore looked at the emerging trends in computer circuits and noted that circuit costs, sizes, and execution times were dropping by roughly 50% every year. This general trend came to be called *Moore's Law.* The law's predictions aren't exact, but the general trend has continued to this day. A more recent restatement of Moore's Law said that the amount of computation available at a given price would double every 18 months. Computing became both faster and cheaper as time went on.   *see Note 14.*

In Section 2.4, we looked at trial-and-error attacks on passwords; clearly Moore's Law was feeding the attack risk by the late 1970s. But it was not until the 1990s that public attacks on DES began in earnest. In 1993, Michael Wiener produced a detailed and convincing design for a $1 million DES-cracking machine that, in theory, could crack one key every 3.5 hours. In 1996, a group of cryptographers and others interested in computer security published a report summarizing the trends in brute force cracking technology, and indicated that DES was no longer safe for commercial applications. But DES cracking remained a theory until 1997, when a loose confederation of volunteers on the Internet cracked a DES message in 5 months using borrowed computing cycles. The next year, a much larger group of volunteers cracked a DES message in 39 days.   *see Note 15.*

But this achievement was overshadowed in the summer of 1998, when the Electronic Frontier Foundation (EFF) unveiled their DES

Cracker. The Cracker was a custom-built machine that, for $250,000, demonstrated a guess rate of 88 billion per second. In its first public demonstration it cracked a DES-encrypted message in three days. While it may be possible that an agency such as the U.S. National Security Agency (NSA) has a faster device for cracking keys, the DES Cracker has the highest guess rate of any publicly acknowledged device.

see Note 16.

THEORETICAL GUESS-RATE LIMITATIONS

The successful attacks on DES leave us with an unsettling question: just how many bits of entropy *should* a base secret have, if it must resist brute force attacks for a long time? In the mid-1990s, the NSA introduced the Skipjack encryption algorithm with 80-bit keys as a candidate to protect "sensitive but unclassified" government information. Noting public concern about 56-bit DES keys, the NSA offered Skipjack for nongovernment use as part of its unsuccessful Escrowed Encryption Standard. Skipjack was never widely adopted, however, because of public outrage regarding escrowed encryption plus a concern that 80 bits no longer gave enough of a safety margin against computational progress. Other commercial encryption algorithms like IDEA and RC4 were already widely used, and both relied on 128-bit keys. Financial institutions that still used DES relied on Triple DES constructions that used 112-bit or even 168-bit keys.

Moore's Law itself doesn't suggest an endpoint: the equation doesn't converge on some maximum value. Indeed, research in quantum computation suggests that we may someday build computers that use individual particles as logic elements. In such a world, only quantum physics itself can provide a convincing upper limit on trial-and-error attacks.

The physicist Seth Lloyd argues that computation speeds at that level are limited by the amount of energy poured into the computing system. If somehow we can build a perfectly efficient *quantum computer* at that level, then the machine could achieve over 10^{33} bit transitions per second on only one watt of power (keep in mind that a 32-bit processor operating at 1-gigahertz produces maybe 10^{11} transitions per second). At that rate, the 1-watt quantum computer could cover a space containing 113 bits every second.

see Note 17.

Of course, this represents a theoretical ideal: there really aren't any machines that achieve anywhere close to that speed or efficiency, not even experimental quantum computers. But it's interesting to consider just how powerful a quantum key-searching computer could be. We can use that information to decide how many bits a secret key should be to defend against really outlandish attacks.

For example, imagine that we can redirect all of the sun's energy, and prevent it from warming the leaves of plants, Earth's oceans, Jupiter's atmosphere, or anything else within the solar system or beyond its borders. Instead, we channel that energy into the guessing process. We assume ideal conditions under which all of the energy is fed to state transitions that correspond to individual trial-and-error guesses. Using all of the sun's energy, we can sustain a rate of 2.33×10^{60} guesses per second, which covers a 201-bit search space every second. Given that it takes 25 bits to represent the number of seconds in a year, we see that an entire year of solar energy will exhaust a 226-bit search space. If we choose to be less greedy and use only the energy falling on Earth itself, then we can crack a 175-bit search space every second.

This suggests to some people that a base secret with a couple hundred bits should resist trial-and-error attacks for the foreseeable future. However, the physics of computation is a relatively new field and continues to evolve in both theory and practice. Some theoreticians find this estimate plausible, but it needs to stand the test of time.

5.4 KEY-HANDLING ISSUES

No matter how strong our encryption algorithm is, the safety of encrypted data is only as good as the safety of the secret key. We must choose keys that are hard to guess and we need to keep the key safe from attackers. On the other hand, we face disaster if we lose or forget the secret key that encrypts some critical data. The problem might be more than a personal one, especially if the encrypted information belongs to an employer or other proprietor. Encryption also has political implications because of its historic role in World War II and the Cold War.

MEMORIZED KEYS

Strong encryption is pointless unless the secret key is hard to guess. If the data is valuable and the attacker is highly motivated, use a relatively long and hard-to-guess passphrase for a workstation encryption key. For example, use a short piece of prose that an attacker is unlikely to guess. The point of a good passphrase is to substitute the difficulty of protecting the computer's data with the difficulty of protecting the passphrase. A good passphrase will be too difficult for attackers to guess even by using a dictionary attack.

A complementary problem, particularly with volume encryption, is that users will lose their data if they lose the secret key. Strong encryption is intended to resist attempts to retrieve the data through trial and error. If encrypted data can be retrieved by a legitimate user despite a forgotten password, then others may also retrieve this information regardless of the user's intentions.

A sensible strategy for file encryption is to use the same passphrase to encrypt all files that are likely to be shared by a particular group of people. For example, a user might write reports for several different projects. The user can encrypt all of the reports for one project with one passphrase and the reports for another project with a different one. The user shares the appropriate passphrase with the people associated with a particular project. This puts the minimum burden on everyone by minimizing the number of secrets to share. The author keeps secrets separate by using separate secrets.

Encryption also yields a situation in which people may need to keep a written copy of their memorized base secrets. In other access-control and authentication systems, users can usually ask an administrator to replace a lost or forgotten password. Recovery isn't so easy with encryption. If the user forgets the passphrase for strongly encrypted data, the data is effectively lost. For that reason, it is practical and even necessary to write down the passphrases for encrypted data. However, once the passphrase is written down, the paper containing it must be very carefully protected.

KEY-HANDLING POLICIES

Encryption keys pose a dilemma because they do more than simply authenticate the authorized user: knowledge of the key also controls access to the encrypted data. This leads some proprietors and other authorities to want to treat encryption keys differently from passwords.

If the proprietor relies on passwords to authenticate people, then there is usually a rule against disclosing the password to anyone else. The proprietor can then hold the password's owner accountable for things done when the password gets used. Moreover, a strong rule against disclosing one's password also reduces the risk of social engineering attacks (Section 1.4). Users are less likely to fall for such trickery if they know with confidence that administrators will *never* ask for their password.

On the other hand, passwords used as encryption keys control the availability of the information, and arguably play a secondary role as far as accountability goes. Anyone who needs to retrieve the data must know the password that encrypts it. It doesn't really matter who uses the password as long as they're supposed to know it. This, in turn, leads some proprietors to demand that encryption keys always be shared with administrators to ensure availability of encrypted data.

Since memorized encryption keys are probably indistinguishable from passwords as far as most users are concerned, this produces an apparent contradiction in policy. One way proprietors can deal with this is training: make it clear what the difference is and why some passwords should be disclosed but not others. This is tricky, since most people won't understand the mechanisms to understand the differences. If users know they're supposed to disclose encryption passwords, then an attacker might manage to convince them that their logon passwords really are encryption passwords, too.

KEY ESCROW AND CRYPTO POLITICS

Another way to provide separate access to encrypted data is to use *key escrow* or *key recovery* technology. Some encryption products provide a way by which the proprietor can supply an additional encryption key: this key will allow the proprietor to decrypt the data without having to know the key chosen by the data's creator. Thus, the creator can keep the key secret but the proprietor still has access to it.

Key escrow has a bad reputation in the computer security field because it evolved as part of the political controversy surrounding commercial encryption technology. Until DES was introduced, there was no strong encryption available to protect commercial or private telecommunications traffic. DES enabled the development of world-wide electronic financial transactions by protecting the transactions from sniffing and forgery.

However, DES also interfered with surveillance activities of the NSA and the FBI. In the United States, encryption technology was classified as a "munition" according to export control laws passed following World War II. Those laws were officially intended to restrict the development and sale of military encryption products, but they also applied to commercial products. Hardware and software systems using DES could be sold to overseas customers only after a special license was issued by the State Department.

As digital telecommunications flourished with the growth of the Internet, export restrictions on encryption technology became a major political issue. In the mid-1990s, the NSA developed the Escrowed Encryption Standard (EES), which became FIPS 185. EES incorporated secret encryption keys that would allow U.S. surveillance agencies to sniff encrypted messages. The best-known implementation was embedded in an integrated circuit called the "Clipper Chip." Few U.S. vendors or foreign customers showed much interest in the technology. The government tried to coerce vendors into implementing EES by exerting pressure through export regulations, but most vendors still refused. By the end of the 1990s, export restrictions on encryption products were mostly eliminated, and the EES was abandoned. But the distaste for escrowed encryption keys still lingers.

see Note 18.

As a practical matter, key escrow can provide a valuable mechanism by which proprietors establish back-up keys for encrypted files or volumes. This reduces the risk of losing data by losing personally chosen encryption keys, especially if files are stored in encrypted form for a long period of time. Few people know how to ensure that an encryption key will remain secret but not get lost over the course of several years. Back-up keys, like those provided through key escrow mechanisms, may reduce the risk of losing the data by losing the key.

see Note 19.

On the other hand, escrowed encryption doesn't make much sense in telecommunications systems. The data on the communications line is ephemeral; the valuable data is the information constructed at either end as a result of the communication. If a proprietor needs to eavesdrop on communications as part of regular business activities, there are much simpler ways to do it. Moreover, the key escrow mechanism proposed by the government involved sharing keys with third-party organizations: the surveillance agencies. We face greatly increased risks to our keys when we share them with larger and larger groups.

5.5 SUMMARY TABLES

TABLE 5.1: *Attack Summary*

Attack	Security Problem	Prevalence	Attack Description
A-33. Retrieve original plaintext	Recover hidden information	Trivial	Retrieves the plaintext file used to produce an encrypted file
A-34. Magnetic data retrieval	Recover hidden information	Sophisticated	Uses laboratory techniques to retrieve overwritten data from a magnetic surface
A-35. Disk scavenging	Recover hidden information	Trivial	Uses "undelete" software or browser to locate sensitive data in plaintext form
A-36. Home-grown encryption algorithm	Recover hidden information	Sophisticated	Find and exploit a weakness in the encryption algorithm to decrypt the data in a practical amount of time

TABLE 5.2: *Defense Summary*

Defense	Foils Attacks	Description
D-33. Overwrite original plaintext	A-33. Retrieve original plaintext	Write other data over the data in the plaintext file that is to be protected by encryption
D-34. Three-step overwriting	A-34. Magnetic data retrieval	Use a three-step process to overwrite the data in a plaintext file to make it harder to recover
D-35. Volume encryption	A-35. Disk scavenging	Encrypts all information on a disk volume so that nothing is left in plaintext
D-36. Open review of encryption algorithms	A-36. Home-grown encryption algorithm	Use encryption algorithms whose capabilities have been thoroughly analyzed and discussed by the open cryptography community

CHAPTER 6

PICKING PINS AND PASSWORDS

*(I cheat and make all my computer accounts use the
same password.)*

— Donald A. Norman, *The Design of Everyday Things*

IN THIS CHAPTER

Password systems are often limited because it's too easy to find out
what the passwords are. This makes it hard to find a balance
between passwords that are easy to remember and easy to guess.

- Limitations human memory places on password safety
- Internal versus external passwords
- Protecting passwords
- Sharing passwords
- Groups and sequences of passwords

6.1 PASSWORD COMPLEXITY

Since passwords were introduced in the 1960s, the notion of a
"good" password has evolved in response to attacks against them. At
first, there were no rules about passwords except that they should
be remembered and kept secret. As attacks increased in sophistication, so did the rules for choosing good passwords. Each new rule
had its justification and, when seen in context, each one made
sense. People rarely had trouble with any particular rule: the problem was with their combined effect.

The opening quotation illustrates one well-known assumption
about proper password usage: it's "cheating" to use the same password for more than one thing. This is because passwords may be

intercepted or guessed. If people routinely use a single password for everything, then attackers reap a huge benefit by intercepting a single password. So, our first rule for choosing passwords might be:

1. *Each password you choose must be new and different.*

An early and important source of password rules was the *Department of Defense (DOD) Password Management Guideline*. Published in 1985, the *Guideline* codified the state of the practice for passwords at that time. In addition to various technical recommendations covered in other chapters, the *Guideline* provided recommendations for how individuals should select and handle passwords. In particular, these recommendations yielded the following password rule:

see Note 1.

2. *Passwords must be memorized. If a password is written down, it must be locked up.*

Password selection rules in the *DOD Guideline* were based on a simple rationale: attackers can find a password by trying all the possibilities. The DOD's specific guidelines were formulated to prevent a successful attack based on systematic, trial-and-error guessing. The *Guideline* presented a simple model of a guessing attack that established parameters for password length and duration. This yielded two more password rules:

3. *Passwords must be at least six characters long, and probably longer, depending on the size of the password's character set.*

4. *Passwords must be replaced periodically.*

The *DOD Guideline* included a worked example based on the goal of reducing the risk of a guessed password to one chance in a million over a one-year period. This produced the recommendation to change passwords at least once a year. Passwords must be nine characters long if they only consist of single-case letters, and may be only eight characters long if they also contain digits. Shorter passwords would decrease the risk of guessing to less than one in a million, but that still provided good security for most applications. The *DOD Guideline* didn't actually mandate eight-character passwords or the one-in-a-million level of risk; these decisions were left to the individual sites and systems.

In fact, the chances of guessing were significantly greater than one in a million, even with eight- and nine-character passwords.

This is because people tend to choose words for passwords—after all, they are told to choose a *word*, not a secret numeric code or some other arbitrary value. And there are indeed a finite number of words that people tend to choose. Dictionary attacks (Section 2.5) exploit this tendency. By the late 1980s, dictionary attacks caused so much worry that another password rule evolved:

> 5. *Passwords must contain a mixture of letters (both upper- and lowercase), digits, and punctuation characters.*

Now that we have these five rules in place, it is time examine Figure 6.1. The evolving rules, and the corresponding increases in password complexity, have now left the users behind. None but the most compulsive can comply with such rules week after week, month after month. Ultimately, we can summarize classical password selection rules as follows:

> *The password must be impossible to remember*
> *and never written down.*

The point isn't that these rules are wrong. Every one of these rules has its proper role, but the rules must be applied in the light of practical human behavior and peoples' motivations. Most people use computers because they help perform practical business tasks or provide entertainment. There's nothing productive or entertaining about memorizing obscure passwords.

FIGURE 6.1: *Do password guidelines* **prevent** *information services?* Password guidelines did not start out with such complicated rules; the rules evolved in response to evolving attacks. Each extra requirement (minimum length, monthly changes, etc.) made life slightly more difficult until it became impossible for users to comply. DILBERT © 1998 United Feature Syndicate. Used by permission.

TABLE 6.1: *Password Systems Are Not User Friendly*

Golden Rules of User Interface Design (from Shneiderman, see Note 2)	True for Passwords?
1. Strive for consistency	YES
2. Frequent users can use shortcuts	NO
3. Provide informative feedback	NO
4. Dialogs should yield closure	YES
5. Prevent errors and provide simple error handling	NO
6. Easy reversal of any action	NO
7. Put the user in charge	NO
8. Reduce short-term memory load	NO

PASSWORDS AND USABILITY

Traditional password systems contain many design features intended to make attacks as hard as possible. Unfortunately, these features also make password systems hard to use. In fact, they violate most of the accepted usability standards for computer systems. Of the eight "Golden Rules" suggested by Ben Shneiderman for user interface design, password interactions break at least six of them (see Table 6.1). People can't take shortcuts: the system won't match the first few letters typed and fill in the rest. Most systems only report success or failure: they don't say how close the password guess was, or even distinguish between a mistyped user name and a mistyped password. Many systems keep track of incorrect guesses and take some irreversible action (like locking the person's account) if too many bad guesses take place. To complete the challenge, people rarely have a chance to *see* the password they type: they can't detect repeated letters or accidental misspellings.

To appreciate another truly fundamental problem with passwords, consider what happens when changing a password. Imagine that Tim needs to change his password, and he wishes to follow all of the rules. While it's possible that he might have a particular password in mind to use the next time the occasion arises, many (perhaps most) people don't think about passwords until they actually need to choose one. For example, Windows NT can force its users to immediately change a password during the logon process, usually because the existing password has become "too old." If Tim hasn't thought of another good password ahead of time, he must think of one, fix it permanently in his mind, and type it in twice without ever seeing it written.

This presents a significant mental challenge, especially if Tim tries to follow the classic password selection rules. He has to remember and apply the rules about length, reuse, and content. Then he must remember the password he chose. This is made especially hard since the system won't display the password he chose: Tim must memorize it without the extra help of seeing its visual representation.

Human short-term memory can, on average, remember between five and nine things of a particular kind: letters, digits, words, or other well-recognized categories. The *DOD Guideline* spoke of eight- or nine-character passwords, which lie on the optimistic end of peoples' ability to memorize. Moreover, Tim's short-term memory will retain this new password for perhaps only a half minute, so he must immediately work at memorizing it. Studies show that if Tim is interrupted before he fully memorizes the password, then it will fall out of his working memory and be lost. If Tim was in a hurry when the system demanded a new password, he must sacrifice either the concentration he had on his critical task or the recollection of his new password. Or, he can violate a rule and write the password down on a piece of paper.

A-37

see Note 3.

Passwords were originally words because it's much easier for people to remember words than arbitrary strings of characters. Tim might not remember the password "rgbmrhuea," but he can easily remember the same letters when they spell out "hamburger." Tim more easily remembers a word as his password because it represents a single item in his memory. If Tim chooses an equally long sequence of arbitrary characters to be his password, he must mentally transform that sequence into a single item for him to remember. This is hard for people to do reliably. While there are techniques for improving one's memory, they are difficult to learn and require constant practice to retain. Strong passwords simply aren't practical if they require specialized training to use correctly. Later in this chapter we examine a few simple and practical memory techniques for producing memorable passwords. The techniques do not necessarily provide the strongest possible secrets, but they are within the reach of most peoples' abilities.

see Note 4.

FORCING FUNCTIONS AND MOUSE PADS

If strong security depends on strong passwords, then one strategy to achieve good security is to implement mechanisms that enforce the use of strong passwords, like those introduced in Section 3.5. The mechanisms either generate appropriate passwords automatically or they critique the passwords selected by users. While these approaches can have some value, they also have limitations. In terms of the user interface, the mechanisms generally work as *forcing functions* that try to control user password choices.

D-37

see Note 5.

Unfortunately, forcing functions do not necessarily solve the problem that motivated their implementation. The book *Why Things Bite Back*, by Edward Tenner, examines unintended consequences of various technological mechanisms. In particular, the book identifies several different patterns by which technology takes revenge on humanity when applied to a difficult problem. A common pattern, for example, is for the technological fix to simply "rearrange" things so that the original problem remains but in a different guise.

see Note 6.

Forcing functions are prone to rearrangements. In the case of strong password enforcement, for example, we set up intractable forces for collision. We can implement software that requires complicated, hard-to-remember passwords, but we can't change individuals' memorization skills. When people require computers to get work done, they will rearrange the problem themselves to reconcile the limits of their memory with the mandates of the password selection mechanism.

Coincidentally, mouse pads are shaped like miniature doormats. Just as some people hide house keys under doormats, some hide passwords under mouse pads (Figure 6.2). The author occasionally performs "mouse pad surveys" at companies using computer systems. The surveys look under mouse pads and superficially among other papers near workstations for written passwords. A significant number are found, both at high-tech and low-tech companies.

D-38

People rarely include little notes with their passwords to explain why they chose to hide the password instead of memorize it. In some cases, several people might be sharing the password and the written copy is the simplest way to keep all users informed. Although many sites discourage such sharing, it does take place, as discussed in Section 6.5. More often, people write down passwords because they have so much trouble remembering them. When asked about written passwords, poor memory is the typical excuse.

An interesting relationship noted in these surveys is that people hide written passwords near their workstations more often when the system requires users to periodically change them. In the author's experience, the likelihood of finding written passwords near a workstation subjected to periodic password changes ranged from 16% to 39%, varying from site to site. At the same sites, however, the likelihood ranged from 4% to 9% for workstations connected to systems that did *not* enforce periodic password changes. In some cases, over a third of a system's users rearranged the password problem to adapt to their inability to constantly memorize new passwords.

These surveys also suggest an obvious attack: the attacker can simply search around workstations in an office area for written passwords. This strategy appeared in the motion picture *WarGames*, in a scene in which a character found the password for the high school computer by looking in a desk. Interestingly, the password was clearly the latest entry in a list of words where the earlier entries were all crossed off. Most likely, the school was required to   *A-38*

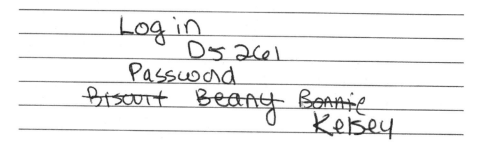

FIGURE 6.2: *Passwords hidden under a mouse pad.* This handwritten list of passwords was found under a mouse pad in a professional office. Each time the system demanded a new password, the user chose a new one, wrote it on the slip of paper, and stuck it back underneath the mouse pad. As many as one out of three people do something like this.

TABLE 6.2: *Mouse Pad Searches and Average Attack Spaces*

Example	Style of Attack	Average Attack Space
Trial-and-error attack on 56-bit DES encryption keys	Off-line	54 bits
Attack on automatically generated passwords	Off-line	39.5 bits
Dictionary attack on eight-character Unix passwords	Off-line	22.7 bits
Attack on a biometric with an FAR of 1 in 100,000	Interactive	16 bits
Trial-and-error attack on four-digit PINs	Interactive	13 bits
Best-case result of a mouse pad search	Interactive	4 bits
Worst-case result of a mouse pad search	Interactive	1 bit

change its password periodically (for "security" reasons) and the users kept this list so they wouldn't forget the latest password.

Using the statistics from mouse pad searches, we can estimate the average attack space for the corresponding attack. Table 6.2 compares the results with other average attack spaces. In the best case, the likelihood is 4%, or one in 25, so the attacker must, on average, search 12 or 13 desks to find a password. That yields an average attack space of four bits. The worst case is 39%, which is less than one in three. Thus, the attacker must, on average, search one or two desks to find a written password. So the worst-case average attack space for a mouse pad search is only *one bit*.

The mouse pad problem shows that we can't always increase the average attack space simply by making passwords more complicated. If we overwhelm people's memories, we make certain attack risks worse, not better. The reason we want to discourage single-word passwords is that they're vulnerable to off-line dictionary attacks. Table 6.2 shows that such attacks involve a 22.7-bit attack space. We don't increase the average attack space if forgettable passwords move to the bottom of people's mouse pads.

6.2   DIFFERENT SECRETS FOR DIFFERENT USES

For many people, the most important memorized secret they have is the PIN for their cash card. Why are banks satisfied with a four-digit PIN that yields a paltry 13-bit average attack space? And, if passwords are to have any value at all, how do we balance our need for security against the risk of mouse pad searches?

The answer is that we must identify the operating environment for the password system and adapt our password rules to fit. For the purposes of this discussion, we consider four password environments:

- **Sniffable passwords**—memorized secrets that protect information of relatively low value. The remote connection may travel over untrustworthy communication links like the Internet. The proprietors don't worry about the threat because the information resources don't justify the expense of more sophisticated protection. Such passwords protect us against only the least motivated attackers.

- **PINs**—memorized secrets, often containing four digits, that are used with a token like a bank's cash card. In most cases, attackers can guess a PIN only by submitting the guess to the card's server.

- **Internal passwords**—secrets that are used only within the physical confines of a reasonably safe site. We would consider it a safe site if insiders don't pose a significant threat to one another.

- **External passwords**—secrets that are used to establish a remote connection to a site, where the site may contain valuable information resources. The remote connection may travel over untrustworthy communication links like the Internet, and attackers can intercept authentication traffic. In general, the passwords are crypto protected. Attackers can often mount a trial-and-error guessing attack on them in encrypted form.

Technically, two things distinguish these cases: confidentiality and dictionary attacks. Confidentiality, enforced through physical security or cryptography, establishes whether or not potentially threatening people have access to the passwords or to the machines they protect. Dictionary attacks plague external passwords but don't pose as much of a threat to the others.

Because attackers can often use dictionary attacks against external passwords, such passwords should be chosen to resist those attacks. Internal passwords may also provide opportunities for dictionary attacks, but only to people who already have physical access to the protected computers. Thus, external passwords need to be chosen to resist dictionary attacks, while internal passwords do not.

If we must use memorized secrets in all these cases, then we need to use different strategies for choosing and handling the different secrets. Ideally, we should have separate passwords for each so that easy-to-use internal passwords aren't used for remote access, where they might be easily cracked.

SNIFFABLE PASSWORDS

An attacker can sniff a password if there are opportunities to intercept it in an unprotected form. The prime example of a sniffable password would be one sent unprotected across the Internet: attackers anywhere along its route can make a copy and use it later themselves (see Section 1.5). Many Internet applications use sniffable passwords. In fact, one should probably assume that Internet passwords are sniffable, unless the application includes some form of challenge-response authentication (Chapter 10) or an encryption feature like SSL (Section 13.6). Without extra protection, almost all Web and e-mail authentication can be sniffed by attackers.

Given that attackers can simply listen for these passwords and then use them, it almost doesn't matter what passwords the victims choose. Passwords that resist dictionary attacks are just as easy to sniff as any others. It makes sense to choose a hard-to-guess password, but it's pointless to choose one that's hard to remember.

PIN APPLICATIONS

A four-digit PIN presents the attacker with only a 13-bit average attack space, but this is sufficient if the system can always detect and thwart a trial-and-error guessing attack. For example, systems whose design fall into the "local" authentication pattern (Section 4.4) can be built to detect trial-and-error attacks. The same is true for systems that deny verifiable plaintext to attackers. The system can do this by using supplementary encryption; this is how ATMs tend to handle PINs. Another approach is to use an authentication protocol that combines the PIN with a larger base secret in order to construct the right protocol message to send. Section 9.5 contains examples of this.

INTERNAL PASSWORDS

An internal password is a memorized password that is used within a site that excludes outsiders but provides little physical protection among insiders. The password is used to authenticate people within the confines of the site. External connections, if allowed at all, must use a different password or a different authentication mechanism entirely.

The earliest network password systems were used primarily on LANs with little or no external access. This includes early versions on networked Unix workstations, Novell Netware, Microsoft LAN Manager, and Apple's Appletalk. In most cases, external access (that is, modem dial-in and Internet connections) appeared later and required a separate software package.

The essential feature of an internal password is that the attacker must be physically present at the site to use it (Figure 6.3). Outsiders must physically break into a site in order to use an internal

FIGURE 6.3: *Internal passwords for computers used locally.* If we keep outsiders away from our computers and forbid remote connections, then we reduce the risk of attacks on the password system. Attacks can come only from insiders who are physically present. Strong, hard-to-remember passwords aren't needed for internal passwords, since attackers don't need passwords if they can physically touch the computers they want to attack.

password. As described in Section 4.2, an attacker with physical access to a computer has several effective attacks at his disposal that do not require knowledge of passwords. Thus, the password may simply be "icing on the cake" for the attacker.

Moreover, an inside attacker can indulge in a mouse pad search, which will probably uncover some passwords. If the site's LAN relies on older, Unix-like passwords for server access, an inside attacker can install sniffers on the network; if not, the attacker can install keystroke capture software on victims' workstations. Attackers can install keystroke software most easily on traditional desktop systems with no protection, like Windows 98 or 95, as well as traditional Macintosh systems.

Inside attackers have so many attacks at their disposal that it's pointless to overburden local users with complicated password requirements. This leads to the following objectives and recommendations for internal password security:

- Encourage users to choose memorable passwords that are hard to guess. See Section 6.4 for recommendations on how to choose internal passwords. Such passwords are vulnerable to dictionary attacks, but such attacks are less of a threat than mouse pad searches or other local intrusions.

- Disable password expiration features, since they force some users to write passwords down instead of memorizing them. Encourage users to change passwords when some other major event occurs. For example, encourage users replace their passwords whenever their workstation hardware or software receives a significant upgrade. Users should also be told to change passwords if a security incident suggests that there are inside attackers that have acquired users' passwords.

- The site's servers should, of course, reside in a locked computer room. Nobody should be able to enter that room except the administrators assigned to those servers.

- Workstations dedicated to critical applications, like payroll, should reside in their own separate, locked office area. Nobody should be allowed into that area unattended except the people assigned to that area. Internal passwords for those computers should work only within that office area.

- Some systems, notably those that provide "single sign-on," will always use the same password for both internal and external access. Under those circumstances, there are no "internal" passwords: all passwords are essentially "external" and should follow the recommendations for them. This restriction can be eased for particular users if it is possible to forbid remote access to their accounts.

- Administrative passwords need to be stronger than other internal passwords, since they represent a more valuable target to attackers. A few people at a site may be tempted to try to guess administrative passwords simply as a technical challenge, regardless of the ethical issues involved. Stronger passwords reduce the risk of such attacks, and are probably worth the inconvenience as long as the administrators handle them safely. See the subsection on administrative passwords in Section 6.4 for suggestions on password selection.

The point of these recommendations is to strike an effective balance between usability and security. Attempts to sacrifice usability in favor of security can sacrifice both.

EXTERNAL PASSWORDS

An external password is one that is cryptographically protected when used, but vulnerable to dictionary attacks by outsiders. In particular, these include passwords used with Microsoft networking protocols (Chapters 10 and 11) and Kerberos (Chapter 12). External connections carry a lot more risk than internal connections, since potential attackers include all outsiders as well as insiders. History has shown that there is always a significant population of outsiders with the means and motivation to attack remote connections.

Cautious sites often build their network so that remote connections receive different treatment from internal connections. Typically, an external connection must traverse a security device, like a "network access server" (NAS) or firewall that performs remote authentication before the remote connection is accepted. Sites generally use an NAS to control dial-in connections (see Chapter 11) while firewalls control inbound connections from the Internet. These devices are often responsible for authenticating inbound remote connections.

Ideally, external passwords should resist dictionary attacks. This usually relies on two separate mechanisms: choosing complicated passwords and changing them periodically. Dictionary attacks take time, and many such attacks use otherwise idle computing cycles to test passwords over a long period. If the passwords change faster than the dictionary search proceeds, then the attack will never succeed. Sites can reduce the cracking risk by using complex passwords and changing them periodically.

However, these two mechanisms will drive many people to write down their passwords. Ideally, people who can't memorize passwords under those conditions should protect them from mouse pad searches as described in Section 6.6.

If the remote system protects a really valuable resource (for example, payroll, order entry, or other systems that manipulate valuable assets) then the system needs more protection than passwords can possibly offer. Such systems should use a stronger, token-based alternative. These are introduced in Chapter 9 and include one-time password tokens, smart cards, and newer devices like USB tokens. These devices provide a larger average attack space than we can get from any memorized password, and it is much harder for attackers to crack or steal the card's secret.

Here is a summary of objectives and recommendations for external password security:

- If the external password is protecting a system that manipulates really valuable assets, then the proprietor should *not* rely on memorized passwords for security. Instead, the system should use one-time password tokens or smart cards. Unfortunately, such systems are expensive. Some enterprises need to suffer a large financial loss before they decide to pay for such protection (see the example in Section 9.3).

- External connections should use protocols that resist rerouting.

- External passwords should resist dictionary attacks. See the subsection on external passwords in Section 6.4 for suggestions.

- External passwords should be changed periodically.

- If an external password is written down, it must be physically protected from insider attacks, if such attacks are judged likely. This judgment should be based on the value of the remote system and the motivation of insiders to attack it.
- If external passwords are used with a laptop or other portable computer, the external passwords should not be stored near the computer itself.

While it's true that people should exercise caution in choosing external passwords, some people will always choose easy-to-guess passwords. There is no foolproof remedy to this. Although we can train people to choose strong passwords, research and practical experience suggest that this provides only a modest improvement. A group of researchers at Cambridge University ran an experiment to measure the effect of training on user password choices, and found that the frequency of bad password choices declined from 30% to 10%. However, the researchers also recognized that some sites can't tolerate having "only" 10% of their passwords weak. If we enforce the selection of complex passwords, then we need to acknowledge that some users will keep written copies of their passwords.   *see Note 7.*

6.3 IMPROVING INTERNAL PASSWORD ENTRY

When we look at the overall shortcomings of most password systems, there are several obvious ways of improving password usability without necessarily sacrificing security. This is especially true when handling internal passwords at a low-risk site. Password systems are often designed to handle the worst possible security situation when in fact the system might be used in a fairly benign environment.

When handling passwords internally, the petty inconveniences of typical password interactions don't necessarily improve security. People in such environments often already know the user names associated with other people. Workstations often operate in environments where shoulder surfing or van Eck sniffing is either unlikely or pointless. We can make password authentication easier to use by taking advantage of this. Here is a summary of possible improvements:

- Operator-controlled echo
- Report incorrect user names
- Allow many password guesses
- Report incorrect password attempts
- Avoid periodic password changes

The strategy for improvement is to provide better feedback whenever it won't cause a significant security problem. To achieve the highest degree of safety and practicality, people should have the option to enable or disable particular features according to their immediate situation. Laptops, for example, may be used in either a crowded airliner or a private hotel room. Either the site or the individual must be able to configure the password dialog to achieve a reasonable balance between safety and usability. Never assume that "one size fits all."

OPERATOR-CONTROLLED PASSWORD DISPLAY

Let the operator decide whether or not the password dialog displays the actual characters while typing the password. It is much easier to type a password correctly if you can see what you've typed. This is particularly important when choosing a new password. It's much easier to memorize some text when we can see it as well as think it.

Most systems "blank out" passwords when typed in. This is a very old tradition, dating back to the days of timesharing. The technique protects against shoulder surfing and some simple forms of van Eck sniffing. Typically, the typed password isn't even displayed when collecting a newly chosen one. This clearly places an extra burden on people's ability to remember the new password.

Today, many systems reside in reasonably private, "internal" areas. Shoulder surfing and van Eck sniffing are reasonably unlikely, since all potential attackers are already insiders. Anyone with means and motivation to attack a computer can just physically attack the workstation of interest. If outside attackers manage to sniff a password using a van Eck receiver, they would still have to break into the company premises to make use of the passwords they find. Under such circumstances, there is little security benefit to blanking out the passwords.

An interesting point is that people have a better chance of spotting a Trojan login attack if they can see the password they typed. As described in Section 1.5 (Attack A-11), the Trojan login program mimics the login process for the purpose of collecting passwords. For example, Cathy sits down at her workstation, sees a login prompt on the screen, and immediately types her user name and password. If in fact the login prompt comes from a Trojan login program, it will simply save her user name and password to share with the attacker, and announce "Password incorrect." However, if Cathy had the password echo enabled, she would be able to tell that she had typed the correct password but the login program didn't recognize it—a clear indication of a Trojan login program.

Even if password echoing can be turned on for some situations, it needs to be turned off in others. For example, people using laptops on airliners or in public places are no longer in an "internal" environment and should disable password echoing. Likewise, administrators should regularly disable echoing when typing their passwords, since such passwords protect more assets than a typical user's password.

REPORT INCORRECT USER NAMES

If an operator makes a mistake when logging on, the system should say whether the problem is with the password or the user name. This helps the operator focus on correcting the right error when attempting to log on again.

The tradition of generating a nonspecific response is intended to increase the amount of work for a remote attacker, since the attacker must be able to guess a legitimate user name as well as guess the password. Today, many users operate in an environment where they are familiar with other people's user names. Some systems, like the eBay auction site, publish legal user names as part of routine activities, and users don't generally expect their user name to be kept secret. Under such circumstances, the system does not reduce its login security by reporting invalid user names. It simply improves usability.

The capability to report invalid user names should be enabled or disabled depending on the environment. It is usually safe to report incorrect user names in internal password environments, or if the system routinely publishes user names during normal system operation. If not, then the system should not distinguish between an incorrect user name and an incorrect password.

ALLOW MANY PASSWORD GUESSES

Many systems, including Windows NT, can configure the authentication system so that a certain number of incorrect password guesses will "lock" the account. The account's owner must then find an NT administrator to "unlock" the account before it is possible to log on again. The number of attempts is often set at five or some other low number. While this capability may be justified for remote connections, it will simply interfere with internal password users. Legitimate users are very likely to type incorrect passwords these days, particularly when they have so many passwords to remember, and if they have been forced to change their passwords regularly.

If a system has a relatively user-hostile password prompt (that is, one that doesn't report incorrect user names, or doesn't echo typed characters in a password) then the system should accept a much larger number of incorrect guesses, perhaps as many as 20, before locking an account. If the system has a friendlier password prompt, then it should work acceptably with a lower bad-password tolerance.

In either case, there is a simpler mechanism that won't lock out a legitimate user but will make attacks more difficult. The password system can introduce a timed delay each time it receives a bad password from a user, and it can increase the delay for each successive bad password. This gives the proprietor a way to make password guessing unattractive while not locking out forgetful users.

REPORT INCORRECT PASSWORD ATTEMPTS

The password system *must* keep track of incorrect password guesses. Otherwise, there is no way to detect an interactive trial-and-error guessing attack. If the system simply ignores bad passwords, then attackers simply have to produce a large list of candidates and try them one by one. This is especially true if the system is allowing numerous bad password attempts. Ideally, the system should report the occurrence of numerous bad password attempts to the system administrator.

The system should also report to each user the number of incorrect password attempts on their user account since the last successful login attempt. Individual users are likely to have some notion of how often they mistype their password. If the system tells them that it received numerous bad password attempts when the users themselves didn't make them, the users can detect trial-and-error attacks themselves.

AVOID PERIODIC PASSWORD CHANGES

Although it is a good idea to change passwords periodically, there is no good time to arbitrarily force users to change their passwords. The worst choice is probably to require a password change during a logon operation when the user might be trying to complete some important task. This often happens when a system like Windows NT forces people to change passwords according to some rigid period, like every two or three months.

If the system interrupts the user's work to demand a password change, the person is probably in the worst possible frame of mind for choosing and memorizing a good password. The person is more likely to either write down the password or choose an obvious one, to avoid the embarrassment and inconvenience of forgetting what was chosen. If system security is not threatened by having passwords written down, then perhaps passwords do not really need to expire, either.

Recent version of Windows NT and Windows 2000 attempt to reduce the impact of password changes by giving users some warning. Instead of demanding an immediate password change, the system announces that the password will expire soon, and asks if this is a good time to change the password. Ideally, the user can defer the password change and think up a memorable password to use. However, some users will undoubtedly ignore the password change until it is forced upon them.

The best time to perform a password change is during a hardware or software upgrade. People expect disruptions at such times anyway. Furthermore, the administrative staff can talk to users about changing passwords when briefing them about other changes to their computer. A successful password change requires that the user have time to think up a new password without interfering with other activities.

6.4   PASSWORD SELECTION

This section describes some simple techniques for choosing local and external passwords. These techniques are not, of course, the only ones for choosing appropriate passwords. The fundamental objective in any case is to resist attacks. Be sure to adapt these recommendations to reflect a site's particular requirements or limitations.

INTERNAL PASSWORDS

As described in Section 6.2, internal passwords are intended to be memorized but not necessarily to resist dictionary attacks. In a sense, these are "weak" passwords since the dictionary attacks can crack them. Their advantage, however, is that typical people can memorize such passwords. Many people at a reasonably diverse site will lack the skill or motivation to memorize stronger passwords. By using these weaker passwords we reduce the risk posed by mouse pad searches.

While these passwords might reside in a dictionary, they should still resist casual guessing attempts. A good password should not occur to an attacker, even an attacker that knows people at the site. People should not choose passwords that others are likely to associate with them, their family, or their activities. By choosing kids' names; pets' names; favorite sports, foods, or other activities; or similar words, people make themselves vulnerable to "Psychic Hotline" sorts of attacks in which a cleverly crafted set of personal questions will provide the right hints. Some particularly bad examples include those in Figure 6.2 (names of family members and coworkers), the password "Joshua" used in the movie *WarGames* (the name of the scientist's son), and the smart card password "Buddy" used by President Clinton to sign a piece of legislation "electronically" for the first time (his dog's name).   *see Note 8.*

A good password uses a word that you never discuss with other people. Don't limit your thoughts to proper names, locations, activities, or things, but consider all such words associated with such events. To start with, consider the following:

- People you knew long ago and won't come up in conversation.
- Obscure towns you rarely visited and never discuss.
- Particular things you avoid and never talk about (obscure dislikes in food, songs, places, entertainers, TV shows, etc.).
- Seasoned technical people might choose obscure acronyms or oddly constructed variable names from obsolete systems.
- Details from some embarrassing personal secret—the person involved, or the place, or some other aspect of the incident. Such passwords aren't likely to be voluntarily disclosed to other people.

There are also simple ways of incorporating digits into memorable passwords. This makes a password a little more obscure, although a well-designed dictionary attack can probably accommodate such things. One popular technique is to substitute digits for similar letters: a zero for the letter "o" or the digit one for an "i" or "l." This can lead in other directions; for example, a digit's sound can substitute for a word's syllable, like using "gr8est" for the password "greatest." The only shortcoming of such passwords is that the owner must remember the correct substitution of letters and digits: it requires remembering more than just the word itself.

Remember that these are *not* strong passwords: they will not withstand a well-designed dictionary attack. However, they represent reasonable choices for passwords that are memorable, never shared, and never written down. These passwords can adapt to other needs: if passwords require the combination of letters with digits or punctuation, then the extra character fits comfortably and memorably between syllables. Simple and thoughtful strategies can make passwords memorable and tolerably hard to guess.

EXTERNAL AND ADMINISTRATIVE PASSWORDS

When Klein performed his password-cracking experiments and managed to crack over 24% of the encrypted Unix passwords he encountered, he found it impractical to try to crack *pairs* of words

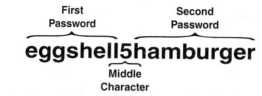

Average Attack Space: 22.7 bits + 4 bits + 1+22.7 bits = 50.4 bits

FIGURE 6.4: *Constructing a strong password.* We can construct a strong password that resists dictionary attacks by combining two passwords. We choose the two passwords and a digit or punctuation mark to stand between them. We construct the strong password by placing the extra character between the other two passwords and using the result as a single password. Such passwords should pose an average attack space of over 50 bits, as long as the individual passwords and the middle character are unrelated and truly random choices.

concatenated together. Therein lies a strategy for constructing strong passwords that aren't so difficult to memorize. *see Note 9.*

Dictionary attacks exploit our bias toward choosing memorable things like words as passwords, and our tendency to use fairly simple tricks to obscure those words. Klein's sophisticated dictionary attack showed that such strategies yield a 22.7-bit average attack space, which will not resist a determined attacker. Strong passwords must provide a much larger average attack space. This suggests we can construct strong, memorable passwords as follows:

1. Randomly choose a single password, using the instructions in the previous section on internal passwords.

2. Randomly choose a second, preferably different, password in the same manner.

3. Randomly choose a digit or punctuation character as a middle character.

4. Construct a stronger password by concatenating the first password, the middle character, and the second password.

5. Look at the resulting password and try to find some pattern, rhythm, or "meaning" of some sort in it. That's the key to memorizing it.

Figure 6.4 illustrates such a password. If the password system works correctly, this procedure should yield a password with an average attack space of over 50 bits. An attacker will have to try every word in the dictionary combined with every other word in the dictionary, and repeat this for every possible middle character. Each password by itself presents a 22.7-bit average attack space. Since each attack space represents only half of the search space, in binary, we must add one bit back to one of the attack spaces. Thus, the combined attack space will be more than twice that large, and the middle character should add another four bits. If the middle character is a digit or punctuation mark, but not a hyphen, then the resulting password will never appear in a dictionary by itself and a one-word dictionary attack will never succeed.

There are, however, certain pitfalls to avoid when choosing passwords in this manner. In particular, people must avoid choosing words and numbers to intentionally make patterns. For example, it's easy to remember a password that sounds like a phrase where the middle digit sounds like a word. Phrases with prepositions like "to" ("2") and "for" ("4") produce passwords like "hard2guess." Unfortunately, such passwords are easier to search for than ones where there's no relationship between the pieces, like "catfood%engine." The safest way to choose random words is through reasonably random processes. For example, choose words by picking a random word on a randomly chosen page of a randomly chosen book. Choose the middle character by rolling two or three dice: results greater than 10 should select a punctuation character from the keyboard (but *not* a hyphen, which could produce a legal compound word).

The principal weakness of this strategy is not in the passwords themselves, but in the underlying systems. The classic, eight-character Unix passwords described in Section 2.3 don't contain enough characters to capture an entire password, particularly when individual words are longer than three or four letters. While this reduces the practical average attack space, it posed an insurmountable computational challenge to Klein in 1990. Microsoft LAN Manager passwords can be cracked in sections (see Section 10.4), and this may allow an attacker to efficiently crack part of a two-word password. The safest techniques use 14 characters or more as part of an integrated cryptographic operation. Examples include the Windows NT hash procedure described in Section 10.6 and SSL encryption described in Section 13.6.

To summarize, here are recommendations for choosing strong but memorable passwords:

- Follow the five steps listed earlier in this section.
- Choose the two passwords randomly, perhaps by picking words randomly from two different books.
- Choose the middle character randomly, perhaps by rolling dice. Do not use a hyphen for the middle character, or anything else that might yield a compound word.
- If you try to choose random words out of your head, do *not* construct the password as a phrase, like "easy2recall." There are a relatively small number of such phrases and an attacker can easily construct a dictionary attack against them.
- Memorize the password by finding a pattern in it. People can find patterns in anything, even in a totally random construction. But be sure to look for the pattern *after* choosing the password. Otherwise, you sacrifice some of its unpredictability.

Some users need to manage several external or administrative passwords. Section 6.7 provides some strategies to help generate groups of memorable passwords.

6.5 SHARED PASSWORDS

There are two general cases of shared passwords. The first case is when one person uses the same password with several different systems: the *multiple-use password* case. The second case is where several people share a single password when using a particular system: the *password delegation* case.

MULTIPLE-USE PASSWORDS

Many people reuse a familiar password, especially these days when every e-commerce site on the Web demands a unique user name and a password. People might be willing to write down their Amazon user name but keep their password secret. It's less of a memory challenge to use the same password for the same purpose on several different systems.

The reason this is a bad idea, however, is that one never knows   *A-39* how carefully a given site might handle one's password. If John, for example, uses five or six different e-commerce sites and one of them has poor security, then attackers might be able to recover his password from the weakest site. For example, not all e-commerce sites are "secure sites" that use the SSL protocol to protect data sent between the site and visitors' browsers. An attacker could sniff passwords or credit card numbers traveling to such sites. If attackers intercept John's password and they know of other sites he uses, they can masquerade as him at those other sites. Thus, John may end up ordering unintended "gifts" for his attackers.

Aside from the traditional rule of different passwords for different sites, John can share passwords among sites depending on the level of risk and trust he has in the different sites. To do this, John classifies the sites according to the potential risk of a particular site disclosing his password, combined with the personal risk to him of someone masquerading as him at those sites. We can call this *risk grouping*. Different sites are assigned to different risk groups, according to the type of risk involved. John then uses the same password for sites within each risk group.

D-39

For example, John uses a password at work to protect proprietary company information, he uses passwords at home to protect personal financial data, he uses passwords on Internet news and information sites, like the *New York Times*, and he uses passwords for e-commerce sites like Amazon.com. He also purchases used books over the Internet from numerous booksellers, most of whom don't know how to use encryption or other forms of transaction security. These different sites can produce the following risk grouping:

- **Proprietary company remote access**

  John has a professional obligation to protect his company from attack. He needs to choose a unique password to use on remote connections to the company network. He does not want to run the risk that a successful attacker of an e-commerce site might figure out how to hack into his company's site with his e-commerce password. If John has only local access to company computers, then he might not need to make this a separate risk group.

- **Personal financial data**

  John uses password-protected personal finance software. He shares joint bank and brokerage accounts with his wife, and they share the password for those accounts. Their shared password protects the financial software files and their remote access accounts for banking and brokerage. However, John should be careful to use this password only with "secure sites" that use cryptographic protection.

Be warned that not all financial sites use cryptographic protection. There are a few otherwise reputable sites (notably quicken.com at the time of this writing) that cryptographically protect financial data sent to some parts of their site but not to others. Users must keep an eye on URLs to look for the "https:" indicator of secure communications, and the padlock or other visual indicator in the browser that indicates a secure connection.

- **Internet information subscriptions**

  John uses the same password for the *New York Times* and other subscription sites. If an information site "leaks" his password, then at worst he's providing free access to a few hackers. These sites share a single risk group as long as the lost password doesn't leave John liable for higher subscription fees or inconveniences.

- **Reputable e-commerce sites**

  This includes well-known sites belonging to successful companies as long as they run secure sites that use cryptographic protection (the "https:" indicator in the URL) when collecting passwords, credit card numbers, and other sensitive personal data. Successful sites have a strong business reason to protect the privacy of customers' identification data: they need to maintain their reputation, avoid liability for negligence, and keep competitors from trying to target their customers. Thus, it's unlikely, though not impossible, that a reputable site will leak a customer's password.

Risky sites abound, and it's difficult to produce a good risk grouping for them. Auction sites don't always encrypt password traffic, which could allow attackers to sniff customer passwords and revoke bids or damage reputations. While it might be appealing for John to have an "auction site" risk group, he has to balance the convenience against what an attack might do to him. If John has different user names on the different sites, this might provide some protection, but a clever sniffer could unravel this ruse.

PASSWORD DELEGATION

A secret is something you tell people one at a time.

— Anonymous

Most authentication systems strive to identify individual people. Typically, each user name belongs to one person. Any action associated with that user name is assumed to have been done by the corresponding person. But this isn't always true, especially in password systems. It is very easy to share passwords, both intentionally and unintentionally.

However, password sharing isn't always motivated by fraud or malice. Some senior executives share their passwords with their private secretaries. While this undermines accountability, it reflects a level of trust that is not unusual in such professional roles. Some organizations have established expensive or complicated procedures for providing computer service, and the lucky people there with computer access sometimes feel obligated to share their passwords with less lucky employees who also need computing services to do their jobs. Password sharing is almost inevitable.

The fundamental problem with a shared password is that there's no way to control how much it gets shared. Anyone who knows the password can easily share it with someone else. We call this *transitive delegation*: once we delegate permission to use a computer to another person, that person can delegate permission to others. *A-40*
While most people tend to keep personal passwords secret, it's easier to share a password that's already been shared by others. There's less of a feeling of personal ownership since the use of the password isn't associated with any particular person that knows it.

6.6 STORING WRITTEN PASSWORDS

There are cases in which it's impractical to avoid written passwords. Some people just have too many passwords assigned by too many different organizations to memorize them all and keep them straight. Some projects distribute low-value passwords by e-mail, which means that they're "written down" already. Systems administrators must often keep a written record of certain critical passwords so that alternate administrators can take over management if the usual administrators aren't available. Naturally, such a list requires highly effective protection, since it would be of immense value to attackers.

In a sense, we turn a password into a physical token when we write it down. Authentication then depends on something you have: the paper with the password written on it. However, it doesn't provide a very safe token, since anyone who sees the password can "duplicate the token" by copying it. Security still depends on keeping prying eyes away from the written list.

Just like there is a range of risks associated with written passwords, there is a range of strategies for protecting them. Three general strategies are physical custody, locked storage, and computer storage. We examine these below.

PHYSICAL CUSTODY

In such cases, people keep a written list of passwords on or near them personally. At one end of the scale we have that list of passwords hidden under the mouse pad: the list might be safe from outsiders, but not from coworkers at the same site. At the other end, the user wears a piece of jewelry that holds a list of passwords. Ideally, the list should always be in the owner's possession so that nobody can look at the list without the owner's realizing it. The owner can also change the listed passwords if the list gets lost or may otherwise have fallen into the hands of attackers.

The jewelry approach is best from a security standpoint. For example, Cathy might have an old-fashioned locket that holds passwords instead of miniature portraits. She is unlikely to leave the locket or other pieces of jewelry lying about her desk, so it's always in her possession. It's possible that she will wear the locket much of the time and only rarely leave it unattended, perhaps somewhere at her home. Thus, it's unlikely that anyone will be able to open the locket and look at the passwords without her knowledge. Compare this with the mouse pad list: Cathy would never know if someone looked under her mouse pad when she's out of the office.

While Tim might not own a locket, he does have a wallet that carries a cache of valuables, notably cash and credit cards. Wallets provide a tolerably safe place to store password lists, particularly for people who always carry the wallet in a pocket. By cultural tradition, people never hand a wallet over to someone else to examine; at best, the owner might remove various items as needed ("Let me see your driver's license and registration"). The wallet is so valuable that Tim will probably realize very quickly if he loses his wallet and can change passwords if necessary.

Purses also offer a place to carry password lists. Unlike wallets, purses are usually too large to fit in a pocket, so they aren't always in the owner's custody. It's common in some offices for people to leave purses in desk drawers during the workday. This gives the motivated attacker ample opportunity to search for a password list undetected. In some places, however, searching another person's purse is a criminal act, or close to one. This may deter some attackers.

Other storage areas, like lists stored in books, file cabinets, or even under mouse pads, might be searched by coworkers who have access to the owner's work area. Such places provide acceptable storage only if coworkers are unlikely to cause damage even if they do manage to collect the passwords. Never assume that a clever but unlocked storage place is safe, no matter how obscure and hard to find it might seem. A thorough search of an office, even one piled high with paper, is far quicker than any trial-and-error password search.

LOCKED STORAGE

It's not always practical to keep physical custody of a password list: we must occasionally change clothes, take a bath, or perform other personal activities that leave our wallet, purse, and jewelry behind. The classic strategy is to lock things up in an adequately strong cabinet with a comparably strong lock.

For example, most information systems staffs have at least one small safe that holds written copies of essential passwords. Even a basic commercial safe can resist a certain amount of tampering. If the attackers just steal the safe (a common practice among safecrackers), then the staff has a clear indication that the password lists have been compromised.

Locked cabinets are usually less effective, simply because most office cabinet locks can't resist a knowledgeable attacker armed with paper clips, much less one with a crowbar. Moreover, the paper clips will probably open a cheap lock without leaving evidence to suggest the passwords were compromised. Locking cabinets that use strong, hard-to-pick locks are not very common. Low-cost safes with combination locks tend to be more common.

In either case, we find ourselves again trading off one security problem for another. If we use a safe, we trade off the problem of memorizing the long list of passwords for the problem of memorizing the one safe combination, and of opening and closing the safe to use the password list. If we use a cabinet with a key lock, then we trade off the problem of carrying the list of passwords around for the problem of carrying around the cabinet's key. In fact, the key lock loses much of its value if both the lock and key often sit unattended on the same premises.

For extra protection of password lists, or even of individual written passwords, we can seal them in envelopes. Administrative staffs often do this: each important password is sealed in its own envelope. If John is a staff member and he needs a particular password, he retrieves the password's envelope from the safe. Then he opens the envelope, uses the password, and reseals it in a new envelope marked with his signature, perhaps countersigned by another staff member. Staff members can tell which passwords have been retrieved by whom, and they can count the envelopes to ensure that no passwords have been lost. While it is true that there are centuries' worth of tricks for opening and resealing a sealed message, these techniques usually require a lot of time and skill to escape detection.

ELECTRONIC STORAGE

There are three distinct candidates for electronic storage of passwords: stand-alone personal organizers, synchronizing personal organizers, and general-purpose computing systems. Each poses its own strengths and weaknesses for safe password storage.

Stand-alone personal organizers generally provide simple storage for an address list and calendar. The organizer includes a simple keyboard for typing in words as well as numbers. To store passwords, we can treat system names as "names" in the address list and provide the password as some other piece of information, like address or city. Many include a "security" feature that will block some of the address list entries from view unless the operator provides a secret code, usually a password. This provides an extra measure of protection when we store sensitive information like passwords.

This mechanism is probably safe enough for typical commercial applications. An attacker would need physical access to the organizer, which is usually in the physical custody of its owner. If the owner uses the secret code feature, then a casual attacker probably won't be able to extract passwords from it. However, these organizers aren't designed to resist sophisticated attacks. With the right hardware, an attacker might be able to bypass the secret code and extract all of the data on the organizer. There is also a risk that some vendors may incorporate back-door codes so they may unlock data for customers who forget their organizer's secret code. Attackers with such a code would be able to read blocked data on any organizer of that make and model.

Synchronizing personal organizers are similar to other organizers, except that the vendor provides a mechanism to share data with the owner's PC. The Palm and Pocket PC products are well-known examples of this. Many simpler organizers manufactured by vendors like Sharp can also synchronize with PCs. Unfortunately, attackers can steal such organizers and extract the contents by synchronizing them with their own PCs. This gives the attacker a copy of all of the organizer's files, including the blocked or otherwise protected files.   *see Note 10.*

Personal organizers typically use very simple blocking techniques. If one examines the synchronized files directly with a simple text editor, for example, one often sees the contents of all files, including blocked ones, without having to provide a password. Attackers can use the same technique to extract passwords from the files.

To prevent such an attack, we can install encryption software on the organizer and encrypt lists of passwords. At least one vendor provides a package that will encrypt memoranda on a Palm organizer using 128-bit encryption. This can provide good protection for the password lists, assuming the organizer isn't suffering from other security problems. For example, the owner might install software with an unexpected Trojan horse capability that could extract encryption keys or make copies of data before it is encrypted. Another risk is that the owner might choose an easy-to-guess encryption key, in which case an attacker might mount a successful dictionary attack against it.

see Note 11.

A standard workstation can pose a dilemma as storage for a list of passwords. As discussed in Section 5.2, it is hard to reliably protect an individual file stored on a workstation or laptop, even with encryption. To store passwords on a workstation safely, it is best to use an application that is intentionally designed to store passwords. One approach is to provide a filing program for passwords, like the Password Safe utility. Another approach is to integrate the password storage with other software that uses passwords; then the software can automatically retrieve passwords without making the owner retype them. This is the password "bundle" approach discussed in Section 4.3.

Password Safe is a free utility program from Counterpane Internet Security that stores passwords in an encrypted file. If Tim puts his passwords into a Password Safe file, he must provide a password that generates the encryption key. The file is automatically encrypted when it is saved on the hard drive, and Tim must supply the password to open the list again later. For convenience, each password is stored with its corresponding user name and other identifying information. Generally, Password Safe's display does not show the actual passwords it stores; instead, it shows only identifying information. If Tim wants to use one of the passwords, he can select it based on its name, "cut" it to the clipboard, and "paste" it into a password dialog without ever actually seeing the password.

see Note 12.

Programs like Password Safe can eliminate some of the risks inherent in using a word processing program to maintain lists of files: the password utility doesn't need to create temporary files that might contain parts of the document after it's finished. If we use a word processing program to construct a list of passwords, we then have no way of knowing if there are discarded temporary files somewhere on the hard drive that contain another copy of our password list. A properly designed file encryption program systematically erases the contents of the original plaintext file, but there's no way it can chase down all of the corresponding temporary files and wipe their disk space as well.

Password bundling programs make password lists more useful by automating some of the password handling. Modern Web browsers, like Netscape Navigator 6 and Microsoft Internet Explorer, can store passwords associated with Web sites and supply them automatically without making the person type them. Apple has taken a more ambitious approach with the Macintosh "keychain," which it reintroduced in Mac OS 9 and in later systems. Its operation reflects the basics of such a mechanism.

see Note 13.

The Macintosh system incorporates certain features that require passwords, notably file encryption and network file sharing. The keychain is similar in function to a Password Safe file, except that it has integrated the Mac OS password operations. The file contains a list of resources along with a password for each resource, and it's stored in encrypted form, protected with a memorized password. If Tim has a keychain, he can activate it by typing its password. Whenever the system asks for a password for some resource, it gives Tim the opportunity to save the password in the keychain after it's been typed in. If the system needs a password, it will use the corresponding password from the keychain if one exists.

When initially distributed with Mac OS 9, the keychain feature used relatively weak 56-bit encryption, but this did not generate much enthusiasm among people interested in using Macintosh security features. Later releases were upgraded to use 128-bit encryption, starting with Mac OS 9.1.

see Note 14.

A general dilemma with password bundles is that they are worthwhile only as long as they store worthwhile passwords. Web server password bundles are useful because many Web sites use well-known hooks in the Web protocols to exchange passwords. However, not all Web sites do this, so not all Web site passwords can be beneficially stored that way. If a browser's user doesn't visit sites that use passwords in the right format, then it's not worth it to memorize yet another password just to use the bundling feature. As standard interfaces evolve and improve, bundles of passwords should become more practical.

6.7 SEQUENCES AND GROUPS OF PASSWORDS

Many people have no trouble choosing a single password, but fail when handling groups or sequences of memorable passwords. Here are some strategies to simplify the task. Groups of passwords provide individual passwords for different systems, or they can be used sequentially when required to periodically change passwords.

A good group of passwords must balance two different goals: memorization and *forward secrecy*. In previous sections we focused on memorizing a few possibly complicated words instead of memorizing numerous random characters. People memorize patterns, not randomness. We must find patterns that are easy to remember but hard for attackers to recognize. Once we ourselves memorize the pattern, we can remember the passwords.

The concept of forward secrecy emerged from cryptographic key management. It can be a challenge to distribute a secret key safely, and the challenge is multiplied if we must distribute new secret keys on a regular basis. Each new key should pose a completely new problem to an attacker. If we don't set up new keys safely, then previously used keys will give strong hints about the new keys. We achieve "perfect" forward secrecy if old keys don't give the attacker any hints about newer keys. In passwords, we pursue "not so perfect" forward secrecy so that attackers can't easily guess the rest of the passwords in a group even if they intercept a single password.

D-40

As with individual passwords, different groups of passwords serve different purposes, so we can use different strategies to deal with different threats. Simple sequences should be fine in low-risk situations: when either the risk of attack or risk of damage is small. Riskier situations call for more sophisticated strategies like theme words or lines from poems and songs.

PASSWORD SEQUENCES

The simplest password sequence generates a series of passwords based on some simple, sequential rule. The easiest approach is to simply append some digits or a textual representation of a number on the end of a password. This approach is also obvious to attackers.

A more sophisticated approach is to adapt the external password strategy from Section 6.4 to generate sequences. We can easily generate a sequence of 10 passwords if we use a digit as the middle character. We generate the sequence by incrementing or decrementing the digit. If we need more than 10 passwords, and the system accepts large passwords, we can use two or more digits instead of a single middle character.

This strategy produces fairly strong passwords, but doesn't provide forward secrecy. At best, we can add variations so that other passwords aren't totally obvious. One approach is to choose middle digits arbitrarily or based on some nonobvious rule, instead of using them in sequence. For example, choose digits in the order they appear in a telephone number or Social Security number. However, these sequences might not resist a modest trial-and-error attack.

FORWARD SECRECY WITH THEME WORDS

We achieve a certain degree of forward secrecy when a given password from a group provides as few hints as possible about how it was chosen. It is probably impossible to achieve true forward secrecy with groups of memorable passwords, since there's always a memorable pattern that ties the passwords together. However, there are a few techniques that minimize this.

One approach that gives an attacker minimal help is based on "theme words." Jan, a security administrator, had to assign safe combinations to cabinets with multiple combination locks and still have a way of remembering them all. She would pick a "theme" word for each cabinet, and use each letter of that word to correspond to an example of that theme. If we choose "songs" as a theme, we can establish five passwords, each starting with a different letter of the word "songs," and each being appropriate to that word. For example, the five passwords could be SwaneeRiver, OldFolks, NoelNoel, Greensleeves, and Schubert.

If we look at our group of passwords, however, we don't see much forward secrecy. An attacker that intercepts Greensleeves might be tempted to try other song names. It's important to choose a theme name that could relate to several different parts of speech: nouns, verbs, adjectives, prepositions, and so on. One approach would be to choose an adjective for the theme word and nouns for the pass-

Theme Word:	Passwords:
H A P P Y	**H** o e # d o w n
	A n i m a l # c r a c k e r s
	P a r t y # f a v o r s
	P r e t t y # h o u s e
	Y u l e # g r e e t i n g s

FIGURE 6.5: *Group of passwords based on a theme word.* We pick a theme word or phrase that's memorable and long enough to provide the number of passwords we need. Then we assign a word to each letter in the theme.

words, or vice versa. Figure 6.5 demonstrates this, using "happy" as the theme word. Each derived password shares its first letter with the theme word, and (at least for some people) there's a relationship between each password and the theme.

Unfortunately, we seem to sacrifice some password strength here, since our passwords contain pairs of words that naturally fall together in written text anyway, like "party favors." Note how the two words making up the sample password in Figure 6.4 really don't make sense together. Randomly chosen words should not usually make up part of a phrase. The fact that our theme-derived passwords make sense suggests that they carry less entropy. This makes them weaker in theory, though there's no known attack today that can exploit that weakness.

PASSWORDS FROM SONGS AND POEMS

We can also generate password groups from poems or song lyrics. British spies during World War II used poems extensively as the basis for secret codes because they were easy to remember and contained a lot of information. We can exploit those same properties to generate passwords. Here are two techniques:

- Use word pairs from songs or poems. For example, a famous Stephen Foster ballad would produce a group of passwords including "waydown," "uponthe," and "swaneeriver." We can embed middle characters between the word pairs if desired.   *see Note 15.*
- Use letter patterns from the words of songs or poems. For example, we could extract the first letter from each word in a line of the chosen poem, and repeat until the password is long enough. For example, "Twas brillig, in the slithy toves, did gyre and gim-

ble in the wabes," would yield "tbitst-dgagitw." The next password in the group would be taken from the next line or two of the
poem, and so on.   *see Note 16.*

These passwords will usually resist classic dictionary attacks, since
they're built of either pairs of words or concatenated letters. The
word pairs are, of course, slightly more vulnerable to attack since
the words do in fact occur in that order in written text. It's theoretically possible that attackers might construct "dictionaries" of poetry
and song lyrics that they use to search for word pairs or patterns of
letters. However, this seems unlikely unless numerous users clearly
choose to use such a system.

Regarding forward secrecy, these techniques weaken as the
attacker senses the patterns. Clearly, the game is up if the attacker
knows which song or poem is used. If the attacker guesses the song,
he can quickly construct a small collection of likely passwords to
try. This makes the word pair strategy less appealing, since the
attacker might see a password like "ravennevermore" or
"swaneeriver." The letter pattern approach would be much harder to
detect from just looking at a password or two.

The real shortcoming to this technique is that people don't always
remember songs and poems perfectly. This caused the British
numerous headaches when they used poem codes. Although spies
were drilled and tested to ensure they knew their poems, it was easy
to transpose a letter or substitute a word, and the result was an
indecipherable message. In the case of passwords, we will find people who remember a stanza with one wording when they set up their
latest password, but remember a different wording when they actually try to authenticate themselves. Encryption was a tedious but
essential task for British spies. Passwords must be convenient to
work effectively.   *see Note 17.*

6.8 SUMMARY TABLES

TABLE 6.3: *Attack Summary*

Attack	Security Problem	Prevalence	Attack Description
A-37. Forgotten password	Denial of service	Trivial	Not really an attack, but has the effect of one
A-38. Mouse pad search	Masquerade as someone else	Trivial	Attacker searches the vicinity of workstations for passwords written down on paper
A-39. Multiple password exploitation	Masquerade as someone else	Trivial	Attacker finds victim's password from one system, uses same password on others
A-40. Transitive delegation	Masquerade as someone else	Trivial	A shared password is inappropriately shared with someone who uses it in an attack

TABLE 6.4: *Defense Summary*

Defense	Foils Attacks	Description
D-37. Force good password selection	A-16. Precompiled dictionary attack A-20. Dynamic dictionary attack	Implement procedures that prevent users from choosing easy-to-crack passwords and that force users to change passwords periodically
D-38. Written password	A-37. Forgotten password	Write down a copy of the secret password and store it in a safe place
D-39. Password risk grouping	A-39. Multiple password exploitation	Share a password among sites if sites' usage carries similar risks
D-40. Forward secrecy	A-39. Multiple password exploitation	Choose groups of passwords so that attackers get no obvious hints of other passwords

RESIDUAL ATTACKS

A-38. Mouse pad search—As noted in the text, the site should avoid hard-to-remember passwords to avoid written passwords.

A-40. Transitive delegation—As noted in the text, a site can protect against such attacks by using tokens or smart cards.

CHAPTER 7
BIOMETRICS

By the pricking of my thumbs
Something wicked this way comes
Open locks,
Whoever knocks.

— William Shakespeare, *Macbeth, Act IV, Scene I*

IN THIS CHAPTER

Biometrics use unique personal traits to authenticate people. There are a variety of biometric techniques, each measuring a different personal trait. Biometrics can provide incredibly convenient authentication, but can also suffer from a variety of shortcomings.

- Biometric uses and basic limitations
- Summary of common biometric techniques
- How biometric authentication works
- Measuring biometric accuracy
- Improving biometric security with cryptographic techniques

7.1 BIOMETRICS: SOMETHING YOU ARE

Biometrics use personal features instead of facts to authenticate a person. When we step away from computer technology, we see that biometric authentication has been used for centuries in one form or another. Passports almost always carry a physical description of the bearer, and have carried photographs as well for the past several decades. Photo ID cards have been used at least since the 1930s; during World War II they were used in various high-security military projects. Although there was no automation involved, these passports and cards served as a portable credential. People could inspect the credential and satisfy themselves regarding the identity of its owner.

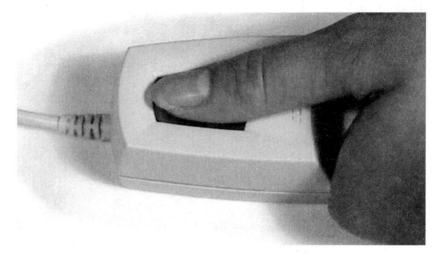

FIGURE 7.1: *Biometric authentication based on fingerprints.* The user has placed her thumb on a device that reads the thumbprint. To authenticate her, the system compares this reading with a previously collected thumbprint. (Scanner courtesy of Informer Systems, Ltd.)

Of course, it's not practical for computer-based authentication to rely on people to manually examine and verify biometric credentials. Instead, computers use special devices to perform the biometric reading (Figure 7.1) and use a computational procedure to verify the user's identity. The procedure compares a biometric reading against a corresponding reading stored in that person's user record. If the two readings match closely, then the system authenticates the person. If the two do not match very well, then the system refuses to recognize the person.

Unlike passwords and other base secrets, the biometric data rarely matches perfectly. Instead, the authentication mechanism measures how close the latest reading matches the reading in the user record. Readings from the right person are supposed to match closely while readings from other people should not match closely.

PROMISE AND REALITY

Many people and organizations are enthusiastic about the promise of biometrics for authentication. This attitude is summed up by a popular slogan among biometrics proponents: "The body is the password." With biometrics, people won't be locked out by forgotten or automatically changed passwords. Biometrics also inspire enthusiasm because they seem to represent the ultimate in personal authentication. Since biometrics are based on a person's unique traits, some observers believe the techniques offer the highest possible confidence in a person's identity.

see Note 1.

But appearances can deceive. First, there is the problem of matching biometric readings. The process generally takes a picture of the person's trait and then tries to match it. The match may fail to authenticate a legitimate user if the biometric has changed or been injured, if it is presented in an unusual fashion, or if dirt or noise works itself into the system. In other words, the user can suffer a *false rejection* by the authentication system. If we adjust the system to be more tolerant of noise and poor matches, then we increase the risk of authenticating a user based on a biometric trait from the wrong person. In other words, we risk *false acceptance* of a masquerade, the same problem we have when an attacker guesses the right password.

Another problem is the threat of replay attacks. An attacker can collect a victim's biometric reading, either through an external recorder or by copying the reading's binary data representation. Too often, an attacker can fool the biometric system by presenting the copy of the biometric reading. Some biometric systems are sophisticated enough to distinguish between a live measurement and a fake (that is, the difference between a fingerprint on a real finger and a reproduction on paper, rubber, or plastic). Sophisticated sensors are always more expensive. Moreover, attackers may generate a plausible binary version of a biometric reading and use such data for replay attacks on networks. There is no way to combat such attacks on networks except with additional authentication measures that typically require a base secret (see Section 7.7).

Biometrics are safest and easiest to use with the local deployment pattern described in Chapters 4 and 5. The local pattern places the entire authentication mechanism inside a physically secure perimeter. This eliminates the risk of an attacker's capturing and replaying the digital representation of a legitimate user's biometric reading. This does not prevent forgeries or recordings of the original biometric reading; the biometric reading device must be designed to detect replayed readings. Biometrics can also be safely used in conjunction with random base secrets as described in Section 7.7. However, the costs of a biometric system can outweigh the benefits if the system still requires us to manage base secrets.

USES OF BIOMETRICS

Since biometrics are based on unique personal characteristics, we can use them for three different but related applications:

- **Authentication**

  This is the problem addressed by most other mechanisms in this book: given a user name, can we confirm that it belongs to the person who presents it? The biometric reading serves the role of the base secret or verifier, and it must closely match the entry in the corresponding user record.

- **Identification**

  This is the classic law-enforcement use of fingerprints: given a biometric sample, can we associate it with a unique human being or, at worst, a small number of "suspects"? This application requires a comprehensive database of biometric samples that is likely to contain the sample being searched for. The most effective identification systems are those with the largest database of biometric samples. The U.S. Federal Bureau of Investigation (FBI) has systematically collected fingerprints since the early 20th century, and this collection is now the centerpiece of their *automated fingerprint identification system* (AFIS).

- **Uniqueness**

  This variant of the identification application has become practical with the advent of low-cost computer-based biometrics: given a biometric sample, can we determine if its owner is already in the database? The technique is used by government-sponsored benefits organizations to ensure that recipients don't register more than once for welfare checks or other valuable services.

The distinction between identity and uniqueness is subtle but important. Both applications use the same technology but they strive for different goals. Identity applications strive for completeness: the ideal database contains every living person, or at least everyone within a particular population. Uniqueness applications involve people associated with a particular institution or enterprise and use biometrics to ensure that each person is registered no more than once. Identification systems have a compulsion for completeness that uniqueness systems usually lack. An important technical difference between the two applications is in their scale: biometric pattern matching gets much harder as the size of the pattern collection grows. Identification systems may grow arbitrarily large.   *see Note 2.*

In 1990, Los Angeles County deployed a pilot project that authenticated welfare recipients with fingerprints and verified uniqueness. The three districts using the new system saw an immediate decrease in welfare applicants while surrounding districts continued to see an increase. This was considered a promising result, so the project was rapidly expanded to other districts, eventually covering 32 district offices and over 700,000 clients. By the end of 1998, changes in welfare enrollment patterns led the county to claim that the $42.4 million system had yielded a $87.8 million savings. Other governments, including the state of Connecticut in 1996, have deployed similar systems with similar results.   *see Note 3.*

These applications underscore another issue with biometrics: privacy. Since each biometric measurement is supposed to be unique to each person, it becomes possible to track individuals by following their biometric readings. For example, anyone who happened to have visited the scene of a crime might be called in for questioning simply because his or her fingerprint or other biometric is similar to one collected at the scene. If e-commerce companies routinely collected biometrics, one could track an individual by searching on-line transaction records for that person's biometric pattern. Some people worry that fingerprints collected for biometric applications might find their way into an identification database like the FBI's AFIS.   *see Note 4.*

At present, few promoters of biometric systems are intent on violating people's privacy. In fact, public concern about privacy has led many biometrics promoters to emphasize security and privacy features of their systems in order to ensure their adoption. This does not always satisfy the critics. There is always a risk of "function creep" in that biometric information could find itself serving new and different functions as the system evolves over time. While it is possible to omit features from a system (like the ability to look up a fingerprint collected from a crime scene), there is no way to guarantee that the feature never appears later. Once an institution possesses the biometric readings, there is no foolproof technique to prevent those readings from being used for other purposes. The systems know *how* to match a biometric reading to the patterns they have collected, but they can't possibly understand *why* a particular reading has been presented.

7.2 BIOMETRIC TECHNIQUES

Just about every device ever built to measure a unique human characteristic has been pressed into service for biometric authentication. Some devices cost tens or hundreds of thousands of dollars, while others try to use equipment already available on a personal computer, like the keyboard or perhaps a microphone. A recent book on biometric technology identified 14 different types of biometrics that have been used, experimentally or in practice, for authentication. These different techniques fall into two categories: those that measure behavior and those that measure physical traits.   *see Note 5.*

MEASURING PHYSICAL TRAITS

These techniques measure physical features of human bodies that should be unique among most or all of the population. Ideally, the measured feature is not affected by normal human behavior or cosmetics, and does not significantly change in a matter of days or weeks. Described below are the five major techniques.

- Fingerprints

  These systems typically use a relatively small image scanner to read the user's fingerprint (Figures 7.1 and 7.2). The technology evolved from earlier systems used to match printed fingerprints in law enforcement applications. Today's fingerprint biometric systems yield a very practical combination of cost and reliability.

FIGURE 7.2: *Fingerprint scanners.* Like computer circuitry, their size and cost has dropped over time. Leftmost is the Model 250 Verifier from Cross Match Technologies. Next is the original Bio-Mouse from American Biometric. Rightmost is a recent fingerprint scanner built by Compaq.

However, a small portion of the population does not have good enough fingerprints for the scanners to recognize reliably. Numerous vendors produce hardware and software for finger-print authentication, including the following:

see Note 6.

- American Biometric
- AuthenTec
- Biometric Access
- Compaq
- CrossCheck
- DigitalPersona
- Identix
- Informer Systems
- Mytec Technologies
- Sony

- **Hand geometry**

  These systems use special readers that sense a user's finger size, thickness, and palm geometry. Mechanical systems of this type were first developed in the 1970s for physical access control. One application provided access control for families to their apartments, and the system successfully adapted to the growing hands of children over a period of several years. These systems are manufactured commercially by Recognition Systems, Inc.

- **Eye features: retina**

  These systems use a retinal camera behind a special eyepiece. Users must place an eye against the eyepiece and the camera records the distinctive pattern of veins on the person's retina. The systems are used in a few high-security government and military applications. Some users find the process uncomfortable and even threatening, although the process cannot damage the eye.

- **Eye features: iris**

  These systems use a special camera that examine's the user's iris from a distance of a few feet and extracts its distinctive texture. Like fingerprints, individuals have unique irises even when they have similar or identical genes (that is, identical twins). Commercial iris authentication systems are produced by the following companies: *see Note 7.*

  - IriScan
  - Sensar

- **Face**

  These systems recognize people by examining images of faces. In authentication applications, the system has a camera that searches for a user's face and matches it against the face stored in the user record. The technology is widely used by law enforcement to search "mug shot" files. A shortcoming of face authentication is that it cannot distinguish between identical twins. Commercial face recognition systems are produced by the following companies: *see Note 8.*

  - Miros
  - Visionics

In addition to these techniques, researchers have studied several others, including body part thermograms, ears, odor, and DNA. Thermograms use expensive infrared imaging devices to detect internal physiological features that are unique among individuals, even identical twins. Ear imagery extracts fairly complex structures that vary significantly between individuals. Odor-based systems use sensitive (and rather temperamental) sensors that measure chemical contents of the air to detect distinctive personal smells. DNA is widely used in criminal trials to associate individuals with genetic material found at crime scenes. These techniques will most likely remain in the laboratory until someone develops a practical and cost-effective method to measure the particular physical feature in real-world situations.

MEASURING BEHAVIORAL TRAITS

These techniques measure some type of human behavior, and use that measurement to generate a unique biometric reading. Unlike physical traits, these biometrics do not have to measure the exact same phenomenon each time: a person could be directed to speak, write, or walk a certain way in order to reduce the risk of a replay attack.

- **Speaker recognition**

  These systems prompt a user for some spoken words, and authenticate the user based on distinctive speech patterns ("voiceprints"). Some systems rely on specific microphones or other restrictions on the speaking environment, while others try to use microphones included in modern "multimedia" personal computers. Speaker recognition can fail in noisy environments, or in some cases be fooled by tape recordings of the user's voice. Apple's Mac OS 9.0 included speaker recognition for authenticating different users of a shared Macintosh computer (Figure 7.3), which has made biometric authentication widely available to the general public. The following vendors produce speaker recognition systems for authentication: *see Note 9.*
    - Apple Computer

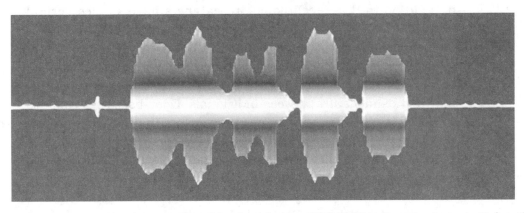

FIGURE 7.3: *Spoken passphrase collected by Apple's Mac OS 9.0.* This is a "voiceprint" for the passphrase "My voice is my password" collected by Apple's Mac OS 9.0. The system matches the way a user says the passphrase against previously collected patterns generated by the same phrase.

- Keyware Technologies
- T-NETIX
- Veritel

- **Written signature**

  These systems collect a written signature from the user and compare it against a record of that user's signature-writing behavior. In order to reduce the risk of forgery, the systems rarely rely on the signature's image alone: reliable systems measure the dynamics of pen motion as well. However, these systems are rarely used for authentication; they are more often used to capture a written signature in a digital form that makes forgery easier to detect. Software for signature authentication is produced by the following vendors:

  - Communication Intelligence Corporation
  - Cyber SIGN

- **Keystroke dynamics**

  These systems sense a user's behavior while typing at a computer keyboard and use unique features of that behavior to authenticate the user. The systems collect information about the time delay between hitting various pairs of keys and the amount of time a person takes to hit and release each key. Researchers have found that this information is distinctive among different individuals. A few recognition systems exist that use this technique. One obvious advantage is that the technique does not require additional equipment to sense user behavior.

Researchers have also built systems to collect information about how a user walks and use distinctive features of the user's gait for authentication. Such systems rely on special camera systems to collect the information. At present, no practical implementations have been demonstrated or used.

7.3   HOW BIOMETRICS WORK

Despite the range of sensors and measurements used for biometrics, all systems share the same fundamental design (Figure 7.4). All systems use a device that collects digitized measurements of a personal trait. The first step is to use the right equipment to measure the particular trait associated with the biometric. For example, an iris pattern system uses a specialized camera that focuses specifically on the iris and collects its image. Fingerprint systems typically use specially designed scanners to collect the fingerprint, and the scanners intentionally do poorly at detecting patterns in other types of surfaces.

Next, a biometric system performs *feature extraction* on the digitized data to identify the distinctive features associated with the particular biometric. In a fingerprint system, features consist of splits and junctions in the print's concentric ridges, combined with information about the features' relative locations. The extraction process yields a data item called the *biometric signature*. We use the term "signature" here in a general sense, and not just to refer to digitized versions of written signatures. Different biometric systems produce their "signatures" from a user's fingerprint, voice, or other personal trait.

To authenticate a particular user, the system looks up the user's record, retrieves the *biometric pattern* associated with that user, and compares the derived signature against that pattern. The comparison process is generally designed to expect partial matches and to specify the degree to which the signature matches the pattern. If the two match closely enough, the system authenticates the user.

The system requires a biometric pattern for every recognizable user. The system constructs these patterns during an enrollment process that collects one or more biometric signatures from each user. The enrollment process uses additional signatures from a user to construct patterns that reflect likely variations in that user's signatures. This makes the system less likely to falsely reject a legitimate user.

Biometric systems designed for the uniqueness and identity applications can establish a user's identity without asking for the user's name. To do this, the system collects a biometric signature from the user and matches that signature against each biometric pattern in user database. The system identifies the user by finding the pattern with the closest match to the biometric signature.

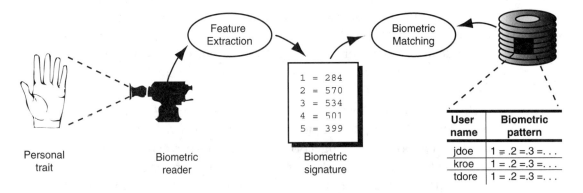

FIGURE 7.4: *Elements of a biometric system.* First, the biometric reader produces a digital representation of the trait. Next, the feature extraction procedure generates a biometric signature containing the individual's distinctive measurements. To authenticate someone, the system extracts the user's biometric pattern from the user record and compares how closely the person's biometric signature matches the user's biometric pattern. Close matches are accepted.

7.4   TAKING A BIOMETRIC READING

The first step in any biometric procedure is to take a reading of the personal trait. The biometric reader in Figure 7.4 performs this task. The reader yields a digitized representation of the trait, which is converted into the biometric signature. This process is the first point where errors can work themselves into biometric authentication.

In some cases, the biometric reader might actually be a general-purpose device, like a flatbed image scanner or a computer's built-in microphone. For example, the speaker authentication process used by Apples's Mac OS uses a built-in microphone to collect the user's passphrase. Some face-recognition systems are also designed to use standard, off-the-shelf video cameras. While general-purpose devices can lower the cost of biometric authentication, they put more of a burden on the feature-extraction software. For example, different cameras might produce a "standard" video signal, but there will still be subtle differences between them that can affect the biometric pattern. The feature extraction process must be able to filter out the variations between different input devices.

Other systems use special-purpose biometric readers. In theory, fingerprint systems could use standard flatbed scanners, but in practice they tend to use specialized devices. Hand geometry readers collect three-dimensional information that a scanner cannot. In some cases, the reader may perform some or all of the biometric signature processing, so that the authentication system only has to perform a match on the resulting data.

FEEDBACK DURING BIOMETRIC INPUT

An interesting feature that shows up in many systems is a mechanism that displays the user's biometric image as the system tries to collect a reading. For example, fingerprint-recognition systems like the one provided with the BioMouse, from American Biometrics, displays a window with the image of the user's fingerprint. Users quickly learn how to place their finger correctly on the print reader, since correct placement has a distinctive appearance, and incorrect placement is generally rewarded with a false rejection.

FIGURE 7.5: *Recognizing a passphrase in a voiceprint.* These two voiceprints represent a six-sylla-ble passphrase, followed by noise. In the left example, a small burst of background noise followed the passphrase. In the right example, the user coughed after reciting the passphrase. Ideally, the system should isolate the phrase from other sounds, since that increases the likelihood of cor-rectly matching the corresponding biometric pattern.

Apple's Mac OS 9 displays a waveform when someone uses its voiceprint authentication, as shown in Figure 7.5. Users can quickly learn to identify excessive background noise and other audio prob-lems that may interfere with correct authentication. The figure shows two waveforms produced when the user uttered the phrase "My voice is my password." In both cases the system produced a group of waveforms that obviously correspond to the six-syllable phrase. In the left-hand example the phrase is followed by a small burst of noise, and in the right-hand example it is followed by a cough. A sophisticated recognition system can automatically isolate the passphrase from the noise. However, the display also helps out users of less-sophisticated systems. If the system rejects the pass-phrase, the user can "see" the noises by looking at the waveform. This at least gives the user the opportunity to try to prevent the troublesome noises when speaking a passphrase.

FORGING A PHYSICAL TRAIT

The biometric reader is an obvious point of attack on a biometric system. If the reader simply collects a digital image from a sensor and passes it on, then we can masquerade as someone by feeding the sensor the same data that the victim would provide. The strat-egy is obvious for fingerprint systems: we produce an image of the victim's fingerprint and present that to the system instead of the vic-tim's finger. The strategy could work, too, if fingerprint systems typ-ically used standard scanners to collect fingerprints.

A-41

As we noted earlier, however, fingerprint systems tend to use specialized scanners to collect fingerprints. These scanners are usually designed to detect the three-dimensional structure of fingerprint ridges and troughs as opposed to their simple two-dimensional appearance. While this may prevent masquerades using photocopies of fingerprints, it doesn't always prevent more sophisticated ones.

For example, the product-testing laboratory at *Network Computing*, a trade magazine, tried out two sophisticated fingerprint forgery techniques against several fingerprint readers. In one case, they collected "latent" fingerprints from a table using techniques similar to those of police detectives. Then they photocopied the latent prints onto transparency material and used the transparency to masquerade as a person's fingerprint. This technique actually succeeded in tricking a couple of fingerprint systems. This could be a serious problem since it suggests that an attacker can pick up a user's fingerprint left casually on a glass, doorknob, or other surface and then masquerade as that user.   *see Note 10.*

In another experiment, the lab took wax impressions of users' fingers and constructed fake fingers out of rubber. These copies succeeded in tricking most scanners. Fortunately, this technique requires the victim's cooperation.

The basic countermeasure for such attacks is to use more sophisticated sensors that measure additional properties of the physical   *D-41* trait. This is why many fingerprint readers try to detect the print in three dimensions, so that the ridges must actually be separate from the troughs to appear in the biometric reading. Some fingerprint readers sense skin capacitance or temperature in order to spot fakes.

A similar type of replay can take place in behavioral biometrics, notably speaker recognition. For example, an attacker can collect a high-quality recording of the victim's passphrase. In many systems,   *A-42* the microphone will filter out most differences between live speech and the playback of a high-quality recording. An extreme and fictional example of this appeared in the 1992 film *Sneakers*.

A countermeasure to prevent such replay is to require a different behavior for each authentication attempt. This is the same basic idea as the "challenge response" passwords described in Chapter 10. Some speaker-recognition systems achieve this by prompting the

user for a different passphrase each time. A relatively simple example is to have the user recite a sequence of digits and randomly
choose a new sequence for each authentication. A more sophisticated approach would be to collect an arbitrary sentence of spoken
words. However, any of these strategies will place a significant burden on the biometric system. While it may be tolerably convenient to
teach a system to recognize the user when reciting a fixed phrase,
varying phrases will take a lot more training. The system must be
trained to recognize any words that might be used and to recognize
any peculiarities about how the user might use pairs of words
together. Thus, such systems might not be practical for some environments.

D-42

7.5 BUILDING AND MATCHING PATTERNS

Once the system has collected a biometric signature, the next problem is to match it reliably with the right user. If Cathy produces the
biometric signature, then it should match the biometric pattern
stored in her user record. It should not match Tim's record.

A physical trait makes a good biometric if it yields a set of unique
measurements for each person. The trait's individual properties, like
its overall size or basic arrangement, might not provide unique measurements by themselves. For example, we could try to use people's
glove sizes as a biometric, except that lots of people share the same
glove size. The biometric is vulnerable to successful masquerades if
many people share the same measurement.

A practical biometric system must collect enough measurements
of the personal trait so that their aggregate will vary from one person
to another. A single spoken word or cough doesn't provide enough
information for a speaker recognition system to distinguish between
different people, so people often have to recite a phrase to such systems (Figure 7.5). Longer speech gives the system a better chance to
detect the inevitable differences in the way that different people
speak.

EXAMPLE: A TRIVIAL HAND GEOMETRY BIOMETRIC

A sophisticated hand geometry system might measure finger lengths, widths, thicknesses, and the relative location of crucial features like knuckles and other joints in order to construct a unique pattern for each person. However, we can easily illustrate the essential features of biometric matching by looking at the grossly simplified version in Figure 7.6: a biometric based on the lengths of the person's fingers. The biometric measuring process generates a signature that is an array of five numeric values, one for each finger in order, thumb first.

It should be obvious that biometric finger-length measurements will not be precise; that is, we can get subtly different measurements each time we measure the same finger lengths. Although adult fingers don't tend to lengthen or shorten significantly over time, the elastic nature of skin makes it impossible to get the same measurements consistently. To measure the length of a finger from a palm image, the system must be able to identify enough features of the hand to compute each finger's length. While fingertips may be easy to recognize, the location of each finger's base depends on folds

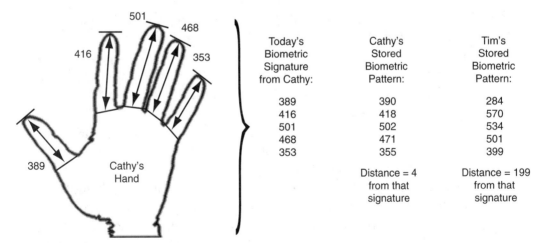

FIGURE 7.6: *Biometric example using trivial hand geometry.* We construct the biometric signature of Cathy's hand by measuring her finger lengths as the features of interest. The signature consists of a five-element array, with the elements representing measured finger lengths. We match the signature against Cathy's pattern by computing the mathematical "distance" between them. Note that the distance is lower (4) than the distance between the signature and Tim's pattern (199).

of skin and other elastic hand features. The length of a given finger can vary with changes in the hand position and finger pressure, since these properties affect the folds of the skin between fingers.

In Figure 7.6, Cathy's hand yielded a particular set of lengths that are reflected in the signature. If Cathy submits to another biometric reading, the next signature might yield a thumb length of 392 instead of 389, a middle finger length of 503 instead of 501, and so on. Similar variations appear in any biometric measurement. Fingerprint features will be slightly farther apart or closer depending on how the finger is placed on the reader. Spoken phrases used for authentication will be said more quickly or with different emphasis regardless of how careful the speaker is (see Figure 7.5). A well-designed biometric system tries to factor out such variations as much as possible, but variations will inevitably crop up.

When we try to match Cathy's signature against her biometric pattern, we want the signature to match regardless of the imprecision. Naturally, this requires a completely different matching strategy from what we use for passwords or other more traditional base secrets, since we're matching approximate values instead of exact values. For the finger-length biometric, we can use the simple strategy of computing the mathematical "distance" between a given signature and a given pattern. In other words, we treat the signature's five values and the pattern's five values as representing geometric points in five-dimensional space, and we measure how far these points would be from each other. Thus, a close match yields a small number. In Figure 7.6, Cathy's own pattern is obviously a close match, and it yielded a distance of 4. Tim's pattern, on the other hand, yielded a distance of 199.

Real-world biometric systems tend to be more complex than the simple finger-length computation. Most biometric signatures require a lot more than five integers to represent their measurements. Some signatures include graph representations to indicate positional relationships between features as well as, or instead of, relative locations. The pattern-matching procedure likewise will be tailored so that results are accurate even if the signature's measurements aren't always precise. It is a delicate balancing act to design a biometric system. The system must pick up the features that make different people distinct but avoid picking up "noise" or other information that confuses the reading. If the system rejects too much apparent noise, it may also reject the details that distinguish one user from another.

ENROLLING A USER

In the simplest case, biometric enrollment isn't particularly different from enrolling a user with a password. Instead of typing in a new password, however, the new user provides a biometric reading. The system uses the reading to construct a biometric pattern to store in the user record. However, this doesn't provide a reliable pattern in all cases. Some biometric systems require *training* so that the system can reliably recognize the person.

Training is necessary when the biometric trait, like a spoken phrase, is subject to too much variation from one instance to the next. In order to construct a reliable biometric pattern, the system must collect several biometric signatures from the user and combine them to construct the pattern. In some cases, the combining process simply takes an average of the different readings and perhaps retains information about the readings' variance. In other cases the system might analyze the signatures' differences in detail to figure out which of the user's measurements are distinctive, and then build a pattern to detect those measurements.

From a usability standpoint, the best systems require only a single biometric signature to enroll a user. Physical traits like fingerprints or hand geometry usually require a single reading. Behavioral traits like voice or written signature are more subject to variation and often require multiple readings to train the system to recognize each user. If fingerprint systems take multiple readings, the readings are usually taken from different fingers. The separate readings then allow the user to authenticate using different fingers, in case one or another is injured.

7.6   BIOMETRIC ACCURACY

For a biometric technique to work, it must be *accurate;* that is, it must be able to reliably associate the biometric signature taken from a particular person with that person's biometric pattern. A perfect system would never generate either false acceptances or false rejections. We measure a biometric system's accuracy by estimating the percentage of false acceptances and false rejections the system should typically produce.

An accuracy estimate is usually based on experiments that test a large number of biometric signatures to see how closely they match a set of biometric patterns. In general, the experiments try to collect a large number of readings from a large number of randomly selected people, preferably from the population that is likely to use the biometric system.

The graphs in Figure 7.7 show what the results might look like, given that the matching procedure measures the difference (or distance) between a signature and a pattern. Ideally, whenever a user like Cathy uses the system, it should compute a difference of zero between the biometric signature it collects and Cathy's pattern. In practice, of course, the difference will vary with each signature. As more and more people use the system, we should find that most signatures yield a low difference, but users will occasionally produce signatures that yield a relatively high difference. This is shown on the left-hand graph. If one of Cathy's signatures yields a difference that is high enough, the system will conclude that someone other

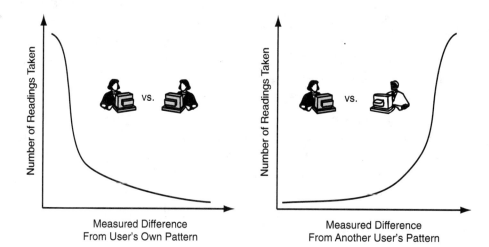

FIGURE 7.7: *A reasonably accurate biometric system.* These graphs show how a biometric system should match readings to individual users. On the left, we collect readings from authorized users and measure the difference between those readings and the users' own biometric patterns as collected by the system. On the right, we collect readings from arbitrary members of the population and measure their difference from randomly selected patterns belonging to authorized users.

than Cathy produced the signature and reject her authentication attempt.

The right-hand graph shows what we find if we calculate the difference between a signature produced by a random person and a biometric pattern belonging to someone else. Ideally, all such computations should yield a very large value. In practice, most such computations produce a large value, but a few produce smaller values, as shown on the graph. Thus, we will occasionally encounter successful masquerades if enough people try.

TRADING OFF USABILITY AND SECURITY

Figure 7.8 combines those two graphs to show how we can tune the system to trade off security and usability. The trick is to balance the likelihoods of false rejection and false acceptance, so the system rarely locks out legitimate users and it doesn't fall for masquerades. To some extent, this depends on the shape of the two curves, which depend on the design of the biometric signature and the matching procedure.

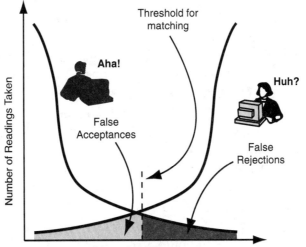

FIGURE 7.8: *Balancing usability and security.* This graph combines the two curves from Figure 7.7. Biometric readings from a particular user should closely match that user's biometric pattern; at worst, the difference should never exceed the matching threshold shown by the dashed line. We reduce the risk of masquerades (false acceptances) by moving the threshold to the left, which reduces the amount of gray area on the left. However, this reduces usability because it increases the likelihood of false rejections (the gray area on the right).

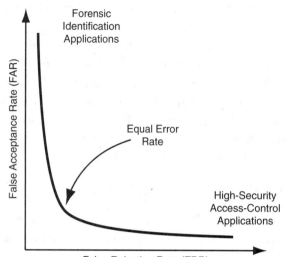

FIGURE 7.9: *ROC-curve and biometric applications.* Each point on this curve represents a different threshold value for biometric matching, and plots the resulting FAR against the resulting FRR. As noted in the upper left, forensic identification applications seek a low false rejection rate and can tolerate a high false acceptance rate. Access-control applications, on the other hand, will place a larger premium on a low false acceptance rate even at the cost of numerous false rejections.

In addition, the trade-off depends on the amount of difference the system is willing to tolerate when matching a signature. If a signature exceeds the system's tolerance threshold, the system will reject the match. The dashed vertical line in Figure 7.8 represents this threshold. The shaded area to the left of the threshold indicates how often random masquerades might succeed. We can generally decrease that risk by moving the threshold to the left, reducing its value. The shaded area to the right indicates how often the system might reject legitimate authentication attempts. As we reduce the threshold and reduce the risk of masquerade, we increase the risk of occasionally locking out a legitimate user.

Developers and analysts of biometrics typically use the results of these experiments to compute error rates based on different choices for the threshold value. This yields the *false acceptance rate*, called the FAR, and the *false rejection rate*, called the FRR, for different threshold values. These rates are scaled as percentages or fractions of the number of matches attempted. Since a particular threshold value will yield a particular FAR and FRR, we can plot one against the other to produce a *receiver operating characteristics curve*, or ROC-curve, as shown in Figure 7.9. The curve will generally contain a point, called the *equal error rate*, at which the FAR and FRR are equal. A low equal error rate usually indicates that the system can achieve strong security without excessive numbers of false rejections.

AVERAGE ATTACK SPACE

We can also use the average attack space concept from Section 2.7 to roughly compare attacks on passwords with attacks on biometrics. In particular, we can use the FAR to compute an average attack space for a biometric system. This is because both computations are based on similar types of large-scale random attacks. To find the attack space (V) from the FAR (A_{FAR}), we compute the following:

$$V = \log_2\left(\frac{2}{A_{FAR}}\right)$$

Some biometric systems, like those for fingerprint recognition, support a range of threshold values that allow each site to choose their own trade-off between safety and ease of use. In particular, some systems calibrate this threshold in terms of the false acceptance rate. Table 7.1 compares different FAR values with other average

TABLE 7.1: *Biometrics and Average Attack Spaces*

Example	Style of Attack	Average Attack Space
Biometric with a "one percent" FAR (1 in 100)	Interactive	6 bits
Random 10-letter English text	Off-line	16 bits
Biometric with a FAR of 1 in 100,000	Interactive	16 bits
Biometric with a FAR of 1 in 1,000,000	Interactive	19 bits
Personally chosen 8-character Unix password	Off-line	22.7 bits
Password from a FIPS 181 10-letter password generator	Off-line	39.5 bits
56-bit Data Encryption Standard (DES)	Off-line	54 bits
128-bit Advanced Encryption Standard (AES)	Off-line	127 bits

attack spaces. Biometrics can rely on relatively small average attack spaces because a well-designed system is not vulnerable to the off-line attacks that plague encrypted password databases. A well-built biometric system will accept only interactive authentication attempts, in which case a 10- to 20-bit average attack space should suffice.

7.7 BIOMETRIC ENCRYPTION

Cryptographic techniques like encryption provide a way to incorporate biometrics into the modern world of network computing. By themselves, biometric signatures can be easy to forge. Moreover, many people are worried about the privacy risks inherent in sharing their biometric readings. The most practical way of addressing these problems is to use cryptographic techniques to protect biometric information. Because most cryptographic techniques require base secrets, we must manage base secrets as well as biometric patterns.

PRESERVING SECRECY

Section 7.1 noted how many people are concerned about privacy risks in biometric systems. If an attacker can intercept a person's biometric data, then the attacker might use it to masquerade as the person, or perhaps simply to monitor that person's private activities. In any case, biometric systems are more likely to be accepted by a user community if the system takes steps to preserve the privacy of people's biometric information.   *A-43*

While systems built along the lines of the local authentication pattern can rely on physical security for privacy assurances, this obviously won't work for networked and distributed systems. They must use encryption. Some models of fingerprint readers even provide encryption to protect the fingerprint data as it travels from the reader to the computer.   *D-43*

Figure 7.10 sketches the basic strategy for cryptographically protecting biometric data. The biometric reader collects its data and cryptographically protects it before transmitting it to other devices in the system. The reader resides within a physically protected perimeter established by the reader's case or within a physically secure office environment. The device stores a base secret within that perimeter, and uses the base secret to cryptographically protect the biometric data. The device that receives the biometric data must also reside within a physically safe environment, and it maintains its own copy of the base secret in order to decrypt and verify the biometric data.

The biometric data remains safe as long as the base secrets are kept safe and attackers can't breach the physical perimeters. Base secrets can complicate the process of managing biometrics, since they represent another sensitive data item to distribute and maintain. One way to simplify the handling of encryption keys is to use public key encryption, which is discussed further in Chapter 13. A shortcoming of public key encryption is that it can be easy for an attacker to masquerade as a legitimate biometric reader. However, there can be similar weaknesses in other encryption techniques, so a careful implementation may still consider the authenticity issues discussed later in this section.   *see Note 11.*

In Section 1.3 we introduced hashing as a strategy to protect passwords from theft. There is no practical way to deduce the original data from the hashed information, so it might seem like a promising strategy to protect biometric privacy. Unfortunately, we cannot hash biometric data and use the resulting hash in the biometric matching procedure. An essential property of a safe hash function is that the hashes of two similar data items aren't at all likely to be

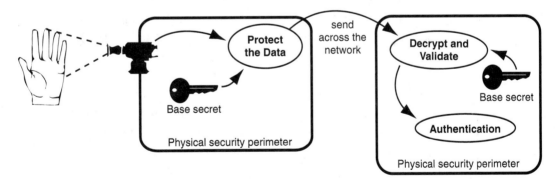

FIGURE 7.10: *Using cryptography to protect biometric data.* In distributed applications, we need to protect biometric data as it travels between devices. We can cryptographically protect it from eavesdropping and/or from modification. On the left, the biometric reader collects a reading. The reader uses a base secret to protect the reading as it is transmitted to another device. On the right, the recipient uses the base secret to decrypt and/or validate the biometric data.

similar. Thus, we can detect the match between a biometric signature to a similar biometric pattern, but we can't expect their hashes to match at all. This makes hashing an impractical strategy for protecting biometrics.

AUTHENTICITY OF BIOMETRIC DATA

The fundamental value of biometric authentication is that it relies on information that only a specific individual can provide. In practice, of course, anybody can provide any piece of information that they happen to have a copy of. While John Doe might not have the same thumbprint as Cathy Roe, he might have a digitized copy of it. If he does, then he might be able to send it to a computer and claim to be Cathy Roe. This is the essence of the biometric replay attack: the attacker intercepts the victim's biometric feature somehow, constructs a biometric signature that matches it, and transmits the signature to masquerade as the victim.

A-44

In a sense, this puts us back where we started. The computer needs to authenticate Cathy Roe. If she sends a biometric for authentication, the computer can't tell if someone forged her biometric signature. The solution is, of course, to authenticate the biometric authentication data. To do this, we must install a base secret in the biometric reader as shown in Figure 7.10. The base secret is used in conjunction with a cryptographic integrity check. If an attacker tries to forge a biometric signature, its integrity check will fail, because the integrity check depends on the base secret. The integrity check will also detect attempts to modify a legitimate biometric signature. Section 8.5 describes how these integrity checks work.

D-44

In other words, we can't trust biometric authentication on an untrustworthy network, unless we distribute base secrets to authenticate the biometric readers. This largely eliminates the perceived benefit of biometrics for some proprietors, since they still need to distribute and manage base secrets to make the system work. On the other hand, this is an acceptable expense in some applications. Many biometric uniqueness applications will require distributed biometric readers and a centralized biometric database. The benefits of the uniqueness check can outweigh the costs authenticating the biometric data.

THE PROBLEM OF BIOMETRIC EXPLOITATION

Even if a particular system isn't explicitly designed to support individual surveillance or law enforcement, some observers fear that the system might someday be exploited for those purposes. Some organizations with large-scale biometric systems have established privacy guidelines and even legislation that restricts the use of biometric data in order to address those concerns. Such systems may also incorporate special technical measures, like biometric encryption and tight security around the biometric database, to ensure the privacy of biometric data.

Nonetheless, some privacy advocates remain skeptical and even alarmed at the remaining privacy risks. The fundamental problem is that we cannot prevent "function creep." Even if today's policies, guidelines, and laws protect users' biometric privacy, there is nothing to prevent new legislation from stripping away the privacy protection. Some observers have suggested that a form of biometric encryption might be able to prevent an existing biometric database from being exploited in an unanticipated way. Such protections might, in theory, prevent a system from accepting any query except from one of its own live sensors. The protections might also prevent third parties from merging the system's databases with those of a large-scale identification system, like FBI's AFIS database.   *see Note 12.*

Despite the hopes of some observers, there really is no technological fix to prevent misuse of biometric systems. The problem is a simple one: computing equipment is completely amoral and cannot tell whether it is being used for "good" or "bad" purposes. If a system can find an identity based on a biometric signature, then there is no purely technological way of controlling *why* a given search is performed. Given enough collusion among system operators and proprietors, there is always a way to fool the system into performing its function for unintended purposes.

The most promising technique for controlling the use of biometric systems is to place the system in the custody of a consortium of interested parties. The consortium becomes responsible for protecting users' privacy and for ensuring that the system operates efficiently and reliably. The consortium can establish procedures to monitor the system's integrity and satisfy all members that biometric data remains under the system's control. While it is not clear whether technology exists to prevent a highly motivated conspiracy from subverting the system's privacy, the consortium can use multi-person control techniques and separation of duty to minimize the risks.

7.8 SUMMARY TABLES

TABLE 7.2: *Attack Summary*

Attack	Security Problem	Prevalence	Attack Description
A-41. Forged biometric trait	Masquerade as someone else	Physical	Attacker makes a copy of the user's physical trait and presents the copy to the biometric sensor
A-42. Replay user behavior	Masquerade as someone else	Physical	Attacker records the user's behavioral trait and replays it for the biometric sensor
A-43. Biometric interception	Masquerade as someone else	Common	Attacker sniffs a victim's biometric sensor reading or signature while being transmitted between devices, invading the user's privacy
A-44. Biometric signature replay	Masquerade as someone else	Common	Attacker replays a biometric sensor reading or signature so that it is treated as having been collected from the actual person

TABLE 7.3: *Defense Summary*

Defense	Foils Attacks	Description
D-41. Detailed sensing	A-41. Forged biometric trait	Collect additional biometric measurements from the person since a simple copy of the biometric will not have all of the properties of a live person
D-42. Varied behavior	A-41. Forged biometric trait A-42. Replay user behavior	The system requests a different action from the person for each authentication attempt so that a simple recording and replay won't be accepted
D-43. Biometric data encryption	A-43. Biometric interception	Encrypt biometric data when it is transmitted between different devices
D-44. Biometric signature authentication	A-44. Biometric signature replay	Apply authentication measures to biometric data to ensure that it came from a trustworthy source

CHAPTER 8

AUTHENTICATION BY ADDRESS

Tell me, who are you, alone, yourself, and nameless.

— J. R. R. Tolkien, *The Fellowship of the Ring*

IN THIS CHAPTER

There are many situations in which the authenticity of a remote command is based on where it came from, as indicated by a location or an arbitrary numerical source address. This takes several forms:

- Authentication through the telephone network
- Network address authenticity, especially on the Internet
- Unix LAN services based on address authentication
- Source authentication of network messages
- Authentication based on device locations

8.1 WHO VERSUS WHERE

The world of remote computing often assumes that authentication yields accountability. Good security has traditionally demanded that every computer user have a unique user name, and passwords ensured that such names were rarely misused. On the other hand, noncomputerized remote controls have not tried to automatically authenticate their operators, even in fairly critical applications. Instead of placing confidence in who gives commands, those systems pay attention to *where* commands come from.

For example, abuse of the "remote controls" operating a large ship could lead to both loss of life and property damage amounting to tens or hundreds of millions of dollars. The engine rooms of large ships have operated by remote control for over a century without providing authentication information from the ship's bridge to the engine room. The engineers obey the remote commands because of *where* the other end of the engine room telegraph resides (the ship's bridge) and because of who is allowed to use it there (the bridge watch conning the ship). Moreover, the bridge watch controls physical access to the ship's bridge to ensure that the remote controls only transmit valid orders.

In the computing world, we may also authenticate a message based on where it originated. As with the ship's bridge example, we then infer that the person operating a particular computer is responsible for messages that carry that computer's address. Some systems do this automatically through built-in assumptions about who uses which computers. In the extreme case, some sites assign a computer's network name to match the name or role of its usual user.

But this brings up another question: how do we establish the origin of a message? Do we need the physical location of the origin, like its latitude and longitude? Or is it enough to have an identifier that's associated with a particular computing device, regardless of its location? Both strategies play a role.

A device's physical location can authenticate messages as long as the recipients have confidence in the physical security at that location. Effective physical security would block unauthorized people from reaching the equipment and allow only authorized people to use the equipment. Attackers would have to infiltrate the location in order to generate bogus traffic.

Naturally, even slightly mobile equipment cannot authenticate itself based on its physical location. Instead, it must establish "where" based on some other property. These properties fall into three categories:

1. **Arbitrary addresses**—The proprietor establishes unique identifiers for each device and configures the device's software to use that identifier. Depending on one's point of view, an identifier assigned to a computer may be either a "name" or an "address." Internet addresses are assigned in this manner.

2. **Hard-wired addresses**—The address is built in to the owner's device, "hard wired" as it were. This is used in most modern

LANs. Each LAN interface has a built-in unique identifier that is used by default as its network address. Since the address is built into hardware, the person who controls that hardware has some control over the address used.

3. **Network enforced addresses**—The device is identified by a network address that is established and enforced by the network's carrier. Typical network end users have no control over such addresses. End users can only receive messages directed at their assigned address, and that address is automatically applied to every outbound message. The telephone system is an example of this, as is network addressing on early computer networks, including the original ARPANET.

The address may be augmented with a base secret to provide additional confidence of authenticity. This is particularly true of the first two cases, since the end users are responsible for managing addresses. When properly used, the base secret can detect and prevent bogus addresses generated by outsiders.

8.2 TELEPHONE NUMBERS AS ADDRESSES

The telephone system plays an important role in computer networking, and occasionally it plays a role in authentication. Except for mobile phones, a telephone number generally implies a physical location, the "customer premises." Telephone numbers are network-enforced addresses, as noted earlier. The local telephone company maintains an absolute address for every telephone subscriber, based on the "local loop" wires connected to that particular subscriber. The telephone number is associated with that local loop by the telephone signaling system.   *see Note 1.*

Computer systems can rely on telephone numbers for authentication only if the subscriber's physical premises are secure and the telephone carrier itself has not been subverted. But the telephone system, and even the numbers themselves, do not always work as expected. And technological progress has wreaked its own havoc on the certainties of the telephone system.

In the early days of dial-up modems, proprietors didn't always worry about authenticating remote connections. After all, the connection would work only if it was called from another computer.

Even if someone else had both the equipment and motivation to use the connection, how would they find out about it? The phone numbers rarely appeared in a directory marked as "computer" numbers, if the numbers were listed at all. So telephone numbers seemed a lot like base secrets. Someone who knew the phone number was probably authorized to use it. Naturally, the strategy failed occasionally since an attacker might discover a telephone number through chance or through social engineering.

But the secrecy strategy was defeated once and for all by falling prices of computers and modems, coupled with an obsession for exploration by hackers. The result was dramatized in the film, *War-Games*. In a crucial early scene, the main character demonstrated a program on his home computer that would locate every dial-in modem within a chosen range of telephone numbers, like those within a single telephone company central office. The program simply dialed one number after another and kept a record of which telephone numbers yielded a modem answering tone. The character later dialed those numbers manually to see what he could get those computers to do. Since the film was released, programs that perform modem searches have been called *wardialers*.

A-45

see Note 2.

Wardialers prey on victims' faulty assumption that telephone numbers can serve as base secrets. Phone numbers make poor base secrets because they really aren't secrets. While the telephone company does not intentionally distribute telephone numbers that people try to keep secret, the company isn't usually set up to exercise extreme caution about keeping such numbers secret. The numbers appear on telephone bills and often in directories. In addition, telephone numbers are hard to change. The obvious defense against wardialers is to implement an effective form of authentication.

IDENTIFICATION VIA DIAL-BACK

Unfortunately, it wasn't easy to insert authentication into every computer program that needed it at the time. Between the 1960s and the 1980s when the film *WarGames* appeared, countless computer systems had evolved that were controlled by relatively simple computer terminals. Although their keyboards and video displays made terminals look like modern desktop PCs, the terminals could do little more than display text on the screen and collect it from the keyboard. The real work was performed by a central computer, often a "minicomputer" about the same size as a household refrigerator.

Most minicomputer system developers assumed that their customers would wire all the terminals directly to the computer. This in turn allowed them to assume that authentication wasn't necessary, since the customers could control physical access to the terminals. But modem prices fell and the cost of trained computer operators rose. Many customers found it worthwhile to replace hard-wired terminals with dial-in modems, instead of staffing every computer with its own on-site operator.

Since many systems didn't have built-in authentication, they were ready targets of wardialers and other casual attackers. Moreover, commercial software systems of that kind were very expensive already. Customers couldn't generally afford to pay for possibly costly modifications to add authentication if the vendor wasn't already inclined to add such a feature.

Instead, many customers purchased *dial-back modems* to provide a basic level of authentication. These devices were similar to other modems in that they could accept dial-in connections from other standard modems. The crucial difference was that the modem didn't simply accept the incoming connection. Instead, it would hang up and try to call the caller back on a predetermined telephone number. If the incoming connection was legitimate, then the caller would be in place to answer the phone and set up the connection. If an attacker had made the call, the connection would fail because the attacker wouldn't receive the dial-back call.

D-45

While a basic dial-back modem would connect only to a single preestablished number, more sophisticated products would accept calls from any of a number of preestablished users. The modem would prompt the user for a name and then perform the dial-back based on that user's preestablished phone number.

Although dial-back modems were obviously designed to resist attacks, not all vendors understood the range of possible attacks against dial-in computer systems. For example, one vendor included a feature that would allow its technical support personnel to dial in to a customer's modem and diagnose problems the customer was having. This feature was protected by a secret password, but the

A-46

password was embedded in the device, literally "burned in" to it, during manufacture.

Thus, the modem contained a "back door" directly into the modem's security features, and purchasers could not disable the back door. If a service technician working for the modem vendor was told the password for that particular product, the technician could connect to any computer protected by that product and bypass the dial-back protection. Since the modems were often used when no other authentication was available, the back door could provide immediate access to the computer. Moreover, any attacker that happened to sniff the product's burned-in password could likewise penetrate customers' dial-back defenses. While it is not known if the product's password made its way into the hacker community, the modem's security features would have been worse than useless if it had.   *see Note 3.*

DIAL-UP IDENTIFICATION: CALLER ID

Many telephone companies now provide a *Caller ID* service (more accurately but less commonly called Calling Number ID, or CNID) in which the carrier provides a caller's telephone number to the recipient of the call. The carrier transmits the number as part of ringing the called telephone. With the right equipment, the call's recipient can display the incoming number, or use the incoming number to look up and display a name belonging with that number.

This technique could be used to authenticate a call's source when dialing in to a modem. This approach can defend against connections by unauthorized people if the computer rejects connections from unauthorized telephone numbers. The modem must be able to *D-46* receive Caller ID information and pass it to the computer's dial-in software. Then the Caller ID information can be looked up in a database of accepted telephone numbers.

A number of organizations use this arrangement to provide customer service keyed by the customer's telephone number. In essence, such systems authenticate their users based on the Caller ID information. For example, some households can order "pay per view" films through the local cable TV system simply by calling a particular telephone number. The cable system uses Caller ID to associate the incoming call with a particular household, and then activates the corresponding cable TV box so that the household can watch the movie. There are also companies that use Caller ID to automatically redirect an incoming call received by a general number so it is answered at the store nearest to the customer's phone.

A problem with these systems is that the Caller ID system is not 100% reliable. Many systems allow callers to block Caller ID when placing a call, and this may also affect the reliability of the information. It is possible that Caller ID blocking could cause some systems to report incorrect numbers instead of "no number" to the called station. In fact, the Oregon Public Utilities Commission proposed that certain sensitive locations, like battered women's shelters, should generate randomly chosen numbers for the Caller ID.

see Note 4.

Caller ID's accuracy is further eroded by the risk of crackers penetrating the telephone company switching equipment. If crackers penetrate a telephone switch, they can reroute lines so that calls from one phone appear to have originated from another. A penetration could also produce side effects that cause mistaken identification of phone calls.

A-47

Although telephone carriers usually work hard to prevent penetrations, they are not immune from them; such crackers are traditionally called *phone phreaks*. In the late 1960s, an Air Force enlisted man named John Draper figured out how to use a free whistle from a cereal box to make free long distance calls from his overseas duty stations, and earned his famous nickname, "Captain Crunch." The phone system didn't know how to distinguish between legitimate control signals between long distance centers and bogus signals embedded in an active phone call.

see Note 5.

During the 1970s, the long distance system was upgraded to separate the control signals from the voice channel, but this did not stop sophisticated crackers and phone phreaks. In the mid-1980s, Kevin Mitnick collected the necessary hardware and know-how to penetrate telephone switching systems. This allowed him to monitor and reroute phone calls, and change what telephone numbers connected to which telephones. Following some prison time, Mitnick repeated his penetrations in the mid-1990s and extended his skills to the world of cellular phones. One observer claimed that Mitnick used his ability to penetrate telephone switches in order to keep tabs on FBI agents who themselves were tapping phones to try to track him down. Although Mitnick's case is perhaps the most dramatic, he is not the only person with the skill and motivation to penetrate telephone switches.   *see Note 6.*

While some phreaks, notably John Draper, seemed mostly motivated by curiosity, other crackers have penetrated the phone system to make money. Mitnick allegedly used his skills to win radio station dial-in games ("The seventh caller will win $1,000!"), making relatively modest amounts of money through phone cracking. In late 1999, however, investigators uncovered a group called "Phonemasters" that penetrated the system to make money. The group used their abilities to collect sensitive information, which they sold to anyone willing to pay for it. They even posted a price list: $25 for a motor vehicle record, $75 for someone's credit report, $100 for a report from the FBI's crime computer, and $500 for information on celebrities and important people.   *see Note 7.*

Despite uncertain reliability, many automated systems that use Caller ID face only limited risks. If Caller ID is used only to redirect a call, then bogus information causes very little damage. There is little risk of fraud in the pay-per-view ordering application, since the Caller ID information both bills the recipient and transmits the film to the recipient's location. An attacker only causes a nuisance by providing another customer's phone number through Caller ID; the attacker cannot provide one number for the film's destination and a different number for billing. On the other hand, Caller ID spoofing could yield big rewards for crackers if it were used to authenticate a home banking application.

8.3 NETWORK ADDRESSES

The very first computer networks were private affairs, developed by particular organizations to support the organization's own system. Some say that the first true computer network was the Semi-Automatic Ground Environment (SAGE), developed by the U.S. Air Force in the 1950s to manage continental air defense. SAGE incorporated some of the earliest "modulator-demodulator" circuits for sending digital data over telephone connections, which became the "modems" familiar to today's computer users.   *see Note 8.*

A crucial feature of the earliest networks was that the system's proprietor controlled the digital network as well as the computers doing the communication. This made the proprietor responsible for assigning network addresses. Early networks relied heavily on specialized hardware to implement network connections, so network addresses were often embedded in the circuits themselves. The network address of a particular device was often established by a row of wires called "jumpers" on the circuit board. A technician could establish a specific address by cutting or soldering jumpers to produce the right pattern of binary values. In such an environment, forged network addresses were rare, since an attacker would need a soldering iron and access to the right hardware in order to mount such an attack.

ADDRESSING ON THE ARPANET

The ARPANET was the first computer network operated by an independent carrier: Bolt, Beranek, and Newman (BBN), who operated the network on behalf of the Department of Defense. The network provided a general-purpose communications service between general-purpose host computers; its e-mail, remote terminal, and file transfer mechanisms are still used today on the Internet. The ARPANET consisted of numbered routers, called Interface Message Processors (IMPs). Host computers were attached to IMPs through a specially designed host interface.

Address forging was not a problem on the ARPANET because the network itself assigned addresses to hosts and enforced how addresses were interpreted. A host's address consisted of the serial number of its IMP combined with the port number connected to that host. Data received from a host was automatically stamped with the host's unique address, providing a sort of Caller ID capability. Data addressed to a particular host port on a particular IMP always went to the host connected to that port. This arrangement made address forging almost impossible. An attacker could cause trouble on the ARPANET by physically modifying an IMP's configuration, but this was prevented with physical security. IMPs resided in physically secured computer rooms belonging to ARPANET customers: military bases, large universities, and defense contractors. In addition, most IMPs were encased in special tamper-resistant cabinets. *see Note 9.*

Following the ARPANET, network-enforced addresses became a feature of many wide area networks. The X.25 protocol, promoted by the International Telephone and Telegraph Consultative Committee (CCITT), was used by several vendors, notably the national telephone organizations in a few European countries, to provide an ARPANET-like service for general-purpose computers, and X.25 used a variable-length address that was assigned and managed by the network. More recently, the Asynchronous Transfer Mode (ATM) networking service, also provided by many telephone companies, uses network-assigned addresses. It is probably no coincidence that these services were developed by telephone companies and rely on the tradition established by telephone number assignment.   *see Note 10.*

If we look at the 802 standard for local networking, published by the IEEE (the Institute for Electrical and Electronics Engineers) we find a different example of network address assignment. Following a tradition developed with the original Ethernet, 802 LAN interfaces generally provide a default address that is guaranteed to be unique among all standard LAN interfaces ever built. This is supposed to guarantee that any interface can be connected to any compatible LAN without encountering a duplicated address. Typical addresses are 48 bits long and divided into two parts: a 24-bit number assigned to the interface's manufacturer and a 24-bit number assigned by the manufacturer to a particular interface. This address is guaranteed to be unique among all IEEE 802 LAN addresses, assuming the manufacturers are careful to assign each address only once. However, many customers have found practical reasons to assign their own addresses to LAN interfaces, so many interfaces allow the owner to change its address.   *see Note 11.*

INTERNET PROTOCOL ADDRESSES

Network-specific addresses, like those processed by LAN interfaces or enforced by wide area networks, have played only a limited role in creating today's ubiquitous Internet. The magic of the Internet is based on the notion of assigning each computer a separate network address that's not tied to particular network hardware like an IMP or a LAN interface. The underlying "physical" network address moves data between one host and another on that particular network. To travel longer distances, the data uses Internet addresses, which can hop across different types of networks until the data arrives at the physical network connected to the destination host.

Each time data arrives at the router standing between two networks, the data must be sent across the next network using a physical address. The router looks at the Internet address of the data's destination and chooses the physical address that will get the data closer to that Internet address. This routing process is repeated until the data reaches the network on which the destination host resides. Then the data is sent directly across the network to its destination.

Unlike the other network addresses we've discussed, Internet addresses are "soft" addresses, unrelated to physical devices or attachments. Internet service providers (ISPs) and other organizations with Internet hosts are assigned a range of addresses by the Internet Addressing and Numbering Authority (IANA). Organizations assign individual host addresses from their assigned address range. A numerical Internet address may indicate the host's ISP or other organization, but it doesn't necessarily imply anything about the host's physical location. The host may physically reside anywhere from an organization's home office to a local office, or even to an employee's private residence.

see Note 12.

Modern networking software in general, and Internet software in particular, is usually developed and sold in "layers" as shown in Figure 8.1. The topmost layer is the application software, like a World Wide Web browser, a database client, or a server. The bottom layer is the device driver used within the host's operating system to communicate with interface hardware, like a networking card. The middle

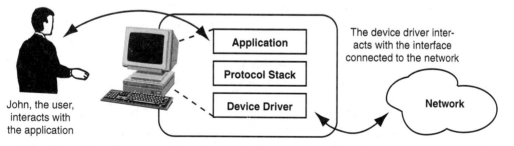

FIGURE 8.1: *Network software involves three separate components.* The application software provides networking services to the user. The protocol stack provides a standard set of networking services to application software via the socket interface. The protocol stack uses device drivers via a standard interface to communicate with networking interfaces and the underlying network hardware.

layer is the *protocol stack*, which performs all standard networking functions that don't vary with different applications or networking hardware. For example, the protocol stack takes a stream of data from the application, breaks it into a series of data "packets," and transmits them to the destination host and, upon receipt, the stack reassembles the data correctly. Internet stack software also converts Internet addresses into physical network addresses before giving a message to the network device driver.

The protocol stack discovers the host's assigned Internet address through one of several ways: it may be entered in a data field stored on the host, or it may be retrieved through a discovery protocol, or dynamically assigned to the host through an address assignment protocol. Although a host's Internet address must be unique across the global Internet, there are a number of mechanisms for sharing addresses. For example, sites may use a special range of "local" host addresses as long as all traffic is restricted to within that site; external traffic must use a firewall or router that performs "dynamic address translation" to communicate with hosts on the global Internet.

see Note 13.

8.4 ATTACKS ON INTERNET ADDRESSES

Since Internet addresses are enforced entirely by software in the protocol stack, it is trivial to fool a host's software into using the wrong address. Each Internet message contains two numerical addresses: the source of the message and the destination of the message. If an attacker wishes to send an Internet message that appears to be from somewhere else, the attacker simply constructs the message so that it contains the desired source address. In some systems, this is simply a matter of changing the host's Internet address in the protocol stack's configuration information. Another approach is for the attacker to write special software to construct Internet messages and feed the bogus messages directly to the network device driver, bypassing the protocol stack entirely. Such address forgeries can serve a number of purposes. Later in this section we will look at the role of forgery in denial of service attacks; Section 8.6 describes a forgery example involving Network File Service.

A-48

Although basic Internet software has no mechanisms to detect such forgeries, there are a couple of mechanisms that make them hard to use. First, the Internet is designed under the assumption that no two hosts in the network have exactly the same Internet address. If two hosts *do* have the same address, then Internet routing procedures don't always work correctly when trying to deliver messages to that address. The problem is that some parts of the network will deliver messages to one of the hosts while other parts will deliver messages to the other host. While this is not really a defense against address forgery, it can make the results sufficiently unpredictable to deter some attacks.

This unpredictability works in conjunction with a second defense: the synchronization protocol used to establish connections under the Internet's Transmission Control Protocol (TCP). This is the protocol used to establish a reliable connection for exchanging sequential data between two hosts. TCP carries a lot of important Internet traffic, including e-mail, Web connections, and file transfers. The synchronization protocol makes it very difficult for an attacker to send data to one of these services with a forged source address.

D-47

see Note 14.

When establishing a TCP connection, the source and destination hosts participate in a three-step handshake. This ensures that both hosts can send and receive information from the other. If an attacker initiates a connection but uses a bogus address for the origin, then the connection probably won't be completed. The recipient will transmit a handshake response to the originating address, which the Internet will route to the originating address, not to the attacker's host. If the host exists, it will discard the handshake response, since it doesn't correspond to any connections it was trying to establish. If the host doesn't exist, the handshake response will eventually be discarded by the Internet. In any case, the destination host won't establish the connection and accept data for it.

These features were not really designed as strong antiforgery mechanisms. Instead, they were designed so that the Internet would respond correctly to unexpected errors and to changes in network connectivity. While these features discourage some simple cases of address forgery, they won't prevent all attacks that use forged addresses.

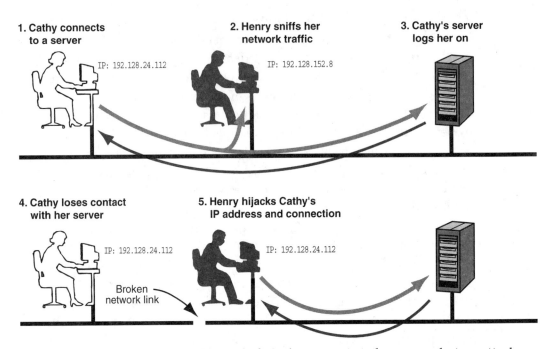

1. **Cathy connects to a server**   IP: 192.128.24.112

2. **Henry sniffs her network traffic**   IP: 192.128.152.8

3. **Cathy's server logs her on**

4. **Cathy loses contact with her server**   IP: 192.128.24.112

Broken network link

5. **Henry hijacks Cathy's IP address and connection**   IP: 192.128.24.112

FIGURE 8.2: *Man in the middle IP address theft.* Cathy connects to her server, but an attacker controls part of the network route her messages must travel. The attacker monitors her connections so that he can "jump in" to her active connections. When he is ready, the attacker breaks Cathy's network link to the server and changes his address to match hers. The network, including Cathy's server, now treats the attacker's computer as if it is really Cathy's computer.

IP ADDRESS THEFT

Although the Internet's connection-handling mechanisms interfere with some trivial approaches to forgery, they don't prevent one host from completely taking over another host's IP address. If done correctly, one host can masquerade as another and take over all traffic destined for that IP address.

However, the Internet protocols do manage to make this a tricky proposition. An attacker could, for example, simply update the IP address used by the host protocol stack, and act as if this is the host's legitimate address, even though the address belongs to some other host.

For example, an attacker named Henry might configure his host to have the same IP address as the system administration host for some Internet banking concern. If Henry simply changes his host's

A-49

IP address and then tries to establish a TCP connection to one of the bank's servers, the Internet probably won't be able to transmit the handshake response back to Henry's machine. The routers sitting between Henry and the servers probably have not yet realized that Henry's Internet address has changed. So either they won't know how to route data to his stolen address, or they will route it to the bank's own host that uses that address. In either case, Henry can't send data to the server reliably because the server can't finish the three-way handshake.

If Henry persists, then Internet routers may eventually update their tables and start treating Henry's host as the legitimate owner of the administrative host's IP address. At that point, all traffic addressed to the administrative host should be delivered to Henry instead. This can happen fairly cleanly if the legitimate owner of the stolen address (the administrative host) fails to exchange any Internet traffic while Henry's masquerade takes place. Of course, chaos will ensue if the legitimate administrative host awakens and starts sending traffic.

Henry can pull an even better address theft by performing a *man in the middle* (MIM) attack. Figure 8.2 illustrates how this attack would work. Henry positions himself on the network somewhere between his victim and the victim's server, such that all of the victim's traffic must pass through that part of the network. In this example, we'll assume that Cathy is a bank administrator, and her host is known to the bank servers as an administrative host.

Henry starts by monitoring Cathy's traffic and collecting any information he might need to take over Cathy's existing connections. If Cathy is using a Telnet remote terminal connection, for example, Henry will have to monitor TCP sequence numbers so that he can continue using the connection. Once he has the necessary information, Henry breaks the network connection leading to Cathy's *A-50* machine and simultaneously announces that his computer owns Cathy's Internet address. In effect, Henry "splices" the TCP connections and reconnects them to his own computer. This type of attack is called *TCP splicing*. Once complete, the entire network will treat Henry's computer as if it is really Cathy's computer, and that includes the bank's server. *see Note 15.*

TCP splicing is an example of the more general threat of *connection hijacking*. If Henry can hijack Cathy's connection, then Henry never needs to steal Cathy's password: he simply waits until she has logged on and then steals the authenticated connection itself. Crackers allegedly have done similar things to telephone connections, as discussed in Section 8.2.

Although TCP splicing requires sophisticated timing and monitoring, there are tools to do it, notably IP-Watcher. Such attacks are feasible, though they still require a bit of planning, coordination, and expertise. Ideally, Henry penetrates Cathy's ISP so that she has no choice but to transmit messages that he can intercept. However, that's not always an essential step. Internet routing protocols provide Henry with a lot of flexibility as to exactly what might constitute the "middle" of Cathy's connection; at least, Henry isn't tied down to a specific geographical location. If the computer that hosts the attack is a router on the only path to Cathy's computer, then Henry doesn't even need to change the computer's Internet address. *see Note 16.*

DENIAL OF SERVICE ATTACKS

Even without stealing a legitimate host's address, attackers find ways to exploit forged Internet addresses. Perhaps the most popular use for forged addresses today is in *denial of service* (DOS) attacks. A DOS attack doesn't try to steal or modify information; it simply tries to disable an Internet host so that people can't use it. Such attacks don't provide a direct benefit to the attacker, and most such attacks are nothing more than vandalism. Unfortunately, some relatively common DOS attacks can prevent almost any Internet server from operating. Given that a busy commercial Internet site can yield hundreds of thousands of dollars per hour in revenue, a successful DOS attacks may be "only vandalism" and still cause a serious financial loss.

One DOS attack that appeared in the late 1990s was called the "SYN Flood" because it relied on the "synchronization" or SYN packets that opened a TCP connection. The attacking host would generate thousands and thousands of separate messages, each trying to *A-51* begin a TCP three-way handshake. Each message contained a different forged source address so that each appeared to open a separate connection. The victim host then tried to generate the appropriate TCP response and send one back to each forged address. If a response to the forged request actually arrived at a host, the host would probably ignore it since the host wasn't trying to open that connection anyway. Other responses would simply disappear into the Internet, since they referred to nonexistent hosts.   *see* Note 17.

Meanwhile, the victim host would hold on to these "half-opened" connections, waiting for a response that would never come. At the same time, the attacking host kept sending more forged packets, pretending to request more and more connections. Many hosts, even those used for large-scale e-commerce, couldn't handle millions, or even hundreds of thousands, of half-opened connections. Eventually, these half-opened connections would use up all of the host's connection resources, and subsequent connection requests from legitimate customers would be rejected.

The practical defense for this attack was to improve how the protocol stack handled half-open connections, particularly when faced with large numbers of them. Several techniques were proposed and   *D-48*
implemented, and the results have been fairly successful. One strategy is to keep half-opened connections in a list in order of receipt, and discard older ones when new connection requests arrive. While this may occasionally discard a legitimate request when faced with a flood, it will most often let legitimate connections through, even during a flood.

A more serious DOS attack is the distributed denial of service (DDOS) attack. These rely on special attack programs that the attacker must install on numerous hosts and invoke remotely.   *A-52*
Thus, the attacker must first attack and subvert a large number of computers on the Internet, and use these hosts as the stage for mounting the DDOS attack on the real target. A strong attack might involve dozens or even hundreds of computers. To perform the attack, the attacker sends a message to each of the subverted hosts, telling them to start the DDOS attack. Then each host sends a flood of data at the targeted computer.   *see* Note 18.

In 1999, DDOS attack software appeared in several forms, with names like Trinoo, Tribal Flood Network (TFN), and Stacheldraht ("barbed wire" in German). Several Internet sites were hit by DDOS attacks later that year. This prompted CERT to sponsor a conference on the problem in November 1999. The conference issued warnings about DDOS attacks and made several recommendations for reducing the threat. However, these warnings did not prevent several attacks in early February 2000 against some very well-known Internet sites, including the Yahoo Internet portal site, the eBay auction site, and the Amazon.com retail site. An estimate based on Amazon's projected sales figures suggested that Amazon by itself may have lost $244,000 per *hour* (U.S. currency) in sales during the three-day attack.

see Note 19.

There is no way to block such an attack once it has started, except to find the attacking computers one by one and shut them down. Unfortunately, this is complicated by the fact that the attack traffic contains forged source addresses. Moreover, there isn't necessarily any way of finding the actual attacker by looking at one of the subverted computers that is actually performing the attack. The only general defense against such attacks is to practice a form of "good hygiene" on a site-by-site basis. In other words, if an Internet site ensures that it does not transmit forged addresses on the Internet, then the site becomes inhospitable for the DDOS attack software.

D-49

8.5 EFFECTIVE SOURCE AUTHENTICATION

The general defense against address forgeries is to apply cryptographic protection to the data while it travels across untrustworthy carriers. Applications can provide such protection, like the SSL protocol used by Web browsers (see Chapter 13), and in Section 8.6 we see how applications can use generic cryptographic services to protect remote procedure calls. The *IP Security Protocol* (IPSEC) provides a generic source authentication mechanism that can be applied to any Internet messages.

see Note 20.

Figure 8.3 illustrates a basic strategy for authenticating a message's source. We assume that each source, be it a host computer, a particular process on a computer, or some other device, has a unique source name (a "source ID") that we will include in any message it transmits. We also assume that there is a base secret associated with that source. Whenever the source wants to send a message, it feeds the text of the message, including its source ID and its base secret, to a one-way hash function. The result of the hash is then added to the message being sent.

D-50

At the receiving end, the message's recipient repeats the computation and compares the resulting hash with the one included in the message. If an attacker modified data in the message, then the message's hash will not match the one computed by the recipient. The attacker can't replace the message's hash with the correct one unless he also has a copy of the base secret. Thus, the attacker can't forge a message because the message won't pass the authentication check.

The message authentication process contains two important and somewhat separate components: the one-way hash and the "hash construction." The one-way hash is the same type of function used to hash passwords in Section 2.4. Modern protocols often use either Message Digest #5 (MD5) or the latest version of the Secure Hash Algorithm (SHA) for the one-way hash.

see Note 21.

The hash functions are then used with a particular "construction" that combines the base secret with the data being protected and then computes the hash in some particular way. Figure 8.3 illustrates the simplest construction: we simply append the protected data and the base secret, and hash the resulting data stream. The initial version of IPSEC used a slightly more sophisticated construction that appends a copy of the base secret at both the beginning and the end of the protected data, and then hashes the result. How-

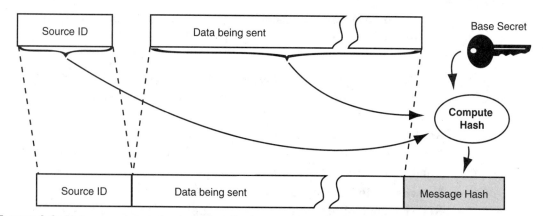

FIGURE 8.3: *Using cryptography to authenticate a message's source.* We append a secret key to the message's contents and compute a one-way hash. To send the message safely, we transmit the message's data along with its source ID and the computed hash. The recipient uses the matching secret key to recompute and validate the message hash. The hash won't match if an attacker forged or modified the message.

ever, the most recent recommendation is to use the Hashed Message
Authentication Code (HMAC) construction, which applies the hash
multiple times to different arrangements of the data and the base
secret. Experts prefer HMAC because it is the least sensitive of any
construction to potential weaknesses in the hash function being
used.   *see Note 22.*

In addition to these constructions, there is also the *message
authentication code* (MAC), which uses a block encryption algorithm
like DES to generate the hash result. The concept was the basis of
ANSI X9.9, which was used to protect banking messages against
forgery or modification (see Section 10.1). Cryptographers have also
proposed alternatives to DES MAC to use with the new AES algorithm but, as of this writing, none of these alternatives have been
selected by NIST for standardization.

8.6 UNIX LOCAL NETWORK AUTHENTICATION

Unix systems have a set of LAN-based "single sign-on" mechanisms
that rely heavily on Internet address authentication. These mechanisms appeared in the 1980s to allow hosts on Unix-based LANs to
share resources. Unix-based workstations used Unix-based servers
to store commonly used files and provide shared services like printing and e-mail. To facilitate this, Unix developers produced three
network services:

- **The "r" commands**—versions of the login command, the command shell, and the copy command that could be invoked
  between computers.

- **Network File Service (NFS)**—a protocol based on the Remote
  Procedure Call (RPC) protocol that allowed workstations to treat
  files stored on servers as if they were stored locally on the workstation. Supplemental protocols allowed workstations to do all
  file operations with NFS and omit local disk drives entirely, producing diskless workstations.

- **Network Information Service (NIS)**—another protocol based on
  RPC, this one shared user authentication information, host configuration data, and other administrative files between workstations and servers within a single site.

These services all make strong assumptions about the trustworthiness of the computers that request or provide the services. They also assume that the underlying network is relatively safe from Internet address forgery. In other words, the services assume the computers and the network connecting them reside within an "internal password" environment, as discussed in Section 6.2.

THE "R" COMMANDS

The "r" commands were developed as part of the Berkeley version of Unix. They provide basic commands that operate between mutually trusted computers. The "rlogin" command allows users on trusted hosts to log in to other trusted hosts without having to type a password. The "rsh" command allows users on a trusted host to run a single command on another trusted host without typing a password.

The "r" commands don't ignore the concept of authentication completely. Rather, they try to take advantage of the fact that a person has already logged in. Once John Doe has logged on, his Unix workstation will rely on that fact and authorize him to log on to other nearby hosts as long as both hosts trust each other.

Consider a local network with several workstations, including one named *bat*, and two servers, named *fox* and *hen*. John Doe has logged on to the workstation *bat*. The two servers are configured to trust all of the workstations to some degree, and this allows John to use the rlogin and rsh commands with them. This trust is established by the contents of configuration files. Both servers contain the file /etc/hosts.equiv, and the files contain an entry for each workstation in the LAN. This allows users at those workstations to execute rsh or rlogin on the servers as long as the user name of the logged-on user matches the name of an authorized user on that server.

For example, John Doe has logged on to *bat* as jdoe. He executes an rlogin command to *fox*. The rlogin server software on *fox* first checks its hosts.equiv file to verify that *bat* is a trusted host. Since it is, *fox* next checks its password file for an entry for the user jdoe. Because the entry exists, *fox* accepts the rlogin command and automatically logs jdoe on without asking for a password. Later on, after John has logged off, Tim Dore logs into *bat* as tdore and then tries to rlogin to *fox*. However, *fox* does not have a password file entry for tdore, so it rejects his rlogin attempt.

These commands also look for a file called .rhosts in a user's home directory. If a user with the same name tries to rlogin or rsh from a host whose name is listed in that .rhosts file, then the command is permitted. This allows individual users to establish trust relationships with other computers on which they have accounts.

The rlogin and rsh commands work conveniently because they place a lot of trust on the security of computers on the local network. This is also their essential weakness. If an attacker penetrates a trusted host, then the rlogin and rsh functions allow the attack to spread to all other trusted hosts. This is an inevitable risk of this type of trust. The commands rely on two types of information to establish trust:

- **location authenticity**—that the host names and addresses are accurate, and are correctly mapped from one to the other
- **message authenticity**—that the rlogin or rsh message contains the user name of a user that has really logged on to a trusted Unix host

If an attacker can generate messages that contain believable host address information, then the server will assume that the information inside the message is correct. In theory, an attacker could intercept an rsh message traveling between two trusted hosts and modify its contents so that the destination would execute whatever command the attacker wanted. Such attacks have not been reported, but they are theoretically possible if an attacker resides on the internal network and can intercept the traffic. But if the attacker is already on the internal network, it is much easier to exploit trust relationships, or even physical access, than it is to capture and modify messages in transit.

However, attackers have developed a technique for forging the source location of an Internet packet for the purposes of tricking an rsh server. The technique is called *IP spoofing*. It played the central   *A-53* role in a widely publicized Internet breakin that occurred over Christmas in 1994. A computational physicist involved in cellular telephone security had configured his host computers to use rlogin and rsh between particular internal hosts at his site. To his surprise, someone managed to execute the rsh command, and used the command to allow any host on the Internet to use rsh or rlogin on the target computer. Once that occurred, the attacker could enter the site's computers directly.

see Note 23.

In theory, the attack should not have worked, since rsh requires a TCP connection. As described in Section 8.4, the three-way handshake used in TCP should have prevented rsh from opening the connection and accepting bogus data. In particular, the attackers can't produce the right packets to complete the handshake with a forged address *unless* they can predict the packet sequence numbers. But, as noted earlier, attackers have found ways to do this.

For the Christmas attack, the attacker sent two messages. The first message was a SYN to open the rsh connection, but it contained the address of a trusted host on the local network. The target host replied by sending a SYN back to the same address. In theory, the target host wouldn't open a connection until it received an "acknowledgment" (ACK) message that had to contain the hard-to-guess sequence number from that packet. Even though the attacking host never received the sequence number, it sent a believable ACK that completed the handshake and provided data to the newly opened connection. The data was a series of commands to modify the victim's hosts.equiv file to let any Internet host in.

see Note 24.

The attack succeeded by exploiting an obscure weakness in certain versions of TCP software. The sequence numbers on TCP packets were mostly intended to handle lost or duplicated packets, and to ensure that long-delayed packets from a closed connection would be properly discarded. However, it proved possible for an attacker to collect information about how the host generated its sequence numbers and then generate the initial packets for a TCP connection that correctly guessed the sequence numbers being used. This possibility first had been explored a decade earlier, but had never been applied to a real attack before.

see Note 25.

The IP spoofing attack began by generating numerous failed connections, which the attacker would examine in order to determine how the victim host generated its TCP sequence numbers. Then the attacker sent the two initial packets to the rsh "remote shell" command, and inserted sequence numbers in the second packet that coincided with what the host should expect. This trick connection only needed to persist long enough for the rsh command to start execution, and that is exactly what happened.

Two basic defenses quickly appeared to resist this attack. The first was for Internet sites to tighten down their firewall filtering. In particular, sites would program their firewalls to be sure to block any packets from outside the site that claimed to originate from inside the site. A message arriving from outside the site should never carry the source address of a computer inside the site in any case—such a message would obviously be a forgery. Firewalls could easily detect and block such traffic.

The other defense was to make the sequence numbers hard to guess. Originally, the security implications of sequence numbers were only of interest to a few researchers. Following the IP spoofing attacks, unpredictable sequence numbers became a standard feature of TCP/IP protocol stacks. This was a case in which an obscure security problem was largely ignored until someone found a way to exploit it and do mischief.

D-51

REMOTE PROCEDURE CALLS, NFS, AND NIS

RPC was developed by Sun Microsystems as a basis for providing simple and efficient services to Unix computers on a LAN. It is the protocol underlying the local file service of NFS and the host and user configuration files exchanged by NIS. Authentication is an essential aspect of such services, since file permissions must be enforced and password data must be consistent with what the individual users have specified. Both of these services rely heavily on RPC for security. RPC, in turn, relies on the security and integrity of the site's hosts and internal network. Like the "r" commands, NFS and NIS are intended for environments made of trustworthy users and equipment.

see Note 26.

The first source of weakness in RPC and the protocols it carries is in the User Datagram Protocol, or UDP. This is the lowest-level protocol provided to application software by the Internet protocol suite. Unlike TCP, UDP provides a simple "datagram" transmission capability without detecting lost data or keeping messages in order. The connection handshaking and sequence numbers used in TCP provide a limited degree of validation of the source address for data it carries, but there is no such validation in UDP. It is trivial to generate a UDP message with a completely bogus source address.

The ability to forge RPC traffic is particularly significant to NFS messages. A typical NFS message requests to read a block of data from a file or write a block of data to a file. Most NFS transactions are considered "stateless," which is taken to mean that a duplicated message (that is, one that was retransmitted due to network problems) can always be processed by the NFS server and the results will be correct. Unfortunately, this also means that there is no protection against forging NFS messages as suggested by Attack A-48 in Section 8.4. An attacker can construct a UDP message containing the RPC header that identifies a user authorized to access some sensitive data, and then construct the appropriate NFS request to actually manipulate the data. The NFS server will not be able to detect the forgery. The contents of all of the message fields are assumed to be authentic.

The first and most important defense for NFS is to block access to it from untrustworthy computers and people. If the people are slightly untrustworthy, then exclude their computers from access permissions to the NFS server. If the people are outsiders, then firewall the NFS service so outsiders cannot reach it.

A second defense for NFS is to use Secure RPC with it. This service provides encryption and a degree of cryptographic authentication for NFS usage. However, this service may simply substitute weaknesses in NFS for a different set of weaknesses, since Secure RPC is not very sophisticated. One observer noted that it relies on Needham-Schroeder, which has a well-known weakness (see Section 12.1), it relies on unauthenticated files for authentication data, and its original public key system was so weak that it was soon broken.

D-52

see Note 27.

As noted earlier, NIS is used to exchange administrative files, including Unix password files that contain user names and password hashes. This information is usually transmitted in plaintext, which makes it vulnerable to sniffing. Thus, NIS eliminates the benefits of the shadow password file if the environment contains attackers who like to sniff network traffic. Another problem is that NIS relies on the ability to trust other hosts on the network. It is possible to trick hosts into using a bogus password file that contains forged password hashes for legitimate user accounts. Like NFS, NIS is best restricted to a trustworthy network.

8.7 AUTHENTICATING A GEOGRAPHICAL LOCATION

Physical security measures are usually associated with static physical locations like office buildings, so a large number of security-critical computing functions occur in such places. In such cases it would be reasonable to use an authentication strategy that ties a message to its physical origin.

Unfortunately, there is no natural phenomenon that distinguishes one point in space from another. A landmark experiment by the physicists Michelson and Morley in the late 19th century helped establish this conclusion, explained by Einstein's relativity theories in the early 20th century. As a practical matter, seafarers had found it incredibly difficult to estimate the geographical position of a ship at sea until the development of highly accurate timepieces, notably the Harrison chronometers, in the 18th century. However, these techniques simply allow an observer to estimate a position. They do not produce evidence of the observer's position that is hard to forge.

In a sense, location information isn't significantly different from addressing information used in computer networks. A proprietor can establish a way of labeling geographic locations and require messages to contain geographical identifiers. The labels can be largely arbitrary, like Internet addresses, or assigned systematically, like geographical latitude and longitude. Regardless, an attacker can just as easily claim to be at an arbitrary geographical location as he could claim to possess a particular identity. Not even base secrets can ensure the accuracy of geographical information: a legitimate user may move a device, including its base secret, to a different location and not realize the security implications.

However, the advent of the *Global Positioning System* (GPS) has changed matters. GPS consists of a set of 24 satellites that maintain precise orbital locations above the Earth. Each satellite transmits a continuous stream of identifying information that, when combined with signals from other visible satellites, will accurately indicate a geographical location. GPS was originally developed for military applications by the DOD, but commercial GPS receivers are now a common feature in aircraft, in commercial and pleasure boats, in cars, and in backpacks.

see Note 28.

Each GPS satellite transmits a unique sequence of signals that arrive at a receiver at a particular time. Generally, a GPS receiver can use the satellite signals directly to compute its geographical location. In addition, a receiver can double check its result, and often increase its accuracy, by using a technique called *differential GPS*. This technique computes the geographical location by analyzing the differences between different satellites' signals.

In the mid-1990s, a group of researchers in Colorado developed a technique to use differential GPS to remotely distinguish between different physical locations. Figure 8.4 shows the basic arrangement. Both Tim and Cathy receive signals from particular GPS satellites. Tim receives the GPS signals in a particular sequence that depends on the distance to the different satellites. He can collect and correlate that data and then transmit it to Cathy. Meanwhile, Cathy collects the same GPS data from the same satellites. But Cathy receives the data at different times because the satellites are

D-53

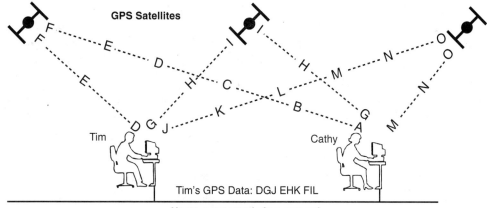

FIGURE 8.4: *Concept for GPS authentication of geographical locations.* This is a greatly simplified example to illustrate the concept. If Cathy knows Tim's geographical location, she can use GPS data to authenticate messages sent from his location. Both Tim and Cathy receive the same time-dependent, unpredictable sequences from the GPS satellites, but their differing locations mean that the sequences arrive at different times. Tim combines the data he receives in real time to create a 20KB package of GPS authentication data. Cathy uses the GPS data stream she receives in order to verify that Tim's authentication data could have originated only from his location at the time his authentication data was sent.

at different distances from her than from Tim. If she adjusts the GPS signals accordingly, she can compute how the data should have been received by Tim at his physical location at a particular time. If the GPS data sent to her by Tim matches the GPS data she expects, then she can be confident that the messages from Tim originated from the physical location she expected. The merged GPS data is both time and location dependent.

see Note 29.

Cathy knows with confidence that the message originated from Tim's geographical location even though she doesn't really know that Tim himself is sending the message. This is sufficient for many security applications, particularly ones that involve dedicated host computers in physically secure locations.

In order to forge Tim's location, an attacker must be able to collect GPS data that Tim might collect. Then the attacker must correlate the data in exactly the same manner that Cathy would expect Tim to correlate it, and send it to her in a timely manner. Since the GPS data is time dependent, the attacker's forgery is only valid for a very limited time. In practice, the attacker shouldn't be able to collect the necessary information and transmit it to a victim in time to achieve a successful masquerade.

This technology does, however, face certain shortcomings. First, it requires an antenna that can receive GPS signals from several satellites, while most standard GPS receivers need to receive a signal from only two or three satellites. Second, the technique works only when the sender and recipient are able to see a few of the same satellites. Third, there may be a privacy risk, since the authentication information identifies the location of the data's source. Unless the data is encrypted, a sniffer will be able to associate data with the physical location of its source.

As of this writing, GPS location authentication is still a relatively new technique, and little has been reported about its behavior in the face of sophisticated attacks. It is not clear, for example, how the evolving threat of GPS jamming might affect its operation. It seems likely that GPS jammers available today could prevent location authentication from functioning. Depending on how the rest of the system works, the attack might force the system to fall back on an authentication mechanism that's easier to attack.

see Note 30.

A related risk is that of forged GPS signals. GPS satellites transmit a well understood signal to civilian receivers, and it may be possible to simulate the signals of several GPS satellites. In theory, such signals might be able to trick a GPS location authenticator, especially if operating in conjunction with a subverted host computer that is trying to authenticate itself. However, a well-designed GPS location authenticator might still work correctly in the face of jamming, since it uses as many satellite signals as it can, and the jammer might not be able to override and mask all visible GPS signals. While GPS location authentication provides a promising capability, further experience is needed to tell how well it operates in the real world of operational needs and sophisticated threats.

8.8 SUMMARY TABLES

TABLE 8.1: *Attack Summary*

Attack	Security Problem	Prevalence	Attack Description
A-45. Wardialing	Recover hidden information (telephone numbers)	Common	Software uses an autodial modem to test all phone numbers within a chosen range to locate modem connections
A-46. Dial-back back door	Masquerade as a different host computer	Physical	Attacker uses built-in back door to bypass the dialback
A-47. Phone line redirection	Masquerade as a different host computer	Sophisticated	Attacker uses special knowledge to penetrate the carrier's telephone switch, and redirects the line from within the switching system itself
A-48. Packet address forgery	Masquerade as a different host computer	Common	Construct a message with the forged address instead of the correct one
A-49. IP address theft	Masquerade as a different host computer	Common	Attacker takes over the victim's IP address and masquerades as the victim's host

TABLE 8.1: *Attack Summary (Continued)*

Attack	Security Problem	Prevalence	Attack Description
A-50. TCP splicing	Masquerade as someone else	Common or Sophisticated	Intercept an authenticated TCP connection and redirect it to talk to the attacker's session
A-51. SYN flooding	Denial of service	Common	Send messages to start opening different connections but don't complete the process
A-52. Distrib-uted denial of service	Denial of service	Common	Penetrate multiple hosts and use them to transmit a flood of traffic at the victim host
A-53. IP spoofing	Masquerade as a different host computer	Common	Trick the receiving host into believing the incoming message comes from a trusted host

TABLE 8.2: *Defense Summary*

Defense	Foils Attacks	Description
D-45. Dial-back modem	A-45. Wardialing	Special device that establishes a remote connection by calling the remote user back with a preestablished phone number
D-46. Caller ID	A-45. Wardialing A-46. Dial-back back door	Use the "Caller ID" feature of modern phone systems to determine if an incoming connection comes from an authorized location
D-47. TCP synchroni-zation	A-48. Packet address forgery	TCP uses a three-way handshake to establish a connection, and the handshake won't generally work unless both hosts successfully exchange the three messages
D-48. Connection resource manage-ment	A-51. SYN flooding	Manage TCP connection resources so that service is still provided even in the face of a SYN flood

TABLE 8.2: *Defense Summary (Continued)*

▼ Defense	Foils Attacks	Description
D-49. Site forgery filtering	A-48. Packet address forgery A-51. SYN flooding A-52. Distributed denial of service A-53. IP spoofing	Discard all messages that obviously contain forged addresses. Examine messages entering a site and discard any containing a source address belonging to the receiving site. Examine messages leaving the site and discard any containing a source address that doesn't belong to that site
D-50. Message authentication	A-47. Phone line redirection A-48. Packet address forgery A-50. TCP splicing A-51. SYN flooding A-52. Distributed denial of service A-53. IP spoofing	Use a cryptographic protocol like IPSEC's authentication mechanism to validate the source address and contents of messages exchanged on an untrustworthy network
D-51. Random TCP sequencing	A-53. IP spoofing	Ensure that TCP software generates truly unpredictable sequence numbers
D-52. Secure RPC	A-47. Phone line redirection A-48. Packet address forgery A-50. TCP splicing A-53. IP spoofing	Deploy Secure RPC service with NFS to provide cryptographic protection to its traffic
D-53. GPS location authenticating	A-48. Packet address forgery A-49. IP address theft	Transmit mingled GPS signals to authenticate one's location at a given moment in time

CHAPTER 9

AUTHENTICATION TOKENS

DARK HELMET: So the combination is 1-2-3-4-5. [Lifts helmet and yells]
That's the stupidest combination I ever heard in my life! That's the
kinda thing an idiot would have on his luggage!

— Mel Brooks et al., *Spaceballs*

IN THIS CHAPTER

Password sniffing has been especially troublesome in remote access
and networking environments. This led to several technical strategies and commercial products to generate unsniffable passwords.

- Passwords using hardware tokens
- Making passwords unsniffable with one-time passwords
- One-time password tokens using internal counters or clocks
- Tokens with PINs
- Configuring one-time passwords
- Attacks on one-time passwords

9.1 TOKENS: SOMETHING YOU HAVE

The essence of token-based authentication is that you must have
the token in your possession in order to authenticate yourself to the
computer. The computer will not recognize you without the token,
regardless of whether the token was lost, lent, or stolen. This is the
way tokens have worked for thousands of years. Important people
have used personal seals to authenticate important documents, and
the recipients of the documents would treat the seal's impression as
evidence that the person really produced the document. The seal
served as an authentication token for documents.

Key-operated mechanical locks are probably the most common authentication tokens used today. Section 2.2 shows how a key carries a base secret (Figure 2.2), and authentication tokens likewise carry a base secret. In fact, the familiar benefits and shortcomings of keys often also apply to computer-oriented authentication tokens.

Everyone has a personal trove of stories about keys: losing them, finding them, locking them in the car, and so on. Much of this translates into the behavior of computer authentication tokens. Here is a summary of the fundamental properties of tokens from a security standpoint:

- A person must physically possess the token in order to use it.
- A good token is hard to duplicate.
- A person can lose a token and unintentionally lose access to a critical resource.
- People can detect stolen tokens by taking inventory of the tokens they should have in their possession.

Numerous authentication products use tokens, for both computer and noncomputer applications. One reason for their popularity is that they take away much of the burden of memorization. A token can reliably carry a much more complicated base secret than most people can memorize. Few people have the memory or motivation necessary to memorize a really strong password. Tokens can carry very complicated base secrets without burdening the owner with any memorization. At most, a token might require a PIN.

Tokens generally fall into two categories: passive and active. In both cases the token incorporates a base secret, and one must copy the base secret in order to make a working copy of a particular token. A *passive token* is simply a storage device for the base secret. Examples include mechanical keys, ATM cards, most employee badges, and some specialized devices like "datakeys." An *active token* can generate different outputs under different circumstances. For example, an active token can take part in a challenge response authentication protocol, or provide other crypto functions that use the token's base secret. Traditionally, active tokens have been either commercial one-time password tokens or smart cards, though other models have evolved that plug into existing ports on desktop and laptop computers.

PASSIVE TOKENS

Passive tokens work by presenting their base secret to the authentication mechanism: a lock responds to the notches on a key, or a card with a magnetic stripe transmits its stored data via a card reader. ATM cards, for example, emit the bank account number stored on a particular card. Aside from these, there are numerous other examples: "datakeys" from Datakey, Inc., that look like keys but contain a read-only memory chip, plastic cards with patterns of punched holes, cards with data encoded in optical bar codes, and wire coils that emit a specific signal when passed near the appropriate reader.

The wire coil systems are often referred to as proximity cards since they are recognized when they are near the card reader. Examples include the XyLoc from Ensure Technologies and the Sage-ID from Tri-Sage. Some models work only when they are right next to the reader, while others work at a distance of a few feet or even a hundred feet. The cards that work at the greater distances usually contain a battery; they are often referred to as "active cards" although they only emit a fixed code. One vendor provides a workstation security system that activates a lock screen whenever the proximity card leaves the workstation's vicinity.

The most common passive tokens are, of course, plastic cards with a magnetic stripe ("mag stripe cards"). Today, they appear everywhere, including ATM cards, credit cards, drivers' licenses, and on employee badges to operate electronic door locks. The cards, their sizes, and their data formats are fully standardized and available from countless manufacturers. One estimate claims that mag stripe readers cost as little as $10, and mag stripe writers as little as $20 (purchased in quantity, U.S. currency).   *see Note 1.*

The problem with passive tokens is that they are often too easy to copy. People often assume that tokens won't be copied because they require special equipment like a key copier or a mag stripe reader. In fact, such technologies are often victims of their own success. Consider mechanical keys: we find key copying equipment everywhere since it's a simple and profitable activity, and a determined attacker can even copy a key without using a copying machine. Even mag stripe equipment is now cheap and relatively common. In late 1999, a clerk in a fancy department store allegedly took advantage of modern miniaturization by copying customers' mag stripes with a compact reader she had attached to her Palm Pilot.   *see Note 2.*

Many, if not most, of today's mag stripe cards deal with the problems of theft and copying by incorporating a PIN. Many companies that use card-controlled locks will demand a PIN before opening important doors, like those from the street. And, of course, ATMs require both the card and its PIN before they perform banking functions. The combination of card and PIN produces two separate authentication factors: something you have plus something you know. This reduces the risk of masquerade, since the attacker must copy the card and also uncover the PIN.

This is not to say that mag stripe card security is foolproof. We've already seen that attackers can make copies of cards; thieves have been equally resourceful at acquiring the PINs to go with those cards. A trivial strategy is to simply stand next to a victim using the ATM and note the PIN as it is typed in (an example of Attack A-9, Shoulder surfing). Some banks would transmit PINs from remote ATMs over conventional phone lines with no additional protection, and thieves would simply eavesdrop on the transmission to recover both PINs and card numbers. Other banks would store the PIN on the card in some form, and thieves would use a variety of techniques to either recover the PIN or to substitute a different account number if the card's PIN is already known.

Some attacks involved PIN recovery by bank employees. About 1% of all bank employees are discharged every year for disciplinary reasons like petty theft, so the risk of embezzlement by staff is very real. Cases have been reported in which bank staff sold PINs to the local crime syndicate. Dishonest bank programmers have even been caught modifying the bank's PIN assignment software to make the PINs easier for their partners in crime to guess. Such problems can't be fought by changing technologies; the bank must use strategies like separation of duty instead.   *see Note 3.*

ACTIVE TOKENS

An *active token* doesn't need to emit its base secret to authenticate its owner. Instead, it uses the secret to do something else—like generate a one-time password. Tokens for computer authentication don't have to implement one-time passwords, but this is what traditional token products do (SafeWord, SecureID, CryptoCard, etc.). More sophisticated tokens connect directly to a workstation and can often perform a variety of crypto functions in addition to authentication. Figure 9.1 illustrates some active tokens.

Active tokens can use crypto techniques for authentication that are immune from attacks via sniffing and replay. Clearly, sniffing is a problem when we authenticate across a network. Token-based authentication will essentially generate a different set of messages each time its owner tries to authenticate, and it does the attacker no good to try to replay a previous set of messages. Moreover, the attacker can't predict what a correct set of authentication messages should be, assuming that the token's authentication protocol is well designed and implemented.

Traditional one-time password tokens evolved in the days of time-shared remote access. Originally, these tokens were the size of pocket calculators and often included a keypad, but more recent tokens also show up on key rings. These tokens generate authentication data to be typed in on a keyboard, so they can work with any interactive computer system and don't require special hardware. However, this also limits the complexity of their authentication pro-

FIGURE 9.1: *Seven examples of active tokens.* These tokens come in a broad range of shapes, sizes, and technologies. *Clockwise from upper left*, a SafeWord Silver 2000 one-time password token from Secure Computing; another SafeWord token—the SafeWord Gold 3000; an iKey USB token from Rainbow Technologies; *right*, a Fortezza crypto card—an NSA-developed PCMCIA card; an iButton ring from Dallas Semiconductor designed to be worn as jewelry; a SecurID one-time password token from RSA Security; a typical credit card-sized smart card produced by Schlumberger.

tocols, since they rely on the user to transcribe authentication data between the token and the computer.

Other active tokens plug directly into a computer and handle more complicated authentication protocols. Today, these come in a variety of packages, as shown in Figure 9.1. The principal example of such tokens is the *smart card*, a device the size of a credit card that contains a small processing system and memory. A few active tokens have also been implemented as "PC cards," which are also known as PCMCIA cards, named after the Personal Computer Memory Card International Association that established the standard. Recently, several vendors have introduced "USB tokens" that connect directly into the Universal Serial Bus: an emerging standard for connecting peripherals like printers to personal computers, desktop and laptop alike. Other tokens, like the iButton, require a special-purpose reader.

Smart cards have been used extensively in Europe, so the technology has seen a good deal of real-world use. European credit cards have been smart cards since the 1980s. Another early application was as value storage cards. For example, a public transit authority could use smart cards to hold a passenger's prepaid fares. When a passenger like Tim entered a train or bus, he would put his smart card in a reader, and the reader would deduct the cost of the fare from his card. When the card ran low, Tim went to a special machine, inserted some money, and the machine added value to the card.

Internally, the card would be programmed with a protocol that worked only in conjunction with computers belonging to the transit commission. This usually involved secret data shared between all valid cards and the transit commission. Even if Tim had a smart card reader on his home computer, the card wouldn't let him add or deduct from the fares stored there.

Recently, credit card vendors in the United States have started offering smart cards intended to provide security for e-commerce transactions. As of this writing, many of these cards work by sharing a base secret between the cards and the credit card vendor, and the secure transaction protocol works only in conjunction with the card issuer's Web site. To some extent, this is because it is so hard to share secret keys safely across enterprises; this reflects fundamental differences between the indirect and off-line design patterns discussed in Chapter 4. Public key cryptography may provide broader applications for smart cards, so further discussion of them appears in Section 15.3.

Smart cards and other plug-in tokens share certain security strengths and weaknesses. All of them usually present the attacker with a security perimeter that can be difficult to physically penetrate, since the internal logic is usually embedded in a single integrated circuit. However, these devices aren't immune to attack. Unlike conventional password tokens that may contain their own keypad and display, these tokens must rely entirely on other equipment for input and output. Attackers can exploit that if they subvert the software that talks to the token and possibly trick the card, its user, or the proprietor. Moreover, some devices are not well designed to resist probing, and a knowledgeable attacker can extract critical data from them while using modest resources.   *see Note 4.*

As of this writing, the major limitation facing plug-in active tokens is that they depend on connections that aren't present in many, often most, desktop computers. Obviously, Cathy can't log on if her workstation won't take her smart card. Tokens built as PCMCIA cards can usually be plugged into laptops, but few desktop systems routinely include a PCMCIA interface.

The connection problem might tilt some proprietors in favor of USB tokens: although such tokens may cost more to manufacture than smart cards, they cost less than the combination of a smart card plus its reader. From a security standpoint, USB tokens appear to offer the same theoretical promise of hardware-enforced security as smart cards. Experiments have also found, however, that a knowledgeable and properly equipped attacker can penetrate the hardware protection of many USB products.   *see Note 5.*

9.2 NETWORK PASSWORD SNIFFING

The story of Ali Baba, which opened Chapter 1, begins with overhearing the password to the thieves' cave: a sniffing attack. In Section 1.5 we see passwords recovered through shoulder surfing and even by copying them out of RAM within a computer. But today's users on modern wide area networks face a much broader threat. Today, attackers often sniff unprotected passwords out of messages

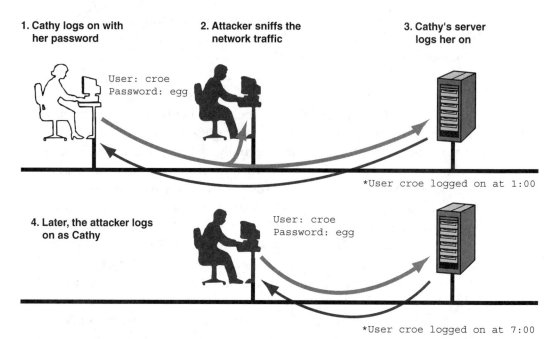

1. Cathy logs on with her password

2. Attacker sniffs the network traffic

3. Cathy's server logs her on

```
User: croe
Password: egg
```

```
*User croe logged on at 1:00
```

4. Later, the attacker logs on as Cathy

```
User: croe
Password: egg
```

```
*User croe logged on at 7:00
```

FIGURE 9.2: *Sniffing passwords on a network.* First, Cathy types in her "reusable" password to log in to the server. Next, an attacker sniffs it while it travels across the network, and uses it to masquerade as Cathy.

in transit between computers. Some attackers install sniffer software within computers belonging to an Internet service provider. The sniffer software snoops on all traffic passing through that part of the Internet. This provides the attacker with a lot of passwords to exploit.

Figure 9.2 shows the network sniffing strategy. Cathy Roe logs on to a service by typing her user name and password. As that information travels across the network to her service, an attacker sees it and copies it down. Neither Cathy nor her service can reliably detect the attacker, and Cathy logs on successfully. Later, the attacker uses Cathy's user name and password to log on himself. The service can't tell the difference between the attacker and Cathy, so the attacker logs on successfully.

A-54

Sniffing the password data from the masses of other network traffic isn't particularly difficult. There are several indicators that will tell an automated sniffer program that a message is part of someone logging on. Obviously, the program can look for prompts like "User name" and "Password." Also, the program can simply look for the beginning of a connection. In the days when many people used line-oriented terminals, it was simple to look for the start of a Telnet connection and copy the first several dozen characters sent back and forth.

Sniffing is one of those problems (if not *the* problem) that distinguishes internal password environments from external ones, as discussed in Section 6.2. Sniffing makes authentication on public networks much trickier than on small private networks and LANs. While reusable passwords might pass safely across a small LAN in some environments, it is an invitation for attack on the Internet.

An obvious solution is to encrypt the password: to transform it into a nontextual form that the attacker can't transform back into text. If the password isn't in a readable textual form, then the *D-54* attacker can't type it in when he tries to log on as Cathy.

Unfortunately, the solution isn't as simple as it looks. Classic encryption requires a secret key that Cathy shares with her server. Setting up and sharing that secret key is at least as complicated as managing Cathy's password. In a sense, straightforward encryption gives her two passwords to worry about instead of one (the SSL protocol neatly addresses this problem in Chapter 13).

Instead of straight encryption, we could compute a one-way hash of the password and transmit that instead. This doesn't require a shared secret key. If the attacker intercepts the hashed password, he can't easily turn it back into the original textual password, and he can't use the hashed password directly to log in.

However, the hashed password opens us up to a replay attack: the attacker could modify his system to simply provide an encoded password when he tries to masquerade as someone else. If the service simply expects a hashed password, the attacker can simply *A-55* replay Cathy's hashed password. The server won't be able to tell if the password was generated from the original textual version or was simply replayed. The hashed password is really a *password equivalent* that provides only a modest amount of security over using the plaintext password itself.

Imagine if the 40 thieves had used a hashed password: the word would probably have just sounded like gibberish instead of a genuine word in Hindustani. Regardless, Ali Baba and his brother could still have been able to intercept it and use it to open the cave's door (assuming, of course, they could pronounce it accurately).

On the other hand, what if the cave's door used a whole series of passwords, changing the password each time one was used? The incantation "Open, Sesame" would work only once. When Ali Baba tried it again later, it would not have worked, the thieves' treasure would have been safe, and Ali Baba's story would have been forgotten.

If we do this with computer services, then the sniffed password does the attacker no good. This is the basic concept behind *one-time password* mechanisms. The service expects a new password each time the person logs on. The protocol used by the particular one-time password mechanism establishes how to generate the correct password.

D-55

But it's hard enough to remember a single password, and most people would find it impossible to figure out the next password to use each time they had to log on. That's where the tokens come in: commercial one-time password systems use hardware or software to generate the user's next password.

9.3 ONE-TIME PASSWORDS

There are two general strategies for generating one-time passwords. *Counter-based* tokens combine the base secret with a synchronized counter to generate one-time passwords. *Clock-based* tokens use a synchronized clock to generate one-time passwords. One vendor has even developed a product that combines both techniques. All these techniques rely on a random base secret stored in the one-time password token. New passwords combine the base secret with some arbitrary value: a counter, a clock, or both.

COUNTER-BASED ONE-TIME PASSWORDS

In 1994, an international team of thieves gained unauthorized access to the Citibank Cash Management System, which allows major Citibank customers to transfer money from their Citibank accounts to other financial institutions around the world. As with many crimes, the details may never be known for sure, but certain things seem likely based on reports about the incident. In particular, the reports suggest that thieves never needed to burglarize Citibank's cash management computer center in Parsippany, New Jersey. Instead, they accessed the system remotely using stolen passwords.

The scheme was apparently masterminded by 24-year-old Vladimir Levin, the head systems operator at A O Saturn, a computer company in St. Petersburg, Russia. Levin and his accomplices acquired and shared passwords that authorized over 40 transactions, totaling over $10 million. The thieves authenticated themselves as legitimate account managers and moved money between bank accounts in Finland, Russia, Germany, the Netherlands, the United States, Israel, and Switzerland. Some team members, like Alexei Lashmanov, 28, provided access to particular accounts to receive stolen funds, while others actually extracted money from unlucky accounts. *see Note 6.*

The team's efforts finally unraveled in October 1994 after five months of activity. The final package of transactions, totaling $2.8 million, ended as an accomplice was arrested in San Francisco while attempting to open a bank account to receive the stolen funds. Citibank managed to cancel or reverse all except $400,000 of the thieves' transactions.

To prevent a repetition of the problems, Citibank installed a counter-based one-time password system for authenticating cash management accounts. Each account manager was issued a token and could not perform transactions without it. This by itself eliminated a major problem with passwords: there was no way someone could induce an account manager to share an account's password without giving up the token as well. In addition, it prevented people with trusted access to cash management messages (like systems operators) from intercepting and reusing an account's password.

Counter-based tokens incorporate an internal counter and use it to generate a fresh password each time its owner needs one. Typically, the owner presses a button on the front of the token; the button increments the counter and the token displays the new password on a built-in display (Figure 9.3). If an attacker intercepts a password and tries to reuse it, the system won't recognize the password as valid (Figure 9.4). Furthermore, the attacker can't guess the next password by examining the sequence: the token com-

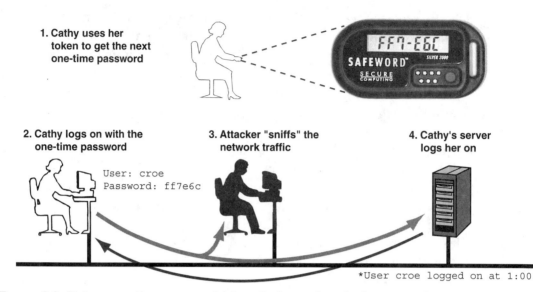

1. Cathy uses her token to get the next one-time password

2. Cathy logs on with the one-time password

3. Attacker "sniffs" the network traffic

4. Cathy's server logs her on

```
User: croe
Password: ff7e6c
```

```
*User croe logged on at 1:00
```

FIGURE 9.3: *Using a one-time password token.* Cathy pushes the button on her password token to display her next one-time password. She types it in to the password dialog. Her server accepts the login. An attacker sniffs the one-time password, but can't use it to log in (see Figure 9.4). The card shown here is a SafeWord Silver 2000 token from Secure Computing Corporation.

putes each new password by encrypting the counter with an internally stored base secret.

SafeWord, a product of Secure Computing Corporation, is a counter-based token. As shown in Figure 9.5, the token increments its internal counter, combines it with the owner's base secret, and generates a one-way hash value from them. The token displays the result in its window. The ActivCard token, a product of PC Dynamics, uses a variant of this technique discussed in the next section.

The exact process for producing the one-way hash depends on the particular product in question. There are a variety of techniques for producing a hash, as noted in Section 8.5. SafeWord, for example, uses 56-bit DES in a MAC construction to produce each one-time password.

The one-time password token generates a correct password as long as both the token and the destination computer have matching copies of the token's internal counter and base secret. Initially, an administrator inserts these values into the token using a special wand that connects through a cluster of seven contacts on the front. The token in Figure 9.3 shows these contacts on the lower right. The

FIGURE 9.4: *An attacker trying to replay a one-time password.* The attacker has sniffed a one-time password and tries to use it to log on as croe. The server accepts the password only once, so the attacker fails.

SafeWord administration software generates the 56-bit base secret randomly and saves the result in the token's account record along with an initial 20-bit counter value.

Besides the initial password values (the base secret and the initial counter value), the token programmer can also configure the token in particular ways. For example, tokens can often display passwords in several different formats that vary the number of digits or the character set used in passwords. The token uses the format selected when it is programmed. More elaborate tokens like the SafeWord Platinum card (Figure 4.3) can store two or more different sets of initial counter values. This allows the card's owner to log in to different systems that use different secrets. The owner uses the keypad on the front of the card to choose among the systems. Some tokens may also be programmed to require a PIN before emitting a one-time password.

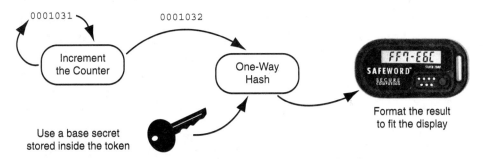

FIGURE 9.5: *Computing a counter-based one-time password.* The owner pushes the button on the token. The token increments the internal counter, combines it with the owner's unique base secret, and computes a one way hash result. The token formats the result and displays the new one-time password.

Counter synchronization is an important design issue for counter-based systems. Ideally, the token's owner should only press the password button (and thus increment the token's counter) when actually logging on to the system. Otherwise, the token's counter increments by one while the corresponding counter in the server remains the same. This can cause a mismatch between the server and the token. To resynchronize, most tokens assume that the person will try to log in again immediately and use the token's next password in sequence. Then the server examines the pair of passwords to verify that they could have been generated by the owner's token.

In short, this strategy uses a double-length password that would be significantly harder for an attacker to guess at random. The Safe-Word server always saves the previous password it received from the token and, if the user tries to log on twice in a row, the server checks to see if the pair of passwords could in fact have been generated by that particular user's token. To do this, the server increments the counter and tests the corresponding password against the first incorrect password, repeating several times and looking for a match. If the server finds a match, it increments the counter again and compares the result against the second password from the token. If the server can match two passwords in a row like that, it authenticates the user and updates the counter to reflect the second of the pair of passwords. According to the vendor, the process is designed to keep the likelihood of successful guesses below one in a million.

see Note 7.

Note that the "one in a million" likelihood yields an average attack space of 19 bits, and the attacks must be performed interactively. Off-line attacks might be performed against the base secret by examining the stream of one-time passwords. Cracking the 56-bit DES key off-line would, of course, involve an average attack space of 54 bits.

The ActivCard token uses a slightly different procedure to resynchronize the counter it uses with a counter on the server. ActivCard passwords incorporate a low-order digit from the counter in each password it generates. If the digit doesn't match the counter on the server's side, the server will try a higher counter value with the same low digit, within a predefined range of values. If the result succeeds, the server accepts the authentication and updates its internal counter. Otherwise, the authentication fails and the counter remains unchanged.   *see Note 8.*

An interesting feature of the counter-based approach is that the system does not behave well if someone makes a copy of a token. If people use both the original token and a copy of it to log on, some attempts will fail and others will cause resynchronization. Although both tokens will work some of the time, the system will not behave correctly. In some cases it may be possible to identify this failure pattern to detect duplicated tokens.

CLOCK-BASED ONE-TIME PASSWORDS

The SecurID token, a product of RSA Security, uses internal clocks instead of counters. SecurID tokens combine an internal clock value with a 64-bit secret key to generate a time-based password each time the user needs one (Figure 9.6). The token reads its internal clock, which reports the number of seconds since the beginning of 1986. Then it computes a one-way hash that combines the clock value with the owner's base secret. The token displays the result, which the owner then uses as the password when logging in.

The server performs essentially the same process by combining its own clock value with a copy of the token's secret key. To account for the time required to transmit the password, as well as clock drift between token and server, the server accepts any password derived from a clock value within an established "time window." In some

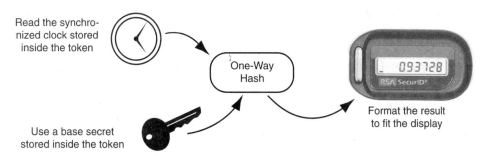

FIGURE 9.6: *Computing a clock-based one-time password.* The owner activates the token. The token reads the internal clock, combines the time with the owner's unique base secret, and computes a one-way hash result. The token formats the result and displays the new one-time password. The token shown on the right is a recent SecurID model sold by RSA Security.

environments, the server's time window has been as short as 30 seconds, though today's network oriented systems typically use a three-minute window.

The technical details of SecurID password generation are proprietary, but they have been leaked to the security community and widely distributed. If we assume that the hash function is computationally secure, the 64-bit key should present attackers with a 63-bit average attack space. As of this writing, the cryptographic community has begun open discussions of the strengths and weaknesses of the SecurID hash function. As yet, no serious weaknesses have been found that would cast doubt on its effectiveness as a one-time password token. Its principal vulnerabilities are shared with all one-time password tokens, as discussed in Section 9.4.   *see Note 9.*

In an ideal world, the clock-based tokens would not have to deal with resynchronization like counter-based tokens. SecurID tokens and servers in modern systems are synchronized with Universal Coordinated Time (UCT). For most purposes, UCT is the same as Greenwich Mean Time (GMT); while there are subtle technical differences, they don't affect tokens. In practice, however, the clocks built into the tokens inevitably drift away from UCT as they age. Although the design could account for this problem by increasing the window size, a larger window size also increases the threat of password interception and replay by an attacker.

Modern SecurID servers incorporate a strategy to adapt to clock drift in individual tokens. First, the server maintains clock drift information for each token and updates the information whenever the token successfully logs in. If the owner does not log in for a long time and the token drifts too far out of sync, the server falls back on a two-password resynchronization strategy similar to those used by counter-based tokens. If the first password falls outside the synchronization window, the SecurID server will reject it so that the owner has to provide a second password. If both passwords reflect the same clock drift factor, then authentication succeeds and the server updates the token's clock drift factor.   *see Note 10.*

An interesting feature of clock-based tokens is that a token's owner could in theory use the same token to log on to several different servers in completely different sites. Each site would need the token's base secret, clock drift information, and the corresponding user name. Then each site could authenticate the token's owner without requiring separate tokens or base secrets. However, such an arrangement makes it easier for an attacker to sniff the password sent to one server and replay it to connect to a different one.

The ActivCard token noted in the previous section combines both a counter and an internal clock. ActivCard provides a much broader range of timer increments than SecurID: a single tick may be as long as one hour. This could provide an unacceptably wide window within which an attacker might capture and replay a password, except that the ActivCard password also incorporates a counter. This yields different passwords within a single clock tick. Each ActivCard one-time password contains eight decimal digits. Six digits represent the actual password and the other two provide resynchronization information. As noted in the previous section, one of the digits contains the low-order digit of the counter. The server also expects to find the low-order digit of the timer as one of the digits. The server uses the digit from the timer to adjust for clock drift.

The ActivCard strategy uses a different resynchronization strategy than that used by SecurID, but it also yields longer passwords with no corresponding improvement in safety. In general, a longer password should reduce the risk of successful guessing or of other attacks. Instead, ActivCard uses the extra two digits to simplify resynchronization on the server side.

9.4 ATTACKS ON ONE-TIME PASSWORDS

Although there are subtle differences between the various one-time password technologies, all face certain major attacks. All are at risk of attacks that divert an authenticated connection, like phone line redirection (Attack A-47 in Section 8.2) and IP address theft (Attack A-49 in Section 8.4). Below, we examine two additional attacks. The first is a man in the middle attack in which an attacker interferes with the victim's authentication process and then replays the one-time password. The second attack is an attack on IP connections that yields a similar result to an IP address theft. Although some observers have occasionally suggested other types of attacks, particularly against SecurID, the other attacks generally involve more sophistication, risk, and effort than the attacks described here.   *see Note 11.*

MAN IN THE MIDDLE ATTACK

In this attack, the attacker eavesdrops on someone who is trying to log on to a server with a one-time password token. When the person sends the one-time password, the attacker intercepts the password, interrupts the communications path between the person and the server, and then uses the password himself to log on. The victim will most likely assume the problem was caused by network errors and is unlikely to suspect that an attack occurred. The person may try   *A-56* to log on again, and the server may accept this attempt if people are allowed to be logged on more than once at a given time. If the server rejects the attempt, the user might still not suspect foul play. Meanwhile, the attacker is successfully masquerading as the legitimate user.

This is a very sophisticated attack. The attacker must have control of the right portions of the network to be able to monitor the victim's traffic and interrupt the communications path to the server when necessary. The attack requires impeccable timing, particularly if the victim uses a clock-based one-time password token.

In this situation, an "asynchronous" challenge response mechanism (Chapter 10) has a security advantage over the "synchronous" tokens discussed in this chapter. A challenge is generally associated   *D-56* with a particular host or connection on the network, since it is supposed to represent the attempt to establish an authenticated session. If the same user attempts to complete the process of logging on from a different host, then the server is going to issue a new challenge. Thus, the attacker can't intercept a response and use it to log on from a different site or connection. Note that this does not resist a more active attack, like IP address theft.

IP HIJACKING

The first known case of the *IP hijacking* attack took place at the same time as the IP spoofing attacks described earlier (Attack A-53 in Section 8.6). The IP hijacking attack relied on special software that, once installed in a system, allowed an attacker to steal an established connection.

The original attack, which took place near Christmas 1994, began with an IP spoofing attack, which was used to transmit "r" commands to the victim's computers. The spoofed commands gave the attacker enough privileges to install software into the victim's operating system—software to perform the IP hijacking attack. IP hijacking became the first widely available, practical example of a connection hijacking attack.

see Note 12.

IP hijacking works by attacking a connection at one of its endpoints: when a victim tries to connect to another host, the attacker steals the connection at the victim's end. The hijacking software is a special software package that gets installed as part of the operating system, and runs with the processor operating in privileged mode. The hijacking software then lets the attacker take over any connection that is currently set up. Ideally for the attacker, the connection should be a Telnet connection to a command shell, or a similar connection set up by an "r" command.

A-57

It is hard to defend against IP hijacking. The attack relies on software that becomes part of the operating system, and this can make it difficult to block, until we detect the presence of the hijacking software. This represents our principal defense: to check the integrity of the host's operating system in order to detect the presence of suspicious software. A well-known package for tracking the integrity of critical computer files is *tripwire*, developed at Purdue.

D-57

see Note 13.

As of this writing, IP hijacking software only exists for Unix. It isn't clear how many systems the existing attack scripts can be used against, or how easily the scripts might be adapted to other systems. So while the attack is available, and in some sense even common, it might not actually be particularly prevalent.

9.5   INCORPORATING A PIN

The problem with tokens in general is that they can be stolen and then used to perform a crime. Most people are very familiar with this in the context of auto theft prevention: "Lock your car and take the keys." An unattended token may represent too much of a temptation, even if outright theft is unlikely.

A-58

The general solution to this problem is the Personal Identification Number, or PIN. Most people are familiar with PINs because they are used with virtually all automated teller machines (ATMs). A PIN is like a reusable password, but it is almost always used as part of a two-factor authentication mechanism: the PIN is "something you

D-58

know" while a password token or ATM card serves as "something you have." Typically, any token that includes a key pad may be configured to require a PIN in order to generate a one-time password.   *see Note 14.*

Although some systems allow longer PINs, many PINs are limited to four decimal digits. This means that determined attackers should be able to guess a PIN by systematically trying every possible value. Sometimes the attacker can apply cultural information to improve the chances of guessing the correct PIN, especially if users are allowed to choose their own PINs. Some systems are also vulnerable   *A-59* to more sophisticated guessing attacks if their PINs are based on special mathematical relationships to the authentication process.   *see Note 15.*

Below, we examine three techniques for implementing PINs: PIN appended to an external password, PIN as an internal password, and PIN as part of the base secret. If our goal is to prevent attackers from guessing the PINs, then the second and third techniques are the most promising. The second technique uses the PIN as a password to grant access to the token. The third technique uses the PIN to generate the base secret and detect guessing at the server.

PIN APPENDED TO AN EXTERNAL PASSWORD

In this approach, we combine the PIN with other information, like the output of a one-time password token, and send them together as an external password to a remote system. This is also called a "soft PIN," since it works with tokens that don't have keypads. When faced with a password prompt and a password token, the user types the password displayed on the token, and then types in the token's PIN. This approach is used by SecurID and other token vendors to provide a PIN with a token that lacks a keypad.

This approach does keep attackers from using any token they might manage to steal, or from applying any PIN they happen to sniff from an authentication. However, there is a risk that an attacker will manage to sniff a particular PIN (or perhaps all PINs used at a site) and then steal the corresponding token. This is a sophisticated attack, since it involves coordinated physical and sniffing attacks. For some sites, this is an acceptable risk to take in exchange for lower-cost tokens that omit the keypad.

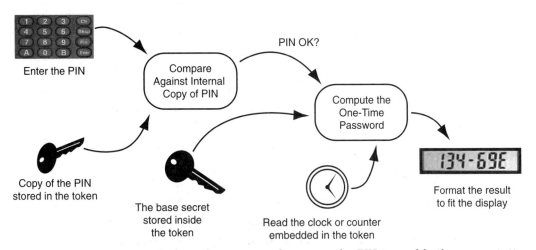

Enter the PIN

Compare Against Internal Copy of PIN

PIN OK?

Compute the One-Time Password

Copy of the PIN stored in the token

The base secret stored inside the token

Read the clock or counter embedded in the token

Format the result to fit the display

FIGURE 9.7: *Using a PIN to unlock a token.* Many tokens use the PIN to enable the computation of the one-time password. The token compares the PIN typed in against an internal copy. If repeated PIN entries are wrong, the token takes steps to resist a PIN guessing attack.

PIN AS AN INTERNAL PASSWORD

Figure 9.7 shows how to use the PIN as a password to grant access to the token. We call the PIN an "internal password" since it is keyed directly into the token and is only seen by the token. Bad PINs either disable the token or introduce delays. If the PIN's value is stored in the token, then the token can detect incorrect PINs and try to foil the guessing attack.

PINs implemented this way can also provide the basis for a duress signal, as described in Section 1.4. For example, many SafeWord tokens will recognize the entered PIN as a duress signal if the last digit entered is one less than in the user's correct PIN. The one-time password generated by the duress PIN then signals the server that the user is under duress. This implementation actually provides a lot of flexibility for implementing the duress signal: the signal could simply change the password generation slightly, or it could select an entirely different base secret to use, or it could even send a fixed response. *see Note 16.*

It is probably safer to handle the duress PIN inside the token than to send it combined with an external password. In the latter case, it's possible that the attackers already know the victim's legitimate PIN value; this would make it risky to use the duress PIN.

An obvious strategy for foiling a guessing attack is to simply disable the token after a fixed number of guesses. Once disabled, the owner needs to take the token to a system administrator for reprogramming. Until then, the token will not allow the owner to log on. SafeWord tokens, for example, may be configured to disable themselves after as few as three bad PINs or as many as fifteen are entered.

D-59

However, this strategy can seriously interfere with the system's usability. Keep in mind that one-time password mechanisms are more complex than traditional reusable password systems, and this increases the likelihood of usage errors. Legitimate users are more likely to encounter problems that are hard to diagnose because of the added complexity. This in turn increases the likelihood that someone will key in an incorrect PIN if he or she is having trouble logging on.

Another strategy to foil a guessing attack is to take longer and longer to report the incorrect PIN to the person each time he types in the wrong PIN. This is reasonably practical with hardware tokens, since the goal is to prevent the attacker from using the token until the legitimate owner can report it missing. The increasing delay reduces the risk of misuse without necessarily disabling the token. If the bad PINs were actually mistakes made by the token's legitimate owner, the increasing delay is a less painful security measure than the alternative of disabling the token. This is particularly true if the token provides authentication to users on travel: it would be extremely difficult to get a token reprogrammed while its owner is traveling.

D-60

These two strategies are well suited for implementation in special-purpose hardware tokens like those shown in Figure 9.1. However, the technique is not as safe if the one-time password token is implemented in software, as described in Section 10.3. If the token is able to verify whether the PIN is correct all by itself without contacting a separate server, then there is enough information embedded in the software token for an attacker to recover the PIN. Then the attacker can analyze the personal credentials embedded in the software token and determine the PIN's value. Security researchers have demonstrated this in practice.

A-60

see Note 17.

A capable software token designer will take steps to resist such an attack, but the steps cannot succeed for long. For example, the software token can store the PIN in a hashed form, and also use the valid PIN value to encode the base secret. But the attacker can quickly mount a systematic attack against the hashed PIN, since most PINs are only a few digits long. For the moment, nobody so far has reported the existence of PIN-cracking programs to perform such an attack. However, it remains a realistic if sophisticated risk against software tokens.

PIN AS PART OF THE BASE SECRET

The third approach to PIN handling is to incorporate the PIN into the base secret. This approach, shown in Figure 9.8, solves the problem faced by software tokens. The token does not store a copy of the PIN at all. In fact, the token does not even store a complete copy of the base secret. Instead, the actual base secret is constructed from a combination of the PIN and the token's partial base secret. If the attacker guesses the PIN incorrectly, he generates the wrong base secret value. The error doesn't appear until he actually tries to log on to the server, at which point the server detects and logs an incorrect one-time password. The attacker can't verify the PIN based on information within the software token, he must try to log on to the service, and that will produce a record of his attempt.

D-61

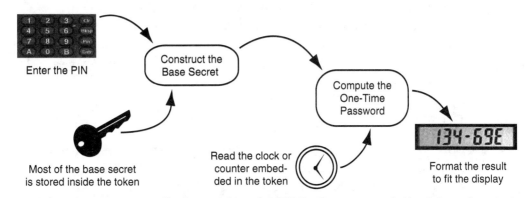

FIGURE 9.8: *Base secret partially derived from the PIN.* In this approach the token does not contain a copy of the PIN in any form and cannot detect incorrect PINs. The token can only generate the correct base secret if the owner provides the correct PIN. If the owner types the wrong PIN, the owner gets an invalid password and cannot log on. This helps the server detect PIN guessing attacks.

A major strength of this last method is that it forces the attacker to go to the server in order to verify his PIN guesses. This opens up his attack to detection, which gives the defenders a chance to identify the attack and resist it. Unfortunately, this is not the only way the attacker can verify a PIN guess. If the attacker can intercept several legitimate one-time passwords from the right software token, he can use those passwords to validate his PIN guesses. Fortunately, this is a relatively sophisticated attack: it requires the attacker to make a copy of the victim's soft token and intercept several uses of that token. Then the attacker needs a program to exhaustively try each possible PIN in conjunction with the software token's credentials to see if they would generate the intercepted passwords. While this is possible in theory, it requires a lot of work on the part of the attacker. Furthermore, each vendor uses a different strategy for generating passwords and for protecting data within their software tokens. A successful attack on one vendor's product would not apply to other vendors' products.

A-61

One can also implement a duress PIN as part of the base secret. In this case, however, the token device itself would not be aware of the fact that a duress PIN was used. The duress PIN would change the cryptographic results, and the server would itself have to perform the extra checking to see if an incorrect password is really a duress signal.

PINs are not passwords: they have never been intended to resist lengthy, systematic attacks. They are intended to be used with special hardware to reduce the risk of token theft. Hardware tokens, or the hardware elements of an ATM, protect the PINs against theft and against systematic attacks. PINs become vulnerable when used in less-protected environments.

9.6 ENROLLING USERS

Enrollment is the process of telling the authentication system about a person the system should be able to authenticate. When tokens are used for authentication, the system must be able to associate tokens with individual people, and associate base secrets with the tokens that carry them. Thus, enrollment involves two separate activities: token programming and user management. In fact, this distinction appears in many products. Most vendors provide a token programming application that generates base secrets, programs them into tokens, and exports a table of new user records for importation into the server authentication software.

Token programming in general involves the following steps:

1. Prompt the operator for the token's serial number and the user name of the owner.

2. Generate a random number to use for the base secret.

3. If the token uses a PIN, generate a random number to use as the PIN.

4. Program the token with this information.

5. Create a database entry containing the user name, token serial number, and the base secret for on-line authentication. The PIN should not appear in this database.

6. If the token uses a PIN, print a separate "PIN report" for each token that identifies the user name, token serial number, and its initial PIN. In high-security applications, PIN reports should be printed on special forms that hide the PIN's value until the form is split and opened.

Once the operator has finished programming a group of tokens, the token programming software will export a database identifying all of the newly programmed tokens. The operator must now import that database into the server. Once the data is installed, the newly programmed tokens can be used.

The token programming software contains the necessary procedures to communicate with the token programming device (Figure 9.9). Each brand of token has its own electrical characteristics, and establishes its own expectations as to how it must be programmed. The token programming software formats the data as needed to program a token and transmits that data to the token programming device.

Although administrators may generally be trustworthy people, there are cases in which the proprietor must address the risk of some administrators' misusing the card programming system. A bank does not want its employees issuing themselves copies of customers' ATM cards, complete with PINs, but such things have indeed happened, as we saw in Section 9.1. A subverted administrator can

A-62

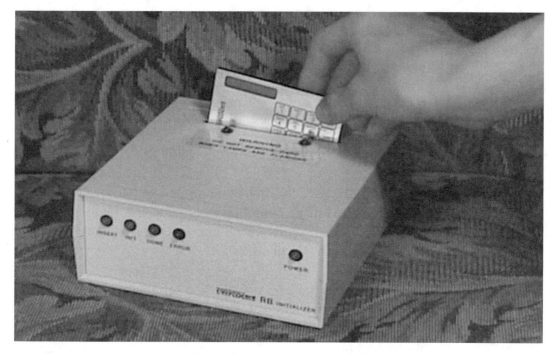

FIGURE 9.9: *Token programming device.* This programming device or "initializer" accepts an authentication token in the slot on top. Internally, the device contains probes that touch a set of contacts on the card. Each card must be programmed individually. The programming process loads a base secret into the token and configures it for any site-specific features, like preferred password formatting. This is an older programming device built by CryptoCard.

cause serious problems in a token-based authentication system. If the administrator has a number of blank tokens at his disposal, he can program them in different ways to circumvent server security. Obviously, he can create bogus new users and assign tokens to them. He might also be able to program blank tokens to mimic existing tokens belonging to authorized users. This could allow the administrator to masquerade as other users.

The solution is to establish two or more separate duties within the card programming activity: require the participation of at least two separate people whenever we add a token to the system. The following list gives examples of activities that the token programming process could keep separate. Sites can implement some of these activities by establishing and staffing the appropriate procedures and responsibilities. Some activities rely on technical features of

D-62

vendors' token programming software. In practice, different vendors' products provide different capabilities for separation of duty, and these capabilities can vary from one release to the next. Here are examples of things that could be separated:

- Assign one person to manage the inventory of unused tokens and another person to perform the programming. Require strict accounting for all tokens used. This makes it harder to create bogus cards without detection.

- Assign one person to program tokens and a separate person to import the list of new users into the site server. This prevents a single person from independently creating a new user.

- Use card programming software that keeps a strict log of every time it programs a token. This is most effective if the token programming software can extract the serial number from each token. The log should be included every time the program exports a list of newly programmed tokens.

- The card programming software should not disclose the base secrets it generates. If the software generates an export file that must move to a different computer, then the base secrets should be encrypted or otherwise hidden. For example, the S/Key password system in Section 10.1 uses one-way hashes.

- The card programming software should protect the programming log from modification. This may involve cryptographic hashes if the log is transferred between computers.

Separation of duty is not the perfect solution. It places a significant burden on the technical features of the authentication system and requires clear understanding by the site's security administrators. Not every site can afford the time, effort, and inconvenience it takes. Sites rarely implement such measures unless they suffer a security incident that is costly enough to justify them. Financial institutions implement very sophisticated procedures to ensure separation of duty when generating PINs, but this happened after many years of costly experience with PIN fraud.

9.7 SUMMARY TABLES

TABLE 9.1: *Attack Summary*

Attack	Security Problem	Prevalence	Attack Description
A-54. Network password sniffing	Masquerade as someone else	Common	Monitor traffic on a network link, intercept any plaintext passwords seen, and exploit them
A-55. Exploit password equivalent	Masquerade as someone else	Common	Intercept a hashed or otherwise encoded password and use in forged network messages where hashed, not typed, passwords are expected
A-56. Interception and replay	Masquerade as someone else	Sophisticated	Intercept a one-time password and replay it while blocking the legitimate user from successfully logging on
A-57. IP hijacking	Masquerade as someone else	Common or Sophisticated	Intercept an established connection and reattach it to a program controlled by the attacker
A-58. Token theft	Masquerade as someone else	Physical	Steal the token belonging to an authorized user
A-59. PIN guessing	Masquerade as someone else	Trivial	Steal a token and manually try every possible value for the token's PIN
A-60. Extract PIN from software token	Masquerade as someone else	Sophisticated	Copy the victim's software token, analyze its contents to identify the encoded PIN, do brute force attack to determine the PIN value, then use it with the software token

TABLE 9.1: *Attack Summary (Continued)*

Attack	Security Problem	Prevalence	Attack Description
A-61. Test PIN against intercepted passwords	Masquerade as someone else	Sophisticated	Intercept several of the victim's one-time passwords, copy the victim's software token, extract the partial base secret encoded with the PIN, do brute force analysis to find a PIN that matches the generated passwords, then use the PIN
A-62. Subverted token administrator	Masquerade as someone else	Trivial	Trusted person who programs tokens also programs extra tokens used for penetrating legitimate accounts

TABLE 9.2: *Defense Summary*

Defense	Foils Attacks	Description
D-54. Encoded password	A-54. Network password sniffing	Encrypt or hash a password when it must traverse a public or other untrustworthy network
D-55. One-time password token	A-54. Network password sniffing A-55. Exploit password equivalent A-61. Test PIN against intercepted passwords	Generates a new password for each attempt to log on. An attacker cannot log on by trying to intercept and reuse a password, since passwords only work once
D-56. Challenge-response one-time passwords	A-56. Interception and replay	Use challenge-response one-time passwords instead of synchronous one-time passwords
D-57. Check the host OS integrity	A-57. IP hijacking	Check the software components of the host OS to see if they have been modified to insert subverted software

TABLE 9.2: *Defense Summary (Continued)*

Defense	Foils Attacks	Description
D-58. PINs on tokens	A-58. Token theft	Require the owner to enter a PIN before the token will generate a valid one-time password
D-59. Lock-up after incorrect PINs entered	A-59. PIN guessing	Disable the token after the user enters too many incorrect PINs, so that attackers can't find the PIN through exhaustive trial and error
D-60. Increasing delay for incorrect PINs	A-59. PIN guessing	If the wrong PIN is entered, delay before accepting another attempt. Increase the length of delay with each incorrect PIN entered.
D-61. PIN forms part of the token's base secret	A-59. PIN guessing A-60. Extract PIN from software token	Incorporate the PIN into the base secret so that the token will not contain the correct base secret unless the correct PIN is entered. Do not detect the wrong PIN at the token.
D-62. Separation of duty in token programming procedure	A-62. Subverted token administrator	Require the participation of two or more people in the process of programming and enabling tokens for authentication

CHAPTER 10

CHALLENGE RESPONSE PASSWORDS

PRESIDENT SKROOB: 1-2-3-4-5? That's amazing! I've got the same combination on my luggage!

— Mel Brooks et al., *Spaceballs*

IN THIS CHAPTER

This chapter examines a more general mechanism for one-time password authentication in which the person must respond to a mathematical challenge by the authentication mechanism. The response is mechanized in various ways.

- Evolution of challenge response authentication
- Challenge response with X9.9 and S/Key
- Microsoft LAN Manager authentication
- Microsoft Windows NT LAN Manager authentication

10.1 CHALLENGE RESPONSE

In 1979, the "personal computer revolution" was in full swing, with new products vying for hobbyists' attention. Although many computers appealed to hardware hackers and arrived in kit form, a newer breed appealed to software hackers. These computers, like the Apple II and the TRS-80, arrived prebuilt and ready to plug in, with some extremely simple but usable software development tools. The TRS-80, built by Tandy and sold through its Radio Shack stores (hence the "TRS"), caught the attention of engineer Bob Bosen.

In his spare time, Bosen wrote a game for the TRS-80 called *80 Space Raiders*, and advertised it for sale in hobbyist magazines. At that time, many hobbyists considered software piracy a routine activity, or even a moral imperative, so Bosen embedded a copy protection mechanism in his game. As it was, the income from game sales had barely paid its advertising bills, even though the game had received positive reviews and satisfied reactions from customers.   *see Note 1.*

Bosen's copy protection consisted of a *challenge response* mechanism. When someone started the game running, it displayed a randomly selected number, called the *challenge.* The game's owner had to look for that number in a table supplied with the game, and type in the corresponding *response.* The game would check the response to verify that it went along with that particular challenge. Thus, one needed a copy of the table in order to play the game. Bosen also took steps to make the table hard to copy: he printed it on red paper and attached to the side of the curved tube that served as the "box" for 80 Space Raiders.

The game wasn't a real commercial success, but several people suggested that a variant of the copy protection scheme could authenticate people to timesharing systems and mainframes. Bosen took the idea and started Enigma Logic, Inc., to produce SafeWord challenge response authentication tokens. Bosen also filed for patents on challenge response tokens in 1982–83. A British patent was issued in 1986, but the U.S. patent application encountered lengthy, unexplained delays and was never issued.

Challenge response authentication still works essentially the same as 80 Space Raiders copy protection: the system displays a number, called a *challenge* or *nonce,* and the person must provide the corresponding response. These days, however, most systems use a one-way function to compute the response instead of embedding the responses in a printed table. People often generate responses to authentication challenges by computing the one-way function on a specially built calculator: the password token. There are several commercial tokens that support challenge response authentication, including SafeWord, WatchWord, ActivCard, and CryptoCard.

People sometimes refer to tokens that use challenge response as *asynchronous* tokens, when compared to the *synchronous* tokens described in Chapter 9. We could say that synchronous tokens are also challenge response tokens, except that the challenge is predictable and is generated automatically by the token and the server. What makes them synchronous is that the server and token must remain synchronized with respect to the challenges they generate.

More recently, many people use client software on their workstations to automatically handle challenge response authentication. Many vendors provide software versions of their authentication tokens, and challenge response is also used by Microsoft for its network server authentication, as described later in this chapter.

Figure 10.1 illustrates a typical challenge response system. In the example, Cathy needs to log on to a server using a challenge response system. She starts by telling the system her user name ("croe"). The server generates a nonce and sends it to Cathy as a challenge ("493076"). Cathy types the challenge into her one-time password token, and the token generates the correct password to send back in response ("319274"). The server looks up Cathy's base secret and uses it to compute the response that should match the challenge. If the server's computed result matches Cathy's response, then it lets Cathy log on.

A major advantage of the challenge response mechanism is that the servers do not need to maintain synchronization with people's tokens. By generating a random challenge each time, the server ensures that previously valid passwords are unlikely to be valid for the next login. No timers or counters are needed. On the other hand, users must key in additional numbers when using the challenge response token.

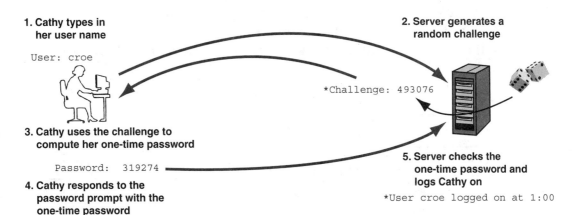

FIGURE 10.1: *Generating a challenge response password.* The server sends a random number to Cathy. She uses her one-time password token to compute the correct response to that challenge. The correct response depends on the value of her base secret. If she has the right base secret, her response will match the response expected by the server. Then the server will log her on.

CHALLENGE RESPONSE AND X9.9

Unlike clock- and counter-based systems, challenge response is an "open standard" authentication mechanism. This makes it easier for the security community to examine these products and make more accurate judgments regarding the security they provide. Furthermore, open standards provide a mechanism by which products from different vendors can interoperate.

The U.S. government and the American Bankers Association have adopted a consistent standard for data authentication called FIPS 113 and X9.9, respectively. These standards used DES to serve the purpose of a one-way hash function. Figure 10.2 illustrates a form of this authentication in which the one-time password response "authenticates" the random challenge. Most challenge response tokens, including SafeWord, ActivCard, CryptoCard, and Watch-Word, provide at least one mode that is X9.9 compatible.   *see Note 2.*

The password generation process shown in Figure 10.2 is very similar to the synchronous processes described in Section 9.3. Internally, challenge response tokens operate in the same general manner as clock- or counter-based tokens. Both use the base secret plus some varying data to generate the one-time password. Instead of using the clock or counter as the varying data, the challenge response token uses the challenge. X9.9 works as shown in the figure: the Data Encryption Standard (DES) takes the challenge as input and encrypts it using the base secret as the key. The challenge is padded with zeroes to make up the full 64-bit block of data that DES requires. Most vendors truncate the response to fit the

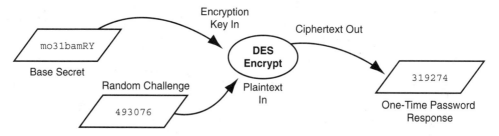

FIGURE 10.2: *Challenge response authentication.* The token stores the base secret internally. The owner types in the challenge. The token computes the one-time password response by encrypting the challenge using the base secret as the encryption key. The server uses the same process to verify the response.

TABLE 10.1: *Password Tokens and Average Attack Spaces*

Example	Style of Attack	Average Attack Space
Biometric with a 1% FAR (1 in 100)	Interactive	6 bits
Four-digit PIN	Interactive	13 bits
Biometric with a FAR of 1 in 100,000	Interactive	16 bits
ANSI X9.9 token with six-digit response	Interactive	19 bits
One-time password token	Interactive	19 bits
Eight-character personal password	Off-line	22.7 bits
ANSI X9.9 token using 56-bit DES	Off-line	54 bits
SecurID one-time password token	Off-line	63 bits

hardware token's display or to conform with a site-specific choice of the length of responses.

Table 10.1 compares the average attack space of ANSI X9.9 challenge response authentication with other authentication methods discussed in earlier chapters. The "interactive" attacks are those that must directly interact with an authentication mechanism; this usually slows the attack down and provides a way to detect the attack. The "off-line" attacks are computer-driven trial-and-error attacks that can't be detected by the targets of the attack.

A security advantage of challenge response passwords is that each password is associated with a particular attempt by the owner to log on. If the attempt fails for any reason (for example, the connection is lost), then the authentication process starts over with a new challenge. This mitigates the risk of an attacker's intercepting and reusing a one-time password (Attack A-56 in Section 9.4).

S/KEY AUTHENTICATION

S/Key is a one-time password system developed at Bellcore in the early 1990s as a technique for logging on to Unix systems. The technical concept was first proposed by Leslie Lamport and published in 1981. Unlike other challenge response techniques, Lamport's approach does not maintain a database of secret keys, so attackers cannot compromise the system by stealing the database of base secrets.   *see Note 3.*

Instead, Lamport's scheme uses a sequence of one-way hash values that are computed from a memorized password (Figure 10.3). As with more traditional Unix passwords, the system takes advantage of the fact that it's easy to compute the hash of a password, but impractical to derive a password from its hash. Lamport's scheme uses a sequence of hashes, each computed from the previous one in the sequence. The server stores the last hash in the sequence. To log on, Cathy provides the next-to-last hash in the sequence as a one-time password. The server takes her one-time password, hashes it, and compares it to the stored hash. Both should match. Then, the server replaces the hash in Cathy's password entry (the *fourth* hash) with the password she just provided (the *third* hash). The next time Cathy logs on, she provides her *second* hash and the server follows the same process.

S/Key is a practical implementation of Lamport's scheme. Strictly speaking, the technique uses synchronous one-time passwords rather than challenge response passwords. After all, the user always needs to provide the hash-before-last as the one-time password. This requires the user to keep a perfect count of which passwords have been used, and in practice, users aren't good at that sort of bookkeeping. Instead, S/Key servers generally prompt the user with the sequence number of the next hash expected. This makes S/Key act like a challenge response system, though the information is really optional and is only provided for the user's convenience.

The S/Key hash also incorporates a random value called a *seed*, which is combined with the base secret when generating the hashes. The seed prevents S/Key from generating the same hash sequence if a user tries to reuse a base secret or uses the same one on different computers. Although Figure 10.3 shows only the hash stored in the password file entry, S/Key will also store the seed value and the hash sequence number. When an S/Key server issues a "challenge" containing the user's current sequence number, it will also display the seed used to generate the user's hashes.

S/Key users generally use software tokens to generate a one-time password. To use the software token, Cathy (the user in Figure 10.3) types in her base secret (her "password"), the sequence number, and the seed. The token applies the hash iteratively to generate the correct value in the sequence, and then displays the resulting hash. Cathy then copies the hash value into the waiting password prompt. Software tokens exist for Unix, Microsoft, and Macintosh. Where possible, the token software tries to detect an S/Key challenge so that it can automatically compute the correct one-time password. Where possible, the token software supports cut and paste to avoid typing errors when copying the challenge or the response. There is also a utility program that will print out hashes on paper for users that can't run a software token. Although it is technically possible to build S/Key hardware tokens, there don't appear to be any in commercial production.

see Note 4.

As long as the server stores only the last hash in the sequence, and the user provides the next-to-last hash as a password, the attacker cannot easily retrieve a valid password. An attacker can't extract a hash from the password file and invert the computation in order to retrieve the previous hash in the sequence, or the base secret for that matter.

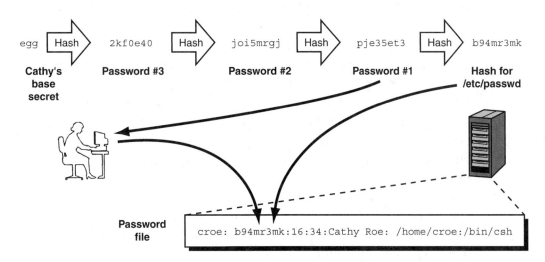

FIGURE 10.3: *Lamport's one-time password scheme, used by S/Key.* Cathy computes a sequence of passwords so that she can log on three times. She hashes her memorized base secret *four* times and stores the final hash in her password file entry. When she logs in next, she invokes the hash function *three* times to generate the right one-time password. The server verifies her password by hashing it (the fourth time) and matching the result with her password file entry. If they match, the latest password replaces the existing hash value in Cathy's password file entry, so that the process works the same when Password #2 is used.

10.2 CHALLENGE RESPONSE ISSUES

This section examines two important concerns with respect to challenge response. First, there is the issue of user interaction, particularly for conventional challenge response tokens. Second, the traditional ANSI X9.9 standard is vulnerable to trial-and-error attack, since it is based on the DES algorithm.

USER INTERACTION

Challenge response works only with software and protocols that provide a way to transmit the challenge as part of the authentication process. Another problem is that it requires even more typing than other authentication methods. It is difficult to build software clients to simplify the typing problem.

Challenge response violates a very common assumption about authentication: that a server can always authenticate someone by collecting a user name and a password at the same time. This interferes with challenge response authentication because it provides no way to give the challenge. This is a problem with several important systems widely used today. For example, the Web page authentication extensions within the Hypertext Transfer Protocol (HTTP) bundle all of the authentication data in the same message that identifies the page being accessed. So there is no opportunity for the server to provide a random challenge to the person being authenticated.

If the software system is able to display the challenge to the user somehow, there is also the problem of getting that challenge into the challenge response computation. First, the person has to locate the challenge within some window on today's ever more cluttered display screens. Then the person has to type the challenge correctly. This is where the system can start to break down. The average person has enough trouble typing a password correctly; a hardware challenge response token may require the transcription of 15 to 20 digits, or more, including a PIN. This provides people with numerous opportunities to make a trivial typing mistake. Since password interfaces rarely echo the data typed, even when handling one-time passwords, the typing error won't be evident until the server rejects the attempt. Logging on becomes a very difficult process.

This is a situation in which software-based authentication clients provide an important benefit. Most users of Microsoft network authentication don't even know that challenge response authentication is taking place, since the underlying software handles it transparently.

Software versions of hardware tokens (the "soft" tokens described in Section 10.3) also provide usability benefits. For example, the workstation operator can often use window cut-and-paste operations to move the challenge and response between the token's window and the window being used to log on. This reduces the risk of typing errors, though less-sophisticated computer users are not as comfortable with this type of window manipulation.

KNOWN CIPHERTEXT ATTACK ON ANSI X9.9

One-time passwords generated with the X9.9 standard are vulnerable to attack by trial-and-error search. If an attacker collects several challenges and corresponding responses from a single X9.9 user, the attacker can try to deduce the user's base secret through a trial-and-error search of all possible DES keys. This is because X9.9 uses DES with the traditional 56-bit keys. As described in Section 5.3, DES has succumbed to several trial-and-error cracking demonstrations. The X9 committee has issued a report regarding this vulnerability.

A-63

see Note 5.

The only defense against the weakness in X9.9 is to migrate to a stronger mechanism. This is the recommendation of the X9 committee. Their analysis identifies nine existing standards that could be used to replace X9.9 functionality. Some alternatives are variants of existing techniques like DES encryption and one-way hashes but use longer secret keys. Another alternative would be to substitute AES for DES, to benefit from its higher performance and longer keys. Other alternatives rely on public key authentication techniques, like digital signatures, which are discussed in Chapter 13.

D-63

10.3 PASSWORD TOKEN DEPLOYMENT

This section examines three issues related to password token deployment. First, it looks at the use of "soft" tokens, that is, software implementations of the mechanisms that were traditionally implemented in hardware tokens. Next, it looks at the use of one-time passwords with multiple authentication servers. Finally, it briefly reviews the issue of using proprietary algorithms in security products.

SOFT TOKENS

Soft tokens are alternatives to hardware tokens that provide one-time passwords. Such tokens appear most often as software implementations of hardware tokens. In some cases, vendors also provide "codebooks" for one-time passwords. These approaches are discussed below.

Many existing hardware tokens, including both SafeWord and SecurID, are available as software tokens. The software version installs on the owner's remote computer, often a home computer or a laptop. Major vendors also provide palmtop versions of their software tokens to run on palmtop organizers like the Palm. The site generates the initial base secret, the same as for hardware tokens, but delivers them to individual users as data files. Once the owner installs the files correctly, the software token will work the same as a hardware token as far as logging on is concerned: the owner invokes the token to generate a one-time password, and then provides that password while logging on.

The principal benefit of software tokens is cost. While a hardware token system may cost as much as $100 per user to implement, including tokens, a software token system may cost only a third or a fourth as much.

Software tokens are much more vulnerable to theft than hardware tokens. Since the entire software token, including the base secret, is stored on a conventional personal computer, an attacker can easily make a copy of it. Unlike hardware tokens, the victim can still use the token even if a copy has been stolen. This is true of palmtop tokens, too, because desktop synchronization procedures like the Palm's "Hot Sync" automatically make back-up copies of the software token's files. Attempts to prevent copying of software token data files can cause serious reliability problems that often outweigh the intended security improvements.

PINs are an essential part of any software token implementation. They provide the principal, and often the only, protection against token theft. As described in Section 9.5, the software token should use the PIN as part of the base secret. The software token must not contain any information that can verify the PIN's value by itself. When an attacker tries to generate a one-time password with the software token, he should have no way of verifying the PIN or the password except by using the password to log on to the server.

Another type of soft token is the *codebook*, a paper listing of one-time passwords to use. Bob Bosen used this approach to implement the copy protection scheme that led to SafeWord. Codebooks may list passwords in their sequence of use, but more often they are used with a challenge response procedure. Typically, the authentication system will generate a separate codebook for each user that needs one. The codebook will be marked with the user name and have a range of validity dates to reduce the possible damage caused by one falling into the wrong hands.

A significant shortcoming of many soft tokens is that they make it possible for people to share their access permissions with other people by sharing the soft token's base secret. For example, if John has just been hired and he needs to use the home office system on his trip next week, someone else in the department (Cathy, for example) could share her soft token with him. By doing this, Cathy delegates her capabilities on the system to John. The system will associate all of John's actions with Cathy, even though John performed them. This might not be a serious problem in some environments, but the results can be expensive, as shown in the Citibank story that opened Section 9.3. Soft tokens are a good choice if the principal threat is password sniffing. They are not a good choice if the site needs to prevent delegation by individual users.

HANDLING MULTIPLE SERVERS

Today, most people don't complain about having to memorize a single password to use their computer: they complain about having to memorize a handful or two. If the computers in question use token-based one-time passwords, then password management needs extra planning. Tokens are expensive, and their proliferation is simply going to increase the number that get lost. The practical strategy is to allow people to use a single token to authenticate to any of their servers.

There are essentially three strategies. The first is to share the token's base secret among multiple sites. The second is to build slightly more complex tokens that can handle multiple base secrets. The third is to use indirect authentication through an authentication server. Consider the problem of Cathy, for example, who needs to talk to six different servers, each doing direct authentication.

While Cathy can do this simply by sharing her base secret, the results can be complicated and risky. In theory, she simply needs to share her base secret with the proprietors of those six different servers so that they can install the base secret in her password entry. If, however, she is using a synchronous token, then she could run into synchronization problems or open herself to a replay attack, or both. Separate servers will have to keep their own synchronization data for Cathy's token, and try to keep that information in sync. However, if Cathy ever has to resynchronize with one server (that is, send it a sequential pair of one-time passwords), then an attacker could sniff those and use them to log on to a different server. This is because the other server would treat the pair of passwords as a valid attempt to resynchronize the token.

Even if Cathy doesn't use a synchronous token, history has shown that secret sharing is a bad security strategy. It was a popular strategy in the encryption world for centuries but has fallen out of favor in the modern world of computer communications. If Cathy shares her secret with all those servers, then she faces several practical, security-oriented problems. First, there is the problem of transitive trust (see Attack A-40 in Section 6.5). Once she gives her base secret to an administrator, she has no way of ensuring that the administrator won't share it with someone else. This was probably the security flaw leading to the Citibank thefts discussed earlier.

An alternative to base secret sharing is to use tokens that store multiple base secrets. Such tokens are available from most major manufacturers, though they tend to be more expensive. To log on, Cathy tells her token which server she needs to use. Most tokens assign different numeric codes to different servers, and Cathy uses the appropriate code to choose the right base secret for a given server. Some tokens provide simple textual tags to choose from. In any case, it becomes the responsibility of individual server administrators to correctly program Cathy's token so that it includes a base secret known to their server. If the base secrets at Server A become compromised, the risks are somewhat contained. Cathy can still log on to other servers safely even if someone actually publishes Server A's base secrets, since Cathy's token uses different base secrets for the other servers. Cathy can add, delete, or otherwise update her base secrets for any of the servers without affecting her ability to authenticate to the others.

The third alternative is to use indirect authentication, so that the server Cathy contacts will in turn contact an authentication server to verify her one-time password. Again, most major manufacturers of one-time password tokens provide authentication servers. If all of Cathy's servers are part of a single site or organization, then an indirect authentication design provides the simplest solution. Chapter 11 talks about indirect authentication in more detail.

PROPRIETARY IMPLEMENTATIONS

Most commercial authentication token vendors sell products that contain unpublished, proprietary mechanisms to some degree. Many do not publish the low-level details of how their tokens perform their computations or how their servers handle resynchronization. Some vendors identify particular algorithms used (usually DES) but don't always explain exactly how DES is used or how keys are generated.

Today, many information security experts argue that the best products are those whose details are publicly available and have been subjected to scrutiny by the community at large. Some experts believe that customers take an unnecessary risk when they purchase a product whose details are proprietary. At the very least, public scrutiny by a diverse community of observers increases the likelihood that serious flaws will be caught, hopefully before any customers suffer damage. Public scrutiny increases the confidence customers can have in new security products.   *see Note 6.*

Public scrutiny also has its drawbacks. There is the possibility that a flaw will be found and exploited before the vendor or other members of the community will find and fix it. In addition, we must recognize that secrecy does play a role in enhancing security: if attackers don't know the technical details of a system, then they have a much harder time attacking it.

Moreover, many vendors have thrived in the password token market without revealing various internal details of their products. There are two likely reasons: longevity and business model. The major token vendors have been in business since the 1980s and have established the reputation of their products. The existing base of satisfied customers provides new customers with the confidence they need to buy the products. In addition, many authentication vendors seek to make money on both hardware tokens and on server software. Both represent an installed base for existing customers that produces sales for the incumbent vendor. By keeping certain product details secret, the vendor prevents third parties from either selling compatible tokens to existing customers or selling replacements for the authentication server.

10.4 EVOLVING WINDOWS AUTHENTICATION

Microsoft's desktop authentication started with typical lock-screen techniques and, with the introduction of LAN Manager (often called LANMAN), embraced challenge response for authenticating network services. As the 1990s progressed, Microsoft developers took an evolutionary approach to authentication so that new products would be able to work with existing, installed software. Windows NT 4.0 brought a capability for indirect authentication to domain controllers (Chapter 11), which uses the acronym "NTLM" for "NT LAN Manager." Windows 2000 has incorporated the Kerberos protocol (Chapter 12). Although the LANMAN and NTLM mechanisms are being replaced by Kerberos, it is still essential to understand the older protocols since they are often used with older, installed software.

see Note 7.

For the most part, Microsoft's products use network-based authentication as a way to control access to network resources. Users on workstations manipulate the data on their workstations, but the final result is often printed on a network printer or stored on a network server. Unlike conventional passwords, or even token-based challenge response, Microsoft's network authentication involves a relatively complicated protocol that is embedded in the desktop client software. The protocol finds its way into file and printer services by transmitting authentication data in Server Message Block (SMB) protocol messages that provide such services across the local network.

Microsoft's LAN and NT password technology incorporated two important features. First, all password databases consisted of hashed passwords. Second, all authentication used challenge response techniques to thwart password sniffing. These features, combined with the evolution from LANMAN to NTLM, yielded a relatively complicated password environment. We look at Windows challenge response in Sections 10.5 and 10.6.

Windows systems store password hashes in a system file and, where possible, provide some degree of protection against attackers stealing the password file. Modern Windows systems include a special storage area called the *Registry*. The Security Accounts Manager (SAM) database in the Registry maintains entries for all authorized users, and stores their hashed passwords as well. Windows NT enforces user-based access restrictions on Registry file entries, and the SAM entry is heavily restricted. While this does not prevent all attempts to extract the Windows password file, it increases the difficulty of such an attack.

Windows authentication has proven to be vulnerable to two types of attacks: off-line password crackers that attack the SAM database, and crackers that work on intercepted challenge response pairs. Basic SAM attacks evolved as a result of work by the Samba Project, which produced a public domain package for sharing files between Unix servers and NT clients. The Unix server needed to extract copies of users' NT password hashes in order to synchronize passwords. Attackers also used the tool, and variants of it like *pwdump*, to extract hashes to perform trial-and-error guessing attacks on them. *see Note 8.*

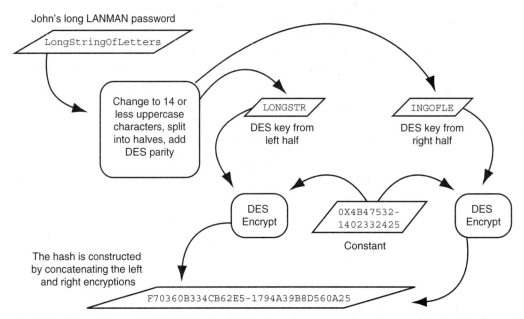

FIGURE 10.4: *Generating a LANMAN hash.* John's typed password is changed to be 14 characters long and any lowercase characters are changed to uppercase. The result is broken into two 56-bit chunks, and each is used to encrypt a constant. The two 64-bit results are combined to produce the hash.

LANMAN HASHING

Figure 10.4 illustrates how the LANMAN hash function transforms a lengthy password belonging to John Doe. First, the function changes the password into a 14-character string, adding or removing characters as needed. Next, it converts all the characters to uppercase. This is a good move from a usability standpoint, since it allows John to make mistakes with the shift key and the system will still recognize his password. However, it also reduces the password's entropy.

Then the function splits the result into two seven-byte chunks, and uses each chunk as a 56-bit key for DES encryption. Each key separately encrypts a 64-bit constant. Unix uses DES in essentially the same way (Figure 2.5 in Section 2.3), but LANMAN omits the "salt." The encrypted results are concatenated into a single string to produce the final hash result.   *see Note 9.*

When creating or changing John's password, the system computes the hash and saves it in the SAM database. When checking a password used for a local logon, the system hashes the password John types in and compares the hashed result with the hash value in the SAM database.

ATTACKING THE LANMAN HASH

Although the LANMAN hash may look complicated to the untrained eye, it carries two critical weaknesses. First, the procedure simplifies a trial-and-error password search by encrypting the password in two completely independent seven-character chunks. Second, the procedure limits characters to a single case, which reduces the password's entropy. Both of these problems reduce the average attack space of a hashed LANMAN password and make it practical to attack.

see Note 10.

To appreciate the first problem, let's look at the average attack space we should achieve if we have 14-character alphabetic passwords. Using the shortcut computation we saw in Section 2.7, we compute the password space like this:

$26^{14} \approx 10^{19}$,

which yields an average attack space of 65 bits.

Unfortunately, LANMAN's arrangement of seven-character chunks allows attackers to search for the password piecemeal instead of having to try all permutations of every character. Figure 10.4 illustrates the problem. Note how the procedure splits the password into the separate pieces "LONGSTR" and "INGOFLE" and encrypts them separately. The attacker can crack the password hash by looking for each seven-byte chunk separately. In other words, the attacker recovers a 14-letter password by testing this many different possibilities:

A-64

$26^7 + 26^7$,

or $2 \times 26^7 \approx 10^{10}$,

which yields an average attack space of only 32 bits.

The problem of password chunks is not new. A celebrated example occurred on the TENEX timesharing system in the 1970s. The

TENEX password checking program maintained a table of plaintext passwords and would check the passwords a character at a time. As soon as Tenex encountered a character in the password that didn't match, it returned a failure without checking the rest of the characters. A clever person realized that the Tenex memory management system would send a signal to his program if the password checking program stepped past the end of his program's available memory. He then used this fact to construct a password cracking program that treated each character as a chunk, and induced Tenex to tell his program whether a particular chunk matched or not.   *see Note 11.*

We solve this problem by making sure we handle the entire password as a single chunk, instead of handling it in two or more pieces. In Tenex, the system programmers solved the problem by having the password checking program copy the password into system memory before checking it. Windows NT solved the LANMAN problem by using a one-way hash algorithm to combine the entire 14-character password in a single cryptographic operation, as is described in Section 10.6.

The second LANMAN problem is that attackers don't need to try all the permutations of upper- and lowercase letters in a password; they can limit the search to uppercase letters and still match the password. Users can choose passwords with a mixture of upper- and lowercase letters, but the LANMAN hashing procedure eliminates the difference when generating the hash value. If attackers had to search both upper- and lowercase characters to crack a LANMAN hash, then the average attack space increases from 32 bits to 39 bits, which increases the attackers' effort by over a hundredfold.

When we combine the shortcomings of LANMAN passwords, we find a straightforward procedure for cracking them. We start by attacking the second half of the hash value. In many sites, most people's passwords will be shorter than 14 characters (most will be *a lot* shorter). If the password is seven characters or less, then the second half of the hash will match the hash value for all nulls. If the password is eight to ten characters long, the second hash will contain only one to three characters, and pose a very simple cracking job. In some cases, the final characters suffixing the password may yield a hint as to the password's first seven characters. For example, the letters "abra" might be the suffix of the password "abracadabra."

A more sophisticated attack might search a dictionary for words matching the suffix and then try just those words.

The second half of the hash is of course the easy part. But the first half will probably fall to some other well-known attack. At worst, a dedicated computer could work through all of the possible passwords and eventually crack it. Although this might not be practical for a single personal computer, a motivated attacker can apply several computers to the task to solve the problem more rapidly.

The problem with LANMAN passwords is tied to the construction of the hash procedure. A better design would provide significantly better security while incurring the same amount of processing overhead. The good news, however, is that at least LANMAN provides some measure of protection to its passwords. For many sites, poor protection is better than none at all, as long as they keep in mind the risks they face.

PLAINTEXT PASSWORDS ON WINDOWS

LANMAN did not always use challenge response passwords, and other LAN products persist that use plaintext passwords. This is particularly important when interoperating with other products. For example, some versions of the Samba package for hosting Windows-compatible network services on Unix used plaintext passwords. Windows products, including NT, provide the necessary hooks to allow a certain degree of automation for logging on to services that require plaintext passwords. Administrators may set a special configuration flag in the Windows Registry to allow the use of plaintext passwords. NT makes it difficult to use plaintext passwords so that administrators are alert to the potential risk of password sniffing.

The support of plaintext passwords does cause a potential problem called the *downgrade attack*. In this attack, the attacker tricks a client into believing that it should provide plaintext authentication to a server. The client responds by automatically providing the password in plaintext instead of hashing the password and using the challenge response protocol.

A-65

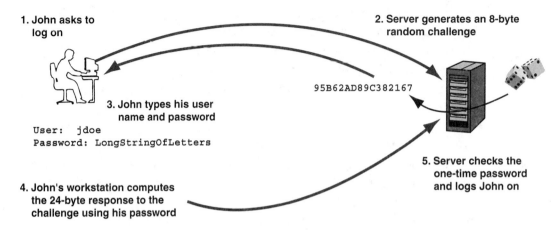

1. John asks to log on

3. John types his user name and password

```
User:     jdoe
Password: LongStringOfLetters
```

4. John's workstation computes the 24-byte response to the challenge using his password

2. Server generates an 8-byte random challenge

95B62AD89C382167

5. Server checks the one-time password and logs John on

FIGURE 10.5: *Windows challenge response authentication.* The challenge response protocol is built directly into the logon software for Windows LANMAN and NT. To log on, John simply types in his user name and secret password. The workstation automatically intercepts the challenge from the server, computes the response, and sends it back without user intervention.

10.5 WINDOWS CHALLENGE RESPONSE

Unlike token-based challenge response, the Windows logon protocol automatically intercepts the challenge and generates the response automatically based on the owner's password. Figure 10.5 illustrates the procedure. When John asks to log on to a server, the server replies with a randomly generated eight-byte nonce. If it hasn't done so already, John's workstation then prompts John for his user name and password. Upon receiving the password, the workstation hashes it so that it does not need to store the plaintext password. The workstation will generally keep a copy of the password hash so that John won't have to type it in again before he logs

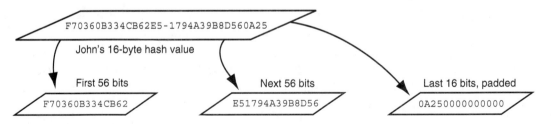

F70360B334CB62E5-1794A39B8D560A25

John's 16-byte hash value

First 56 bits

F70360B334CB62

Next 56 bits

E51794A39B8D56

Last 16 bits, padded

0A250000000000

FIGURE 10.6: *Keys for a Windows response to a challenge.* The user's hash value is broken into three 56-bit keys, padded with nulls. These are used individually to encrypt the challenge

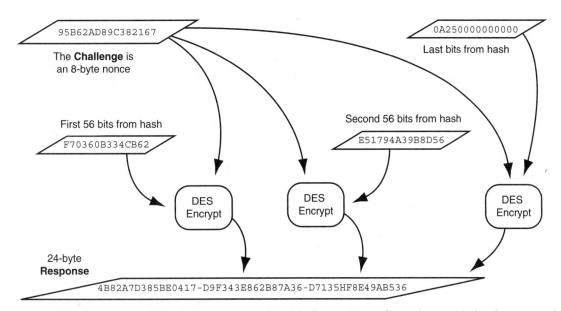

FIGURE 10.7: *Generating a Windows response to a challenge.* Parts from the user's hash are used as DES keys, and the nonce is encrypted once with each of the keys. The response consists of the nonce encrypted with each key.

off. Finally, the workstation computes the response by applying DES encryption to the nonce three times. *see Note 12.*

Figures 10.6 and 10.7 illustrate how Windows software computes the response for an authentication challenge. LANMAN introduced this procedure and NTLM uses a variant of it. First, the procedure takes the user's 128-bit hash value and produces three 56-bit pieces (Figure 10.6). Then the procedure encrypts the nonce three times, using each piece of the hash as a DES key. The procedure combines results of the three encryptions into the 24-byte response.

ATTACKING WINDOWS CHALLENGE RESPONSE

There are essentially two approaches to attacking the Windows challenge response procedure. First, an attacker can search for a password that matches a challenge response pair. Second, the attacker can use a copy of someone's hashed password to masquerade as that person. Both attacks are based on theoretical properties of the challenge response protocol and, as of this writing, are not in any set of tools that attackers are known to use.

The first attack combines the classic sniffer attack with an off-line dictionary attack. Actually, the sniffer attack is slightly more complicated because the attacker must intercept both the server's challenge and the client's response. If the attacker intercepts several challenges and responses, each must be correctly paired up, and each pair must be associated with the user that generated the response. The attacker takes a set of challenge response pairs associated with a particular user and performs a password search attack. For example, the attacker could use a dictionary to generate candidate passwords, generate the hash for each password, compute the appropriate response, and match it against the intercepted response.

The second attack simply exploits a password hash that was stolen from a SAM database. As shown in Figure 10.7, the challenge response relies entirely on the password hash value and not on the password itself. In other words, the hash value serves as a *password equivalent*. The actual base secret used for authentication is the password hash value, not the password.

If an attacker has a copy of some user's password hash, the attacker can correctly respond to a server's challenge and masquerade as that other user. This requires a subverted Windows client which allows the attacker to insert the appropriate user name and password hash into the password database, and then log on without actually supplying a password. This is not normal behavior for Windows clients. However, traditional Windows clients (non-NT systems prior to Windows 2000) have no real protection against attackers patching their software to behave in odd and inappropriate ways.

A-66

10.6 WINDOWS NTLM AUTHENTICATION

Microsoft Windows NT 4.0, the last system labeled "NT," supports three separate types of authentication, which are termed "local," "domain," and "remote." Local authentication has the same meaning as the local authentication pattern discussed in Chapter 4: a person logs on to a device directly and does not establish a remote connection. Domain authentication corresponds to the direct authentication pattern and represents the case in which a person uses his or her personal computer to log on to a different computer across a network. LANMAN authentication is also an example of this. Remote authentication corresponds to the indirect authentication pattern, in which a client logs on to a server who in turn relies on a different server (the NT *domain controller*) to verify a user's challenge response. When we refer to "NTLM" authentication, we generally are referring to the latter two types, which represent NT network authentication.

Developers of Windows NT saw an opportunity to make major improvements over LANMAN authentication. NT supported an extended character set which would greatly increase the number of possible passwords. Several new cryptographic algorithms were available that could reduce computational overhead while maintaining or even improving the level of security provided.

This led Windows NT to use a new password hashing procedure, illustrated in Figure 10.8. NT retains the 14-character limit on password size, but allows people to use any character in the extended Unicode character set. Passwords are read in and stored as a sequence of fourteen 16-bit Unicode characters. To create the 128-bit password hash, NT uses Message Digest #4 (MD4), a commercial hash algorithm developed by Ron Rivest (a newer algorithm, MD5, is widely used in Internet protocols). This improved hash is usually called the *NTLM hash*.

D-64

see Note 13.

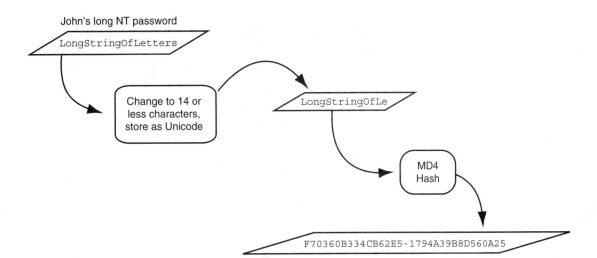

FIGURE 10.8: *Generating the NTLM hash.* John's typed password is changed to be 14 characters long and each character is converted to its 16-bit Unicode representation. MD4 hashes this string of characters into a 128-bit hash value that is used as the NT password hash.

Although NTLM authentication uses an improved hash function for encoding passwords, it still uses the challenge response protocol shown in Figure 10.6. However, NTLM authentication acquired some odd complications in order to retain compatibility with LANMAN. NTLM authentication requires *both* an NTLM hash and a LANMAN hash. Each user password entry in the SAM database contains two password hashes: one computed using the NTLM hash procedure and a second one computed using the LANMAN procedure. When an NT client performs a challenge response authentication, it computes two responses: one using the NTLM hash and another using the LANMAN hash. This approach allows NT systems to interoperate with much older LAN software, but it also opens up some unfortunate weaknesses in NTLM authentication. For many sites, this interoperability feature manages to negate the security improvements brought about by the redesigned NTLM hash procedure.

ATTACKING THE NT PASSWORD DATABASE

Attackers can recover passwords by attacking the hashes stored in NT's SAM database. The first step in this attack is to retrieve hash values from the database. The second step is to crack the hash values once they have been intercepted. We examine the second step first.

Each user entry in NT's password database contains two separate hash values: one computed using the newer NTLM hash procedure and another computed using the older LANMAN procedure. Both hashes are computed from the user's secret password.

The attack takes place in two steps. The first step is to attack the LANMAN password as described in Section 10.4. This recovers the password but does not indicate which letters are uppercase and which are lowercase, since the LANMAN hash maps everything to uppercase. The attacker must recover the case information; otherwise, the attacker can't use the password to log directly into an NT system.   A-67

The second step is to recover the NT password. To do this, the attacker must find which letters in the password are supposed to be in uppercase and which in lowercase. The attacker generates every possible permutation of case changes for the letters in the password, computes the NTLM hash for each permutation, and compares the result against the hash value from the SAM database. The two values match when the attacker finds the right choices of upper- and lowercase letters.

see Note 14.

Unlike less-sophisticated Windows products, NT provides user-oriented access control and can use it to block access to the SAM database (Defense D-20 in Chapter 2). This is the essential defense against attacks on NT passwords. Unfortunately, this is not foolproof. Interoperability requirements often lead sites to export password hashes and install them on other systems. Any time a sensitive file is copied, the risk of its disclosure increases. Furthermore, history has shown that user-based access control isn't enough to ensure the secrecy of a file on a multiuser system.

To reduce attacks on the SAM database, Microsoft released a patch to Windows NT to provide encryption of the SAM database. This mechanism, called the "System Key" or SYSKEY fix, uses a secret key to encrypt the SAM database. The computer's administrator must provide the key to the system somehow, and then the system decrypts the database and allows users to log on.

D-65

see Note 15.

The system key itself poses another security quandary: where should it stay when the computer is shut down? The key should not be accessible by attackers, nor should copies sit around the computer room in case administrators are careless or have been subverted. A hard-to-crack encryption key should be just about impossible for someone to memorize. On the other hand, the key should be available to the computer at all times so that it may reboot itself without operator intervention. Microsoft provided three alternatives: type in the key at boot time, "hide" the key in the Registry, or store the key on a removable diskette. Each of these techniques has its risks and benefits.

Typing the key in at boot time is probably the least appealing because it forces an administrator to be present whenever the computer reboots. Furthermore, the key will have to be provided to every administrator that might be called upon to reboot the computer, and this increases the risk of some types of misuse or disclosure. As a practical matter, many administrators might keep the key written down near the keyboard that is used to boot the computer.

If the key is hidden in the Registry, then the computer can reboot itself without operator intervention. This is very important for availability. On the other hand, it is difficult or perhaps even impossible to hide this type of key in a computer system. There are always ways of locating such keys. Once attackers figure out where the key is located, they can try to extract it from a system backup. A sufficiently privileged user could probably extract the key directly from the Registry.

Storing the key on a diskette has the same advantage as hiding the key in the registry: it becomes possible to reboot the computer without operator intervention. Furthermore, the key becomes somewhat easier to control if it resides on a diskette. Since it is not on the system volume, it will not be copied onto back-up tapes, and this reduces the risk of attackers extracting the key from a backup. Since the diskette is portable, the administrators can remove it and lock it up if necessary. On the other hand, a careless or subverted administrator could make a copy of the diskette and allow it to fall into the wrong hands. Also, a sufficiently privileged administrator could probably extract the key off of the diskette as long as the diskette is installed in the computer's drive.   *see Note 16.*

Many NT systems provide an extra opportunity for attackers to steal the SAM database: the recovery disk. NT systems allow administrators to maintain crucial system configuration files on a diskette called the *recovery disk*. One of the crucial files is, of course, the SAM database. Moreover, many systems maintain a copy of the recovery disk's files on-line to simplify the process of keeping the disk up to date. Attackers have been able to recover the SAM database by stealing it from the recovery disk area of a domain controller. There are two strategies for preventing this attack: (1) put access protection on the recovery disk files, or (2) do not store the files on-line except when actually constructing a recovery disk.   *A-68*

ATTACKING NTLM CHALLENGE RESPONSE

The NTLM challenge response may be attacked in essentially the same way as the LANMAN challenge response. Attackers can try to recover passwords by intercepting matching pairs of challenges and responses and cracking the password. Attackers can also use subverted clients to exploit stolen password hashes. However, the principal difference for NT is in the strategy used to crack passwords from intercepted challenge response pairs.

Since the NTLM protocol transmits both the NTLM response and the LANMAN response, attackers can mount an attack similar to the one against the NT password database, but target it against challenge response pairs. Again, the attack takes place in two steps. The first step attacks the LANMAN challenge response as described in Section 10.5. The next step uses the candidate LANMAN password as the starting point and searches for the NT password by trying permutations of upper- and lowercase characters.

The principal defense is to disable the weaker mechanism so that attackers can't exploit its weaknesses. In this case, NT must be configured to disable LANMAN authentication. This eliminates the LAN- *D-66* MAN hashes from the challenge response transactions. NTLM challenge response pairs may be vulnerable to dictionary attacks, but the stronger hash makes them much harder to attack. Originally, there was no way to eliminate the LANMAN weakness, but Microsoft produced a patch to optionally disable LANMAN authentication to increase security.

10.7 SUMMARY TABLES

TABLE 10.2: *Attack Summary*

Attack	Security Problem	Prevalence	Attack Description
A-63. Trial-and-error attack on X9.9	Masquerade as someone else	Physical and Sophisticated	Intercept several one-time passwords from an X9.9 user, crack the base secret using a DES cracker
A-64. Crack passwords in sections	Recover a user's password	Common	Cracks the password in independent parts, so attack is linear by parts instead of geometric
A-65. Force use of plaintext password	Recover a user's password	Common	Forces server to ask the user for a plaintext password so that it can be sniffed on the network
A-66. Logged in hash substitution	Masquerade as someone else	Sophisticated	Embed a stolen hash in the SAM database and subvert NT so that the user appears logged in

TABLE 10.2: *Attack Summary (Continued)*

Attack	Security Problem	Prevalence	Attack Description
A-67. Use LAN-MAN hash to crack NT hash	Recover a user's password	Common	Use password cracking software that exploits weaknesses of LAN-MAN hash to crack NT hashes
A-68. Copy hashes from NT recovery files	Recover a user's password	Trivial	Extract password hashes from the NT recovery disk files and use a cracking program on them

TABLE 10.3: *Defense Summary*

Defense	Foils Attacks	Description
D-63. Use longer cryptographic keys	A-63. Trial-and-error attack on X9.9	Replace existing technical measures with mechanisms that use longer cryptographic keys so that they better resist trial-and-error attacks
D-64. Interdependent hash computation	A-64. Crack passwords in sections	Every part of the password hash value depends on the value of every part of the password. There is no way to crack part of the password
D-65. Database encryption	A-67. Use LANMAN hash to crack NT hash A-68. Copy hashes from NT recovery files	Encrypt the entire password database so that attackers cannot attack the hashes
D-66. Disable weaker authentication	A-65. Force use of plaintext password	Configure the system to forbid the use of weaker mechanisms provided for backward compatibility

RESIDUAL ATTACK

A-66. Logged in hash substitution—the problem is that the Windows hash *is* the base secret. We foil this attack if we eliminate the need to store the base secret within the vulnerable Windows operating system. Kerberos provides one approach, which is to use a temporary base secret. We examine Kerberos in Chapter 12.

CHAPTER 11

INDIRECT AUTHENTICATION

Any problem in computing can be solved
by adding another level of indirection.

— David Wheeler, via Lampson et al., *Authentication in Distributed Systems*

IN THIS CHAPTER

Indirect authentication relies on shared servers to authenticate people based on information they provide. This allows several servers to use a common authentication database.

- Basics of indirect authentication
- RADIUS protocol for indirect authentication
- Indirect authentication on Microsoft Windows NT
- Server security concerns

11.1 INDIRECT AUTHENTICATION

Indirect authentication was introduced in Chapter 4, along with the other authentication patterns. Such systems make authentication decisions using a shared server with a single database of user records. If Cathy needs to dial in to the site, she doesn't need to worry about which dial-in server answers the phone. All of them authenticate her using the same authentication server. If she appears in the user database of that authentication server, then any of the site's other servers will recognize her. In some cases, the same authentication server can vouch for her whether she connects through a firewall, sends a file to a restricted printer, or connects to a file server.

Networking systems have used indirect authentication for at least 20 years. One of the earliest examples was "TIP login" on the ARPA-

NET. The network switching nodes that made up the ARPANET were called IMPs, and there was a special version called the *terminal IMP* (TIP). People could dial in directly to the nearest TIP and then connect to any computer on the network, much like we do today. Originally, the people managing individual TIPs controlled their use by keeping the dial-in phone numbers secret. This did little to prevent abuse. A humorous observation around 1980 suggested that more high school kids were penetrating computers through TIP connections than had reached puberty.

see Note 1.

To combat this, the TIPs were upgraded to incorporate an authenticated logon feature. This was not a simple thing to do at that time. Direct authentication was the only approach most people had encountered, and it wasn't a practical strategy to use with the TIPs. Computer hardware was very expensive at that time, and TIPs did not have enough memory to hold password checking software, much less the password list itself.

The problem was solved by the *terminal access controller access control system* (TACACS) protocol, developed by BBN, the creators of the IMPs and TIPs. Whenever someone like Cathy connected to a TIP, it would require her to log on with a user name and password. The TIP would forward this information to an ARPANET host that acted as that TIP's authentication server. Those hosts ran the authentication server program "tacacsd," which kept a user database of authorized TIP users. If Cathy's user name and password checked out, the server would tell the TIP, and the TIP would let her use the ARPANET.

see Note 2.

Since then, indirect authentication has been applied to numerous applications. We can summarize its uses in three categories:

- Network boundary control
- One-time passwords
- Resource usage in a LAN operating system

The remainder of this section describes those categories. The rest of this chapter examines two specific implementations of indirection authentication. First, we examine the RADIUS protocol used by several commercial NAS, firewall, and one-time password products. Next, we examine the "pass-through authentication" mechanism implemented in Microsoft Windows. The chapter winds up with a discussion of security concerns for stand-alone servers like authentication servers.

NETWORK BOUNDARY CONTROL

Most networks today have installed boundary protection devices, many of which require authentication. A *network access server* (NAS), for example, does the same job as the old TIP: it authenticates someone who dials in on a phone line before allowing him or her on the network. Unlike TIPs, which supported only character-oriented terminals, a modern NAS will accept one or more tunneling protocols that support the whole range of modern networking activities. Here are some of the tunneling protocols used by NASes:

- Serial Line Internet Protocol (SLIP)
- Point to Point Protocol (PPP)
- Point to Point Tunneling Protocol (PPTP)
- Layer 2 Tunneling Protocol (L2TP)
- Internet Protocol Security (IPSEC) protocol family

Firewalls generally enforce a boundary between different networks that use the Internet protocol family. Typically, a site will run Internet protocols on its interior LAN and connect to the global Internet through a firewall. The firewall is intended to reduce the risk of attacks on the site by people on the Internet. Some sites also use the firewall to restrict what people can do on the Internet when connecting from that site. Some firewalls also support various encrypted tunneling protocols like IPSEC and PPTP that allow people to connect to the site while protecting the data they exchange with the site.

When a firewall must tailor its rules to specific individuals, it usually needs to perform some type of authentication. Some firewalls simply check the Internet host address of the messages, but more sophisticated firewalls will make a serious attempt to authenticate people before allowing certain activities. For example, some firewalls require authentication to surf the World Wide Web or to use the file transfer protocol. Some firewalls will try to authenticate the person associated with a particular Internet host address and then grant permissions to subsequent messages that use that address.

Today, most NASes and authenticating firewalls use the same set of well-known protocols. When the router vendor Cisco started building NAS products, it chose the TACACS protocol to authenticate dial-in connections. Eventually, Cisco developed improved versions called XTACACS and TACACS+, to handle the special needs of its NAS products. Another well-known protocol used by NASes is the *Remote Authentication Dial In User Service* (RADIUS), an open protocol developed and maintained by the IETF. Some products use variations of the SMB protocol to query Windows domain servers and verify a user's identity.   *see Note 3.*

ONE-TIME PASSWORD PRODUCTS

While it's easy to verify a password by simply comparing two strings for a match, one-time passwords are much harder to validate. As seen in Chapter 9, the verification process is often subtle, complex, and proprietary. Vendors of such systems often package their products around a proprietary authentication server program. Well-known examples include the SafeWord Security Server and the RSA Ace/Server.

Buyers of one-time password products install the server package on one computer, or more for higher reliability. All other servers, firewalls, NASes, and other devices pass their authentication requests to the authentication server. All of the necessary data and procedures are present on the server to verify the one-time passwords. NASes and firewalls supporting the latest version of RADIUS will usually work with any type of one-time password system. Other servers need to have special *authentication agent* software installed. The agent replaces the server's conventional logon procedure with one that forwards the authentication data to the authentication server (Figure 11.1).

Aside from packaging, the centralized authentication server plays another important role in one-time password systems: it makes them more reliable. Both clock- and counter-based systems tend to build up a user-specific profile that is used in conjunction with the base secret to correctly authenticate one-time passwords. For example, the counter-based systems must maintain the counter, and clock-based systems often maintain readings of clock drift for individual tokens. The systems are much less reliable, inconvenient, and may even be unusable, if that per-token profile information isn't available. The centralized server makes it much more practical to maintain such information effectively and reliably.

Originally, one-time password servers relied on proprietary protocols. All major vendors today support the RADIUS protocol, and often support TACACS+ as well. A few vendors still use proprietary protocols to support unusual features and maintain compatibility with older versions of agent software.

LAN RESOURCE CONTROL

When LANs were small, resource control wasn't a problem—everyone in the department usually knew the rules. As LANs grew larger, the networks tended to span separate departments within a site. Eventually, people in one department found that they could use resources that were being paid for by a different department. While this situation might not often cause real trouble, it led many organizations toward LAN operating systems that could control which users could use which resources.

It is cumbersome to maintain separate password files on even a few separate systems, so the major LAN operating systems today all provide indirect authentication. Novell used direct authentication in

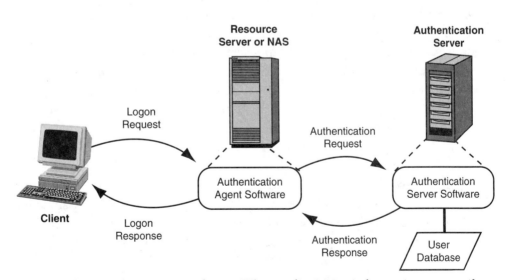

FIGURE 11.1: *Indirect authentication software.* When a client tries to log on to a server, the server's authentication agent forwards the authentication data to the authentication server. The server validates the user's identity and returns the result to the agent, which in turn informs the client.

its Netware 3.x systems and introduced indirect authentication in Netware 4.x. Early versions of Microsoft's LAN Manager and Windows NT likewise provided direct authentication. Microsoft implemented indirect authentication as part of network domains in a LAN Manager add-on. Domains (and indirect authentication) became a standard part of Windows NT in version 3.

Unlike network devices and one-time password systems, however, there is no generally accepted "open standard" protocol for LAN resource sharing. Vendors like Novell, Microsoft, and Apple have developed proprietary authentication and resource-sharing protocols that are used in their products. The Kerberos protocol described in Chapter 12 is the closest there is to an open standard for secure resource sharing, but it only focuses on key management. Microsoft has incorporated Kerberos into Windows 2000 as a replacement for the Windows domain authentication protocol (Section 11.3).

11.2 RADIUS PROTOCOL

The RADIUS protocol follows the general outline of indirect authentication in Figure 11.1. The RADIUS specification refers to the "agent" as the "client," because RADIUS is a client/server protocol, and the agent plays the "client" role. However, we will continue to use the term *agent* here to avoid confusion with the activities of someone trying to log on from a "client workstation."

When someone tries to log on, the RADIUS agent sends an "Access-Request" message. The authentication server responds with either an "Access-Accept" or an "Access-Reject" message. However, the RADIUS protocol contains several additional bits of complication to protect the agent and server against attacks.   *see Note 4.*

In earlier chapters we discussed several ways for attackers to exploit or interfere with authentication messages sent by a client workstation. Such attacks are outside the realm of RADIUS, since it describes messages between the agent and server. However, many of those attacks against messages between a client and an agent may also threaten messages between the agent and the authentication server.

For example, consider what might be done by a team of two attackers, Tom and Henry. Tom is on the outside of the site, trying to log on. Henry is connected to the inside, and uses his position to help Tom masquerade as an authorized user. What kinds of attacks can they perform?

To start with, Henry could place himself on the network between the agent and the authentication server. When Tom tries to log on, Henry could intercept the authentication request on its way to the server and send back a forged authentication response that verifies Tom's logon attempt. If the agent can't detect the forgery, Tom will log on successfully.

A-69

There are several ways a protocol can protect against a rank forgery like that. But even if the protocol includes such protections, there may be other ways to achieve the same end. For example, Henry might intercept packets that travel between the server and agent, modify them "on the fly," and send them on their way. In particular, Henry could then intercept the Access-Reject message sent in response to Tom's Access-Request and transform it into an Access-Accept message. Henry can do this by changing a single bit in the Access-Reject message.

A-70

Even if the protocol protects against forgery or modification, there's still another risk. Henry might intercept legitimate messages passing between the agent and server and try to replay those messages to trick the agent into accepting Tom's logon attempt. If the authentication server sends a "canned" set of responses to legitimate logon requests, then Henry can simply collect the response he needs and send it to the agent. Cryptographic integrity protection won't detect a replayed message without additional anti-replay protection.

A-71

To summarize, there are three basic attacks RADIUS must address:

- Replayed messages in either direction
- Forged messages, especially from the server to the agent
- Modified messages from the server to the agent

Aspects of the RADIUS protocol might seem arcane and peculiar, but they begin to make sense when we see how RADIUS resists these attacks.

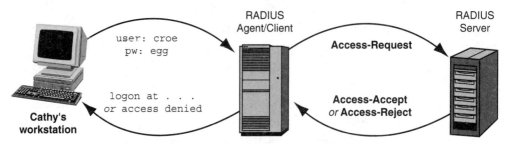

FIGURE 11.2: *Basic RADIUS protocol interaction.* Cathy tries to connect to a device that's running a RADIUS agent. The agent collects her user name and password, and builds a RADIUS Access-Request message with them. When the server receives the message, it checks Cathy's password and other permissions. If all is in order, the server returns an Access-Accept message to the agent. Otherwise it returns Access-Reject. The agent sends the appropriate message to Cathy in response.

A RADIUS LOGON

At a high level, the RADIUS protocol is quite simple. Figure 11.2 shows how RADIUS simply uses one message sent from agent to server, and a response from server to agent. When someone initiates a logon, the agent collects the user's name and password, and puts it in an Access-Request message. The whole message generally contains the following:

- Numeric code indicating this is an Access-Request
- Eight-bit identifier for this particular logon request
- Length of the whole RADIUS message
- A 128-bit nonce called the *request authenticator*
- An identifier for the agent making the request
- The user name (optional, actually)
- The password just entered, encrypted for transmission
- Optional data, like the port the connection has arrived from

Upon receipt, the authentication server extracts the user name, decrypts the password, and compares the information against its user database. If the password matches, then the server sends an Access-Accept message back to the client. The message generally contains the following:

- Numeric code indicating this is an Access-Accept message
- Eight-bit identifier copied from the Access-Request message

- Length of the whole RADIUS message
- A hash, called the *response authenticator*, to detect attacks
- An optional text string that is transmitted to the user
- Optional data describing the user's rights and permissions

The agent receives this message and analyzes its contents to check for forgery. Next, it uses the eight-bit identifier to match this message up with a pending logon. Then the agent looks at the message's numeric code, accepts the logon if the code is Access-Accept, and rejects it otherwise. If the Access-Accept message includes details about user permissions and access privileges, the agent processes those after accepting the logon.

PROTECTING RADIUS MESSAGES

To use RADIUS reliably, we find ourselves doing authentication twice: we must authenticate the *server* to safely authenticate the *user*. When the agent receives an Access-Accept message, it must be confident that the message comes from a server it trusts. We don't want to give Tom, Henry, or anyone else a way to trick the agent. Moreover, we want to protect the overall authentication process as much as possible.

The fundamental building block for server authentication is, of course, a base secret. In the case of RADIUS, the secret is generally a password or passphrase, and it is shared between servers and agents. The secret is used to encrypt passwords before being sent, and it is also used to compute the correct response authenticator hash in an Access-Accept or Access-Reject message.

The Access-Request message contains two defensive measures against attack. The first measure is the 128-bit nonce called the request authenticator. The agent chooses a new nonce value randomly for each logon request it processes. If properly chosen, the chances are extremely remote that an attacker could predict the nonce's value or that the same value would be used more than once. Figure 11.3 shows how the server uses the nonce to construct the response authenticator hash it sends back to the agent. Thus, any legitimate message the agent receives is based on the nonce in the original message.

Access-Request message

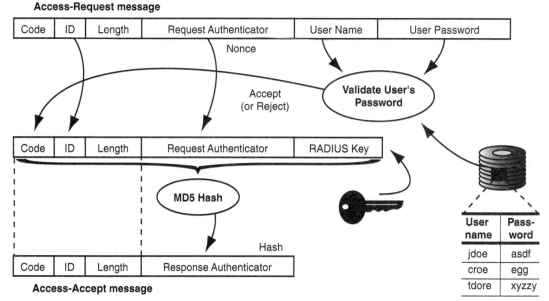

FIGURE 11.3: *Processing a RADIUS Access-Request message.* When a RADIUS authentication server receives an Access-Request message, it starts by validating the user name and password. Then it hashes the response message (Access-Accept or Access-Reject), the nonce (or "request authenticator"), and the server's RADIUS key to produce the "response authenticator" sent back with the response.

The nonce helps the agent detect attempts to replay an earlier, legitimate reply sent by the authentication server. If an attacker *D-67* replays an earlier message, like a valid Access-Accept message with a matching eight-bit request identifier, the response authenticator hash won't have been derived from the corresponding nonce. The agent can detect this by repeating the processes shown in Figure 11.3 (except for the user database lookup, of course). If the MD5 hash does not match the response authenticator hash, then the agent discards the message as invalid.

The second, more obvious, security measure in the Access-Request is user password encryption. This prevents attackers from being able to sniff user passwords while traveling between the agent and the authentication server. Before the agent sends the Access-Request message, it encrypts the user's password. Unlike password encryption on Unix, the authentication server can reverse this encryption when it receives the Access-Request message.

Figure 11.4 illustrates the basic encryption procedure. First, we construct a 128-bit encryption key by computing the hash of a data field containing both the RADIUS secret and the nonce for this request. To encrypt, we simply perform the logical exclusive-or operation on the bits of the password using the bits of the key. If the password is shorter than 128 bits, we pad it with zero bits. If it is longer, we generate additional encryption keys using a simple chaining procedure described in the RADIUS protocol specification. *D-68*

Upon receipt, the authentication server decrypts the password by using the RADIUS key it shares with that agent. The server extracts the nonce from the Access-Request and combines it with the RADIUS key to construct the same key used by the agent. Decryption is the same as encryption: a simple exclusive-or operation between the key and the encrypted password will yield the plaintext password.

One might wonder why we go to the trouble of constructing a different key by combining it with the nonce, since we already have this shared secret, the RADIUS key. This step serves two important purposes. First, it eliminates a crucial weakness we face when using exclusive-or for encryption. If attackers collect two or more different *D-69*

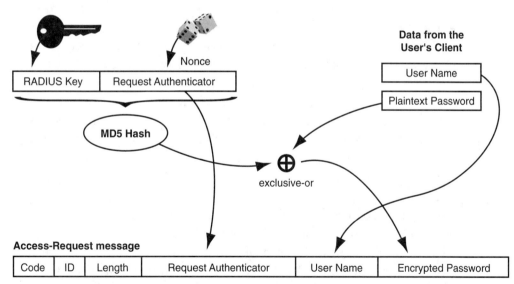

FIGURE 11.4: *Encrypting a password for RADIUS.* The RADIUS agent encrypts passwords before sending them to the authentication server in an Access-Request message. The agent generates the encryption key by hashing the request authenticator and the RADIUS key. The agent encrypts the password by computing the exclusive-or of the plaintext password and that encryption key.

messages encrypted using exclusive-or with the same key, then they can easily strip away the encryption and find the encrypted data. By hashing the secret key and the random nonce, we produce a new key whenever we encrypt another password.

The second purpose is that this combination prevents a slightly more complex replay attack. If we always use the same key to encrypt passwords, perhaps using stronger encryption, attackers could simply copy an encrypted password into a forged Access-Request message. If attackers could simply replay passwords that way, then they could trick the authentication server into logging on the wrong user. By including the nonce in password encryption, attackers can't reuse encrypted passwords sniffed from earlier Access-Request messages.

To protect the agent against forged or modified messages, RADIUS uses the keyed hash it calls the response authenticator. As shown in Figure 11.3, the hash is computed from the contents of the server's response message, omitting the response authenticator (since we don't know its value yet) and appending the nonce and the RADIUS key. The concept is similar to the keyed message authentication described in Section 8.5.

D-70

For both keyed message authentication and RADIUS response authenticator hashes, the hash depends on the message's contents and on secret data not available to an attacker. If an attacker changes the message in any way, the recipient (i.e., the RADIUS agent) can see that the hash value no longer matches the message's contents. Since the attackers don't know the shared RADIUS secret, there is no way they can construct a valid hash for the message. As noted earlier, the nonce prevents a replayed message from matching up with any other server response sent to a RADIUS agent.

For maximum safety, each RADIUS agent should share a unique key with the authentication server. This allows the proprietor to revoke the RADIUS key belonging to a single agent that may have been attacked and penetrated, without having to change the keys used by other agents. However, it is not unusual for all agents at a site to share the same RADIUS key: it is a convenient thing to do until an agent is penetrated and the key is stolen.

RADIUS CHALLENGE RESPONSE

As described so far, RADIUS protocol works fine with conventional passwords and with counter-based or clock-based one-time passwords. But there is no mechanism for passing a challenge to a user with a challenge response token. RADIUS uses additional messages to handle challenge response authentication. Instead of the two-step protocol described earlier, challenge response authentication proceeds as follows:

1. The agent sends an Access-Request message. Unlike the simple password case, this message will not contain a valid password; if the password field appears for compatibility reasons, it will not be checked.

2. The server responds with an Access-Challenge message. This message is similar to an Access-Accept, except that it includes a text string containing the challenge. The agent should transmit that string to the user's workstation. In many systems, this message also includes a state attribute from the server.

3. User receives the challenge and transmits the response back to the agent.

4. The agent constructs another Access-Request message like the first one, but containing a new identifier and nonce, and carrying the user's response in the password field. If the server provided a state attribute in the Access-Challenge message, the agent copies that attribute into the message as well.

5. The server matches up the Access-Request message with the earlier challenge, probably by using the contents of the state attribute. Then the server validates the response and returns an Access-Accept message if all is well.

11.3 ENCRYPTED CONNECTIONS AND WINDOWS NT

Chapter 10 introduced several aspects of Microsoft Windows authentication. This section examines the indirect authentication strategy introduced in Windows NT, sometimes called "remote authentication" or more often *pass-through authentication*. Pass-through authentication is a special variant of Microsoft's domain authentication. In Microsoft's local and domain authentication, we assume that the base secret (a hashed password) resides on the des-

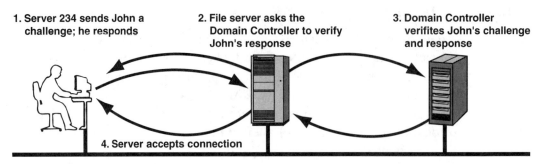

FIGURE 11.5: *Windows NT indirect (pass-through) authentication.* When John attempts to use a server, and the server requires authentication, the server authenticates John by sending him a challenge. John's workstation generates a response based on his hashed secret password (Section 10.5). The server forwards the challenge and response to the NT domain controller, which verifies John's response by using John's hash stored in the SAM database.

tination computer. Pass-through authentication allows certain computers, usually servers, to forward authentication data from a user to the domain controller for authentication so that the server doesn't have to handle its own copy of the domain's SAM (user) database. In Windows 2000, this approach to pass-through authentication has been replaced with the Kerberos protocol.

Figure 11.5 presents the familiar picture of indirect authentication adapted to the *Microsoft Challenge/Reply Handshake Protocol* (MS-CHAP). When John requests service from Server 234, the server sends John's workstation a randomly generated nonce as a challenge. When John types in his password, his workstation computes the correct response for that challenge, and sends the information to Server 234. If John is already logged on, the workstation will retrieve his password hash value from the Registry and use it to compute the correct response. From John's standpoint, there is nothing special about indirect authentication. John sends a request to a server, and that server authenticates him transparently. The actual process invokes the standard "logon" function, but the function is transformed into a remote procedure call from the server to the domain controller.   *see Note 5.*

This process works as follows. When the server receives the response from the user's workstation, it transmits the following information to the domain controller:

- Domain name
- User name

- Challenge (nonce) value
- Response encrypted with the user's base secret hash

The domain controller extracts the user's hash value from the SAM database to compute the expected response from the challenge. According to tradition, the user's hash is generally stored in both LANMAN format (Section 10.5) and NT hash format (Section 10.6) so that the user can transparently log on to both older and newer systems. In fact, the first version of MS-CHAP would provide the response using both hashes, though the latest version only uses the LANMAN hash if required for compatibility with the workstation. Once the domain controller has computed the appropriate hash, it compares the hash with the response from the user. If they match, the controller sends a "success" message back to the server. Otherwise, it reports a failure.

The communications link between the server and the domain controller faces the same risks as those between the RADIUS agent and authentication server discussed in Section 11.2. However, Microsoft's designers chose a different strategy than the RADIUS designers. Most computers using Windows network domain software will automatically establish a "secure channel" to the domain control when they start up. The channel uses an encryption protocol to protect the information from attack. Windows uses this channel to carry pass-through authentication between servers and their domain controller. Instead of constructing a subtle protocol like RADIUS, Windows relies on a fully encrypted connection to protect against the whole range of attacks we examined against indirect authentication.

D-71

ENCRYPTED CONNECTIONS

An encrypted connection uses an encryption algorithm like those discussed in Section 5.3 to protect the data as it travels between sender and recipient. The sender encrypts data using a secret key before transmitting it to the recipient. The recipient uses the same secret key to decrypt the data.

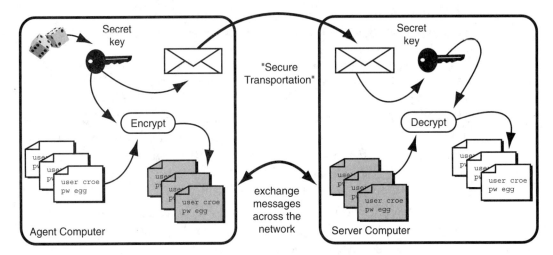

FIGURE 11.6: *Encrypted connection between two computers.* In this example we have an authentication agent that needs to authenticate users by passing information to the authentication server. The agent encrypts the messages to be sent before transmission, and the server decrypts the messages upon receipt. Across the top of the figure we see that secret keys must be distributed separately.

Figure 11.6 illustrates the essentials of an encrypted connection between two entities on a network. The computer on the left is an authentication agent that needs to authenticate Cathy. It takes Cathy's information, encrypts it using a shared secret key, and transmits it to the authentication server. The server uses the same shared secret key to decrypt the data. For the most part, Henry cannot attack this connection as long as he does not know the secret key. If he tries to forge a reply from the authentication server, the agent won't recognize the message's contents because it hasn't been encrypted with the shared secret key.

The envelopes in Figure 11.6 indicate that the agent and server must somehow share a secret key in order to use encryption. The key is often distributed by hand or transported some other way that is difficult to tap or otherwise intercept. The encryption key is similar to the shared password used in RADIUS, and the proprietor runs the same risks to the authentication system if the key is guessed or stolen by attackers. As with RADIUS, a stolen key would allow an attacker to forge messages from the authentication server, like an Access-Accept message.

When designing a secure channel, the security architect must choose an encryption algorithm to use, which is usually either a stream cipher or a block cipher. Microsoft chose RC4, a fast stream cipher, to encrypt the domain secure channel traffic.

INTEGRITY PROTECTION

Many people assume that an attacker can't really attack an encrypted message without knowing the key. Some people might acknowledge that a replay attack doesn't need a key, but still assume that at least an attacker couldn't have modified the message's contents without knowing the key. Unfortunately, this isn't true, especially for stream ciphers.

Figure 11.7 illustrates the problem. If the authentication server decides to reject an authentication request, it sends a well-known message back to the authentication agent. Even if attackers don't know the keys being used by the server and agent, they can reliably "rewrite" the contents of an encrypted message to say something different. This is a *rewrite attack*.

A-72

see Note 6.

The trick is that the attackers must know *exactly* what the message says in order to rewrite it accurately. If they know, for example, that the authentication server will reject a particular logon request, they can watch for an encrypted message sent at the appropriate

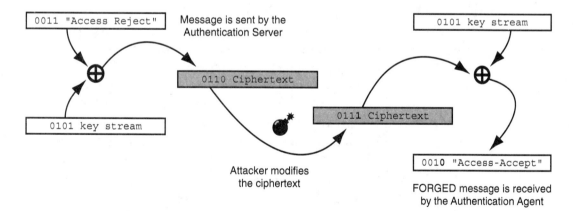

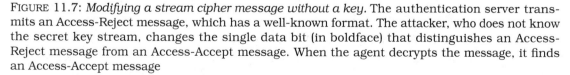

FIGURE 11.7: *Modifying a stream cipher message without a key.* The authentication server transmits an Access-Reject message, which has a well-known format. The attacker, who does not know the secret key stream, changes the single data bit (in boldface) that distinguishes an Access-Reject message from an Access-Accept message. When the agent decrypts the message, it finds an Access-Accept message

time to the appropriate agent containing the appropriate number of bytes. Then they intercept the message and modify the single data bit that distinguishes an Access-Reject message from an Access-Accept message. When the agent receives the modified message, it finds nothing wrong with it. Decryption proceeds normally and the plaintext message appears to match the legal format. Nothing indicates that the message was changed from one type to another.

There are several ways to eliminate rewrite attacks, or at least make them harder to perform. But the problem is a bit more subtle than it might seem at first. Some designers might think they can block this attack if they simply include a checksum or unkeyed hash in the messages. This might make the attack harder, but it certainly doesn't prevent it.

No doubt a designer would try this because it might seem that the hash is safe since its value is encrypted. But this obviously won't work if the attackers know exactly what the original message should say. They can construct a copy of the message and compute the correct checksum. Once they have decided what they want the forged, encrypted message to say, they construct it and compute its proper checksum, too. To produce the forged but encrypted message, they compare the text of the original message with the text of the forged message, bit by bit. Each bit that's different between the two messages must be changed in the ciphertext. When the agent or other recipient decrypts the message, it gets a perfect forgery.

Other designers might consider block ciphers safer, since they scramble bits across an entire block of bits. However, it's still possible to do rewrite attacks on block-encrypted messages. If the message is encrypted by simply applying the cipher block by block to the message, then the attackers can rearrange the blocks or substitute one for another in order to change the contents. In practice, few systems use block ciphers that way. Instead, they use the ciphers according to one of the established *block cipher modes*, which try to tie the encryption of separate blocks together. Modes generally use the output of a previous block's encryption step to systematically modify the key, the plaintext data, or the ciphertext. This makes some trivial cut-and-paste attacks more obvious, but doesn't necessarily detect all rewrite attacks. Some block modes use the block cipher to generate a key stream like the ones used in stream ciphers and then applies the key stream bit by bit. Clearly, such block modes are vulnerable to the same rewrite attacks as more conventional stream ciphers.   *see Note 7.*

The most effective approach is to use a keyed hash. Consider that RADIUS doesn't even use encryption to protect its messages, except for passwords. Instead, it detects modifications by using its response authenticator, which is a keyed hash. Both the SSL and IPSEC protocols use keyed hashes to protect the integrity of their encrypted traffic. Microsoft did not originally provide integrity protection on its secure channels within domains, but this was added to later releases of Windows NT.   *see Note 8.*

Replay attacks also pose a problem, since neither encryption nor simple integrity protection will detect them. RADIUS relied on the nonces to detect replays, since each new transaction required a newly generated nonce. This isn't the only approach, however. If the agent and server have established a shared secret key that will encrypt a whole sequence of messages, they can detect message replay simply by embedding sequence numbers in each new message. This technique is used in IPSEC, PPTP, and SSL protocols.   *see Note 9.*

 D-72

POLITICS, ENCRYPTION, AND TECHNICAL CHOICES

Note that the encryption mechanism shown in Figure 11.6 provides many of the same protections as the more complex RADIUS mechanisms illustrated in Figures 11.3 and 11.4. This is especially true if we incorporate message integrity protection, which is easily worth the trouble. We might then sensibly ask, why did the RADIUS designers develop those arcane protections instead of pursuing a comparatively simple design based on encryption? The answer is export control: a problem we discussed briefly in Section 5.4.

Export control regulations following World War II classed encryption as a munition. In response, commercial product designers avoided general purpose encryption mechanisms, since the State Department allowed the export of products that didn't use encryption to hide free-form messages between people. So RADIUS applied reasonably strong cryptographic technology to the authentication problem without providing general-purpose encryption. The RADIUS security techniques are still effective even though the rationale for the technology has faded with recent relaxations of cryptographic export controls.

see Note 10.

In the mid-1990s, the U.S. government promoted the Escrowed Encryption Standard (EES) as a way to provide encrypted connections while still giving government intelligence and surveillance agencies a way to eavesdrop on communications they were interested in. As noted in Section 5.4, this strategy failed. Although many vendors and system designers avoided EES because their overseas customers didn't want a foreign power eavesdropping on their traffic, many also avoided it for technical reasons. In essence, a key escrow mechanism is a "back door" into some encrypted data. While it should be possible in theory to build such a thing reliably and correctly, it has proven difficult to do so in practice. Shortly after EES was made available on the Clipper Chip, Matt Blaze of AT&T demonstrated a way to circumvent the key escrow mechanism. Moreover, Blaze has not been the only one to discover problems with key escrow mechanisms. While key escrow may provide benefits in some applications, it is difficult to do it correctly and not increase the risk to the encrypted data.

see Note 11.

11.4 WINDOWS NT SECURE CHANNELS

Although Windows NT network authentication relies on challenge response techniques to protect secret passwords from disclosure, it relies on an encrypted connection to protect indirect authentication. The domain controllers act as authentication servers in a Windows environment as well as providing other services. Windows NT maintains a separate base secret between a domain controller and every computer in its domain. The domain controller uses this shared secret to establish an encrypted connection between itself and every computer in its domain.

The shared secret key establishes a "star" network topology in which the domain controller is in the center and all of the other computers talk directly to it. Windows supports both "primary" and "secondary" domain controllers, and the secondary controllers provide higher reliability through redundancy. The shared secrets reside on both the primary and secondary controllers.

SECURE CHANNEL KEYING

The secure channel is established when a Windows computer starts up and attempts to connect to the domain controller. The computer first sends out messages to locate its domain controller. Once the controller is located, the computer and domain controller exchange messages to authenticate one another and to establish a secret key for encrypting their traffic. Figure 11.8 shows how the computer sends a nonce to the domain controller and the domain controller sends a nonce to the computer. Then they each combine the two nonces with their shared secret key to generate a secret key. *see Note 12.*

This is a good strategy for several reasons. First, the process authenticates the computer to the domain controller and vice versa. This works effectively as long as the administrator establishes differ-

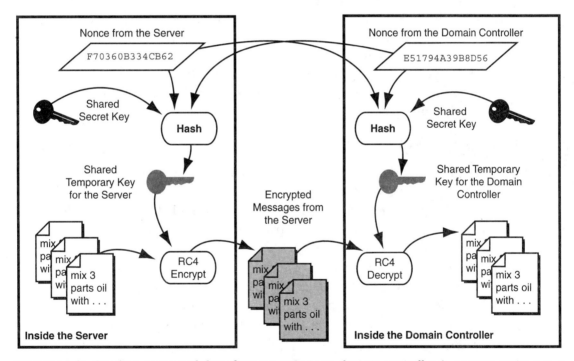

FIGURE 11.8: *Sending encrypted data from a server to its domain controller.* A server sets up a secure link to its domain controller by establishing a shared, temporary secret key and using that key to encrypt messages between them. The temporary key is generated from nonces exchanged by the server and domain controller combined with a shared secret key previously established between them. The RC4 algorithm encrypts the data as it travels between the server and the domain controller.

ent shared secrets between every computer and its domain controller. Second, this strategy does not require the secret key to be sent across the network. Third, the process establishes a new secret key every time the computer starts up. It is a good communications security practice to change encryption keys regularly and to not encrypt too much traffic with a particular key. Fourth, the arrangement makes it impossible for an attacker to masquerade as either the computer or the domain controller and try to reestablish a previously used key. This is true as long as each nonce is randomly generated.

A peculiar feature of this arrangement is that NT requires at least two shared secrets in order to support a user workstation: the user's personal password and the shared secret for domain controller message encryption. This illustrates why one can't simply fix a problem by adding a layer of encryption: each such layer also adds an extra piece to the key management problem. Administrators must contend with managing two secrets instead of only one. The solution to this problem is to use a single, integrated protocol that uses a single key for both encryption and user authentication. This is the approach used by Kerberos, which has been adopted in Windows 2000 (Chapter 12).

ATTACKS ON SECURE CHANNELS

Despite the technical measures provided for its protection, there are ways to attack some implementations of Microsoft's secure channels. As noted in the previous section, it is possible to systematically modify the encrypted message traffic even if the encryption key is not known. Fortunately, this problem was fixed.

However, there is also a flaw in key generation that yields a technique to decrypt encrypted traffic. This problem first came to light because Microsoft originally used the same procedure to generate keys for its PPTP protocol; Microsoft has made changes to PPTP to fix that problem.

The problem is that Windows NT uses the same temporary key to encrypt the RC4 traffic in each direction. This springs another trap for unwary users of stream ciphers. Careful stream cipher implementations never use a particular key stream to encrypt two or more different messages. If attackers intercept two ciphertext messages that were encrypted with the same key streams, they can combine the two ciphertexts with the exclusive-or operation and it will cancel out the two key streams. This yields the same result as taking the original two plaintext messages and combining them by themselves using the exclusive-or operation. A clever cryptographer can analyze the resulting bits and probably extract the original messages. This same problem was originally found and fixed in PPTP.

A-73

see Note 13.

The Soviet Union made essentially the same mistake during and shortly after World War II by reusing "one-time pads" that encrypted messages from their overseas spies. Theoretically, one-time pads are unbreakable, but this mistake allowed U.S. cryptographers to learn about Soviet spying activities, particularly in atomic research labs.

see Note 14.

To eliminate this problem, the encryption system should never use the same encryption key to encrypt two different secret data streams. Clearly, this is what happens in Figure 11.8. Of course, both the workstation and the domain controller need to be able to derive the secret session keys that each are using. The solution is for the two hosts to generate several different keys from the same set of nonces and shared base secrets. One of the keys is used for traffic encrypted by the agent and one for traffic encrypted by the domain controller. To construct different keys, the hosts can append different, predefined numeric constants to the nonces: one value of the constant is used to generate the agent's encryption key and a different value generates the controller's encryption key. This is how Microsoft used to correct this problem in PPTP's key generation.

D-73

see Note 15.

These problems with Microsoft secure channels should not affect Windows 2000, since it contains other, better-engineered mechanisms. The Kerberos protocol already provides mechanisms for protecting the types of messages sent on NT secure channels. In addition, Windows 2000 includes the IPSEC protocol, which provides well-engineered mechanisms to encrypt and authenticate arbitrary data connections. However, the older, less safe protocols may produce security weaknesses because they may still be used for backward compatibility.

11.5 COMPUTERS' AUTHENTICATION SECRETS

Base secrets can pose a security problem for stand-alone systems like NASes, firewalls, and servers. These systems must be able to authenticate themselves to each other to perform security-critical operations like indirect authentication. To keep these operations safe, the systems must protect their base secrets from disclosure. Computers directly operated by people often avoid this problem by using a memorized password for a base secret. Unattended systems pose a different problem. It isn't practical to require operators to enter passwords on unattended systems, so passwords and other base secrets must generally be stored right on the systems.

Some of the problems with storing base secrets on a computer were described when discussing the Microsoft SAM database in Section 10.6. If attackers know where to look, they can steal the secret. We can encrypt the secret, like with Microsoft's SYSKEY, but then we have to store *that* secret somewhere, too.

see Note 16.

Some researchers have described general-purpose strategies to find cryptographic keys stored in large amounts of computer memory. Even if the system puts the key in a really hard-to-find place, such an attack might locate the key by searching a system's entire RAM space and hard drive. The attack searches for "high entropy" areas of storage, that is, blocks of memory that are "more random" in comparison to other areas of the disk. Shamir and van Somerin found that one could identify areas of high entropy by displaying them visually, one bit per pixel. They further experimented with an automated technique that counts the number of unique data bytes in each 64-byte region; a region containing a secret key would most likely yield a higher count than regions containing graphics, text, or computer instructions. This technique could be used to focus an attacker's search for keys hidden on a computer.

A-74

see Note 17.

The basic defense against randomness searches is to use *steganography*, the strategy of embedding a little information in a lot of information. For example, the encryption key can be broken into several separate pieces of four bits each and expanded into eight-bit bytes with the high-order bits taken from an ASCII character. This will dramatically reduce the entropy. Or else the key can be stored in the low-order bits of an image. The image data won't have high entropy, either.

D-74

see Note 18.

Unfortunately, steganography relies entirely on "security through obscurity." Once attackers learn the secret of how the key is stored, they will be able to extract the key themselves without resorting to complicated searches. The most effective defense against key theft is to move the key out of the computer's regular operating environment so that attackers can't reach it. This usually involves moving the key onto a separate hardware device that performs cryptographic functions without passing the key back to the computer. A promising, low-cost approach for this is with smart cards, introduced in Section 9.1.

To summarize, here are recommendations for managing secure servers that must run unattended:

- Don't store the key on the machine; use crypto hardware that stores the key away from attackers.
- If you must store the key on the machine, harden the machine as much as possible.
- If the software gives you several options for storing the keys, try to pick one that is hard for an attacker to anticipate and circumvent.
- A security-critical function, particularly one that stores valuable base secrets, should be hosted on a dedicated computer.

11.6 SUMMARY TABLES

TABLE 11.1: *Attack Summary*

Attack	Security Problem	Prevalence	Attack Description
A-69. Forge access acceptance	Masquerade as someone else	Sophisticated	Forge a message that accepts a bogus access request, masquerading as the authentication server
A-70. Convert reject into acceptance	Masquerade as someone else	Sophisticated	Modify an access-rejection message from the authentication server to say access-accept
A-71. Replay attack	Forge a message	Sophisticated	Retransmit a legitimate message to trick an agent into repeating its previous response
A-72. Rewrite attack	Forge a message	Sophisticated	Modify an encrypted message to approve an authentication query sent to a domain controller
A-73. Duplicated stream cipher keystream	Recover hidden information	Sophisticated	Combine the encrypted data streams that used the same key and decode the result
A-74. Find keys in high entropy regions	Recover hidden information, like base secrets	Sophisticated	Use entropy-measuring techniques to look for likely places in a computer where base secrets have been stored

TABLE 11.2: *Defense Summary*

Defense	Foils Attacks	Description
D-67. Nonce in messages	A-71. Replay attack	Requests contain a random nonce, and legitimate messages incorporate the nonce into the response in a hard-to-forge way
D-68. Encrypt transmitted passwords	A-10. Keystroke sniffing	Passwords sent across a network are encrypted using reversible encryption
D-69. Encryption incorporates nonce	A-10. Keystroke sniffing A-71. Replay attack	Encryption and decryption of data in a transaction incorporates a nonce so that encrypted data can't be replayed in other, forged transactions
D-70. Keyed hash incorporating nonce	A-69. Forge access acceptance A-70. Convert reject into acceptance A-71. Replay attack A-72. Rewrite attack	Include a nonce when sending a message that needs a reply. After constructing the reply, compute a hash that combines the reply's text, the shared secret, and the nonce from the original message
D-71. Encrypted connection	A-69. Forge access acceptance	Agent and authentication server establish a fully encrypted connection between themselves to protect access control messages
D-72. Sequence numbers for anti-replay	A-71. Replay attack	Insert a sequence number into every message and apply integrity protection. If two messages have the same sequence number, they are duplicates
D-73. Generate unique encryption keys	A-73. Duplicated stream cipher keystream	Incorporate predefined constants into the key-generation process to yield different secret keys for different purposes from the same initial secrets and nonces
D-74. Steganography for keys	A-74. Find keys in high entropy regions	Encode random secrets so that there are no concentrated storage areas with high entropy

CHAPTER 12

KERBEROS AND WINDOWS 2000

"That is plain enough," said Gimli. "If you are a friend, speak the password, and the doors will open, and you can enter."

— J. R. R. Tolkien, *The Fellowship of the Ring*

IN THIS CHAPTER

Kerberos provides a mechanism to authenticate and share temporary secret keys between cooperating processes.

- The concept of a key distribution center
- Needham-Schroeder key distribution protocol
- Kerberos tickets and ticket-granting tickets
- Kerberos and Microsoft Windows 2000

12.1 THE KEY DISTRIBUTION CENTER

In the 1980s, the banking industry began to take full advantage of how encryption with the DES could protect electronic funds transfer traffic. As traffic grew, however, the banks struggled with the problem of handling encryption keys safely and effectively, Drawing on network security work by Dennis Branstad, they developed standards for *key distribution centers* (KDCs). Banks used KDCs to generate temporary encryption keys for messages between pairs of bank offices. This eliminated the risk of using a single encryption key for all messages between "trusted" sites. It also eliminated the enormous expense of having to distribute unique keys for every pair of bank offices. The banks' approach was codified in ANSI Standard X9.17.

see Note 1.

Temporary encryption keys provide a similar benefit to one-time passwords: they limit the damage attackers can do if they manage to

341

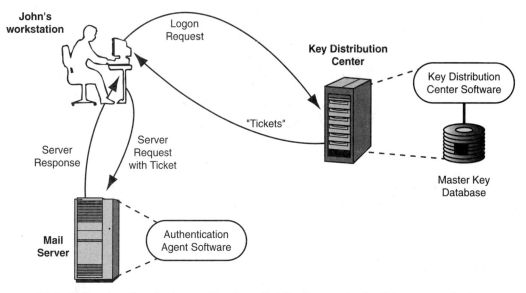

FIGURE 12.1: *Indirect authentication with a key distribution center.* In this approach, two computers mutually authenticate each other by providing a shared secret key that only those two can
possibly share. The shared secret key is embedded in a cryptographically protected data item
called a "ticket." To use the mail server, John Doe contacts the key distribution center, which
gives him two tickets: one encrypted for his own master key and the other encrypted with the
mail server's master key. John decrypts his ticket to retrieve the shared secret key and forwards
the other to the mail server. The server retrieves its own copy of the shared key from its ticket.

find one of the keys, since each key works only temporarily. Each
trusted site has a unique *master key* that it shares with the KDC.
The master key allows each site to talk to the KDC safely. In addition, the KDC can cryptographically "package" temporary keys using
the master keys so that one site can safely forward the right keys to
another site. This reduces the number of network messages by providing a form of indirection.

Perhaps this topic might seem to stray a little from the topic of
authentication, but if we think of these shared temporary keys as
base secrets, the KDC's role emerges. If two computers need to
authenticate each other's messages, the KDC can provide a shared
base secret to do this. For example, imagine that John needs to
retrieve his e-mail from the mail server. Traditionally, John might
provide a reusable secret password to his server, and the server
would use it to authenticate John directly or redirect the password
to a separate authentication server.

TICKETS

Figure 12.1 shows a third alternative: using a KDC. John starts by contacting the KDC, which provides him with encrypted credentials, called *tickets*. John forwards the appropriate ticket to the mail server, which uses that ticket to authenticate John. (As a matter of historical accuracy, the term *ticket* originated with the Kerberos protocol, so we're really looking at prehistoric tickets here.)

In essence, a ticket is an encrypted copy of a temporary base secret. The ticket is encrypted with the master key known only by the KDC and the ticket's intended recipient. Figure 12.2 shows how this works. The KDC maintains a database of reusable shared secrets, the master keys. Each user or server known to the KDC has its own master key. When John contacts the KDC for access to the mail server, the KDC generates a temporary shared secret for him to use with the mail server. Then the KDC encrypts two copies of the secret, one for John and one for the mail server, each using their respective master key from the database.

Finally, the KDC delivers these tickets to John, who delivers a ticket to the mail server. Upon receipt, the mail server uses the mas-

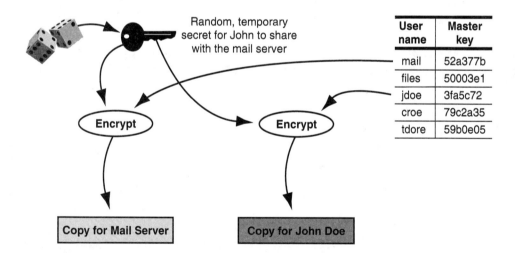

FIGURE 12.2: *Simple "tickets" generated by a KDC.* Fundamentally, a ticket is an encrypted copy of a temporary secret intended to be shared between a particular pair of computers. In this case, John Doe has requested a ticket for use with the mail server. In the upper left, the KDC generates a random secret. Then it produces the tickets by encrypting copies of the secret with the recipients' master keys, taken from the KDC's master key database. This ensures that only the recipients can decrypt the shared temporary secret.

ter key to decrypt the ticket and extract the temporary shared secret. Since nobody else knows the master keys shared between individuals, servers, and the KDC, nobody can decrypt tickets except the intended recipients.

Once the server has the temporary shared secret in hand, John can send the server his e-mail request and use the shared secret to authenticate his request. Trivially, the server could present a traditional password prompt and accept the temporary shared secret as the legal password. More likely, the server will use the secret to perform a challenge response handshake with John's workstation, so that the shared secret doesn't need to be transmitted "in the clear."

This basic approach to key distribution is, of course, too simple to use safely. The fundamental problem is that John has no way of knowing if the key he receives for the mail server is in fact for the mail server. For example, an attacker (someone named Henry, for example) might have intercepted John's request. Henry could then have substituted his own name for that of the mail server. If John uses the resulting keys, Henry will be able to intercept John's messages and read them. To combat such problems, the X9.17 protocol incorporated extra data in key distribution messages, notably message authentication codes, time stamps, and the names of senders and recipients. This followed a number of recommendations produced by computer scientists intrigued by the challenges of key management, starting with Roger Needham and Michael Schroeder.

A-75

NEEDHAM-SCHROEDER

In 1978, Needham and Schroeder published a simple protocol to efficiently address the forgery problems faced by the KDC. This Needham-Schroeder protocol incorporates nonces and a challenge response to detect forged or replayed messages. We can look at the protocol in two parts: first the KDC portion, and then the challenge response portion.

D-75

see Note 2.

Figure 12.3 illustrates the KDC portion of the protocol. John sends the KDC a request that identifies who it's from (John), John's destination (the mail server), and a randomly generated nonce. Like before, the KDC generates a shared key. However, the ticket for the mail server now contains John's user name as well as the shared key. Then the KDC combines the ticket, the nonce, the shared key, and the mail server's name into a single response to John, all encrypted with John's key.

Upon receipt, John decrypts the data from the KDC. John can verify that the response isn't caused by a replay of an earlier request by checking that the nonce value is correct. Likewise, he can verify that an attacker didn't change his request, say, to point to a different recipient, by verifying that the ticket is intended for the mail server. If either of these had happened, the reply's encrypted contents would reflect it.

An important assumption here is that the KDC doesn't use a stream cipher or other encryption technique that's vulnerable to a rewrite attack (A-72 in Section 11.3). Otherwise the attacker could make systematic changes to the reply, like replace one nonce with another, or modify the stated recipient. The KDC must use a cipher that diffuses plaintext bit values across numerous other bits: a

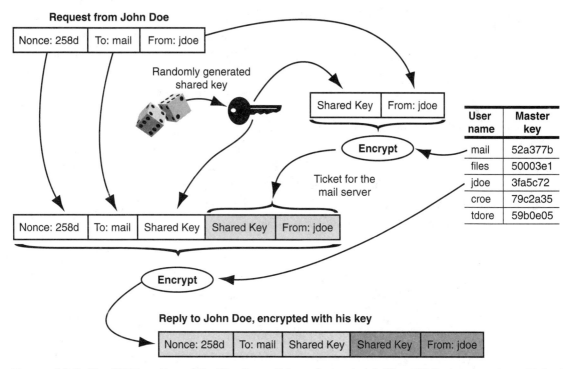

FIGURE 12.3: *The KDC portion of the Needham-Schroeder protocol.* The KDC constructs a ticket that contains a randomly chosen shared secret and the name of the client requesting the key. The KDC then sends back a response encrypted with the client's secret key that includes the client's nonce, the shared key, and the name of the server for whom the ticket was created.

block cipher. Moreover, the block cipher should operate in a chaining mode that makes different parts of the ciphertext depend on one another. This will cause changes to the ciphertext to yield unexpected or invalid results when decrypted.

It might seem that John can finish the key exchange by simply transmitting the ticket to the mail server. John is reasonably certain that he's not using a "stale" message from the KDC that has been replayed by an attacker. On the other hand, the mail server can't be certain that an attacker isn't simply replaying one of John's earlier tickets. If an attacker tricks the mail server into accepting an earlier ticket, the attacker could then replay some earlier session John had with the mail server. For example, the attacker might cause the mail server to accept a duplicate copy of some earlier e-mail message that, perhaps, performs some valuable transaction (like paying money to the attacker an additional time).

A-76

To prevent this, the Needham-Schroeder protocol includes a challenge response portion (Figure 12.4). This verifies that the ticket came from a system that actually possesses a copy of the ticket's shared key. Once the mail server receives the ticket from John, it uses the key it shares with the KDC to decrypt the ticket. It verifies that John's user name is in the ticket. Then the server generates a nonce, encrypts it with the key from the ticket, and sends the nonce to John. Upon receipt, John decrypts the nonce, subtracts one from it, and sends it back to the mail server. This allows the mail server to verify that John does indeed have the other key, since otherwise John could not have decremented the nonce.

D-76

The main reason for using temporary session keys is that there's always a risk that attackers will occasionally get a hold of a session key. They may do it through brute force cracking or perhaps by penetrating one of the computers using that key. Following that logic, the researchers Dorothy Denning and Giovanni Sacco realized that an attacker with a session key could reuse the corresponding ticket with impunity. For example, imagine that the attacker had intercepted one of the session keys shared between John and the mail server, and also had a copy of the corresponding ticket. The attacker could return to the mail server any number of times with that ticket and convince the server to use the ticket again. The mail server would have no way of knowing that the ticket wasn't being used by

A-77

John, since the attacker could use the corresponding session key to handle the challenge response.

see Note 3.

To solve this problem, Denning and Sacco proposed an alternative to the Needham-Schroeder protocol that used *time stamps* instead of nonces. In John's case, his computer would insert the current time in the request being sent to the KDC. The response from the KDC would contain the same time stamp instead of the nonce. In addition, the KDC would include the time stamp in the mail server's ticket. When the mail server decrypts the ticket from John, it can now check that the ticket is from John and that he produced the ticket recently. This greatly reduces the risk of a replay attack, and the technique found widespread use in the Kerberos protocol.

D-77

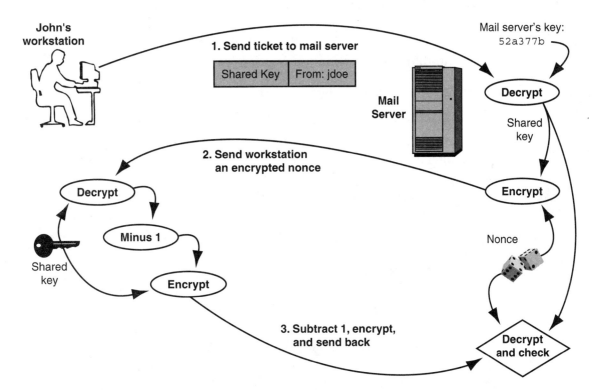

FIGURE 12.4: *The challenge response portion of Needham-Schroeder.* John's workstation has received a mail server ticket from the KDC as described in Figure 12.3. He sends it to the mail server, which extracts the shared key as shown on the right. To ensure that both John and the server are using the same key, the server encrypts a nonce and sends it to John. As shown on the left, John's workstation decrypts the nonce, subtracts 1 from it, encrypts it, and sends it back. The server verifies the response by decrypting it and checking it against the original nonce.

12.2 KERBEROS

In 1983, Project Athena was started at MIT as a model for the envisioned "next generation distributed computing" environment for academic environments. The Project Athena team decided to design their security solution around a KDC based on the Needham-Schroeder protocol but incorporating the work of Denning and Sacco. To make Kerberos work in a large-scale environment, Project Athena had to provide software to handle logons at client workstations and adapt servers to accept the Kerberos protocol. Software adapted to work with Kerberos is generally referred to as having been *Kerberized*.

see Note 4.

By 1989, Steve Miller and Clifford Neumann had produced four versions of Kerberos with help from others at MIT. Version 4 was the first publicly released version, and is still used to some extent. Version 5, however, is the standardized version in the Internet community, and that is the version we look at here.

see Note 5.

THE AUTHENTICATION SERVER

The Kerberos KDC contains several separate servers that provide different functions. The "authentication server" provides a protocol most similar to Needham-Schroeder. In theory, this server can issue tickets to talk to any Kerberized service. In practice, most workstations only use the authentication server to issue tickets to the "ticket-granting service," which we will discuss in a later section. Table 12.1 summarizes the essential contents of a Kerberos ticket.

To collect a ticket from the authentication server, John must construct a KRB_AS_REQ message (Figure 12.5). Like the Needham-Schroeder protocol, John provides his own identity, the name of the desired server, and a nonce when requesting a ticket. In addition, the protocol establishes a time period during which the shared key, called the *session key* in Kerberos, should be valid. Kerberos also incorporates a workstation identifier into the keying protocol, so that it can control which workstations are allowed to use a particular ticket. This reduces the likelihood that an attacker can misuse a ticket. The authentication server responds by constructing a KRB_AS_REP message containing the ticket and its associated status information.

TABLE 12.1: *Essential Contents of a Kerberos Ticket*

Field	Purpose
User name	The client who requested the ticket
Server name	The desired service. This ticket is encrypted using this server's master key
Validity period	The time at which the ticket, and its corresponding session key, begin to be valid, and the time at which the key and ticket cease to be valid
Session key	The secret key being shared between this user and server
Workstation	An identifier for the computer (or computers) on which this user may reside

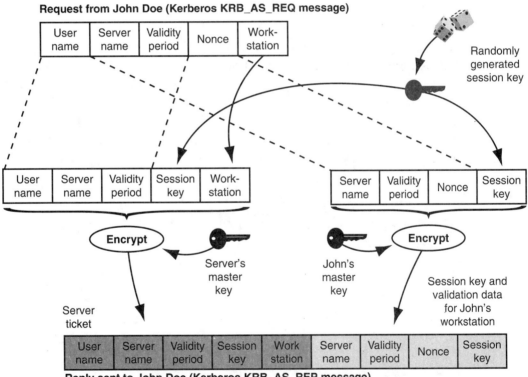

FIGURE 12.5: *The Kerberos authentication server.* Users must go to this server for their first ticket after logging on. The protocol is an improved version of Needham-Schroeder. The validity period establishes when and how long a ticket and its corresponding session key should be used. This addresses the replay problems identified by Denning and Sacco. The workstation identifier establishes which computers may use a particular ticket.

John validates the ticket by checking the status information the server provides in the KRB_AS_REP message. In particular, he needs to verify that the reply contains the correct server name, nonce, and validity period. Then he can safely use the ticket and session key to contact the server.

AUTHENTICATING TO A SERVER

Figure 12.6 shows how John uses his Kerberos ticket and the corresponding session key to construct a KRB_AP_REQ message to authenticate himself to the mail server. In addition to the server's ticket, John provides a Kerberos *authenticator*, which is an encrypted data item containing John's user name and a time stamp. John uses the same session key that appears in the ticket to encrypt the authenticator.

Upon receipt, the mail server first decrypts the ticket. Then it extracts the session key and uses it to decrypt the authenticator. The authenticator's user name should match the one in the ticket, and the time stamp should be recent, usually within the past five minutes. If the request passes these tests, the server constructs a KRB_AP_REP message, if the user asked for one. This reply sends back the request's time stamp, encrypted with the session key. As with Needham-Schroeder, this reply is only meaningful if the

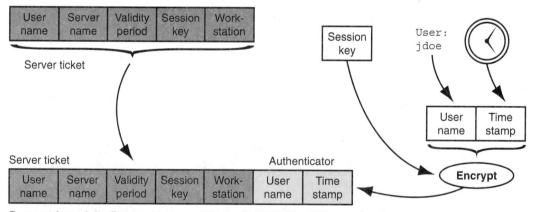

Request from John Doe to the server (Kerberos KRB_AP_REQ message)

FIGURE 12.6: *Authenticating to a Kerberized server.* When John sends a ticket to the server, he must also provide an authenticator, which contains his user name and a time stamp, both encrypted with the session key.

encryption does not permit precise and reliable rewriting or cut-and-paste attacks.

TICKET-GRANTING SERVICE

Although it's possible to use the Kerberos authentication server to generate tickets to individual service, this poses a problem. Kerberos needs to use one's master key to process messages with the authentication server, and most people tend to use many services while working on a computer. If we store the master key on the workstation while someone is using it, we run the risk that someone else will steal it. To eliminate this problem, we need to use the master key for as short a time as possible and erase it from the workstation as soon as we can. But this presents another problem: if we erase the master key once we finish connecting to one server, we'll have to read it in again when we try to connect to another. Traditionally, Kerberos has used memorized passwords as users' master keys, so this would present people with numerous password prompts. Neither alternative is practical.

So here we are facing the same dilemma that led to session keys: we need a temporary key that we can use for issuing other temporary keys. Indeed, we solve the problem in the same way: instead of leaving the master key on the workstation while John is logged in, we come up with a special session key we can use to issue our tickets. This applies a well-known piece of computing wisdom: you can often fix things by adding another level of indirection.

Kerberos implements this additional temporary key by adding a special server to the KDC called the *ticket-granting server*. This server accepts tickets that are called, of course, *ticket-granting tickets* (TGTs). Users can send their TGTs to this special server to request tickets for other services.

In previous examples, we spoke of John Doe's establishing a connection to the mail server via the KDC. In practice, of course, John won't just connect to the mail server. More likely, he'll also routinely connect to two or more different file servers, a print server or two, and various other services. John's workstation will undoubtedly connect itself to several of these services automatically when he logs on. But there may be other services that he doesn't routinely use or that it doesn't make sense to connect with until needed.

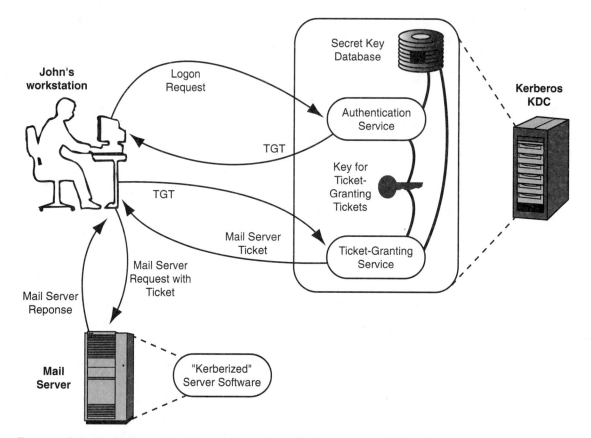

FIGURE 12.7: *Kerberos and ticket-granting tickets.* Kerberos can split the ticketing process into two parts: first, John can retrieve a "ticket-granting ticket" (TGT), and then he uses the TGT with the ticket-granting service to acquire individual tickets to use individual services. He needs to enter his master key only when he requests the TGT, and thereafter it does not need to reside on his workstation and be vulnerable to attack.

Kerberos provides a relatively safe and user-friendly mechanism for single sign-on by using the ticket-granting server (Figure 12.7). When John signs on to his workstation, it immediately contacts the Kerberos KDC's authentication server and collects a TGT. Then the workstation collects John's password (or other authentication data) and uses it to decrypt the reply from the authentication server. Then the workstation passes the TGT to the ticket-granting server to collect a ticket for every service he immediately needs: his usual file servers, the mail server, the print server. Later on, the workstation can again go to the ticket-granting server for more server tickets if

John needs to use additional servers. The workstation never needs to prompt John again for his password: it simply uses the TGT and its corresponding session key to collect additional tickets.

The ticket-granting server issues tickets through an intricate but fairly straightforward process. Figure 12.8 shows the first part of this process. John sends his request, which contains an authenticator, a TGT, and details about this request: which server (the mail server), when and how long it will be used, and a nonce.

Like all other servers, the ticket-granting server has its own private key, which Kerberos uses to encrypt its tickets. Upon receipt of a TGT, the server decrypts it and extracts the session key being used for issuing John's tickets, called the *ticketing key* here. The server uses the ticketing key to decrypt the authenticator and check its

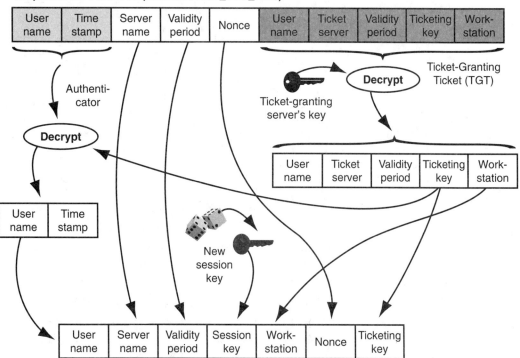

FIGURE 12.8: *Using a TGT request to construct a ticket for a service, part 1.* John sends the ticket granting server a copy of his TGT, an authenticator, and information about the mail server ticket he needs. The ticket-granting server decrypts and validates his request, using their ticketing key. Then it generates a session key for John to share with the mail server.

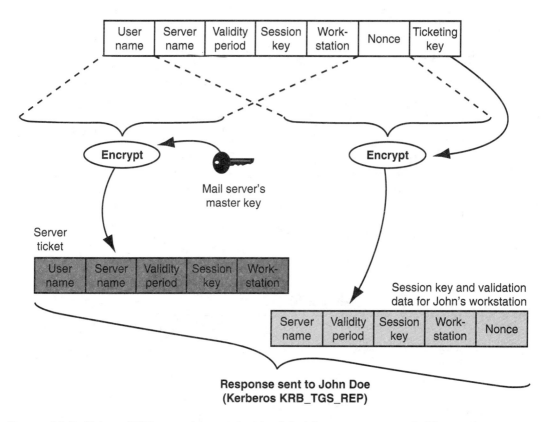

FIGURE 12.9: *Using a TGT request to construct a ticket for a service, part 2.* The ticket-granting server takes the information it has collected and formats it for encryption. The mail server ticket is encrypted with the mail server's master key. The rest of the reply is encrypted with John's ticketing key, taken from the TGT.

validity. The server also checks the validity period of the TGT against the current time and the validity period John's workstation has requested for this new ticket. Next, the server generates a random session key to be used by John's workstation and the mail server.

Figure 12.9 shows how the ticket-granting server takes the data to be returned to John and encrypts it for delivery. First, the server constructs the mail server ticket and encrypts it with the mail server's master key. Next, the server assembles the rest of the data required in its reply, and encrypts that data with John's ticketing key. Both blocks of encrypted data are then combined to produce the reply message that the server sends to John.

12.3 USER AND WORKSTATION AUTHENTICATION

Careful readers may have noticed that the KDC protocols like Kerberos really emphasize the authentication of people to network services. The classic protocols do little or nothing to establish a user's identity for the benefit of a workstation or even the KDC. There is nothing to prevent anyone, including an attacker, from requesting tickets for authenticating someone else to a particular server. Anyone that can communicate with John Doe's KDC can send a message claiming to be John and retrieve a ticket for authenticating John to the mail server. The subsequent protocols simply ensure that attackers can't really use the tickets they receive.

This situation has two interesting implications. First, it means that Kerberos doesn't necessarily treat the workstations themselves as distinct entities that require authentication. Instead, they're assumed to be interchangeable devices, like they might be in an academic lab environment. Second, it means that attackers might be able to collect enough tickets associated with a particular person to try to mount an attack on their master key. Fortunately, these implications aren't cast in stone, and Kerberos implementations can overcome them.

WORKSTATION AUTHENTICATION

A fundamental feature of the KDC protocols we examined in the previous sections is that the protocols rely on a single key, the user's master key, to secure the activities of a workstation. Unlike the Windows NT protocol examined in Section 11.4, the workstation doesn't have a separate key for communicating with the KDC or any other security service. Since Kerberos implements indirect authentication, it doesn't help the workstation itself to authenticate individual users. The workstation simply serves as a vessel by which authorized users can manipulate resources on servers. Anyone with physical access can, in theory, use any workstation since Kerberos itself provides no workstation-specific authentication services.

The Kerberos approach clearly reflects a "thin client" view of distributed computing. If client workstations are simple and fairly uniform across a network, people can use them interchangeably. It doesn't matter which workstation a person uses; the principal objective of authentication is to ensure that a user like John doesn't retrieve server resources that don't belong to him.

However, this vision doesn't fit the reality in sites dominated by personal computers on individual desks. Each personal computer contains local files belonging to its particular owner or custodian. In many cases it contains software that is individually licensed to its owner. If Kerberos will authenticate anyone on any workstation, then it can't control access to these personal resources. In such cases the workstation will have to provide an additional authentication procedure. This could consist of local authentication or it can use Kerberos-based "preauthentication" described later in this section. Microsoft uses a combination of these techniques in Windows 2000, as described in Section 12.6.

In an ideal world that uses perfectly reliable encryption, it shouldn't matter that attackers can request and receive tickets intended for other users. But in fact we never have as much confidence in our cryptographic algorithms as we might wish. Thus, we generally avoid putting information at risk when we don't have to.

In the case of Kerberos tickets, there is a risk that attackers could collect enough tickets intended for some other important user to mount a successful attack against that user's master key. In a classic Kerberos environment this is a serious threat because personal master keys are based on memorized passwords. For example, imagine that some very important person (the Pope, the President of the United States, Bill Gates, Jodie Foster, or some other notable) uses Kerberos for authentication through a large-scale KDC. This means that anyone else who can contact that KDC can retrieve "papal tickets," or tickets belonging to any other VIP there. If the particular VIP is careless with password selection, then attackers might be able to crack the VIP's password by collecting tickets and mounting a dictionary attack on them.

A-78

PREAUTHENTICATION

Kerberos Version 5 introduced *preauthentication* so that sites could authenticate requests sent to the KDC instead of relying on servers to authenticate the requests later. Administrators can configure Kerberos to require preauthentication on requests for tickets or TGTs so that the KDC only distributes encrypted data to those who

D-78

already know the associated key. Typically, the process is used to authenticate a user when retrieving an initial TGT from the KDC, though the protocol can support a broad range of alternatives. Initial preauthentication should be available as an option in any truly interoperable version of Kerberos.

In traditional Kerberos authentication, the workstation collects keys from the KDC before it needs the user's master key. Since Kerberos typically uses people's passwords as their master key, the workstation can defer the password prompt until it hears from the KDC. With initial preauthentication, the workstation must collect the user's master key first, which usually means collecting the password.

Next, the workstation constructs the initial KDC request, which usually requests a TGT. For preauthentication, the workstation adds a specially formatted, encrypted time stamp. The time stamp includes the current time of day and a one-way hash of the rest of the KDC request, all encrypted with the user's master key.

When the KDC receives the request, it checks to see if preauthentication is required and, if so, rejects the request if it is missing. If the preauthentication time stamp is present, the KDC looks up the user's master key and uses it to decrypt the time stamp. If the time stamp's time of day is reasonable, the KDC computes a one-way hash over the rest of the request and compares it against the hash in the time stamp. If they match, the KDC fulfills the request.

Note that the workstation can treat the KDC's response as confirmation of the user's identity. The KDC will send back a legitimate response message instead of an error message only if the preauthentication succeeds. The workstation can decrypt the KDC's response and verify that it contains the correct nonce, server name, and validity period. If not, then the workstation can conclude that the user is trying (unsuccessfully) to masquerade as someone else.

12.4 TICKET DELEGATION

As we've described it so far, John's tickets can be used only by John himself to fetch and use his resources. But as distributed systems have evolved in sophistication, we've encountered situations in which servers may need to contact other servers on John's behalf. For example, the mail server undoubtedly needs to read John's mail queue files, which no doubt reside on a file server somewhere. The e-mail server somehow needs to get permission to read John's queue. Traditionally, administrators grant the mail server the god-like power to read all files, or at least all mail files, but this has also been a source of security problems. If an attacker tricks the mail server into using the wrong identity, the attacker can read the other user's mail. Even worse, if an attacker penetrates the mail server, the attacker could gain free access to everyone's mail file.

The preferred solution is to give the server only as much permission as it needs to perform its authorized activities. If John asks the server to retrieve his mail, then the server should have access only to his mail files and to whatever administrative files are essential for retrieving that mail. The mail server is confident that it speaks to John, because it has a valid ticket from him. But if the mail server turns around and asks the file server for files on John's behalf, how does the file server become confident that the request is honestly on John's behalf? After all, there's always a risk that someone has penetrated the mail server and is making bogus requests. Moreover, Kerberos tickets identify the address of the computer that requested them, and they aren't supposed to be honored if the addresses don't match.

Kerberos Version 5 provides mechanisms so that workstations can delegate their ticketing privileges to servers under limited circumstances. This involves two features added to the TGT. The first feature allows *proxiable tickets*, which permit a TGT's owner to request tickets tied to computers with different network addresses. The second feature allows the TGT to be *forwardable*, which permits the owner to ask for another TGT that is tied to a different network address. Also, Kerberos uses a similar mechanism to authenticate users between different KDCs ("realms") using a special TGT called a *referral ticket*.

PROXIABLE TGT

If John's workstation software wants to use proxy tickets, then it starts by requesting a TGT with the "proxiable" option allowed. When John needs to read his mail, he first collects a mail server ticket, and uses it to authenticate himself to that server as usual. Since the mail server also needs to contact the file server on John's behalf, John's workstation must also request a *proxy ticket* for the file server. This proxy ticket contains the network address of the mail server. John forwards this ticket to the mail server along with a copy of the associated session key. The session key is encrypted using the key that John shares with the mail server, so that the mail server can retrieve that key. The mail server then forwards the proxy ticket to the file server. Upon receipt, the file server sees that the ticket contains the network address of the mail server, so the ticket is accepted. The file server decrypts the ticket and retrieves the session key. Since the mail server and file server share that key, they can authenticate one another and proceed with the processing of John's mail.

FORWARDABLE TGT

A problem with proxy tickets is that the originating workstation must somehow be able to predict which proxy tickets will be needed. Even worse, the workstation and server could find themselves exchanging numerous messages trying to establish an accurate list of the required proxy tickets. The forwardable TGT eliminates this problem by letting the server ask for the necessary tickets itself.

If John's workstation software wants to use a forwardable TGT, then it starts by requesting a TGT with the "forwardable" option allowed. When John needs to read his mail, he again collects a mail server ticket and uses it in the normal way. Then John contacts the ticket-granting server and requests it to issue him another TGT, this one containing the network address of the mail server. John forwards that ticket to the mail server along with an encrypted copy of the TGT's ticketing key. Now the mail server can contact the ticket-granting server directly to retrieve tickets for whatever server it needs to contact. The ticket-granting server honors the ticket requests on John's behalf because the mail server's network address matches the address in the forwarded TGT. Of course, the request also contains a valid authenticator that the server has encrypted with the TGT's ticketing key.

These different techniques reflect different trade-offs between security and operating convenience. While both eliminate the need to give servers unrestricted access to other servers, both pose their own risks and costs. The proxy approach lets the user's software decide what server permissions it will delegate to other servers, but this requires the software to know which proxy tickets will be needed. The forwardable TGT approach lets servers collect whatever tickets they need on behalf of a user, but there's no strong mechanism to prevent a subverted server from abusing this power. The only limit is in the ticket's expiration date and, possibly, in permission fields copied into tickets from the TGT. These permission fields are specific to particular software environments and applications. This trade-off depends heavily on the security needs of particular sites and particular application environments, so these delegation features form an optional part of Kerberos. They are only available if the site or application environment allows them to be used.

REALMS AND REFERRAL TICKETS

A proprietor's enterprise can establish two or more Kerberos KDCs if a single KDC can't satisfy the enterprise's needs. The proprietor can establish separate KDCs to reflect organizational or geographical distinctions, or to implement separation of duty. In Kerberos parlance, the community of users, servers, and other entities registered with a particular KDC represent a single *realm*. Entities within the enterprise are assigned names based on their realm, and multiple realms can be structured hierarchically. Authorized users in one realm can be authenticated to servers in other realms using the Kerberos protocols for "cross-realm authentication." This allows sites to handle user administration locally but still authenticate users across a large-scale networking environment.

For example, let's say that John needs to use a special-purpose printer in another realm to print a document for someone at a different location. John can use that printer if he can get a TGT for the printer's KDC. To do this, John asks his own KDC for a *referral ticket* to the printer's KDC; the referral ticket serves as the TGT he needs. To create the referral ticket, John's KDC uses an "interrealm key" that it shares with the printer's KDC. Once John has the referral ticket, he uses it to contact the printer's KDC to retrieve a ticket for visiting that printer.

For one KDC to create a referral ticket for using another KDC, the two must already share an interrealm key. Since this might not be practical in really large organizations with dozens, or hundreds, of

KDCs, a KDC can retrieve a referral ticket through multiple hops if necessary. The KDC can do this by following the branches of the organization's realm hierarchy, as long as every KDC has shared an interrealm key with its parent and children in the hierarchy.

This approach allows anyone in a large-scale Kerberos network to be authenticated to any server within that network. In theory, cross-realm authentication could even span multiple enterprises. However, there remains the question of how the servers make authorization decisions. Once they identify who has asked for service, they need a mechanism to decide if that person should really receive service or not.

12.5 ATTACKING A KERBEROS NETWORK

A fundamental feature of the Kerberos philosophy is to recognize that some computers in its network will be successfully attacked. This should be obvious, since Kerberos relies on reusable passwords as base secrets. The Kerberos design tries to minimize the system-wide implications of intrusions on individual workstations and servers. The overall security of a Kerberos site also relies on the assumption that all clocks are roughly synchronized on all participating computers. Kerberos should meet its security objectives as long as those assumptions remain accurate.

INTRUSION TOLERANCE

Kerberos tries to provide a practical degree of security with minimum reliance on special properties of computers within the network. Successful attacks on individual workstations or servers cannot compromise the overall security of a Kerberos network. This is because neither the workstations nor the servers require any special permissions to work with the KDC.

This is a practical and realistic strategy, especially in an academic setting. Commercial computer systems are notoriously vulnerable to attack. While it's possible to reduce the risk if administrators put a lot of effort into hardening a particular host, this effort isn't practical in a large-scale networking environment. In any case, people with computers on their desks will, over time, disable some security measures either accidentally or intentionally. Moreover, the distribution of authority in an academic environment does not give a network security administrator a way to reliably install security measures on individual machines.

Kerberos adapts to this situation by tolerating intrusions to a certain extent. If a single computer is compromised somehow, the only possible damage will affect that particular computer and no others. At worst, the attacker might manage to retrieve a master key belonging to the user or server. Most often, however, the only keys available for attack should be the temporary session keys. Loss of those keys should cause only short-term damage. While it is true that attackers can affect large parts of the user population by penetrating a heavily used server, the risk of damage in such a case has more to do with local computing policies than it does with the Kerberos architecture. In such cases, a cautious site can reduce risks by deploying numerous independent servers instead of concentrating users and services on only a handful of computers.

The KDC, however, must successfully resist attack in order to maintain overall network security. If attackers manage to penetrate the KDC's defenses, they can copy the database of master keys and then masquerade as any user. They might even be able to masquerade as the KDC. Cautious Kerberos sites generally assign the KDC to a dedicated computer, and the administrators remove and disable all other services on that computer. This reduces the risk of an attack by reducing the number of entry ways into the computer.

CLOCK SYNCHRONIZATION

Clock synchronization is a crucial requirement of computers operating in a Kerberos environment. Tickets become valid and expire within established time periods; if clocks are wrong, then tickets won't work when they should. Worse, they won't expire when they should.

This provides an opening for an attack. Imagine that an attacker manages to recover the session key corresponding to a particular ticket. The Kerberos approach assumes that such things might happen occasionally, but expects to limit the damage by limiting the validity period of tickets. But what happens if the attacker manipulates a server's clock? There are many ways to do this. An attacker might somehow manage to penetrate far enough into the server to convince its clock to change. More likely, however, the attacker would simply send messages using the Network Time Protocol that trick the server into changing its clock. Then the attacker can transmit the expired ticket and the server will mistakenly accept it as being legitimate.

A-79

The usual solution is to require authentication on messages from the time server. In practice, though, it can be tricky to provide such authentication at a level of confidence that compares well with Kerberos. Classic strategies for time authentication are based on shared base secrets, like passwords, and suffer from the classic risk of sniffing and replay. A more promising approach would be to use "public key" authentication as discussed in the next chapter. Ultimately, however, accurate clocks will need to rely on vigilance and regular checking. Bellovin and Merritt have noted that an attacker could construct a radio transmitter that generated bogus WWV time signals, and that the transmitter might be able to fool the time server itself into distributing the wrong time.

D-79

see Note 6.

12.6 KERBEROS IN WINDOWS 2000

In Windows 2000, Microsoft replaced the Windows NT domain authentication mechanism described in Section 11.3 with Kerberos. Windows domain logon has become a transaction that retrieves a TGT. File server mapping now involves the exchange of tickets and session keys. Master keys and other security-critical information is stored in the *Active Directory* facility. Although the Windows implementation of Kerberos contains a number of distinctive elements, Microsoft states that the implementation will comply with standard Kerberos interoperability requirements. In particular, non-Windows Kerberized applications should be able to process Windows tickets to yield a single sign-on capability between Windows and non-Windows applications.

see Note 7.

The Kerberos protocol has provided Windows 2000 with three particular benefits in comparison to earlier Windows products. First, it provides faster server authentication, since the server doesn't have to contact the domain controller for indirect authentication. Instead, the server simply processes the ticket. Second, Windows uses the ticket delegation features to pass a user's access rights to a server by way of another server. Third, Windows uses Kerberos protocols that allow KDCs belonging to different organizations to grant access to each other's users in a controlled manner.

Naturally, Microsoft could not simply substitute new network authentication protocols for old ones, abandoning its existing products and customers. Windows 2000 still supports the older NT domain protocols. If required, Windows 2000 can even support the older, security-challenged LANMAN authentication protocols described in Section 10.4.

MASTER KEYS AND WORKSTATION AUTHENTICATION

It is inevitable that some adjustments take place when a rather mature product line like Windows incorporates an even more mature technology like Kerberos. Microsoft needs to tread a fine line to maintain compatibility with its existing products while reaping at least some of the benefits of Kerberos' security features. We see this when we look at how Microsoft has adapted Kerberos to the Windows workstation logon process.

The workstation user, of course, is supposed to see nothing different. When a user like John Doe tries to log on, he types the usual magic keystroke and sees the password dialog on his screen. He enters his user name, selects his domain, and types his password. Underneath, Windows converts it all into Kerberos transactions.

A significant difference between traditional Kerberos and the Windows implementation is that Windows workstations are treated as distinct entities. Each workstation has its own identity within the realm and its own master key, separate from the master key of a logged-on user. In this example, John has named his workstation *bat*, and that's its name within the domain. The logon process retrieves a ticket to authenticate the user to the workstation in addition to any other tickets that might be needed.

In Windows 2000, the logon process is divided between three major processes: the *Winlogon* process that prompts John for his user name and password, the *Security Support Provider (SSP)* that communicates with Kerberos, and the *Local Security Authority (LSA)* that protects the workstation itself. This is shown in Figure 12.10. The process takes place as follows:

1. Once Winlogon has collected John's authentication data, it passes the data to the LSA.

2. The LSA converts the password into the master key to be used by Kerberos. The LSA does this by hashing the password as described in Section 10.6. Then the LSA invokes the Kerberos SSP, and passes it John's user name and master key.

   Unlike traditional Kerberos, Windows 2000 retains the master key in a cache. This allows the workstation to use Windows NT domain authentication if necessary for talking to older servers. There is an obvious risk in keeping this information in a cache, and the risk is unnecessary if the entire site uses Kerberos authentication.

3. The Kerberos SSP tries to contact its domain controller and retrieve an initial Kerberos TGT in John's name. The request uses preauthentication based on John's master key.

   If the chosen domain is controlled by an older Windows NT server and Kerberos isn't available, the LSA falls back to using an NT version of the SSP that uses the NTLM protocol described in Section 11.3.

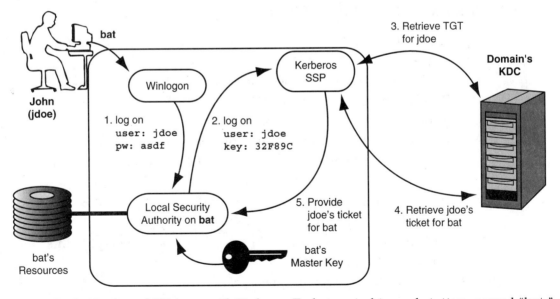

FIGURE 12.10: *Windows 2000 logon with Kerberos.* To log on to his workstation, named "bat," John must collect a ticket for bat from the domain's KDC. John's master key is derived from his memorized password, while bat's master key is a secret value stored in the workstation's Registry. The numbered steps in this diagram are keyed to the discussion in the text.

4. If the SSP receives its Kerberos TGT, it uses the TGT to retrieve a ticket for the workstation named "bat" on John's behalf.

5. Upon receipt of the workstation ticket, the SPP provides the ticket to the LSA, which uses bat's master key to authenticate it. If the key is authentic, the LSA logs John on to bat.

The extra step of collecting a ticket for the workstation itself is an unusual feature compared to other Kerberos environments. The ticket's session key serves no real purpose. Windows 2000 uses this approach because the KDC stores user credentials in each ticket, and this is a relatively clean and consistent way to retrieving a user's credentials from the KDC. Each ticket contains authorization information and other credentials necessary to associate the user with the right resources and access permissions on the workstation. The LSA on a Windows server works the same way: it retrieves credentials from a user's ticket and uses those credentials to run a server process with the identity and permissions of that user. At the workstation, the LSA ensures that applications on the workstation are run in that user's name.

SERVICE AND PROTOCOL SUPPORT

Here is a summary of the services and protocols that use Kerberos authentication in Windows 2000:

- File services, including the usual CIFS/SMB services and distributed file system management
- Printer services
- Web server authentication to the Internet Information Server
- Authenticated Remote Procedure Call (RPC) services for remote server and workstation management
- Queries to the Active Directory using the Lightweight Directory Access Protocol (LDAP)
- Authentication for setting up a host-to-host cryptographic link using the IP Security Protocol (IPSEC)
- Authenticate requests for quality of service levels

12.7 Summary Tables

TABLE 12.2: *Attack Summary*

Attack	Security Problem	Prevalence	Attack Description
A-75. KDC request spoof	Recover or modify hidden information	Common	Attacker intercepts a client's KDC request and returns a different set of shared keys whose value is known by the attacker
A-76. Rekey replay	Masquerade as someone else	Common	Attacker sends an earlier ticket to a server and then replays messages sent earlier by the client encrypted with that key
A-77. Off-line cracking and replay	Masquerade as someone else	Common	Attacker cracks a session key off-line and uses this knowledge to reuse that key's ticket
A-78. Off-line master key cracking	Masquerade as someone else	Sophisticated	Attacker requests tickets in the victim's name and uses them to brute force crack the victim's master key
A-79. Forged time change	Masquerade as someone else	Sophisticated	Attacker sends forged time of day messages to a server so that expired tickets are valid

TABLE 12.3: *Defense Summary*

Defense	Foils Attacks	Description
D-75. Nonce shared with KDC	A-75. KDC request spoof	A nonce is included in requests sent to the KDC and included in responses
D-76. Challenge response by server in KDC protocol	A-76. Rekey replay	Server sends a user a challenge, which requires a response that depends on the user's encrypting data with the session key

TABLE 12.3: *Defense Summary (Continued)*

Defense	Foils Attacks	Description
D-77. Time stamps in KDC protocol	A-77. Off-line cracking and replay	KDC messages include time-of-day information to detect attempts to reuse tickets later
D-78. KDC preauthentication	A-78. Off-line master key cracking	User must provide personal authentication information when requesting a TGT
D-79. Authenticated time messages	A-79. Forged time change	Messages that change a server's time of day must be authenticated

CHAPTER 13

PUBLIC KEYS AND OFF-LINE AUTHENTICATION

Three can keep a secret if two are dead.

— Ben Franklin, *Poor Richard's Almanac*

IN THIS CHAPTER

Public key cryptography uses clever mathematics to simplify and even eliminate several problems we have with shared base secrets. This gives us the tools we need to implement off-line authentication.

- Public key cryptography and its use in authentication
- RSA public keys and attacks on them
- The U.S. Digital Signature Standard
- Challenge response authentication with public keys
- Secure Sockets Layer
- Public keys for Kerberos preauthentication
- Public keys and biometrics

13.1 PUBLIC KEY CRYPTOGRAPHY

Ben Franklin's famous quote captures the essence of the problem with shared secret keys: we can't prevent the secret from spreading further through mistakes or through transitive trust. This can pose real problems when we use cryptography to authenticate important documents, like electronic checks. On the other hand, if we can find a mechanism that lets us safely sign checks, we can adapt it to authenticate people.

Consider the following situation: Tim Dore has written an electronic check to John Doe, payable by his bank ("I owe John $100").

In a perfect world, Tim gives this electronic check to John, and John forwards it to the bank. Both John and the bank must be able to authenticate the check. John must verify that the bank will recognize it as a check from Tim before he hands over whatever Tim bought from him. The bank, of course, must authenticate the check before it takes the money from Tim's bank account and gives it to John.

Imagine what happens if we use shared secret keys, probably with a keyed hash (Section 8.5), to authenticate Tim's electronic checks. Tim has to share his secret key with everyone who might receive one of his checks. Sharing the key with the bank might not raise an immediate worry, since we routinely use shared secrets (PINs for ATM cards) with banks already. But if Tim shares his secret key with everyone else who might want to authenticate his electronic check (John, for example), then anyone could modify or forge one of his electronic checks. All the forger has to do is use Tim's secret key to recompute the correct keyed hash for the forged or modified message. Section 9.1 provided examples of why banks aren't completely reliable for this, citing the occasional troubles they have with dishonest employees abusing customers' PINs.

A-80

Once we share that secret, there's nothing to prevent John or the bank from accidentally (or intentionally) misusing it, or from sharing the secret with others. Early password systems tried to limit the problem of leaked secrets by hashing the password so that its textual form wasn't easily available. This was a step in the right direction as long as attackers really needed the textual form when attacking some cryptographically protected data. But more sophisticated systems like Microsoft Windows now use the hashed password itself as the base secret for its security services (Section 12.6). Attackers can bypass these services by stealing the hashed password stored at either end of a "secured" network connection—they don't need the plaintext password.

Public key cryptography gives us back the benefits we used to get from hashed passwords: a way to do security functions with something other than the base secret itself. In public key cryptography we work with a pair of keys, the *private key* and the *public key*, which have special mathematical properties (Figure 13.1). We embed the base secret inside the private key, which is kept secret by its owner. We perform a special one-way mathematical function to construct the public key. Since the function works efficiently in one direction but not the other (like a one-way hash function), it's not practical for attackers to deduce the private key from the public key. Thus, we can safely publish and distribute the public key, even if it risks falling into the hands of attackers.

Public key algorithms use these two keys to perform *asymmetric encryption*. That is, we use one key for encryption and the other for decryption. In typical public key algorithms, we can use either key for encryption, but then we must use the other key for decryption. For example, if Tim uses his private key to encrypt something, then we must use Tim's public key to decrypt it. Likewise, if we encrypt something with Tim's public key, then nobody can decrypt it except Tim, using his private key.

Public keys always work in pairs. If we receive a message from Tim and use *his* public key to decrypt it, then we know for certain that it was encrypted with *his* private key and nobody else's. If someone else tries to encrypt something with Tim's public key, then we *cannot* decrypt it by using Tim's public key again. As with conventional secret keys, different public key pairs perform encryption differently: a message encrypted with John's private key won't be decrypted correctly by Tim's public key.

Thus, if Tim writes an electronic check and encrypts it with his private key, anyone who wants to verify its authenticity can use his public key to do so. The verification takes place entirely off-line. We *D-80* don't have to perform some transaction with the bank or with some authentication server: if we have Tim's public key, then we can use

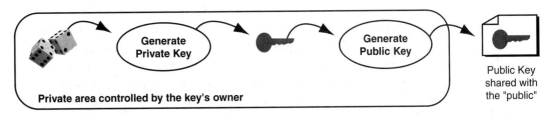

FIGURE 13.1: *Generating a public–private key pair.* First, we generate a random number and use it to choose a value for the private key. Next, we apply a special one-way function to the private key to produce the public key. Attackers can't derive the private key from the public key because the one way function is hard to reverse.

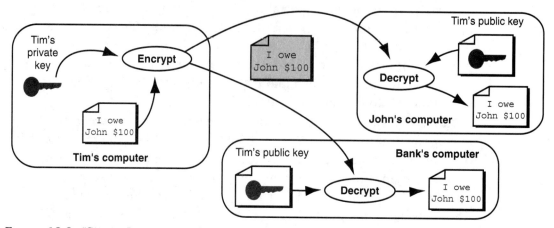

FIGURE 13.2: *"Signing" a message by encrypting it with the private key.* To authenticate his electronic check ("I owe John $100"), Tim encrypts it with his private key. The recipients (John and the bank) authenticate the message by decrypting it with a copy of Tim's public key. Attackers can't forge a message—if they encrypt it with the public key, it will yield gibberish when decrypted with the same public key.

it to authenticate his check. The encrypted electronic check serves as a primitive "digital signature" constructed by Tim to authenticate his message.

Figure 13.2 shows how we can use public key encryption to generate an electronic check that others can authenticate off-line. Tim writes the check and sends a copy to John and to his bank. Both recipients have copies of Tim's public key. Both can use the public key to verify that Tim wrote the message. Neither can modify that electronic check or create a completely different one.

Because of this, we can use public key cryptography to reduce the risks of transitive trust and of leaking base secrets. The key's owner keeps the private key secret and distributes copies of the public key to all potential recipients. Tim, John, and other bank customers generate public key pairs and share their public keys with the bank and with one another. They can validate each others' checks directly, using software residing on their own computers, and so can the bank. While this doesn't solve the problem of overdrawn bank accounts, it reduces the risk of forgery.

For authentication, we can reap the benefits of public key cryptography by replacing secret key algorithms with public key algorithms.

For example, we can replace the algorithms used in a challenge response protocol. Instead of encrypting the nonce with a shared secret key, Tim uses his private key. The authentication server can authenticate Tim using a copy of his public key. Thus, an attacker can't masquerade as Tim by simply stealing the key database, since it only contains public keys. Thus, public key authentication provides greater safety and flexibility.

13.2 THE RSA PUBLIC KEY ALGORITHM

The basic trick behind public key cryptography involves mathematical operations that are easy to do in one direction but hard to do in another. Unlike the one-way functions we use for one-way hashing, these functions have to yield numbers with a carefully tuned internal structure. This allows us to perform a series of one-way operations that won't fall apart when hit with clever mathematics.

Multiplication is a good example of how our one-way function needs to work. It's always straightforward to multiply several numbers together, but it's not always so easy to figure out what numbers were combined to produce a particular result. For example, you can easily use a pencil and paper to multiply 550 by 750 and find 412,500. On the other hand, there's no similar procedure to find which two numbers were multiplied together to yield 401,963. This is called the *factoring problem*, since it's the problem of finding what factors were multiplied together to produce a particular number. At best, one performs a search by trial and error to locate the factors. This can take a long time if the number is the product of multiplying two primes together, since primes aren't divisible by any smaller numbers, except the value *one*. Public key cryptography is based on the notion of using large enough numbers to make the trial-and-error factoring process too difficult to be practical.   *see Note 1.*

The factoring problem is at the heart of the Rivest Shamir Adelman (RSA) public key algorithm, created by Ron Rivest, Adi Shamir, and Len Adelman. RSA is arguably the most widely used public key algorithm, since every modern Web browser program uses it to protect e-commerce transactions (see Section 13.6). RSA is faster, or more flexible, or both, when compared to other public key algorithms. With RSA, we can encrypt with either the public or private key, and then decrypt with the other key. Various protocols and applications use RSA to authenticate people and computers, and to safely distribute keys used with secret key encryption.

An RSA key pair actually consists of three parts: the public part *e*, private part *d*, and the shared value *N*. We construct the shared value *N* by choosing two very large prime numbers and multiplying them together. In practice, we often use a standard value for *e*, like 3 or 65,537, but it can be chosen randomly as long as it meets certain mathematical restrictions. We compute *d* from *e* and the two large primes. The RSA public key consists of the shared value *N* along with the public part *e*. Once we've erased the data used to produce the keys (particularly the two initial primes), only the private part *d* needs to be kept secret.

see Note 2.

RSA encryption and decryption are surprisingly simple in design. If we're encrypting with the public key, then we take the plaintext message (let's call it *P*) and exponentiate it by the public part *e*, and take the *modulus* relative to *N*. In other words, we raise the number *P* to the e'th power, and then find its remainder relative to *N*. The modulus function simply computes the integer remainder (note that the RSA shared value *N* is itself often called "the modulus"). Now we can look at a trivial example using small numbers. If we take *e* = 7, *N* = 527, and our secret message is 2, for example, then encryption looks like this:

$$C = P^e \bmod N \qquad \begin{aligned} C &= 2^7 \bmod 527 \\ C &= 128 \bmod 527 \\ C &= 128 \end{aligned}$$

So, the message, encrypted with the public key, is the number 128. We use essentially the same, simple computation to decrypt it, but we use the other key. The private part depends on the public part, and so we find that *d* = 343 if the public key's *N* = 527 and *e* = 7. The decryption takes place like this:

see Note 3.

$$P = C^d \bmod N \qquad \begin{aligned} P &= 128^{343} \bmod 527 \\ P &= 2 \end{aligned}$$

Now we can implement electronic checks for Tim using RSA. First, Tim must generate the three pieces of an RSA key for himself, and send a copy of his "public key" (his *N* and *e* values) to his bank.

Then he can fill out an electronic check, encode it into a large number, and then encrypt that number using his RSA private key. This takes place exactly as shown above, except that we substitute d for e in the encryption step. Now, anyone with Tim's RSA public key can decrypt his electronic check and see for themselves that Tim produced it.

13.3 ATTACKING RSA

Consider what happens if someone named Henry takes Tim's public key and tries to construct an electronic check that appears to be from Tim. Of course, Henry can encrypt an electronic check with Tim's public key, but the resulting check won't decrypt correctly when the bank uses Tim's public key to decrypt it. To forge Tim's signature, Henry can use either of two general strategies: he can figure out Tim's private key, or he can fiddle with the mathematics of the encryption to try to produce a properly encrypted check. Both techniques might work unless Tim takes the right steps to prevent them.

ATTACKING RSA KEYS

Henry can reconstruct Tim's private value d if he can find the two factors that make up the shared value N. If Tim's key is the one used in the example ($N = 527$, $e = 7$) then Henry has a reasonably easy job. He knows that the shared value N is the product of two prime numbers, and that the private key d is constructed from those two primes. So all he has to do is find which two numbers were multiplied together to produce the number 527. At worst, he could write a program to iterate through all reasonable pairs of numbers, see if their product equals 527, and stumble on the answer after trying, at most, a few dozen alternatives.

In essence, the value N is the "key" value when considering brute force attacks on RSA. For that reason, we generally refer to N as the "RSA key," and the "size" of an RSA key refers to the size of N itself. If the key size is small, like in the example, then it is vulnerable to attack. We need to determine how big our RSA key must be to resist attack. Fortunately, we can increase the size of an RSA key without changing the encryption algorithm. We only have to be sure that the software implementation will handle the key size we choose.

We can crack an RSA key by factoring it and, unfortunately, there are some very efficient techniques for factoring numbers. Unlike brute force attacks on secret keys, these factoring techniques don't have to consider every possible value of the key individually. In fact, classical factorization techniques require $N^{1/2}$ steps, which means that the average attack space contains *half* as many bits as the RSA key. And the story gets even worse.

A-81

see Note 4.

When RSA was introduced in 1977, Ron Rivest predicted that it would take 40 quadrillion years to factor an RSA key containing 125 decimal digits (416 bits), and whimsically offered $100 to the first person to do it. But his prediction proved inaccurate by approximately 40 quadrillion years when a team of researchers broke an RSA message encrypted with a 129-digit key in 1994. To be fair, Rivest's estimate might have been plausible in 1977. Back in 1977, factoring relied on classical techniques, so a 416-bit RSA key presented a 208-bit average attack space. A brute force attack of that size was impractical back then and remains impractical today.

see Note 5.

Although Rivest's challenge started as a bit of a joke, it became serious as mathematicians made incredible progress on the factoring problem. A few years later, RSA Data Security, the company that held the patent rights to the RSA algorithm (now RSA Security), officially established the RSA Factoring Challenge. The challenge consisted of a series of messages encrypted with RSA keys of different lengths, and each challenge was named according to the number of decimal digits in the key. Thus, the RSA-129 challenge contained a message encrypted with a 129-digit (429-bit) RSA key. The successful attack on RSA-129, led by Arjen Lenstra of Bellcore, used a factoring technique called the quadratic sieve.

see Note 6.

Between 1991 and 1999, teams of mathematicians and computer scientists cracked seven RSA challenge messages by factoring larger and larger numbers. RSA-129 was actually the last time that the quadratic sieve was used to crack an RSA challenge. Later successes relied on a different technique: the number field sieve. The quadratic sieve worked efficiently against smaller RSA keys. When key sizes (and challenges) exceed the 429-bit keys of the RSA-129 challenge, the number field sieve becomes the practical choice.

In 1999, a new team (though including a few people from the RSA-129 effort) used the number field sieve to crack RSA-155, a message encrypted with a 512-bit RSA key. The attack was comparable to a 63-bit average attack space. The 512-bit key was a particularly important milestone, since that used to be a standard key size used for e-commerce on the World Wide Web. RSA Security used the occasion to recommend that RSA keys be at least 768 bits long. However, a survey of e-commerce servers the following year found that over 25% of them were still using keys of 512 bits or less.

see Note 7.

RSA's press release is right: the principal countermeasure against factoring attacks is to use larger RSA key sizes. Typically we use heuristics to estimate the number of computational steps a sieve will require to factor an RSA key of a given size; we can use the same heuristic to estimate the average attack space of an RSA key. Table 13.1 compares the average attack space for common RSA key sizes against other cryptographic authentication techniques. Typical secret key sizes rarely approach 200 bits, and the corresponding average attack space is usually only one or two bits less than that. Since the average attack space for an RSA key is dramatically smaller than the key size, we must obviously choose a correspondingly larger key size. Modern RSA keys are often more than a thousand bits long, and in some cases may contain over 2,000 bits.

D-81

see Note 8.

TABLE 13.1: *Comparing Public Keys with Other Average Attack Spaces*

Typical Use	Average Attack Space
Eight-character personally chosen password	22.7 bits
56-bit DES (ANSI X9.9, other DES tokens, encryption, etc.)	54 bits
SecurID one-time password token	63 bits
512-bit public keys for digital signatures	63 bits
768-bit key—RSA Security's minimum RSA key size, 1999	76 bits
1024-bit public keys	86 bits
2048-bit high-security public keys	116 bits
128-bit Advanced Encryption Standard	127 bits

Factoring attacks look incredibly powerful in comparison to the straightforward brute force attacks posed by secret key algorithms, and that by itself might make some people uneasy. If attacks have made so much progress against public keys so quickly, then what's to prevent this "trend" from continuing until public key cryptography is worthless? We can answer that question in several ways.

First, we look at why the factoring attack seems to be the best way to attack an RSA private key. Mathematicians have found a few arguments to support this belief. Attempts to crack the key by attacking other elements of the encryption, like the private part *d* of the private key, turn out to require as much work as attacks directly on the *N* value itself. And, while mathematicians haven't been able to prove conclusively that all attacks on the RSA private key will require factoring of *N*, they have proven it for something similar, the *Rabin cryptosystem*. However, the Rabin system isn't as practical to use, so instead we rely on their similarities to give us confidence in the safety of RSA encryption.   *see Note 9.*

Second, we can consider why it's likely that factoring will remain a hard enough problem to protect our data. For centuries, mathematicians have acknowledged that factoring is a hard computational problem. No mathematician has ever posed a credible argument that there might be a shortcut for factoring very large numbers. There has never been a "last theorem" in which a noted mathematician posed a solution to the factoring problem but omitted the details. There was tremendous progress in factoring in the late 20th century, thanks to the development of the quadratic sieve and number field sieve. However, there is no reason to expect that further developments will make the number field sieve look as obsolete as the classical techniques look today.

Finally, we must keep the risks against RSA in perspective. None of the arguments here absolve RSA of mathematical risk, but that's the nature of modern cryptography. Keep in mind what we know (and don't know) about the strength of secret key encryption. Although we have heaps of practical experience with secret key algorithms, we have no way to prove mathematically that our algorithms are strong. The same is true of RSA.

ATTACKING DIGITAL SIGNATURES

When discussing secret key cryptography we identified some ways to attack the encrypted data without knowing the key. Similar attacks exist against public key algorithms, including RSA. These attacks rely on the mathematical structure of RSA—they work by deriving mathematical factors that will affect encrypted RSA data in controlled, malicious ways.

For example, Henry is still trying to forge one of Tim's checks, and he has adapted one of these mathematical attacks to do so. The crucial trick is that Henry must get Tim to sign a message that looks like gibberish ("I'm just testing something in the system, Tim. Hey, look at the message yourself. Look as closely as you want. It doesn't mean anything!"). If Henry can get Tim to sign such a message, he can exploit the mathematical properties of modular exponentiation to construct a forged message signed by Tim.

This is called a *chosen message attack*, and public key mathematics provides several ways to do it. In one approach, Henry first constructs a message containing random bits, and encrypts it with Tim's public key. Then Henry combines the encrypted result with a *A-82* forged check of Tim's. This yields the gibberish that Henry asks Tim to sign. Remember that when Tim signs the message, he is encrypting it with his private key. After Tim signs the message, Henry combines it with an inverted form of his original random bits, which mathematically deducts those bits from the signature. This leaves Henry with a forged check signed by Tim.   *see Note 10.*

Fortunately, there is a single, well-known technique that prevents the chosen message attack from working: compute a hash of the *D-82* message being signed and encrypt the hash only. Figure 13.3 shows

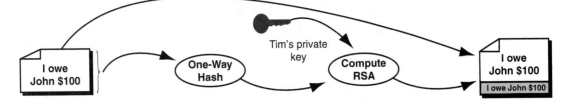

FIGURE 13.3: *Applying an RSA digital signature to a message.* To sign his message, Tim first computes the one-way hash of the text of his message. Then he encrypts the resulting hash value using his private key. Finally, he attaches this digital signature value to the original message. Anyone can verify the contents of the message by checking this digital signature value.

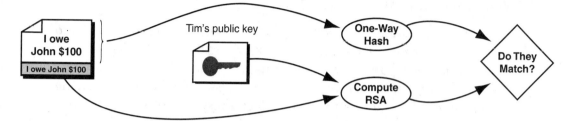

FIGURE 13.4: *Checking the RSA digital signature on a message.* To verify that Tim actually signed the message we received, we must compare the hash of the message against the hash Tim encrypted with his private key. We decrypt that hash using Tim's public key and compare the result with the hash we get from the message's text.

how to construct a digital signature using a hash function. To sign his check, Tim first computes the one-way hash value of its text. Next, Tim encrypts the hash value using RSA with his private key.

If John, the bank, or anyone else, wants to authenticate the check that Tim signed, they use Tim's public key as shown in Figure 13.4. John takes the text and computes the one-way hash, just at Tim did. John does *not* include the digital signature itself in the hashed text, since Tim didn't include that value, either. (Of course, Tim couldn't include the digital signature value in the hash, since he couldn't possibly know its value until after he'd computed the hash —a circular reference he can't possibly resolve.) Then John decrypts the digital signature value by applying RSA with Tim's *public* key. If the check is authentic, then the decrypted value will match the hash value.

Chosen message attacks rely on classic mathematical symmetries, like the associative, commutative, and distributive properties we learned in early arithmetic. Henry's attack against an unhashed signature succeeds because he can do parts of the computation piecemeal, and combine those parts in clever ways. If we add a hashing step to the signature process, we destroy part of the symmetry of the mathematical operations and thus prevent the attack from working.

13.4 THE DIGITAL SIGNATURE STANDARD

By 1990, RSA digital signatures had found their way into a few successful applications, most notably Lotus Notes. However, agencies of the U.S. government could not use digital signatures based on public keys because there were no accepted federal standards for such signatures. To fill this gap, NIST proceeded to develop such a standard. However, the standard NIST proposed in 1991 was *not* based on RSA despite its popularity with commercial users. The actual reason for this wasn't clear. One suggested rationale was that RSA was protected by a U.S. patent, and NIST wanted a standard unencumbered by licensing and fees.   *see Note 11.*

But regardless of the reason, the FIPS Digital Signature Standard (DSS) is not based on RSA or factorization. Of course, factoring isn't the only mathematical problem appropriate for public key cryptography. A different problem, the *discrete logarithm problem*, provides the public key algorithm used in the DSS. When we exponentiate a number, we raise it to a particular power, which in turn involves a series of multiplications. As we noted before, multiplication is a straightforward operation, so exponentiation is fairly straightforward, too. However, it is a bit more difficult to invert the exponentiation, that is, to take its logarithm.

There are a number of practical mathematical techniques for computing logarithms (in fact, tables of logarithms were one of the principal 19th-century goals of mechanical computation). However, there are ways of modifying the problem so that the classic techniques don't work. In particular, we can exponentiate a number and then compute its modulus relative to some base value. The modulus operation discards the high order bits of the exponentiation, and this makes it hard to undo the exponentiation. To make things even more difficult, we compute the exponentiation and the modulus against large prime numbers.

The mathematician and cryptographer Taher ElGamal published a paper in 1985 describing how to apply the exponentiation problem to encryption and in particular to digital signatures. ElGamal had been a student of Martin Hellman, the cryptographer who co-developed the first successful public key algorithm: Diffie-Hellman. Like ElGamal's work, Diffie-Hellman is based on the discrete logarithm problem. Unlike the developers of RSA, however, ElGamal had published a paper describing his technique long before he considered filing a patent application, so his technique was not eligible for a patent.

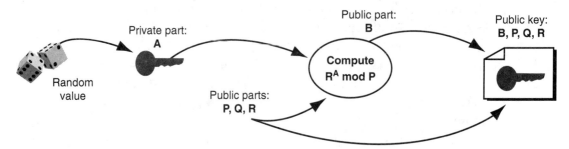

FIGURE 13.5: *Creating a public key pair for exponential techniques like DSS.* Here is how we produce a public key for exponential public key methods DSS, ElGamal, or Diffie-Hellman. First, we select a large (512-bit) prime **P**. Next we select two numbers **Q**, a smaller prime, and **R**, both based on the value of **P**. We pick **A** at random and keep it secret. We compute the value of **B** as shown here. The values of **B**, **P**, **Q**, and **R** make up the public key. **Q** is used in digital signatures.

Figure 13.5 shows how we construct a public key pair for DSS and similar, logarithm-based techniques. The computation involves the exponentiation and modulus pattern we saw in the RSA algorithm, but here we use it to construct the key pair. First, we choose three public numbers: a large prime, **P**, and two other numbers, **Q** and **R**, related to P. For our private secret, we choose the random secret value **A**. We produce the public key by raising **R** to the **A**-th power, and taking its modulus relative to **P**. Since the modulus operation factors out the upper digits of the exponentiation, there's no straightforward way to take the result (called **B** here) and find the value of **A** that produced it.

From the outside, the procedure looks reasonably similar to the RSA procedure of signing a message: it requires a hash of the message's text, the private part of the key pair, and some of the public part of the key pair. Inside, however, the procedure is far more complicated. Figure 13.6 sketches the procedure. First, we hash the function as usual, but then we must generate a random value, **K**, that we use to produce a "check value" used in the verification procedure. The signature consists of two pieces of information: the signature value computed from the hash, and the check value. The verification procedure applies a series of modular exponentiations and modular inverses to verify the signature. Unfortunately, the process is very slow to execute as well as being complicated. *see Note 12.*

An interesting feature of the mechanism is that it can only be used for digital signatures. With RSA, the computation can encrypt

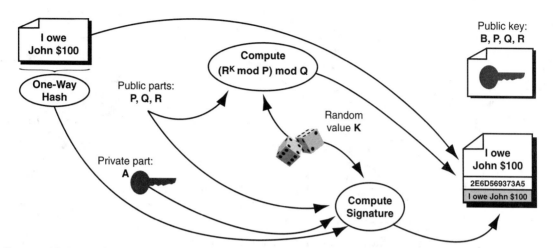

FIGURE 13.6: *Applying a DSS digital signature to a message.* As with RSA, Tim first hashes his message. Then he chooses a random value **K** and computes a check value to be used to validate the signature. Then he uses the key's private part **A** in conjunction with **K** and the public key components to compute the signature value. Then Tim attaches the check value and signature value to the message and delivers it. The recipient authenticates the message by computing a series of equations that use the public key, the signature, and the check value.

data as well as sign documents. This made ElGamal's scheme more appealing in 1991, since the U.S. government heavily restricted exports of cryptographic systems at that time. The DSS, a variation of the ElGamal scheme, was adopted as a federal standard in December 1994.

The basic approach for attacking a DSS key, or any other public key that relies on modular exponentiation, is to apply a relatively efficient algorithm for finding the discrete logarithm. One such algorithm is called the index calculus method, and it is very similar to the number field sieve technique used to factor RSA keys. In fact, the performance estimates are so close that we use the same average attack space estimates for both RSA and DSS keys.   *see Note 13.*

13.5 CHALLENGE RESPONSE REVISITED

The previous sections have used electronic checks as an authentication problem, but it's a bit different from the problem of verifying who is talking to a particular computer at a particular instant. The digitally signed document poses some eternal statement, like "Tim pays John $100 on Flag Day, 2001," or something like that. It

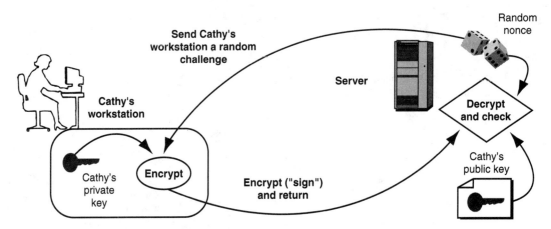

FIGURE 13.7: *Trivial challenge response using public key cryptography.* The server sends Cathy a nonce in response to her request to log on. To authenticate herself, Cathy encrypts the nonce with her private key, which essentially generates its digital signature. The server compares her response to the original nonce's value, after decrypting it with her public key. The server can authenticate Cathy without having to contact another server for authoritative information.

doesn't say that Tim is present at any particular computer at any particular moment. We can use public key cryptography to do that as well.

Figure 13.7 illustrates a simple protocol to authenticate someone using public key cryptography and a challenge response strategy. When Cathy, for example, tries to log in to the server, it transmits a random challenge. To prove her identity, Cathy encrypts the random challenge and sends it back. The server verifies her identity using her public key: her decrypted response should match the challenge that it sent.

This approach provides true off-line authentication, since the server only needs a copy of Cathy's public key. The server does not need to contact a separate authentication server to verify Cathy's identity.

As shown earlier with shared secret authentication, we can use variants of this approach to produce one-time passwords without a challenge (Section 9.3). For example, Cathy could encrypt a clock value, and submit that along with her user name when logging on. The server would decrypt the clock value and verify that it's within some acceptable window. However, Cathy would have to keep her computer's clock very closely synchronized with the server's clock; otherwise the server would have to tolerate a fairly wide clock skew. This in turn could make the system vulnerable to a sniff and replay attack (Attack A-79 in Section 12.5).

As with one-time passwords, we could also use a counter instead of a clock. However, this would not allow off-line authentication. Servers would need to share information about the counter's value, and that would create the need for an on-line authentication protocol.

Although we used challenge response with some success in Chapter 10, this particular approach poses an interesting problem: it might make Cathy vulnerable to signature forgeries. or other attacks. Since public key mathematics are vulnerable to attacks of the type described in the previous section (Attack A-81), we want to avoid using our private key to encrypt arbitrary data received from others.

LOCKOUT FORTEZZA AUTHENTICATION PROTOCOL

A practical solution to these problems was developed to use with the Fortezza card, a special cryptographic module developed by the U.S. government. The Fortezza card was a standard PCMCIA card developed by the NSA to provide a general-purpose cryptographic capability for government and commercial applications. The Fortezza card contained implementations of the DSS algorithm introduced in Section 13.4 and the SHA introduced in Section 8.5.

The authentication protocol was originally called the "Tessera Authentication Protocol," since "Tessera" was the original name for the Fortezza card. The protocol was named "LOCKOut Fortezza" when it was released as a product. The protocol used SHA and DSS, since those were the algorithms provided on the Fortezza card. The basic design could have accommodated RSA as well. The protocol was developed in 1994 for government agencies that required a strong and reasonably automatic authentication mechanism based on public key cryptography, notably the defense finance community. End users installed PC card readers on their workstations, and sites installed the protocol on their firewalls.   *see Note 14.*

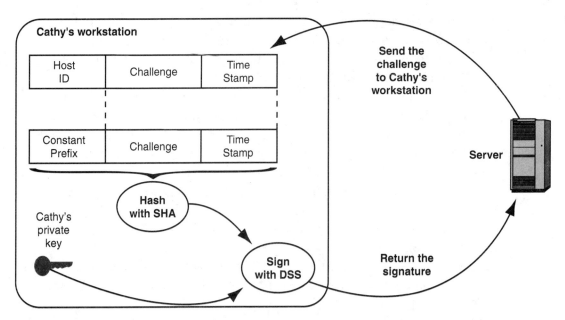

FIGURE 13.8: *The LOCKOut Fortezza authentication protocol.* This protocol uses challenge response with DSS to provide authentication using a public key. Cathy sends her user name to the server, which replies with a host ID, a random challenge, and a time stamp. Cathy constructs her response and sends its signature back to the server. The server uses Cathy's public key to verify that the signature matches the expected hash result.

As with Microsoft's challenge response, the process is embedded entirely in software, since it exchanges too much data for people to type in. Figure 13.8 illustrates the protocol. Cathy begins the authentication process by providing her user name to the server. The server responds with a server identifier known to Cathy, a 12-bit time stamp, and an 80-bit challenge. The server identifier is a numerical value chosen by Cathy's workstation software when she enrolled with the server and provided the server with a copy of her public key. After checking the time stamp for freshness, Cathy's workstation constructs a response. The workstation combines an 80-bit constant prefix, the server's challenge, and the server's time stamp, and then computes their DSS digital signature. Her response consists of the digital signature.

Note that the figure has simplified the DSS picture in comparison to Figure 13.6. Subsequent figures do not show the different DSS public components separately, or separate the check value from the

DSS signature value. Instead, the DSS "public key" includes all public data by implication, and the DSS "signature" includes both the signature itself and the separate check value it requires.

To verify Cathy's response, the server retrieves a copy of the challenge and time stamp it sent her, constructs a copy of the response, including the constant prefix, and computes the hash on it. Then the server extracts Cathy's public key and checks the signature value response against the computed hash. The two should match.

There is actually a situation in which the protocol allows for this match to fail: if Cathy has logged on "under duress," she can secretly signal that fact to the server. One of the problems with off-line authentication is that it can be hard to revoke credentials; we will examine this further in Section 14.6. So, consider a dramatic scenario in which Cathy is taken hostage by an international spy or gangster and forced to log on to a critical military system with her Fortezza card. She can give her workstation a secret signal that makes a subtle, hard-to-detect change in the digital signature. Specifically, it changes the constant prefix from one value to another. If the server's first attempt to verify the signature fails, the server can try again with the duress version of the prefix. If that one succeeds, the server can take appropriate actions. For example, the server can send a silent alarm to security officers, and it can make changes to Cathy's access permissions that take into account the fact that she may be in danger and not in a position to act responsibly. As noted in Section 1.4, it can be relatively easy to provide duress signals, but it is difficult to use them effectively.

A-83

D-83

In Kerberos, the logon process generally authenticated the client workstations to servers, and vice versa as well. The LOCKOut Fortezza protocol also provided this feature through a simple extension to the server's challenge. To authenticate itself, the server combines the challenge data with the normal prefix value and signs the result. Then it sends this signature along with the rest of the challenge message. Upon receipt, Cathy can authenticate the server by checking the signature against the server's public key.

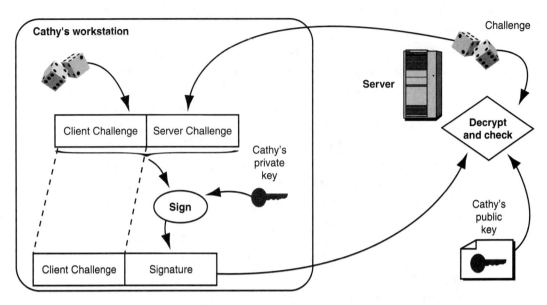

FIGURE 13.9: *FIPS 196 one-way authentication.* The server sends Cathy a challenge in response to her request to log on. Cathy generates a challenge herself, combines it with the server's challenge, and generates a digital signature with her private key. Then she sends the digital signature plus her own challenge back as her response. The server combines its challenge and her challenge, and uses them to verify Cathy's signature with her public key.

FIPS 196 AUTHENTICATION

In 1997, NIST published a federal standard for public key authentication: FIPS 196. Like the LOCKOut Fortezza protocol, it would authenticate the client to the server, and could optionally authenticate the server to the client as well, using public key cryptography. However, FIPS 196 did not define a protocol for interoperability; instead it defined the general transactions required and left details up to the implementers.   *see Note 15.*

Figure 13.9 illustrates the FIPS 196 protocol. The process starts with a request by the client workstation that yields a random challenge from the server. To respond, Cathy generates her own challenge and combines it with the server's challenge. She computes her digital signature using the two challenges, and her response contains her challenge along with the digital signature. Unlike LOCK-Out Fortezza, FIPS 196 relies entirely on nonces and does not use time stamps.

To verify Cathy's response, the server retrieves the challenge it sent to her along with a copy of her public key. The server reconstructs the message that Cathy signed, her client challenge combined with the server's challenge, and verifies the signature against that message.

Although these authentication protocols were used in the defense community, they never achieved widespread acceptance. Clearly, its association with the Fortezza card was a detriment to the LOCKOut Fortezza protocol, since Fortezza proved too expensive for widespread use. Also, Fortezza had a bad reputation in the computer security community because it was associated with escrowed encryption. But the most important reason was probably the emergence of the Secure Sockets Layer protocol, which provided the same features and more and deployed them successfully on the World Wide Web.

13.6 SECURE SOCKETS LAYER

In 1991, a British computer scientist named Tim Berners-Lee developed the World Wide Web at INRIA in Switzerland. The original purpose was to simplify the exchange of technical papers, particularly in physics, stored on Internet servers around the world. Mark Andressen and a team of software developers at the University of Illinois went on in 1993 to produce Mosaic, a general-purpose graphical "browser" for visiting Web pages. Mosaic integrated the World Wide Web protocols with the ability to display graphic images and to support other data retrieval protocols, including the File Transfer Protocol, and Gopher, a menu-driven protocol.

A year later, Andressen left the university to found Netscape, a company seeking to provide software so that businesses could use the Web. Security was naturally an essential part of this, and the young Netscape company arranged to use the public key algorithms from RSA.   *see Note 16.*

Moreover, Netscape's designers looked closely at the capabilities of public key technology, and of "hybrid" strategies that combined it with secret key encryption. The result was a very clever technical approach that put the bulk of public key management problems on the server. This approach was incorporated into the *Secure Sockets Layer* (SSL) protocol.   *see Note 17.*

SSL is undoubtedly the most common public key application on Earth. In 1995, Jim Barksdale, president of Netscape Communications, estimated that there had been approximately 20 million copies of Netscape's SSL-enabled browser distributed worldwide. Here are features of SSL:

- **Safety and convenience:** SSL establishes a strong, cryptographically protected connection between a client workstation and a server, and usually requires no participation by the workstation's operator.

- **Server authenticity:** SSL authenticates the server to ensure that the client is talking to the correct computer. This authentication uses "public key certificates," described in Chapter 14.

- **Automatic client authentication:** A workstation operator can authenticate to an SSL-enabled server using the operator's own public key pair, if the server is set up to accept it.

- **Extensibility:** SSL can use most encryption algorithms and hashing algorithms. The client and server can automatically choose the best algorithms from those they both support.

Although SSL is extensible, there's a relatively standard implementation that's used almost universally for consumer sites on the World Wide Web. The typical site uses RSA public key encryption to establish a set of shared secret keys used with RC4 for encryption and MD5 for integrity protection. A typical server will authenticate itself to clients, but does not support SSL's built-in client authentication. However, some servers do support the built-in client authentication. The next two sections describe these alternatives.

Figure 13.10 illustrates the essential concept behind the SSL protocol. Cathy contacts the server, and the server responds by sending a copy of its public key. Cathy then generates a base secret, encrypts it with the server's public key, and sends it back to the server. If we think of this in Kerberos terms, the public key allows Cathy to act as her own KDC, generating her own ticket to send to the server. As with Kerberos tickets, the shared secret lets Cathy's workstation exchange encrypted and integrity-protected messages with the server. The only difference is that Cathy hasn't really been authenticated in this process.

The complete protocol is, of course, more complicated than this. Part of the complication comes from flexibility: by breaking the protocol up into separate layers and messages, the designers made it easier to support a whole range of options for public key algorithms and other security services. Other complications arose from attacks: as people in the community studied SSL, they saw troubling possibilities. Between 1994 and 1997, Netscape developed three versions of SSL, with each newer version seeking to fix the problems found in the previous one. The last Netscape version, 3.0, is the one described here. Arguably, the safety of SSL 3.0 is comparable to other peer-reviewed protocols like Kerberos and RADIUS. *see Note 18.*

SSL is designed to provide cryptographic protection to messages traveling on a TCP connection, that is, a reliable, bidirectional connection established using standard Internet protocols. SSL provides another layer atop TCP that protects messages against forgery, modification, and sniffing. When a pair of hosts first establish an SSL connection, the messages they exchange are still embedded in SSL transport messages, but no encryption takes place. The hosts must negotiate the use of cryptographic services via SSL's handshake protocol.

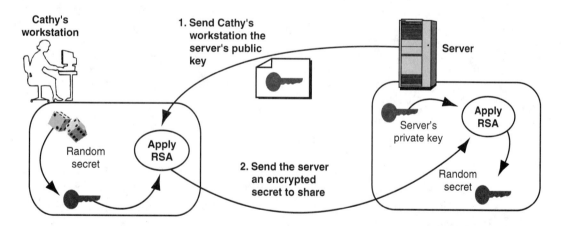

FIGURE 13.10: *Secure Sockets Layer lets the client and server share a secret key.* When Cathy contacts the server and asks for a secure connection, the server sends her a copy of its public key. Cathy randomly generates a secret to share with the server, and encrypts that secret with the server's public key. Only the server's private key will be able to decrypt that secret. Cathy sends the encrypted secret to the server. The server decrypts the secret, and they use the shared secret to encrypt and authenticate subsequent messages, just like with Kerberos session keys. Note that this protocol does not authenticate Cathy to the server.

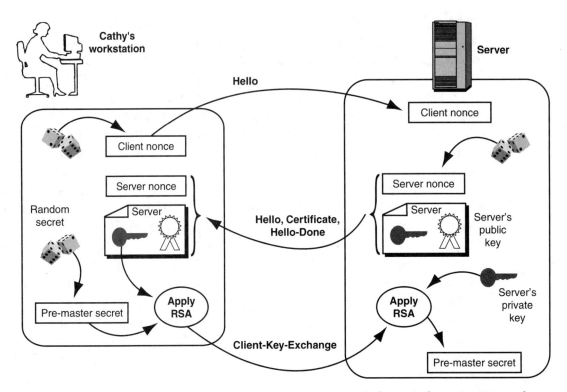

FIGURE 13.11: *Details of the SSL handshake protocol, Part 1.* Cathy's workstation starts the process with a Hello message containing random data. The server responds with a three-message
sequence that provides another nonce and the server's public key (embedded in a "certificate").
The client responds with a three-message sequence, but only one shown here. The Client-Key-
Exchange message transmits a shared secret, encrypted with the server's public key. The server
decrypts the secret with its private key, yielding the "pre-master secret" used to construct shared
keys to cryptographically protect the traffic between the client and server. The client does not
need any preestablished crypto keys to establish the shared secret with the server.

ESTABLISHING KEYS WITH SSL

Figure 13.11 illustrates SSL's handshake protocol. The server and
client take turns sending a series of messages to the other. Once the
exchanges are finished, the cryptographic protections and shared
keys are in place. Here is the process:

- Client says: "Hello."

Once the client has opened the connection, it generates 28 bytes
of random data and transmits them to the server in a "Hello"
message. This is the first message transmitted in Figure 13.11.

- Server says: "Hello, Certificate, Hello-Done."

  Upon receipt of the client's "Hello," the server responds with a sequence of three messages, illustrated by the second message transmitted in Figure 13.11. The first is a "Hello" to echo the one from the client, containing 28 random bytes that the server generated itself.

  The next message is a "Certificate" message, which contains the server's public key embedded in a "public key certificate" data structure. The client needs to check the authenticity of the server's certificate before using its public key. Certificates and certificate validation are described in Chapter 14.

  The final message, the "Hello-Done," simply tells the client that the server is through with this step of the handshake process.

- Client: "Client-Key-Exchange, Change-Cipher-Spec, Finished."

  The client responds with a sequence of three messages. The "Client-Key-Exchange" message is the heart of SSL: it transmits the secret from the client to the server, encrypted with the server's public key. In SSL, the shared secret is called a *pre-master secret*. As shown in Figure 13.11, the client extracts the public key from the server's certificate and performs RSA encryption. Upon receipt, the server retrieves the pre-master secret by

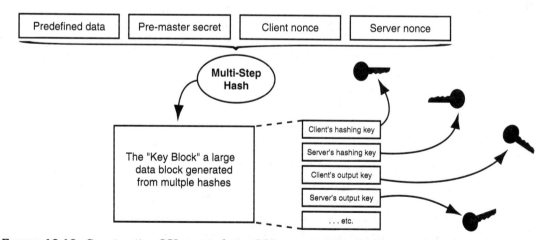

FIGURE 13.12: *Constructing SSL crypto keys.* SSL constructs all of its working keys by hashing the nonces with the pre-master secret and other, predefined data to construct a large data block called the Key Block. To create the individual keys, we subdivide the Key Block into separate sections, one per key. The server and client construct a matching set of keys from the Key Block.

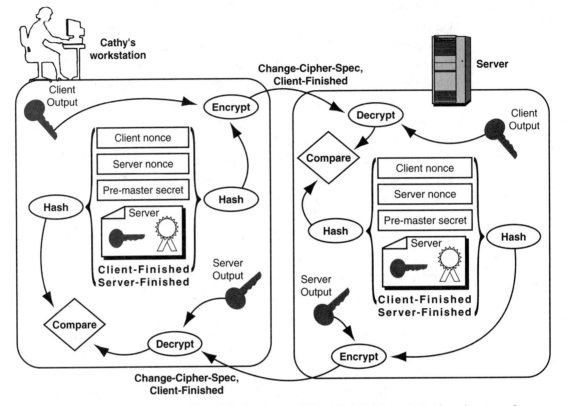

FIGURE 13.13: *Details of the SSL handshake protocol, Part 2.* At this point, the client and server are ready to switch to the newly negotiated keys, and to verify that each has successfully retrieved the same keys as the other. The Change-Cipher-Spec messages each signal when the host is ready to switch to the new keys. The Client-Finished and Server-Finished messages transmit the hash of all the messages received by the respective hosts, so the other host can verify that both received the same series of messages.

applying RSA with its private key. Once this step is finished, both the client and server share the secret and non-secret information they need to generate the SSL session keys. Figure 13.12 illustrates the key generation process.

Figure 13.13 shows the processing of the remaining two messages in this sequence. The client's "Change-Cipher-Spec" message simply signals the point at which the client will start using the keys established during this handshake. The "Client-Finished" message transmits hashes of all of the data shared during the handshake process. The hash is computed twice: once with

MD5 and once with SHA. The resulting hashes are encrypted and integrity protected using the keys just established.

Upon receipt, the server uses the client's output key to decrypt the "Finished" message. Then the server checks the message contents against its own hashes of the handshake messages. If all went correctly, both should match. This tells the server that the client has set up its keys correctly.

- Server: "Change-Cipher-Spec, Finished."

This final sequence echoes the last two message types sent by the client, but from the server's perspective. The "Change-Cipher-Spec" message indicates that the server will now start using the keys that were just established. All subsequent data will be encrypted and integrity protected with the new keys.

The "Server-Finished" message transmits almost the same data hash as the client's earlier message, except that now we must include the hash of the "Client-Finished" message. The server constructs the appropriate hashes, encrypts the message with the "server output" keys, and sends the message to the client.

Upon receipt of the "Server-Finished" message, the client decrypts it with the "server output" keys, and compares its contents with the client's own computation of the correct hashes. If they match, then the client is confident that the server possesses the corresponding private key, and thus must be authentic.

AUTHENTICATION WITH TYPICAL SSL

Now that the client has established the authenticity of the server, how will the server establish the authenticity of the client? In practice, servers tend to use typical authentication methods, and they often take advantage of the fact that passwords can't be sniffed on an encrypted SSL connection. Here is a summary of techniques that can authenticate a client over an SSL connection:

- User names and passwords, self-selected
- E-mail addresses and passwords
- Information about credit card accounts
- Externally assigned user names and passwords

- Quizzes with cultural secrets belonging to a select group
- One-time password systems

An unfortunate legacy of U.S. export restrictions is that many desktops run older versions of SSL that use only 40 bits of secrecy in their encryption keys. While most browsers distributed today provide at least 128 bits of secrecy, the older browsers are still used. Often, the users aren't even aware of the fact that they are using relatively weak encryption to protect their private information.

SSL CLIENT AUTHENTICATION

Clients can also authenticate themselves to servers by using SSL's built-in client authentication. This protocol uses a public key pair belonging to the workstation's user, and performs a challenge response transaction to verify that the user really possesses the appropriate private key.

The process works as shown in Figure 13.14. It is integrated into the SSL handshake protocol, in the server's final message and the client's response to it. The server asks for the client's public key in the form of a certificate, and the client replies with both the certificate and a response encrypted with the corresponding private key.

The server prompts for client-side authentication by including a "Certificate-Request" message along with its "Hello" message sequence. This message includes information about the certificates that the server is willing to accept. If the client can't accommodate the server's expectations, it sends back a "No-Certificate" warning. Upon receipt, the server can either reject the connection or require some other form of authentication.

In response, the client includes two additional messages in its message sequence. The first message is a "Certificate" message containing the client's certificate. The other message is a "Certificate-Verify" message that serves as the "response" portion of a challenge response protocol. For a "challenge," the message uses the computed hashes of the previous messages in the handshake protocol. This is similar to the "Finished" messages shown in Figure 13.13. However, the "Certificate-Verify" computes a digital signature from the hashes, and transmits those results to the server.

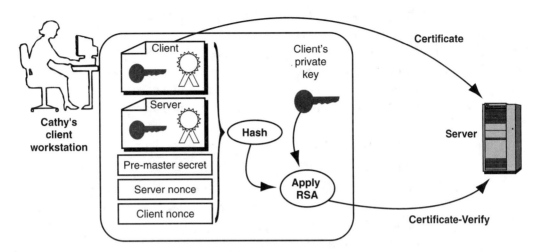

FIGURE 13.14: *SSL client authentication.* Cathy's client sends two separate messages in order to authenticate her. The Certificate message transmits her personal public key certificate. Later, she sends a Certificate-Verify message, containing a hash covering the messages she exchanged with the server during the SSL handshake, encrypted with her private key.

From a security standpoint, the SSL client authentication protocol is reasonably strong. The "challenge" incorporates nonces recently generated by both the server and client, so replay isn't a practical attack. More reasonable attacks would go after either the certificates or after the client's private key. These attacks, and their defenses, are described in Chapters 14 and 15 respectively.

13.7 PUBLIC KEYS AND BIOMETRICS

It may seem to some readers of Section 7.7 on biometric encryption that public keys could "solve" the biometrics problem. As with so many technologies, public key technology simply rearranges the problem without really solving it. Here is a look at two possible applications of public keys to biometrics and their limitations.

- **Protect a biometric reading from sniffing**

  We could create a public key for a biometric system and embed that public key in all biometric readers. Whenever a biometric signature is collected and sent in for authentication, we can encrypt it first with the public key. This will prevent attackers from sniffing the biometric.

While this approach would reduce the risk of someone intercepting a biometric reading collected by the system, it does not prevent an attacker from collecting a victim's biometric in any number of other ways. While there are valid privacy concerns that justify the encryption of biometrics, we cannot assume that such protections will keep biometric readings a secret. This simply gives people a false sense of security, letting them assume that their biometrics can serve as safe base secrets.

- **Authenticate the source of a biometric reading**

  We can take things a step further and embed private keys in biometric readers. The reader's key would be used to digitally sign the biometric so that the system has confidence that the reading originated from an acceptable reader. This gives the system a way to detect spoofed biometrics, if we assume that the readers themselves can reliably detect spoofing.

  Of course, this approach substitutes the problems of biometrics with the problems of managing the private keys that must be installed in all of the biometric readers. If the proprietor is willing to spend the administrative resources necessary to manage those private keys, it may make more sense to simply assign the keys directly to individuals instead of assigning them to biometric readers. This is an architectural trade-off that individual sites and system managers must make.

While we can indeed use SSL's approach to public key cryptography to protect biometric readings from interception, we cannot use it to prevent spoofing. For that, we need to associate a base secret with the transmitter of the biometric reading, so we are sure the reading originates from a trustworthy source. Otherwise, an attacker with a copy of the public key and a convincing version of the victim's biometric reading can masquerade as that victim. As noted in Chapter 7, there are lots of ways to capture biometric readings even without the victim's cooperation.

13.8 SUMMARY TABLES

TABLE 13.2: *Attack Summary*

Attack	Security Problem	Prevalence	Attack Description
A-80. Shared key misuse for forgery	Masquerade as someone else	Trivial	Secret key that was shared with a trusted party is used to forge a message
A-81. Factoring an RSA key	Recover hidden information (RSA key)	Sophisticated	Factor the RSA composite and deduce the private key
A-82. Chosen message attack	Recover hidden information (RSA key)	Common	Construct a message with a special mathematical structure. Victim signs it, and result can be transformed into one for a different message
A-83. Duress logon with private key	Masquerade as someone else	Physical and Sophisticated	Attacker forces the owner of a private key to log on, then uses the established session

TABLE 13.3: *Defense Summary*

Defense	Foils Attacks	Description
D-80. Public key encryption	A-80. Shared key misuse for forgery	Use public key encryption that anyone can verify and associate with the owner of a specific private key
D-81. Significantly larger RSA key sizes	A-81. Factoring an RSA key	Generate RSA keys containing thousands of bits; certainly more than 1,000 bits
D-82. Hashed digital signature	A-82. Chosen message attack	Construct digital signatures by encrypting the result of a one-way hash
D-83. Duress signature	A-83. Duress logon with private key	Construct a special form digital signature indicating that user is under duress

CHAPTER 14

PUBLIC KEY CERTIFICATES

[16] And he causeth all, both small and great, rich and poor, free and bond, to receive a mark in their right hand, or in their foreheads:

[17] And that no man might buy or sell, save he that had the mark, or the name of the beast, or the number of his name.

— Revelation of St. John the Divine 13:16–17 *King James Version*

IN THIS CHAPTER

We use public key certificates to reliably associate a particular identity to a particular public key. Most of the examples here have to do with authenticating Web servers, but the concepts also apply to authenticating people's public key certificates.

- Public key masquerade and the basics of certificates
- Strategies for issuing public key certificates
- Revoking public keys
- Using certificate-based authentication with Kerberos

14.1 TYING NAMES TO PUBLIC KEYS

If we want to authenticate a person or computer off-line, then we need a copy of his or her public key. As long as we can get a copy of the right public key for Cathy or Tim or the Acme.com Web site, then we can accurately authenticate them across a network. However, attackers can undermine this by providing bogus credentials.

The simplest and most obvious approach is for someone named Henry to convince people and software that his own public key is the one used by some important computer, like a bank's server. *A-84* Henry might be able to profit even if he tricks only one or two peo-

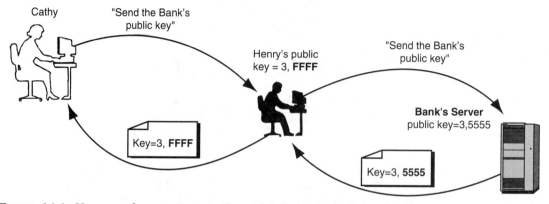

FIGURE 14.1: *Henry performs a "man in the middle" attack.* Cathy asks for a copy of the bank's public key so that she can establish a secure connection to it, perhaps using SSL. Henry intercepts the bank's reply and substitutes his own public key for the bank's. Whenever Cathy uses that public key, Henry intercepts the message and reencrypts it with the bank's public key. Neither Cathy nor the bank can detect Henry's presence.

ple this way. For example, Henry could send a message to Cathy pretending to be the bank, and give Cathy the "bank's public key" when it's really his own key. If Cathy then tries to send secret information to the bank, like password-protected messages, Henry can masquerade as the bank.

Cathy will probably uncover this scam when she realizes that the bank really hasn't received any of her transactions. But this isn't enough to guarantee that Henry's fraud will always be detected. There's also a risk that Henry could systematically participate in all of Cathy's transactions with the bank, substituting his own public key for the bank's. This produces yet another the man in the middle (MIM) attack (Figure 14.1).

A-85

To implement the attack, Henry places himself (or more likely, some software of his) between Cathy and the bank, and intercepts every message they send back and forth. When the bank sends Cathy its public key, Henry substitutes his own key for the bank's key. If Cathy sends the bank some secret information encrypted with its public key, she unintentionally uses Henry's key instead. So Henry intercepts the data, decrypts it with his own private key, reencrypts it with the bank's own public key, and sends it on. Neither Cathy nor the bank can tell the difference. But Henry can eavesdrop on everything Cathy does with the bank.

The solution to this problem is attributed to Leon Kornfelder who, as an MIT undergraduate, proposed the use of *certificates* to thwart such attacks. Figure 14.2 shows the essential contents of a public key certificate. The certificate is a data item containing a public key, the name of the key's owner, and a digital signature. Figure 14.3 shows how a Web browser displays a certificate. We verify a certificate's authenticity by checking its digital signature. Certificates help us detect public key substitutions and MIM attacks. The attacker can't insert a bogus public key if we can verify the key's owner.

D-84

see Note 1.

CERTIFICATE AUTHORITIES

The first question posed by certificates is to decide who signs them. The signer must fulfill two requirements: the signer must be reliable, and the signer's public key must be available to check signatures. We call the signer the *certificate authority*.

By "reliable" we mean that the authority must not sign a certificate without being confident that the name on the certificate really goes along with the public key. Imagine what would happen if Henry could acquire a certificate containing the bank's name along with his own public key: he could sign electronic documents and authenticate himself to remote systems using the name "www.bank.com." This problem actually struck Microsoft Corporation in early 2001: someone posing as a representative of Microsoft submitted public

A-86

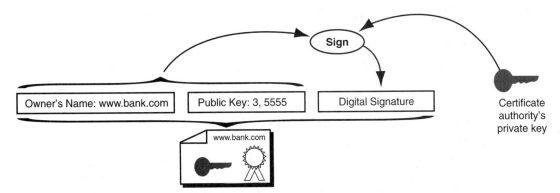

FIGURE 14.2: *Basic public key certificate.* Here is a basic certificate for the bank. Like all public key certificates, it is a data item contains the owner's name ("www.bank.com"), the public key ("3,5555"), and a digital signature. The certificate is produced by a trustworthy third party, the "certificate authority," whose private key is used to sign the certificate. To verify a certificate, we must use the public key belonging to the authority that signed the certificate.

```
╔══════════════════════════════════════════════════════════════╗
║═══════════════════ Netscape: View A Certificate ══════════════║
╠══════════════════════════════════════════════════════════════╣
║ This Certificate belongs to:    This Certificate was issued by:║
║   www.llbean.com                  Secure Server Certification Authority
║   Information Services            RSA Data Security, Inc.      ║
║   L.L. Bean, Inc.                 US                          ║
║   Freeport, Maine, US                                         ║
║ Serial Number: 61:8E:44:C1:B9:17:A6:51:80:FA:E3:25:8B:9F:67:DD║
║ This Certificate is valid from Tue Aug 17, 1999 to Wed Sep 06, 2000
║ Certificate Fingerprint:                                      ║
║   3C:10:EB:A1:51:60:6E:8C:96:B8:9D:94:22:BB:B1:46             ║
╚══════════════════════════════════════════════════════════════╝
```

FIGURE 14.3: *A public key certificate displayed by a browser.* This certificate was issued to L. L. Bean of Freeport, Maine, to authenticate their Web server when customers use the server to buy merchandise.

keys to Verisign, a major certificate authority, and Verisign issued certificates claiming that Microsoft owned those keys. It later turned out that the corresponding private keys were not in fact in Microsoft's possession. The resulting certificates would allow the owner of the private keys to produce software that could masquerade as legitimate software released by Microsoft itself.   *see Note 2.*

The obvious defense is to enforce that first requirement for a certificate authority: the authority must ensure that the name really goes along with the key. This generally means that authorities must ensure that the owner of a particular public key pair is really entitled to use the name. Authorities do this by establishing rules   *D-85* describing how they verify that the person has rights to the name. If Cathy asks for a certificate identifying her as Vice President of Art at Acme Corporation, then she needs to show that she really holds that position. With respect to the Microsoft incident, at the time of this writing it is not yet clear how Verisign was tricked into issuing the bogus Microsoft certificates; Verisign's rules and procedures should have prevented it.

The second requirement for signing certificates is that the certificate authority's public key must be available to check signatures. To be practical, the key can't simply be "published information" that's available after some digging, no matter how little. The key must be

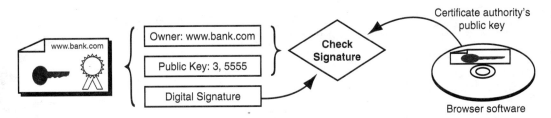

FIGURE 14.4: *Browser authenticating a public key.* This was the original strategy in Netscape Navigator for authenticating a public key. All keys were in certificates, and all certificates were signed by a single certificate authority. The authority's key was embedded in the software. Today, browsers usually contain many such keys in an "authority list," as described in Section 14.4.

immediately at hand so that public key software can use it to authenticate certificates issued by that authority.

Netscape faced this problem when first deploying software to use SSL for Internet electronic commerce. The software ensemble consisted of Web server software, the "Commerce Server," and Netscape's well-known "Navigator" browser software. A server would authenticate itself to a browser by sending a public key certificate. Netscape arranged for RSA Data Security, Inc., to serve as the certificate authority and issue the public key certificates. RSA established a separate organization to do this, which eventually became Verisign, Inc. The authority used a particular public key pair to sign all of those early certificates. Since all certificates were signed with that particular key, Netscape embedded the corresponding public key in Navigator's SSL software, as shown in Figure 14.4. The browser used that key to authenticate certificates used by SSL.   *see Note 3.*

USING THE RIGHT CERTIFICATE

Since the public keys are large and the processing is complicated, we have to rely on our workstation to do the authentication processing. This can be a double-edged sword. For example, it's not enough for our browser to receive an authentic public key certificate when we contact an e-commerce site. We need to receive the certificate for the site we think we're using.

For example, an attacker might be the owner of a legitimate e-commerce site and have a legitimate public key certificate for the site's server. What happens if he implements a second server that   *A-87*

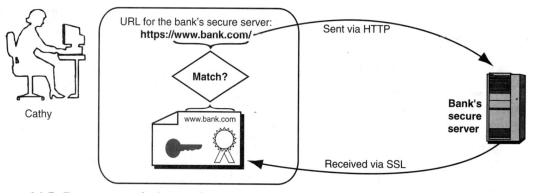

FIGURE 14.5: *Browsers verify the certificate's name.* When Cathy contacts the bank's secure server, the bank's host name appears in the URL. The bank sends back its public key certificate as part of the SSL handshake protocol. The browser compares the host name in the certificate against the domain name in Cathy's URL to verify that it is speaking to the right host.

masquerades as www.bank.com, and intercepts Cathy's messages to the bank? We are essentially back to the problem that opened this section.

In part, this problem arises because the SSL security software operates at one software level, ignoring the data it carries, while the Web server or other application software operates at a completely different level. The solution to the problem is for the application software itself to verify that the name in the certificate goes along with the messages being handled by the application. In the browser environment, Netscape solved this by checking the name in the certificate against the server being asked for in the HTTP (Figure 14.5). This is like checking the name of the account holder on an electronic check against the name in the public key certificate. The check is legitimate if the certificate name matches the account's name.

D-86

Figure 14.6 shows how a browser responds if the check shown in Figure 14.5 fails. The browser has tried to open an SSL connection to the site "www.sprintpcs.com" and received a certificate to use to establish the connection. However, the certificate it received did not contain the host name "www.sprintpcs.com" in it. So the browser displays a dialog that briefly identifies the host name, some basic identifying information on the certificate, and asks the workstation's user to decide if the certificate really goes with the site. This type of problem can occur if the site's proprietor orders a certificate that

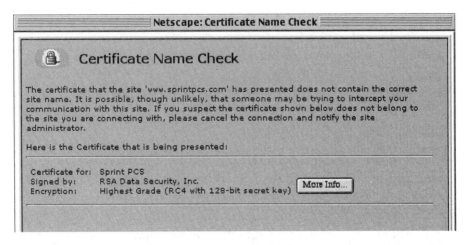

FIGURE 14.6: *Browser warns of a certificate containing the wrong name.* Here, Netscape Navigator has been given a certificate to secure a connection, but the site name in the URL does not appear in the certificate. This may have been caused by installation errors, or it could indicate an attempted MIM attack. Verify that the name on the certificate is appropriate for the site, and that the certificate authority (indicated above by "Signed by") is well known and trustworthy.

contains the wrong host name or no host name, or if the host name needs to be changed later for technical or administrative reasons. However, the problem may also show up as part of a public key MIM attack. Essentially, the user must decide if it's likely that the certificate authority who signed the certificate ("RSA Data Security") would have issued a certificate with the name "Sprint PCS" to someone other than the owner of "www.sprintpcs.com." In this case, the certificate seems legitimate, and might be accepted safely. On the other hand, it might be risky to accept a certificate belonging to "Henry's Internet Company" when we try to connect to "www.bank.com." There is no obvious relationship between the URL and the name in the certificate, and that's a bad sign.

Microsoft faces a variant of the certificate-matching problem with their mechanism to verify that downloaded software really comes from Microsoft. This mechanism is intended to prevent attackers from distributing subverted software that claims to be from Microsoft. Major components that install or run downloaded software include procedures to verify a digital signature on the software. The procedure contains a list of Microsoft certificates to verify those signatures. Verisign unintentionally created some bogus certificates to verify such signatures, but those certificates are not in the list of accepted certificates. So, even though there exists a bogus code-signing certificate that contains the name "Microsoft Corporation," nobody is likely to be tricked by that certificate into loading bogus software.

see Note 4.

14.2 CREATING CERTIFICATES

There's no special trick to creating a public key pair if we have the appropriate software handy, but we usually create the certificate separately. Figure 14.7 shows Cathy creating her key pair and acquiring a certificate. First, she creates her key pair within the confines of her computer and keeps her private key secret. Then she transmits a copy of her public key, along with her name, to the certificate authority that will issue her a certificate. The authority, if it is satisfied that the key really goes along with Cathy's name, will combine the name and key into a certificate data structure and affix its digital signature. After that, the authority can transmit a copy back to Cathy, publish the certificate in its own directory, if desired, or distribute the certificate in other ways.

Modern Web browsers can generate public key pairs and submit the public key for certification. One can visit the Web site of a certificate authority, generate a private key within one's browser, and submit the corresponding public key to the authority for certification. On the other hand, some authorities require higher confidence in a person's identity than one gets on-line. For example, certificates for e-commerce applications often require notarized documents attesting to the applicant's right to use the specified domain name. The applicant would need to submit the paperwork along with a machine-readable copy of the public key via a delivery service.

An alternative strategy that is used in some situations is for the proprietor to generate all key pairs and certificates and to handle the distribution of both. Thus, a user like Cathy needs only to receive her key pair and certificate from the site's proprietor and she doesn't need to bother with the key generation process herself. She only has a single task to perform: to install her key material once she receives it. Lotus Notes traditionally uses this approach for distributing public key pairs. This carries an increased risk simply because the private key is created and a copy may be archived by

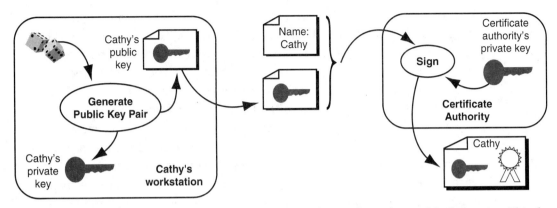

FIGURE 14.7: *Creating a public key certificate.* First, Cathy produces her public key pair within her workstation. Next, she transmits a copy of her public key along with her identifying information to the certificate authority who issues the certificate. The authority verifies that Cathy has the right to use her name, and that she in fact owns the corresponding private key. Then the authority constructs the certificate and affixes its digital signature.

the proprietor. On the other hand, it simplifies configuration for end users and reduces the risk of losing important information if a user's private key is accidentally destroyed.

As a practical matter, modern certificates contain a good deal more information than just the key, the owner's name, and the signature. At least, they need to identify the certificate authority so that we know what key to use to verify the signature. In addition, certificates tend to carry other information to make them easier to use reliably. These include:

- Date of issue
- Expiration date
- Version of this certificate's format
- Indications of types of keys contained
- Owner's name in various formats
- Other properties of the owner (address, for example)
- Owner's rights and privileges

The question of what information really belongs in a certificate is subject to dispute. Some of the information has evolved for practical reasons: the validity dates help minimize problems with invalid keys since they ensure that all keys "die" eventually. The owner's name has to appear in domain name format so that browsers can compare it against domain names in URLs, while "official" owner names tend to appear in a different, incompatible format. Some experts argue that certificates work best if simply restricted to the job of associating names with keys. Others argue in favor of added features, like the owner's citizenship, date of birth (for age information), or other personal data that may be useful in Web applications. Others have suggested adding fields to certificates to store information about computer system privileges and access permissions. Standards for public key certificates can support a number of extensions, but most certificate products omit personal data and privilege information from their certificates.

CERTIFICATE STANDARDS

Public key certificates today are usually based on X.509, a standard originally established for X.400 electronic mail systems. This seemed like a good choice in the early 1990s, since a number of major organizations had announced their intention to use X.400 for future electronic mail systems, including the U.S. Department of Defense. Today, X.400 is primarily of historical interest, except for its impact on public key certificate formats.   *see Note 5.*

In particular, X.509 has had two major impacts on public key certificates: *Abstract Syntax Notation #1* (ASN.1) and *distinguished names*. X.509 defines the contents and arrangement of data in a certificate using ASN.1 statements. Figure 14.8 gives an ASN.1 example from a 1993 Internet certificate specification. The individual statements provide labels for identifying the different fields and type specifications to show what type of information is stored in particular fields. Software developers use ASN.1 compilers to generate the code to build the corresponding data structures and to extract data from them.   *see Note 6.*

A distinguished name is a name containing several separately named elements that make the name identify a particular person uniquely. Often, the elements represent levels of a hierarchy. For example, a distinguished name could be based on geography, so that the highest level identifies the country, then the state, city, street address, and then the individual. For John Doe, this might yield the following distinguished name:

/C="US"/SP="Minnesota"/L="Red Wing"/PA="123 Main Street"
/CN="John Doe"

This hierarchical approach gives us a good way of assigning certification responsibilities and of ensuring uniqueness. We can assign certification authorities to be responsible for different "suffixes" of the distinguished name. For example, there could be a "Red Wing" authority that issues to all Red Wing addresses, and a separate one for each city of each state. These authorities would ensure uniqueness among their own certificates. Since each authority issues certificates with a different city and state, no certificates will be duplicated if each authority avoids local duplicates.

```
Certificate ::= SIGNED SEQUENCE{
        version [0]             Version DEFAULT v1988,
        serialNumber            CertificateSerialNumber,
        signature               AlgorithmIdentifier,
        issuer                  Name,
        validity                Validity,
        subject                 Name,
        subjectPublicKeyInfo    SubjectPublicKeyInfo}

Version ::= INTEGER {v1988(0)}

CertificateSerialNumber ::= INTEGER

Validity ::= SEQUENCE{
        notBefore               UTCTime,
        notAfter                UTCTime}

SubjectPublicKeyInfo ::= SEQUENCE{
        algorithm               AlgorithmIdentifier,
        subjectPublicKey        BIT STRING}

AlgorithmIdentifier ::= SEQUENCE{
        algorithm               OBJECT IDENTIFIER,
        parameters              ANY DEFINED BY algorithm OPTIONAL}
```

FIGURE 14.8: *ASN.1 syntax for a public key certificate.* This definition is taken from RFC 1422, the standards for Privacy Enhanced Mail (PEM), and uses ASN.1 to describe a simple certificate.

CERTIFICATES AND ACCESS CONTROL

This is an open problem—if our software can process a broad range of certificates from numerous sources, then we can reliably authenticate a large population of people and computers. On the other hand, we must then contend with the problem of access control. Note how Netscape would accept any secure server as long as the certificate name matches the host domain name. That level of access control isn't sufficient for every application. It's like using any mag stripe on any card as a credit card. What if the card is a premises-access badge or a driver's license? Neither say anything about the creditworthiness of the owner. Authentication is one problem, and access control is a completely different one.

14.3 CERTIFICATE AUTHORITIES

We've talked briefly about how certificates are created and formatted, but we have only slightly touched on the whys and wherefores of certificate authorities. What makes a particular person or organization into a good choice for a certificate authority? We examine that question here.

The fundamental question is a trade-off between risk and convenience, like so many other security questions. Errors in certificates will yield mistakes in authentication—the system will recognize data as coming from someone who did not create it. On the other hand, extra caution in certification will increase operating costs.

One way to consider this trade-off is to look at a similar system that has evolved over the past 40 years: the credit card system. Credit cards provide third-party authentication for valuable transactions: John Doe shows his credit card to a clerk, and the card attests to the fact that he will pay for a purchase in the future. Credit cards have gone through several phases over the past decades that parallel some issues facing certificate issuance:

- **Phase 1:** Pioneering organizations like American Express produced special cards for charging travel and entertainment expenses from certain merchants.

- **Phase 2:** Every oil company, department store, and airline issued its own credit card for the convenience of its customers. A creditworthy person might have dozens of credit cards.

- **Phase 3:** Cross acceptance in which companies merged their credit operations and accepted one's cards at the other's stores.
- **Phase 4:** Consolidation in which major cards like American Express, Visa ("Bank Americard"), and MasterCard ("Master Charge"), arranged to be accepted by numerous vendors, making individual cards less necessary. The major cards competed with one another by touting the vast number of places where they were accepted for payment.

Credit cards are worth comparing to public keys because, in an ideal world, an individual's public key might serve many purposes much as a Visa or MasterCard does today. While general-purpose certificates might have large benefits, they also pose practical problems not unlike those faced in the evolution of credit cards.

PROPRIETORS AS CERTIFICATE AUTHORITIES

If we follow the traditions of older authentication systems, we would expect a computing site's proprietor to be fully responsible for issuing certificates. So, if Acme Corporation wishes to issue certificates to its employees, then it purchases the necessary hardware and software and issues them from its information services department. This is similar to Phase 2 of our credit card history: the era when individual organizations issued their own cards.

The big benefit of handling the entire process in-house is that the proprietor could control costs. This was also true of credit cards. A company could issue credit cards for free to anyone they wanted if they controlled the issuance. They could ask whatever questions they wanted on the credit application in order to reduce their risks, or ask no questions at all. They could control how long the cards were valid before they expired, and how much people could use the cards before paying.

Much the same is true for a company issuing its own certificates. The company can structure the enrollment and distribution process to meet its own targets for administrative costs. The company can take the risks it thinks appropriate and establish the requirements needed to keep risks in line.

On the other hand, the process requires an infrastructure that the company must pay for. Credit card operations became rather large at some companies and, thanks to interest payments, they actually became profit centers in some cases. It's not clear how certificate authorities would ever become profit centers, since they have the potential to require a somewhat costly infrastructure. The U.S. government spent as much as $40 per telephone per year to maintain public key certificates for STU III secure telephones in the mid-1990s.

see Note 7.

The shortcoming of issuing one's own keys is that the approach can be hard to scale. If we need Acme's certificates to be accepted by most organizations, then most organizations need a copy of Acme's public key. If every company in the Fortune 500 has its own certificate authority and we must check their certificates with those keys, then public key software systems will need to keep track of a huge number of separate authorities.

COMMERCIAL CERTIFICATE AUTHORITIES

Commercial certificate authorities provide a service akin to major credit cards: they're established entities recognized in most places. If a Web site has a certificate issued by a well-known authority, like Verisign, then the certificate will be automatically recognized by most users' browsers. Otherwise, the browser has to take extra steps to accept the certificate, and must generally ask the workstations' operator for permission. Naturally, it's best to avoid the need for such interactions.

Commercial Web sites generally acquire certificates signed by commercial authorities because most browsers will automatically recognize such certificates. This is obviously a good thing. But what about a site that's issuing certificates for individual users? For example, what if a site is using a public key protocol to authenticate people? What does it mean for such a site to hire a commercial certificate authority?

In that case, the proprietor is essentially delegating the enrollment process to the commercial certification authority. Since the authority controls the signature that appears on certificates, the proprietor must depend on the authority doing enrollments correctly. The proprietor must be willing to accept some level of risk associated with incorrect enrollments by the authority. In some cases, the risk might be acceptable in exchange for the convenience of using existing browser configurations. In other cases, like if forged credentials pose a serious risk, then a commercial authority might not be the right choice.

Since certification is a relatively new type of business, commercial authorities are cautious about the services they offer. In general, they will provide certificates when presented with convincing evidence of identity, but they don't in general accept any financial liability for making incorrect decisions. This situation is generally set forth in the authority's *certification practices statement*. Such statements are intended to provide customers with a clear explanation of the services the authority provides. In general, the statement also explains that the authority does not offer the services such that it takes on the potential liability from errors in authenticating people. Ultimately, the liability rests with the proprietor who incurs the loss caused by an improperly issued certificate. This is the principal shortcoming of commercial authorities.   *see Note 8.*

14.4 PUBLIC KEY INFRASTRUCTURE

The *public key infrastructure* (PKI) is the collection of organizations, mechanisms, protocols, and procedures that create, certify, and distribute public keys. A PKI may provide public keys for a small user community, for a single enterprise, or possibly for a nation. A properly working PKI provides the facilities to create certificates and to reliably validate them. We've mentioned at least two PKIs already: the National Security Agency created a PKI to support the STU III secure telephones, and RSA Data Security created a PKI to support SSL-based Web security.

End users need authentic copies of certificate authorities' keys in order to validate certificates off-line. The most convenient approach might seem to involve a single certificate authority whose key resides in all end-user software, much like Netscape's original approach. However, this doesn't scale well as the number of certificates grows.

The natural approach is to delegate certification. We make this work by issuing certificates to these certificate authorities and signing those certificates with the key belonging to a higher level certificate authority. End-user software can then validate keys from

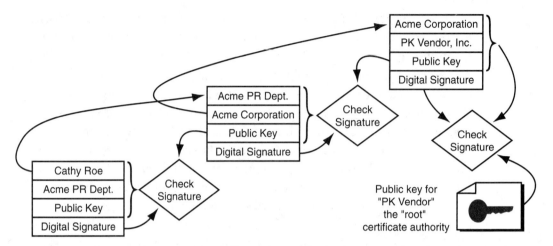

FIGURE 14.9: *Authenticating a certificate chain.* We verify Cathy Roe's certificate by checking its signature with the public key of the "Acme PR Dept" certificate authority. We verify the certificate for the Acme PR Dept by checking its signature with the public key of the "Acme Corporation" authority, and we check that certificate using the key from the authority that issued that certificate. Ultimately, the chain leads to a public key that we already trust, or the authentication fails.

numerous different authorities by validating those authorities' own certificates.

This yields the notion of a *certificate chain.* Each certificate in the chain validates the next earlier certificate, until we reach a "root" authority whose public key we already have. In Figure 14.9, John gets a copy of Cathy Roe's certificate. Note that each certificate has four important entries: the owner's name, the authority that created the certificate, the public key, and the certificate's signature. So John can validate a certificate by retrieving the public key for the authority that created that certificate.

He starts with Cathy's certificate, which was signed by the "Acme PR Department." He retrieves the certificate for the department and uses it to validate the signature on Cathy's certificate. Now he knows that Cathy's certificate is genuine, but only if the PR Department's certificate is also genuine. The department's certificate was issued by Acme Corporation itself, so John must retrieve Acme's corporate certificate to verify the department's certificate. Once John has verified the department's certificate, he still needs to verify the corporation's certificate. That certificate was signed by a commercial certificate authority named "PK Vendor." John already has a reliable copy of the PK Vendor public key, so he can use it to verify Acme's corporate certificate. Now that all the certificates in the chain have been validated, John can believe that Cathy's certificate is valid.

Originally, it seemed that the world of computing would probably be incorporated into a single, universal PKI. There would be a single "root" certificate authority that all chains led to. This did not work out well in practice, and today there are many "roots" that certificate chains might lead to. Applications like browsers contain lists of authorities in order to deal with this situation. A slightly different strategy is for different authorities to cross-certify each others' keys so that chains might still lead to other roots. These alternatives are discussed below.

CENTRALIZED HIERARCHY

A single, centralized hierarchy would seem to provide a straightforward PKI. There would be a single "root" authority that would sign all certificates for other authorities, and all certificate chains would lead to this root. Software vendors could embed the root authority's key in all software, making it easy to verify any certificate.

Such a hierarchy was proposed for the Internet as part of the Privacy Enhanced Mail (PEM) specification. The root authority would be called the "Internet Policy Registration Authority" and it would issue certificates to "Policy Certification Authorities" (PCAs). Each PCA would have its own policy for issuing certificates, somewhat akin to a certification practices statement. PCAs would in turn issue certificates to certificate authorities, who in turn could certify lower-level authorities or end users.

The PCAs were included because it was obvious that certificates would be issued for different purposes, and there needed to be a systematic way of distinguishing between them. In theory, user software could detect which PCA appeared in a particular certificate chain, and could accept or reject a certificate on that basis.   *see Note 9.*

In practice, the centralized hierarchy did not prove practical. Part of the problem was cost. The arrangement forced everyone to purchase a certificate from a PCA, even for prototypes and small-scale tests. Another problem was that no organization had enough goodwill in the community to be able to hold the Internet root key without arousing suspicions from some quarter.

AUTHORITY LISTS

Although browsers started off with all certificates hanging from a single tree, this changed as newer browsers were released. Today, browsers contain a list of certificate authorities whose certificates they recognize. The Netscape Navigator calls this the list of "certificate signer certificates." Figure 14.10 shows part of Netscape's list, as distributed in mid-2000. At that time, the list contained 70 separate keys (13 from Verisign alone). Typically, an authority's key is itself stored in a certificate signed by the authority's own key.

The list structure allows the browser to add new keys as well as recognize the keys already installed. This can happen somewhat automatically when a user visits a site whose certificate can't be authenticated. For example, let's assume that John is browsing a site belonging to a new e-commerce vendor, and the site's certificate was signed by an unfamiliar certificate authority. The SSL protocol generally provides the entire certificate chain when sending certificates to a browser. If the browser doesn't already recognize the highest authority's certificate in that chain, the browser can ask John if it should add that authority to its list.

It is typically a multistep process to add an authority to the browser's list. First, the browser displays the authority's certificate, and then it asks John if and how it should accept the certificate. John can choose to reject the authority entirely, although that will prevent him from being able to open a secure connection with that site. More often, John will add the authority to the browser's built-in list. If John connects to other sites whose certificates were issued by that authority, his browser will recognize the certificates automatically. However, John can also decide to accept the authority only for this particular connection and to discard it afterwards.

Unfortunately, this convenient process isn't necessarily a safe one. It makes things very easy for an attacker who wants to present bogus certificates to a browser. All the attacker has to do is create a public key pair for a certificate authority, give it an honest-sounding name, and sign certificates with that authority's key. The attacker   *A-88* could even create a legitimate site or two whose certificates are signed by the bogus authority. Once John or some other unsuspecting person visits one of those sites, his browser will try to install the bogus authority's certificate. If John adds the authority to his browser's list, then the bogus site can trick John into accepting forged certificates that claim to be from legitimate sites.

For example, the attacker could create a series of bogus sites that masquerade as well known commercial sites like Amazon, Barnes and Noble, or Wells Fargo. When John downloads the site's certificate, signed by the bogus authority, his browser will treat the certificate as genuine. This is because John's browser has essentially been "infected" by the bogus authority's certificate. Of course, it's probably not practical for an attacker to masquerade as a large, complicated commercial site, but the attacker could use a bogus certificate to implement an MIM attack, like we described in Section 14.1.

This attack essentially brings us to the limit of what we can do with indirection. We can only establish confidence in a piece of digital data if we can authenticate it against data we already trust. If we receive a completely new public key, we have no way of establishing any certainty about that key's real identity.

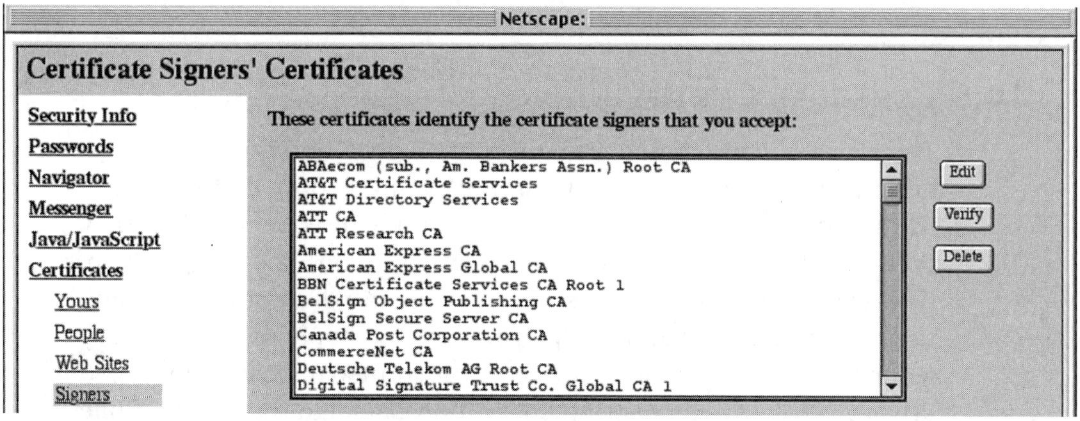

FIGURE 14.10: *List of certificate authorities in the Netscape browser.* This shows part of the list of certificate authorities whose certificates will be automatically authenticated by the browser if received while processing an SSL connection or other secure operation. The user may examine or delete authorities as desired by using the buttons on the right.

CROSS-CERTIFICATION

Although certificate chains were originally intended to support hier-
archies of authorities, they also can allow authorities to certify each
others' public keys. This allows us to use a smaller number of
authority keys to authenticate a broader range of certificates. Moreover, this reduces the risk, since the authority is essentially vouch-
ing for the other authority's legitimacy by signing its key.

The notion of cross-certification was introduced in the Distributed
Authentication Security Service (DASS) developed by Digital Equipment Corporation. DASS identified specific certificate authorities
that could issue certificates containing other authorities' public
keys, even though those authorities weren't strictly subordinates.
The result was that workstations could get by with a small number
of keys belonging to authorities that were allowed to cross-certify
other authorities.   *see Note 10.*

Although cross-certification holds promise, it also poses some
problems. In particular, it's not clear what liability an authority
takes on when certifying another authority's keys. If an authority
certifies keys from a subverted authority, then this subverts the
entire public key system. Moreover, there's the question of exactly
what is being implied by cross-certification. Perhaps an authority
would like to certify another's keys for some purposes but not for
others. Various researchers have been looking at this problem in the
context of "trust management systems."

14.5 PERSONAL CERTIFICATION

The world of certification and authorities does not appeal to everyone in the potential user population. Many people do not want a
third party to produce a costly cryptographic credential when they
themselves have the necessary software on hand. The complexity of
large-scale PKI systems does little to promote grass-roots applications of public key technology. However, the benefits of public key
technology don't all require a large-scale infrastructure. Pretty Good
Privacy (PGP) is a pioneering encryption package that uses public
keys without a sophisticated infrastructure. Instead of relying on
certificate authorities to serve as independent, trusted third parties,
PGP lets people certify their own keys, and the keys of their friends,
colleagues, and acquaintances.   *see Note 11.*

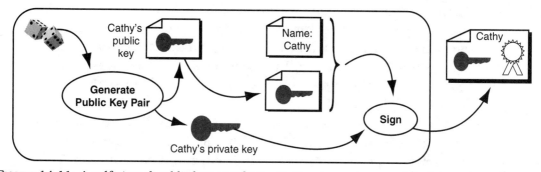

FIGURE 14.11: *A self-signed public key certificate.* Cathy generates a public key pair and generates a self-signed certificate by using her own private key to sign her own certificate. This is a practical approach in environments that establish identity and reputations over time.

The PGP approach can provide a lot of confidence in the authenticity of keys in two particular cases, described below. In the first case, a person's self-signed key can establish authenticity through the "reputation" associated with the key's use in public. In the second case, a key can establish authenticity because other people have vouched for its authenticity.

CERTIFIED BY REPUTATION

The Internet has created a unique public forum in which people can discuss ideas, argue points, and establish reputations based entirely on the strength of one's public statements. Individuals become known and respected for their words, and people refer to this level of respect as *reputation capital.* Most people participating in Internet discussions have no particular public reputation, but many still establish reputation capital based on their performance in the discussions.

A number of people who participate in these discussions will place digital signatures on their messages. The public key for those signatures resides in a *self-signed certificate.* Such a certificate contains the person's name as used on the Internet and is signed with the public key embedded within the certificate. This is illustrated in Figure 14.11.

We can see how this works if we look at what happens when Cathy Roe develops reputation capital based on a series of signed messages. Cathy creates a public key pair and publishes a pubic key certificate that she signs with that same public key. Anyone who gets a copy of that certificate can verify that the key contained therein was used to sign the certificate, and that the certificate contains Cathy's name. As Cathy publishes signed messages, anyone can verify them with the public key in the certificate she has published.

As Cathy's messages are read by other participants, they develop an understanding of Cathy's identity, and they establish certain assumptions concerning her knowledge and capabilities. This understanding of Cathy is based on the messages that she has signed with her public key. Everyone can verify that all messages were generated by a person who holds that particular public key, and that the person claims in the certificate to be Cathy Roe.

Now, what happens if someone else generates a self-signed certificate claiming to be Cathy Roe? Let's assume that Henry has decided to try to ruin Cathy's reputation by forging messages in her name. First, he creates a self-signed certificate containing Cathy's name. Then he publishes the certificate and uses it to sign messages claiming to be from Cathy.

While some readers might be tricked by Henry's stratagem, Cathy can respond by publicly denouncing the certificate in a message signed with her own key. Anyone can use her older certificate to authenticate her message. Henry won't be able to sign messages with that old key; all of his messages must be signed with his bogus key. So people can use the self-signed certificate to reliably distinguish between Henry's forgeries and Cathy's legitimate messages.

CERTIFIED BY A WEB OF TRUST

In a large-scale PKI, the only entities that can sign certificates are the certificate authorities. In PGP, anyone can sign any certificate. In fact, certificates can contain numerous signatures. The signatures serve roughly the same purpose as a certificate authority's signature: it attests to the fact that the given name and key go together. But PGP relies on individuals to certify each others' keys instead of relying on formally established third-party authorities.

In PGP, as in other public key systems, we authenticate a key by checking the certificate's signature against a signature we trust. If John gets a copy of Cathy's certificate directly from Cathy, then he's going to treat it as a genuine certificate. If he gets a copy of Tim's certificate via e-mail, and Cathy has signed Tim's certificate, then he'll probably believe that Tim's certificate is genuine. Now what happens if John gets a certificate from someone named Bob that has been signed by Tim? John essentially has a certificate chain leading from Bob to Tim and then to Cathy, which allows him to authenticate Bob's certificate. This type of chain is called a *web of trust*.

14.6 CERTIFICATE REVOCATION

Indirect authentication is a very convenient thing to be able to do, but we pay for that convenience when we try to revoke a certificate. If someone loses their private key to an attacker, we have no easy way to revoke his or her certificate. We have no way of knowing how many copies of that certificate might reside in various browsers and workstations. Since the software uses the certificate to authenticate people off-line, the software won't necessarily find out that the certificate shouldn't be used.

A-89

There are three general strategies suggested to address this problem. First, there is the *certificate revocation list* (CRL) which publishes a list of all certificates that should be revoked. Second, there is the notion of checking certificates on-line. Third, there is a notion of using short-term certificates to minimize the risk of stolen credentials. These alternatives are described below.

CERTIFICATE REVOCATION LIST

In the world of formal certificate authorities, the revocation list is cited as the standard approach to revocation. Every authority is responsible for producing a list of certificates that should be revoked, and for providing that list to end users on a regular basis. Every certificate contains an expiration date, and a revoked certificate remains on the revocation list until it expires. Unfortunately, revocation lists are often one of the last pieces of PKI technology to be implemented, and computers may be vulnerable to bogus certificates under those circumstances.

D-87

see Note 12.

The principal benefit of the revocation list strategy is that it lets us do off-line certificate checking. Major credit cards used a similar strategy to handle revoked credit cards in the 1970s and 1980s, until on-line credit checking became common. Each card company would periodically publish a list of revoked credit cards and distribute the list to all merchants who accepted their card. In some cases, the companies offered a bounty for every revoked card a merchant might find, giving merchants an extra incentive to check the cards.

The credit card list had an obvious shortcoming: a thief could make heavy use of a card between the time it was stolen and the time the next list of stolen cards was published. The same problem applies to CRLs: the theft may have occurred since the last CRL was issued, or the end user might not have been able to retrieve the latest CRL for some reason. This uncovers one of the places where off-line authentication systems are brittle: an attacker can provide "most" of the evidence to make a key look legitimate, and some end users may be satisfied that authentication has come "close enough" even though partial evidence may well be entirely bogus.

Public key products don't implement CRLs because they represent a complicated mechanism that is rarely used. Early versions of Web browsers ignored CRLs entirely, though recent versions of major browsers do support them. Unfortunately, this doesn't guarantee that CRLs will in fact revoke bogus certificates, since the mechanism depends on detailed technical cooperation between certificate authorities and software product vendors. Vendors might not even know there is a problem until they actually need to use the CRL mechanism.

For example, when Verisign issued a bogus certificate containing Microsoft's name, it uncovered a gap in their CRL processing that prevented the CRL from being used. Microsoft's software relied on a pointer in the certificate to locate the CRL, but Verisign's certificates didn't contain that pointer. So Microsoft issued a specific software patch that installed Verisign's CRL on each computer and forced the certificate-checking software to examine that CRL, ensuring the certificates would be revoked.   *see Note 13.*

ON-LINE REVOCATION

This approach is more akin to what happens today with almost all credit cards: the merchant checks the card's status on-line before   *D-88* accepting it for payment. This approach isn't as reliable as true off-line authentication, since failures in the communication system or other components can cause the transaction to fail. The advantage

of on-line revocation is that it ensures completely accurate information.   *see Note 14.*

In the public key certificate environment, an end user would verify
a certificate on-line by contacting the certificate authority. The
authority could verify that the specified certificate has not yet been
revoked. However, not all certificate authorities support real-time
certificate verification; at most, host computers would be able to
contact the authority for its most recent CRL. In fact, not all public
key applications support CRLs, so there are environments in which
it isn't really possible to revoke a certificate.

TIMELY CERTIFICATION

Ron Rivest, coinventor of RSA, has proposed a different approach to
the revocation problem which relies on recently issued certificates
instead of long-lived certificates. Rivest believes that the risk falls
most heavily on the host that accepts a certificate, and that the way
to control that risk is to control how recently the certificate has been
validated. Depending on the application, a host might want the certificate validated fairly recently. From this point of view, the CRL
strategy is wrong because the certificate authority, not the recipient,
determines how fresh a certificate's validity data can be.   *see Note 15.*

Rivest proposes that it should be up to the signer to provide evidence that a certificate is valid, and that such evidence should be a
certificate with a recent creation date. Certificate authorities should   *D-89*
be able to issue updated copies of valid certificates on demand. If
John needs to provide a certificate to his bank in order to perform a
transaction, he first retrieves a new copy of his certificate, which will
contain a recent time stamp. The bank will be able to look at that
certificate and tell from the time stamp that it is probably a valid
certificate, since it was issued recently.

If Henry manages to steal John's private key, John can tell the
certificate authority about the compromise. When Henry, or anyone
else, asks the authority for an up-to-date copy of John's certificate
containing the compromised key, the authority will report that the
certificate has been revoked. Meanwhile, John can file a new public
key with the authority and start distributing certificates with his
name and a new key.

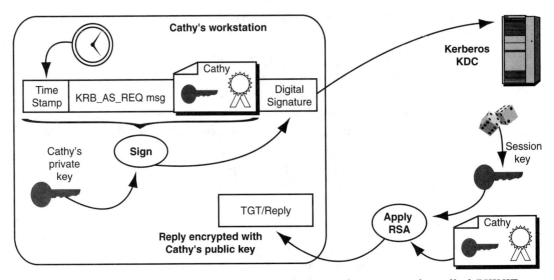

FIGURE 14.12: *Kerberos preauthentication with public keys.* This approach, called PKINIT, uses Cathy's public key certificate instead of a memorized password to authenticate Cathy to the Kerberos KDC. The reply uses a public key to encrypt the TGT's session key.

14.7 CERTIFICATES WITH KERBEROS

In Chapter 12, we briefly noted that there are ways to integrate public key cryptography with Kerberos. While these techniques don't necessarily convert a Kerberos environment into a true off-line authentication architecture (after all, the whole process will always depend on the presence of a Kerberos KDC), it does eliminate the need for a shared secret based on a reusable password.

Figure 14.12 illustrates the technique called PKINIT, for "public key initialization." PKINIT uses Cathy's public key pair in a special version of the preauthentication process described in Section 12.3. Cathy logs on to her workstation and provides her private key. The workstation contacts the KDC, sending a preauthenticated request for a TGT. The request contains the usual information along with a copy of Cathy's public key certificate, and the whole request is digitally signed with her private key.   *see Note 16.*

Upon receipt, the KDC first tries to validate Cathy's certificate. It must be issued by an authority recognized by the KDC or it will be rejected. Next, the KDC generates the TGT for Cathy and encrypts the corresponding session key with Cathy's public key. The entire response is then signed with the KDC's own private key so that Cathy can verify its integrity upon receipt. Once Cathy decrypts the session key, she can use it with the TGT to authenticate herself to other servers. She should not need her private key again until the next time she logs on.

This is not the only way PKINIT can work. It can also use temporary Diffie-Hellman keys in order to generate a shared secret. In that case, Cathy's preauthentication request contains a temporary Diffie-Hellman key. Cathy must still sign the request with a separate key, and must usually provide a copy of the certificate for her signature key. The KDC then verifies her certificate and the signature on the preauthentication data before generating a TGT based on a Diffie-Hellman shared secret.

An important property of PKINIT is that it can eliminate the KDC's role in authenticating users. Instead, the KDC relies entirely on user certificates. The authority that issues certificates will bear the responsibility for verifying user identities. Once the KDC accepts a certificate, it has essentially authenticated the corresponding user. For this reason, the KDC must scrupulously check certificates and only issue tickets if the certificate is one that the KDC can honestly recognize.

Windows 2000 uses PKINIT to integrate public keys with its Kerberos authentication environment. The Kerberos TGT request contains a copy of the user's certificate and is signed with the user's private key. The Windows 2000 KDC confirms that the certificate is valid and that it was issued by an authority recognized by that KDC. Then the KDC verifies the preauthentication time stamp and digital signature.

see Note 17.

Once the KDC has validated the preauthentication data, it constructs a TGT that includes Windows 2000–specific authorization data, primarily consisting of security identifiers for the user and groups the user belongs to. Then the KDC encrypts the response with the public key in the user's certificate and signs it with the KDC's own private key. Upon receipt, the user's system decrypts and verifies the response, and uses the TGT in accordance with the Kerberos protocols to request access to other servers.

14.8 SUMMARY TABLES

TABLE 14.1: *Attack Summary*

Attack	Security Problem	Prevalence	Attack Description
A-84. Public key forgery	Recover or modify hidden information	Trivial	If a recipient accepts an unauthenticated public key, the attacker simply substitutes his own key for the right one.
A-85. Man in the middle	Recover or modify hidden information	Sophisticated	Attacker substitutes own public key for another, and reencrypts messages between two entities
A-86. Bogus name on certificate	Masquerade as someone else	Trivial	Attacker puts the victim's name on the application for a public key certificate.
A-87. Substitute certificate	Masquerade as someone else	Trivial	Attacker uses a legitimate certificate to implement SSL on a bogus site that is masquerading as a different site
A-88. Bogus certificate authority	Masquerade as someone else	Common	Attacker uses a bogus certificate authority to create bogus certificates, and induces browsers to accept his authority key
A-89. Exploit private key	Masquerade as someone else	Software	Attacker relies on off-line authentication to exploit a stolen private key

TABLE 14.2: *Defense Summary*

♟ Defense	Foils Attacks	Description
D-84. Public key certificates	A-84. Public key forgery A-85. Man in the middle	Publish the assignment of a given public key to a given owner, and sign this publication with a trustworthy digital signature
D-85. Key ownership requirement	A-86. Bogus name on certificate	Issue certificates only to the person who owns the requested name
D-86. Validate certificate's host name	A-87. Substitute certificate	Compare the name on the certificate against the name of the host computer on the SSL connection
D-87. Certificate revocation list	A-89. Exploit private key	Issue a periodic list of all certificates that have been revoked
D-88. On-line certificate revocation	A-89. Exploit private key	Provide a mechanism to query an authority to verify that a given certificate has not been revoked
D-89. Timely certification	A-89. Exploit private key	Require that all certificates be issued recently, and provide a mechanism so that authorities can issue such certificates if the certificate has not been revoked

RESIDUAL THREATS

A-88. Bogus certificate authority—The user interface of typical modern browsers provides no reasonable protection against this attack, since there is no way to tell the difference between a new key from a legitimate authority and a key from a bogus authority.

CHAPTER 15
PRIVATE KEY SECURITY

I can't keep secrets—it's no use to try.

— L. M. Montgomery, *Anne of the Island*

IN THIS CHAPTER

Public key cryptography succeeds only as long as a private key's owner can keep it under control—always available when needed but never disclosed to anyone else. There are many ways to try to achieve this.

- Generating private keys
- Storing private keys in files and smart cards
- Storing private keys on servers
- Strong authentication using weak passwords

15.1 GENERATING PRIVATE KEYS

Even before we face the problem of protecting our private key, we must face the problem of generating a private key. If we are using Diffie-Hellman, DSS, or some other key involving modular exponentiation, then it's simply a question of picking an appropriately large random number. If we are using RSA, then we need to pick two large primes. This poses more of a challenge. Large prime numbers are mathematically unwieldy, which is why they provide such good security. But the quality of the security depends on picking numbers that really are primes.

The standard approach for picking prime numbers is to construct a random number that might be a prime, test it mathematically, and discard it if it's not a prime. Unfortunately there are no practical mathematical tests to tell us if a number is really a prime. To do that we would have to factor the number completely, and that shouldn't be a practical computation for numbers we're using in RSA keys. Otherwise, we could use the factoring computation to crack the RSA keys themselves.

We use several tests that try to detect factors of a number in various ways. If we fail to detect any factors, then we conclude that the number must be a prime. By using several different tests we can reduce the likelihood of making a mistake: if there are additional factors in our RSA key, then it becomes much easier for an attacker to crack it.

The first step in constructing a prime is to generate a random binary number of the desired size. Then we set the number's high-order bit and low-order bit to one. By setting the high-order bit, we ensure that the number is of the size we want. By setting the low-order bit, we ensure that the number is odd—even numbers obviously aren't primes.

Once we have constructed this candidate prime number, we test its primality. The first and simplest approach is to verify that the number isn't divisible by "small" prime numbers. Schneier suggests testing the candidate prime against all numbers less than 256 or even all those less than 2,000.   *see Note 1.*

Next, we apply a probabilistic primality test. This is a test that can detect primes with very high probability. There are several probabilistic tests, and they all work by choosing a random value and systematically testing the prime against it. The most efficient algorithm is called the Miller-Rabin test. By applying the Miller-Rabin test four times, one can achieve extremely high confidence that a number is a prime.   *see Note 2.*

This is essentially the same approach used by PGP to generate its RSA keys. First, PGP creates a candidate n-bit prime by generating a random number of n-2 bits with the highest two bits set to one. Next, PGP uses a table of the first hundred primes (through 541) to check the candidate for factors. PGP randomly dives into the table and computes remainders, searching for factors or even hints of factors in the remainders. Finally, PGP applies a probabilistic primality test four times. PGP performs this operation twice to yield the two primes that make up the RSA composite of the key.

see Note 3.

15.2 THE PRIVATE KEY STORAGE PROBLEM

Protecting secret keys is a problem simply because there are two of them—the proprietor faces the problem of distributing the key as well as that of protecting the key at the end points. In this sense, it should be easier to protect a public key pair simply because we don't have to distribute the key or store a second copy at the destination. But we still need to protect that private key.

The most common approach today is to store the key in a file, and encrypt the file with a secret key. The key is usually a password or passphrase. Lotus Notes, arguably the oldest public key application today, uses this approach. The private key for a Lotus Notes user is stored in a file called the *ID file*. In addition to the private key, the file contains the user's identifying data and other user-specific security information.

see Note 4.

We can see several benefits to the file-based approach if we consider how a user like Tim might work with one. The file gives Tim direct control over his private key. He can make as many copies as he might want for back-up purposes. He can use the ID file as a weak form of two-factor authentication by storing it on a diskette: the encrypting password represents "something known" and the diskette represents "something had." This provides mobility if Tim needs to log on from several locations. Of course, this is weaker than a card-based two factor system since it's easy to make copies of the ID file, possibly without Tim's knowledge.

Another benefit is that Tim doesn't have to store his private key on a server, as required with the techniques in Section 15.5. This reduces the risk of a dictionary attack against his password, since the attacker can't harvest the encrypted keys from a server. Moreover, Tim can perform cryptographic operations even when operating off-line, as with a laptop computer. Perhaps the most compelling benefit for many developers is that file-based private key storage is relatively easy to implement. The technique is also used in Web browsers if the browser's owner has installed a personal private key for use with SSL client authentication or e-mail encryption.

PGP also stores the user's private key in encrypted form in the user's key file. The key is encrypted with a passphrase, which may contain dozens of characters. As a practical matter, however, users often protect their PGP key with a short password that's vulnerable to brute force attack. There is even an attack program available to *A-90* try to crack PGP passphrases. The program uses a dictionary of likely choices, like other password-cracking programs, and tries each candidate until one yields a decrypted private key.   *see Note 5.*

Another risk faced by private keys stored in files is that a subverted program might be able to sniff a user's private key while it is decrypted for use by the public key software. For example, Henry *A-91* might write a special add-on for Tim's web browser, and the add-on might look for Tim's private key while the key is decrypted for use. Once Henry's program has sniffed the key, it might transmit the key via some web transaction associated with the add-on program.   *see Note 6.*

15.3 SMART CARDS AND PRIVATE KEYS

Smart cards were introduced in Section 9.1. As seen in Figure 15.1, a smart card is an active token that is generally the size of a credit card. When placed in the appropriate smart card reader, the card will respond to various commands and update information stored on the card. Every card can store a certain amount of variable information even when the card is unplugged. Some vendors have used these capabilities to implement public key crypto functions.

A smart card can store an individual's private key and provide public key crypto functions in a way that protects the private key from theft or disclosure. Several public key vendors have developed smart cards to do this. A workstation using public key encryption *D-90* will perform functions that require the private key by transmitting the requests to the smart card, and the card transmits back the results. The workstation never sees the private key, which never needs to leave the card. In fact, such cards might not even provide a function to divulge the private key.

The smart card overcomes the risks of storing private keys in files. Obviously, there is no way for a sniffer program to steal the private key if the key never resides on the workstation. There is also no encrypted private key file to crack. Although smart cards don't provide absolute protection, they provide far better protection than we find on a typical desktop computer.

There are several different ways to store and use a private key on a smart card, and different vendors use different approaches. A vendor could simply use the card as a variant of diskette storage: the card would export the private key when needed, and the cryptographic algorithms would all reside on the workstation. This approach would of course be vulnerable to a sniffer attack, though it should resist dictionary attacks. Although this approach has limited security benefits, it appeals to some vendors because it is relatively simple to implement and places few demands on the smart card.

There are two other general approaches that offer significantly better security by placing cryptographic processing on the smart card. The first approach generates the private key on a workstation and stores it on the card. The second approach generates the private key on the card itself.

FIGURE 15.1: *Smart cards for handling public key cryptography.* These are Datakey Model 330 cards, designed to carry a private key and perform public key cryptographic functions. The card in the lower center is used by employees of the Federal Deposit Insurance Corporation for secure communications over their enterprise network as well as for building access control. The card in the upper right is a nonfunctioning copy of the card used by President Clinton on July 5, 2000, to sign the Electronic Signatures in Global and National Commerce (E-Sign) Act. Photograph courtesy of Datakey, Inc.   *see Note 7.*

OFF-CARD KEY GENERATION

In this approach, we use software on a workstation to generate the public key pair. Then we download the keys onto the smart card as part of its initialization. This is shown in Figure 15.2. The card pro- *D-91* vides public key cryptographic functions without having to divulge the private key. This eliminates the risk of having the private key disclosed to a sniffer on the workstation.

In its simplest form, this type of card could get by with two operations: *install private key* and *apply private key*. The first function would put the private key into the appropriate storage area on the card. The second function would apply the RSA algorithm to some input data using the private key. There is no function that discloses the private key; we have only the option of replacing the existing key value with a new one.

While it might be tempting to provide a function that exports the private key under appropriate circumstances, it is very difficult to implement such a function safely. It is difficult to define "appropriate circumstances" and enforce them in the face of a serious attack. It is much safer to simply omit any functions that might disclose the private key directly, and only allow the key to be changed. This allows an "expired" smart card to be reused without disclosing an old private key.

When Tim generates his private key, he can make a back-up copy and save it on a diskette in a safe place. If Tim's smart card fails

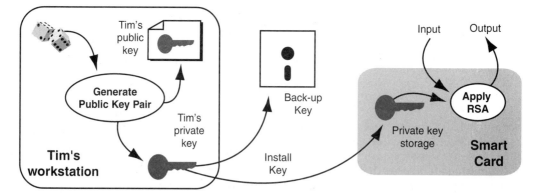

FIGURE 15.2: *Off-card key generation.* Tim generates a public key pair with workstation software and downloads the private key onto his smart card. He can also make a back-up copy of the key.

(after all, hardware isn't 100% reliable) or is damaged or destroyed, he can create a new copy using his backed-up key. This is particularly important if Tim uses his private key to protect stored files. Otherwise, Tim would lose the files' contents if his smart card failed. This strategy carries an obvious security risk: the more copies of a key we have, the greater is our risk that the key will somehow be leaked. Here we must trade off the benefit of a backup against the added risk of disclosure. *A-92*

As a practical matter, smart card vendors often provide additional functions. Some cards provide functions for storing and retrieving the public key certificate associated with the private key. While a minimal card that stores an RSA private key might get by with a single *apply RSA* function as shown in Figure 15.2, other cards may implement separate functions for encrypting, decrypting, and signing with the private key, depending on the algorithms used.

ON-CARD KEY GENERATION

In this approach, we embed the private key generation on the smart card itself, and provide no way of divulging the private key (Figure 15.3). This addresses the risk of stealing a backed-up private key as well as the risks associated with using the private key on a workstation. The only way to use the particular private key is to have possession of the smart card it resides on. *D-92*

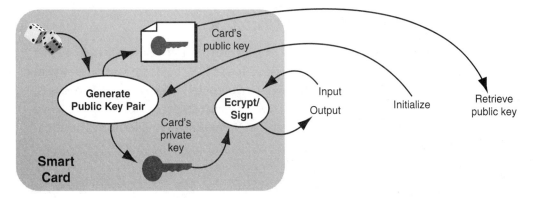

FIGURE 15.3: *On-card key generation.* This type of card generates its own key pair and never divulges its private key. Aside from cryptographic functions using the private key, the cards can emit the public key and can generate new key pairs.

While this approach yields a real security benefit, it also poses some shortcomings. First, it places some serious performance requirements on the smart card. As explained in Section 15.1, RSA keys require a lot of mathematical processing to create and test. This translates into a lot of computing cycles and memory. The Datakey Model 330 card, for example, takes an average of 23 seconds to generate a 1,024-bit private key this way, and takes an average of three minutes to generate a 2,048-bit key. This approach is more practical for Diffie-Hellman and DSS keys. In addition, the card will tie up a certain amount of program storage to hold the software required to generate keys, and the card will use that software only once in most cases.

see Note 8.

Another shortcoming is that such cards should not be used for keys that protect encrypted files. This is because we have to assume that the cards fail occasionally. The card's failure would destroy its private key and render the files unreadable that require that private key for decryption.

On the other hand, such smart cards are ideal for digital signatures on transactions. If a card fails, the owner can get another one, publish the new public key, and start using it on subsequent transactions. The previously signed transactions can still be verified with copies of the old public key. New transactions can be verified with the new public key. In a sense, replacing this private key is like being issued a new credit card number after a card has been lost or stolen.

15.4 SMART CARD ACCESS CONTROL

Many vendors implement two-factor authentication with their smart cards. Usually, the card incorporates a PIN, and the user must provide the PIN before the card will perform its cryptographic functions. Some vendors use biometrics as a method of controlling card access, which, combined with a PIN, yields three-factor authentication.

PINS

Section 9.5 describes several techniques for implementing PINs. The best technique for smart cards is to use the PIN as a password. The smart card would store a copy of the PIN internally and refuse to accept commands until the operator provides the correct PIN. The card can implement security measures to resist attempts to find the PIN through trial-and-error guessing.

When discussing one-time password devices, we examined a different approach in which we incorporate the PIN into the base secret. When the attacker guesses the wrong PIN, the device appears to work correctly but yields the wrong result. The attacker can find out that the result is wrong only by trying to log on to a server using that one-time password. If the attacker does this numerous times, the server detects an attempt to penetrate the system using brute force. Unfortunately, this strategy doesn't work well with public key cryptography. If the smart card uses the PIN to construct the private key, then an incorrect PIN will yield results that don't work with the card's public key. Thus, the attacker can test the PIN's correctness without having to contact a server. This makes it impractical to use the PIN as part of a smart card's private key. The practical approach is for the card to store a copy of the PIN and verify it before granting use of the card's services.

The principal shortcoming for PINs is that subverted software on a workstation might sniff the PIN used to unlock a smart card. Some vendors try to bypass this problem by incorporating a PIN keypad into the smart card reader, though this increases the reader's cost.

BIOMETRICS

Biometrics provide an interesting approach for controlling access to a smart card. In general, the strategy is to store the owner's biometric pattern on the card and to require a reasonable match against a biometric signature. This has yielded three architectural concepts, each providing security improvements over the previous.

- **Biometric pattern storage**

  In this approach, the smart card sets aside storage for a biometric pattern. When a workstation requests access to the smart card, the card emits the pattern, and the workstation compares it to a biometric signature collected from the operator and tells the card whether they match or not. This approach appeals to people concerned about biometric privacy. Individuals retain personal control of their biometric patterns and the system does not need to create a large-scale biometric database. *see Note 9.*

Unfortunately, this approach would also be easy for an attacker to bypass, particularly if the biometric matching relies on software running on the operator's workstation. An attacker could replace that software with a subverted program that simply told the smart card that the biometric matching was a success, without ever collecting a signature from the operator.

One strategy for addressing these problems is to integrate a biometric reader with a smart card reader. The biometric never enters the workstation, and the reader itself is responsible for collecting the biometric signature and performing the match. While this does not eliminate the risk of an attack through a smart card reader that doesn't incorporate a biometric reader, it increases the attacker's work factor.

- **On-card biometric matching**

A slightly better approach is to require the workstation to present a biometric signature before the card will unlock itself. The card then performs the biometric matching against the owner's internally stored pattern. If the signature matches the pattern closely enough, the card allows the workstation to use it.

This approach is similar to collecting a PIN. There is the same risk of an attacker's sniffing the biometric and later replaying it to unlock the card.

A practical problem is that the biometric matching places additional demands on the card's resources. The card must have additional program memory to store the biometric matching procedure, and will require additional working storage for performing the match calculations. Cards containing the necessary resources are expensive, though the prices should drop as smart cards evolve.

- **Embedded biometric reader**

In this approach, we embed a biometric reader on the smart card so that it can collect the biometric pattern directly. This approach is most likely to involve fingerprint recognition, since a fingerprint reader could be constructed to fit the card's form factor.

This approach addresses the problem of an attacker's sniffing and replaying a biometric signature, since the card would accept signatures only from its built-in reader. However, this poses a significant challenge for smart card technology because it requires a lot of processing resources as well as a high-quality fingerprint reader packed into a tiny package.

Figure 15.4 shows the Sony Puppy, an authentication token with a built-in fingerprint reader. However, the Puppy is not a smart card. While its length and width are card-sized, it has the thickness of a credit-card calculator.

This type of card would be practical for digitally signed transactions, since the biometric processing will introduce reliability problems. Biometrics are vulnerable to failure if the person's physical trait suffers injury or undergoes other natural changes. The safest response from a security standpoint would be to replace the smart card in such situations. The alternative would be to install a "back door" to unlock the card in cases wherein

FIGURE 15.4: *Authentication token with a built-in biometric reader.* This is the Sony Puppy, a token with a built-in fingerprint reader. The Puppy provides on-card generation of a public key pair along with standard public-key cryptographic functions. The owner provides a fingerprint to unlock the private key. The wire connects to one of the computer's USB ports.

the biometric fails to recognize the card's legitimate owner, and such back doors could also be exploited by an attacker.

On today's smart cards, PINs provide slightly better overall security than biometrics, simply because the biometric matching doesn't usually take place on the smart card itself. If the card can do its own biometric matching, then the biometric provides similar security to the PIN. If the biometric matching takes place on the operator's workstation, then we face the risk of subverted matching software. The subverted software could trick the smart card into unlocking itself by claiming that a biometric match occurred without actually performing a match. We reduce the risk of such spoofing by performing the match on the card itself.

15.5 PRIVATE KEYS ON SERVERS

Although smart cards carry some clear security advantages, we purchase those advantages at the cost of extra hardware. If we deploy a smart card–based system, then people are limited to using systems containing the appropriate readers. We can use private key files instead, and carry around a diskette in lieu of a smart card, but this still places a practical burden on end users.

A third approach to private key management is to store all such keys on a server. When a person logs on to the network, the server downloads the user's private key to the workstation.

Digital's DASS pioneered this approach. Private keys for users and other entities would be stored on a server called the *certificate distribution center*. During logon, the user's hashed secret password was used to authenticate the person. DASS used public key encryption to distribute a shared secret key, which in turn protected the private key during transmission to its owner. While DASS was not widely used, its architectural concepts have persisted.   *see Note 10.*

Today, there are two general strategies for managing private keys on servers. The key downloading approach pioneered by DASS is used by Novell's NetWare V4 product and by Keon from RSA Security. A different approach, the virtual smart card server, does not download the private key but instead performs the cryptographic services on the server. These two approaches are described in this section.

NOVELL NETWARE: KEY DOWNLOADING

The Novell approach is a commercial implementation of the DASS protocol for downloading the private key. The system consists of a proprietary server running the NetWare Directory Services (NDS) and proprietary NetWare client software for the workstations. Figure 15.5 illustrates the overall process. NDS stores the private key in encrypted form and transmits it to the client when it receives an authenticated request. The request is authenticated with the user's memorized password. The private key works correctly only after it has been decrypted with the memorized password, which isn't permanently stored anywhere *see Note 11.*

Key downloading poses a number of security concerns that are addressed by specific features of the NDS downloading protocol. This begins with user enrollment, shown in Figure 15.6. To enroll, Tim provides his user name and password. The enrollment process generates a public key pair for him, and encrypts the private key

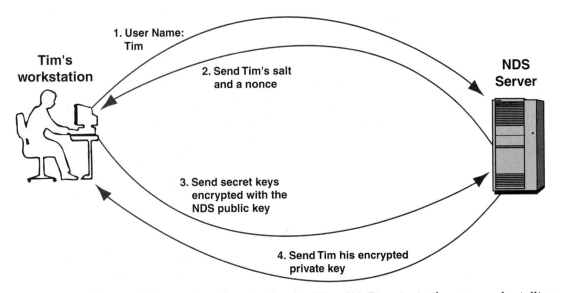

FIGURE 15.5: *Overview of private key download on NetWare V4.* Tim starts the process by telling the NDS who he is. The NDS looks up his information and responds with a copy of his "password salt" and a newly generated nonce. Tim uses this data in conjunction with his password to generate a secret key. He encrypts that key, along with a randomly generated session key, using the NDS public key. Then he sends those keys to the NDS, which decrypts them and uses them to encrypt his private key for delivery.

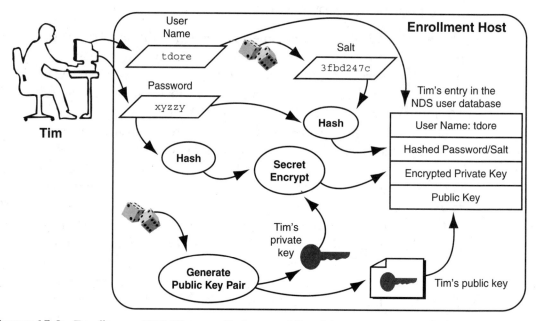

FIGURE 15.6: *Enrolling on NDS.* Tim enrolls by providing his user name and choosing a secret password. The enrollment process generates a public key pair for him and encrypts the private key with a hash of his password. The user database stores a salted hash of his password that it uses to authenticate him. Tim's database entry does not contain enough data to decrypt his private key directly, though a weak password would make it vulnerable to a dictionary attack.

using his hashed password. The process also generates a second hash of his password using a salt value.

The two password hashes work together to authenticate Tim, but they serve different purposes. The first hash protects his private key as it resides on the NDS host. While the NDS does apply operating system security to the file to resist attacks, a successful penetration doesn't give the attacker instant access to private keys. The attacker must at least mount a dictionary attack and crack a user's password in order to decrypt a private key.

The second password hash is used to authenticate Tim when he logs on and attempts to download his private key. The NDS will not download the private key, even in its encrypted form, until Tim has verified that he knows his password. The NDS uses this hashed password in conjunction with a second, randomly generated key to encrypt the private key further when transmitting it to Tim's workstation.

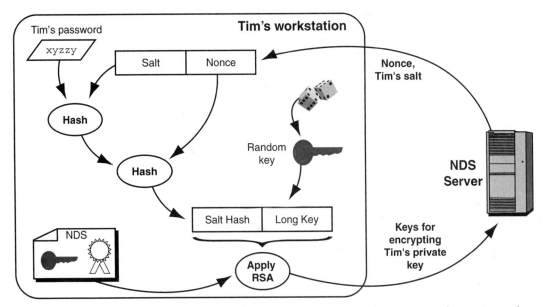

FIGURE 15.7: *NetWare user authentication.* To authenticate Tim, the NDS sends Tim's workstation a nonce and a copy of Tim's password salt. The workstation reconstructs Tim's salted password and hashes it with the nonce to produce the "salt hash." The workstation also generates a random key. Then it encrypts these two results using the NDS public key, and sends them to the NDS. Upon receipt, the NDS computes the same hash using the nonce and Tim's hashed password, and authenticates Tim if the two match.

The authentication and private key downloading process is fairly complicated, so the description here has divided it into two parts. Figure 15.7 illustrates the first part: the process of authenticating a user to the NDS with the secret password. Tim starts by telling the NDS his user name, and the NDS replies by sending Tim's workstation a random nonce and a copy of Tim's password salt.

Tim's workstation responds by generating two secret keys. The first one is constructed by hashing his password twice. First, it hashes his password along with the salt received from the NDS; the resulting value should match the salted password stored in Tim's NDS user database entry. Next, it hashes that result along with the nonce just received from the NDS. This will yield a key we will call the *salt hash*. The workstation then randomly generates a second key we will call the *long key*. This key contains exactly the same number of bits as the private key, and it will be used later as a "one-time pad" key to further encrypt the private key. The worksta-

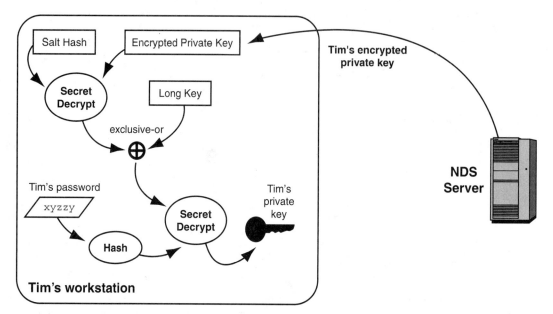

FIGURE 15.8: *Downloading the private key from the NDS.* First, the workstation uses the salt hash as a secret key to decrypt the message. Next, the workstation exclusive-ors the result with the long key. This produces a copy of the private key as stored in the NDS database. Finally, the workstation decrypts the private key by using the hashed password as a secret key.

tion puts these two keys into a message, encrypts the message with the NDS public key, and transmits the result to the NDS.

Meanwhile, the NDS extracts Tim's salted password from the user database and hashes it with the nonce to produce its own version of the salt hash. Upon receipt of Tim's reply, the NDS compares the salt hash Tim computed against its own salt hash result. The two will match if Tim provided the correct password to his workstation.

Once the NDS authenticates Tim, it encrypts his private key for delivery. First, it uses the exclusive-or operation to encrypt the private key with the long key. Next, it uses conventional secret key encryption to encrypt the result, using the salt hash as the secret key. Then the NDS transmits the resulting message to Tim's workstation.

Figure 15.8 illustrates how Tim's workstation decrypts the private key after receiving it from the NDS. First, the workstation decrypts the message using a secret key algorithm with the salt hash as the key. Next, the workstation computes the exclusive-or of the result with the long key. This yields the private key as stored in the NDS database. Finally, the workstation computes the hash of Tim's password and uses it as a key to perform a final round of secret key decryption. This produces Tim's private key.

This elaborate process provides several layers of protection against typical attacks. Attackers can't perform dictionary attacks because the messages do not contain a recognizable data item to test against. If the workstation sent simply the salt hash in response to the NDS, then attackers could test against that message. By including the random long key in the RSA encryption, we deny them a way of verifying their password guesses. The only practical approach is to try to steal the encrypted user database, and the NDS architecture makes this difficult to do.

Once the private key arrives on Tim's workstation, NetWare takes one final step to protect it from leaking. Instead of using the actual private key for encryption or signatures, the NetWare client constructs a different random private key derived from Tim's private key. This other key is used with the Gillou-Quisquater (GQ) digital signature algorithm. Once the workstation constructs this GQ key, it erases Tim's private key. This reduces the risk of a sniffer program retrieving a NetWare private key. The only key usually visible within the NetWare client is the temporary GQ key.

SAFEWORD VIRTUAL SMART CARD: DATA UPLOADING

The virtual smart card server takes a different approach than Net-Ware and DASS: instead of downloading the private key to the client, it uploads a request to perform a cryptographic function and processes it on the server (Figure 15.9). The server is responsible for protecting all users' private keys and for authenticating requests to use those keys. As with NetWare, the only technical requirement is that the site install the necessary servers and the client software on user workstations. The client software interfaces with public key applications through either PKCS #11 or Microsoft's Crypto API.   *see Note 12.*

The virtual smart card protocol combines two separate security mechanisms to protect the traffic between server and client. First, the connection uses a standard SSL connection to provide encryption, integrity protection, and authentication of the smart card server. Second, the server uses a SafeWord-compatible authentica-

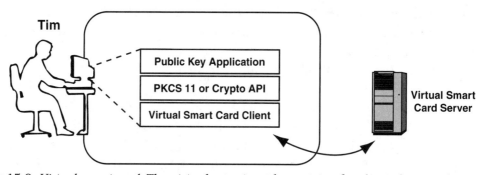

FIGURE 15.9: *Virtual smart card.* The virtual smart card consists of a client that resides on the user's workstation and interfaces with software that uses public key cryptography. The example here shows a public key application using the virtual smart card to implement some type of authentication. The application communicates with the smart card via a standard interface. The virtual smart card client communicates with the virtual smart card server across the network, sending data to the server for cryptographic processing and receiving the results.

tion procedure to authenticate the workstation's operator before granting access to a private key. This authentication procedure may simply require a memorized password or it may use a one-time password token (Section 9.3).

Once the virtual smart card server has authenticated a client connection, it extracts the user's private key from the database. All keys are stored in encrypted form, using a server key, so the server next decrypts the user's private key. As the server receives cryptographic service requests across the SSL connection, it performs the service using the private key, if required, and then transmits the result back across the connection. If the connection exceeds a preestablished time period, it may require the client to reauthenticate itself, which makes the user reenter the password or enter a new one-time password. When the connection closes, the server erases the private key, leaving only the encrypted copy in the database.

The virtual smart card server has access to plaintext versions of users' private keys. While this is not the ideal approach to private key management, it poses the same threat faced by Kerberos KDCs and by commercial authentication servers for one-time password products like SafeWord and SecurID. Large-scale commercial users have found these systems to provide adequate security even in high-threat environments like the financial community.

15.6 PASSWORDS REVISITED

Passwords have a relatively small average attack space because we know how to make a list of likely candidates and compare them against the hashed or encrypted form of the password. If we hash the password to protect it, then attackers simply hash their guesses, one by one, and test them against the hashed target. When we use the password to encrypt some data, like a nonce, during an authentication protocol, the attackers will generally be able to see the nonce's value and use it to perform their trial-and-error attack. But what if we use the password to encrypt some data that the attackers can't easily check?

Researchers started discussing the possibility in the late 1980s, motivated by the observation that there will always be people who choose easy-to-guess passwords. The researchers sought a way of using low-entropy passwords to establish a strong, hard-to-guess secret between two entities, like a workstation and a server.   *see Note 13.*

In 1992, Steve Bellovin and Michael Merritt described several protocols, called collectively *Encrypted Key Exchange* (EKE), that seriously resisted dictionary attacks. The protocols worked by combining public key encryption with secret key encryption. Unlike the public key encryption techniques described elsewhere in this book, EKE kept the public key secret as well as the private key.   *see Note 14.*

To illustrate the protocol, we will have Tim try to log on to a server that uses EKE. First, Tim's workstation generates a public key pair to use for this particular server connection. Then the workstation encrypts the public key using Tim's password and transmits the encrypted public key. Meanwhile, the server does the same thing, encrypting its own, temporary public key with Tim's password. Once they have exchanged public keys, they can use those keys to share another secret key that's large enough to resist trial-and-error attacks itself. EKE could resist trial-and-error attacks because it's not practical for attackers to try all possible values for Tim's password against all possible values for Tim's public key.

In a sense, the protocol "amplifies" the password's entropy. It starts with the low-entropy password and uses it to secretly exchange a public key with higher entropy. This public key can then establish a secret key with enough entropy to resist attack, amplifying the entropy of the original password. Additional protocols have evolved to address limitations of earlier ones. A paper published by Kwon in 2000 identified almost two dozen different protocols derived from EKE and from earlier work by Lomas et al. Although these password-amplifying protocols haven't entered any mainstream applications, some commercial organizations are getting involved in their development. The Institute of Electrical and Electronics Engineers (IEEE) is sponsoring a study group to develop protocols for standardizing strong password-based authentication and key exchange.

see Note 15.

15.7 SUMMARY TABLES

TABLE 15.1: *Attack Summary*

Attack	Security Problem	Prevalence	Attack Description
A-90. PGP passphrase cracking	Masquerade as someone else	Common	Attacker uses a cracking program designed to attack PGP passphrases
A-91. Sniff a private key	Masquerade as someone else	Common	Attacker inserts a sniffer program in the victim's system and sniffs the private key while in use
A-92. Steal a private key backup	Masquerade as someone else	Physical	Attacker steals a copy of the private key stored on a back-up diskette or other device

TABLE 15.2: *Defense Summary*

Defense	Foils Attacks	Description
D-90. Private key on smart card	A-90. PGP passphrase cracking	Store the private key on a smart card instead of in an encrypted file
D-91. Public key crypto functions on smart card	A-91. Sniff a private key	Store the private key on a smart card that provides crypto functions so that the private key never needs to leave the card
D-92. Private key created on smart card	A-92. Steal a private key backup	Generate the private key on the smart card so that the key never exists outside of the smart card

CHAPTER NOTES

This appendix identifies the sources for information in this book. The notes do not amplify the technical information in the text—they only identify sources. Follow the marker from the text if you need to identify the source of a particular piece of information.

If you want to review all of a chapter's notes, then you should simply read the chapter's notes from start to finish once you've read the chapter's text.

These notes contain only the title and author for each source. Full citations appear in the **Bibliography**. If an item contains no author's name and is the product of a particular company, government agency, or other institution, then I list the institution as the author. If the note refers to a vendor or a Web site, check the book's **Web and Vendor Resources** section for contact information and URLs.

NOTES FOR CHAPTER 1

1. Scholars disagree about how and when the tale of Ali Baba was added to the centuries-old compendium called *The Thousand and One Nights*, or just *The Arabian Nights*. Sir Richard Francis Burton published the classic English translation of those folk tales in the 1880s. Burton added Ali Baba's story to the collection in a supplementary edition. The story was probably copied from a 19th-century Hindustani version of *Hazar Dastan* ("The Thousand Tales") compiled by Totaram Shåyåm. Jack Zipes of the University of Minnesota included Ali Baba's story in his abridged edition of Burton's translation.

2. Standards of due care form a central theme of Donn Parker's important book *Fighting Computer Crime*. The concept is also discussed in the classic book *Firewalls and Internet Security: Repelling the Wily Hacker* by Bill Cheswick and Steve Bellovin.

3. The federal standard for risk analysis was published by the National Bureau of Standards (NBS) in FIPS Publication 65, "Guideline for Automatic Data Processing Risk Analysis," though this official approach was withdrawn in 1995. Tom Peltier's book *Information Security Risk Analysis* provides a step-by-step approach to risk analysis. The Computer Emergency Response Team (CERT) has also developed a risk analysis method, described in the paper "An Introduction to the OCTAVE Method" by Alberts

and Dorofee. Parker discusses risk analysis in *Fighting Computer Crime*, though he does not recommend the practice.

4. The description of CTSS and the introduction of passwords is based on reminiscences of CTSS provided to this author in private communications from Fernando J. Corbató, Richard Mills, and Tom Van Vleck.

5. See Steve Levy's book *Hackers: Heroes of the Computer Revolution* for the evolution of hacker culture, particularly at MIT. See Joseph Weizenbaum's *Computer Power and Human Reason* for a less flattering portrayal of the extremes of computer obsession. Weizenbaum didn't object to "hackers" per se, but in Chapter 4 he portrayed "compulsive programming" as a disorder similar to compulsive gambling.

6. The CTSS story served as a major example in Fernando J. Corbató's Turing Award lecture, "On building systems that will fail." Tom Van Vleck provided additional details in his Multics stories "Multics: Security" and "The IBM 7094 and CTSS," and also in private communications with this author.

7. Maurice Wilkes described the Titan timesharing system (which he referred to as "the Cambridge system") in his book *Timesharing Computer Systems*.

8. Wilkes published the earliest known description of "one-way encryption" in his book *Timesharing Computer Systems* and attributed the idea to R. M. Needham. In a private communication with this author, Roger Needham described the origin of the concept and gave credit to Mike Guy.

9. Tom Van Vleck recounts the story of the weak Multics password hash in the "Multics: Security" story on his Multicians Web site.

10. The "Trusted Computer System Evaluation Criteria" (also called the TCSEC or even "the Orange Book"), written by the National Computer Security Center (NCSC), provides a classic outline of requirements for high-security systems. The NCSC also published the report "A Guide to Audit in Trusted Systems" to further describe how auditing should operate.

11. Jerry Neal Schneider's story is told by Donn Parker in *Crime by Computer*.

12. *Cyberpunk: Outlaws and Hackers on the Computer Frontier*, by Katie Hafner and John Markoff, tells the story of the "cheerful technician."

13. CERT reported this attack in CERT Advisory CA-1991-03, "Unauthorized Password Change Requests Via Mail Messages." The e-mail message in the text was copied from the CERT Advisory, misspellings and all.

14. Leo Marks described his wartime experiences with duress signals in his book *Between Silk and Cyanide*.

15. Michael J. McCarthy described business use of keystroke monitors in his *Wall Street Journal* article "Thinking Out Loud."

16. CERT issued their Advisory CA-1994-01, "Ongoing Network Monitoring Attacks," to report the sniffer attacks and recommend countermeasures. Eugene Schultz and Thomas Longstaff described the attacks in their paper "Internet Sniffer Attacks."

17. The TCSEC establishes the requirement to provide a "secure attention" signal as a countermeasure against attacks like Trojan login programs.

18. Wim van Eck's paper was entitled "Electromagnetic Radiation from Video Display Units: An Eavesdropping Risk?"

19. Win Schwartau described his efforts and concerns with van Eck radiation in Chapter 7 of his book *Information Warfare*.

20. The earliest reference that this author has seen to the characterization of three authentication factors is in FIPS PUB 41, "Computer Security Guidelines for Implementing the Privacy Act of 1974." The factors were also reviewed in detail in the 1988 paper "Alternate Authentication Mechanisms" by Steven Carlton, John Taylor, and John Wyszynski of the NCSC.

21. There are many books describing trivial and common attacks (and more), from how-to guides like *The Happy Hacker*, by Carolyn Meinel, to preventative guides like *Maximum Security*, authored by Anonymous.

22. Clifford Stoll's experiences with the Wily Hacker were entertainingly described in his best-seller *The Cuckoo's Egg*.

23. The Brookings Institution has published two books describing nuclear command and control: *Managing Nuclear Operations*, edited by Carter, Steinbruner, and Zraket, and *The Logic of Accidental Nuclear War*, by Bruce G. Blair. Ross Anderson provides a good summary in Chapter 11 of his book *Security Engineering: A Guide to Building Dependable Distributed Systems*.

NOTES FOR CHAPTER 2

1. The book *Techniques of Safecracking* by Wayne B. Yeager provides an appendix with try-out combinations for eight different manufacturers. Chapter 2 discusses the search for written-down combinations as a safecracking technique. Also see the chapter "Safecracker Meets Safecracker" in *"Surely You're Joking, Mr. Feynman!"* by physicist Richard Feynman.

2. CERT reported on a similar problem on the Unisys U5000 Unix systems in their Advisory CA-1990-03.

3. For information about locks and keys, see *The Complete Guide to Lock Picking* by Eddie the Wire, or *The Complete Book of Locks and Locksmithing*, by Roper and Phillips. Jerry Neal Schneider's story is told by Donn Parker in *Crime by Computer*.

4. See *A Quarter Century of Unix* by Peter H. Salus for the early evolution of Unix.

5. See "Multics—The First Seven Years" by Corbató, Saltzer, and Clingen for an overview of Multics.

6. Lions' commentary was published in two parts: "A Commentary on the Unix Operating System," and "Unix Operating System Source Code Level Six." Although AT&T vigorously discouraged its distribution, the commentary achieved a fairly wide, if underground, audience. The commentary was groundbreaking in that it presented source code as "published," readable material. Similar listings are published today, like the *Linux Core Kernel Commentary* by Scott Maxwell.

7. The classic paper "Password Security: A Case History," by Robert Morris and Ken Thompson, presents an overview of the early development of Unix password security.

8. See "File Security and the Unix Crypt Command" by Reeds and Weinberger.

9. Bruce Schneier discussed the risks of modifying existing algorithms in his paper "Why Cryptography Is Harder Than It Looks."

10. Daniel Klein performed an elaborate experiment to assess trial-and-error attacks on passwords and described it in the paper "A Survey of, and Improvements to, Password Security." See nearby notes for the other sources.

11. See "UNIX Password Security—Ten Years Later" by David C. Feldmeier and Philip R. Karn for a description of the evolving attack against DES crypt().

12. An early observation of the dictionary attack problem appears in the paper "A User Authentication Scheme Not Requiring Secrecy in the Computer" by Arthur Evans, William Kantrowitz, and Edwin Weiss.

13. Peter Denning edited the book *Computers Under Attack: Intruders, Worms, and Viruses,* which reprints several classic reports on the Internet Worm. The article "With Microscope and Tweezers: The Worm from MIT's Perspective" by Jon Rochlis and Mark Eichin gives a "blow-by-blow" account of the infection and recovery.

    Note that there are two people named "Robert Morris" to keep track of in this book. Robert T. Morris, the Worm's author, is the son of Robert H. Morris, coauthor of "Password Security: A Case History." References to the son in this book will always include his first name and middle initial.

14. Eugene Spafford's article "Crisis and Aftermath" provides a detailed description of the Internet Worm's operation.

15. John Shoch and Jon Hupp report on pioneering experiences (good and bad) at Xerox PARC with worm programs in "The 'Worm' Programs—Early Experiences with a Distributed Computation." Rochlis and Eichin's article, noted earlier, describes how various network managers at MIT dealt with the Internet Worm.

16. Ray Kaplan described the back door in VMS login in a memorable Usenet posting titled "Diary of a Security Incident." CERT reported the problem in the Advisory CA-1992-14. The Interbase problem was reported in CERT Advisory CA-2001-01.

17. See *Firewalls and Internet Security* by Cheswick and Bellovin for a thorough examination of how firewalling works.

18. *Firewalls* by Cheswick and Bellovin also discusses how chroot() can protect Internet servers. This author's paper "Mandatory Protection for Internet Server Software" compares chroot() with other encapsulation technologies for protecting a host against buffer overruns in a server.

19. Both CERT and CIAC have public Web sites where they post announcements of security incidents, problems, and fixes. See the section **Web and Vendor Resources** for URLs.

20. The *Department of Defense Password Management Guideline* was authored by the NCSC in 1985.

NOTES FOR CHAPTER 3

1. Financial fraud statistics can be found in reports like the "Financial Institution Fraud and Failure Report: Fiscal Year 1998," produced by the Federal

Bureau of Investigation (FBI). The report by the CSI/FBI is published as the "2001 FBI/CSI Computer Crime and Security Survey."

2. In the "Project MAC Progress Report III" from MIT, Mills and Van Vleck gave a report on CTSS security that commented briefly on local hacker activity.

3. Donn Parker recounted this story of "Val Smith (not his real name)" in Chapter 9 of *Crime by Computer*.

4. See CERT Advisory CA-1994-01, "Ongoing Network Monitoring Attacks."

5. The story of fraud on optical telegraph systems was retold in Chapter 2 of *The Early History of Data Networks* by Holzmann and Pehrson. Similar stories involving electrical telegraph systems appear in *The Victorian Internet* by Tom Standage.

6. A form of "mind reading" was widely practiced by "spirit mediums" up to the early 20th century. The famous magician Harry Houdini published a book *A Magician Among the Spirits* which described their techniques for gathering information in Chapter 20.

7. The AT&T experience is described in "Password Security: A Case History" by Morris and Thompson. The Purdue experience is described in "Observing Reusable Password Choices" by Eugene Spafford. This author's own studies of password writing and hiding are described in Chapter 6.

8. Estimates of entropy in English text often appear in cryptographic references, notably *Cryptography Theory and Practice*, by Douglas Stinson (Chapter 2) and *Applied Cryptography: Protocols, Algorithms, and Source Code in C* by Bruce Schneier.

9. These password dictionaries came from the "Security Tools and Techniques Library," a CD-ROM produced by the Forum of Incident Response and Security Teams (FIRST).

10. Eugene Spafford's article "Crisis and Aftermath" provides details of the Internet Worm's dictionary attack.

11. Klein's paper "A Survey of, and Improvements to, Password Security" describes his experiments.

12. The size given for Klein's password space is an estimate based on the description in his paper. Klein does not report the actual password space size.

13. Spafford's password study was described in his report "Observing Reusable Password Choices."

14. The 1998 incident was reported as CERT Incident IN-98-03, "Password Cracking Activity." The study by Yan, Blackwell, Anderson, and Grant is titled "The Memorability and Security of Passwords—Some Empirical Results."

15. Crack is described in the paper "CRACK: A Distributed Password Advisor" by Raleigh and Underwood. The l0phtcrack tool is described by its FAQ, written by "l0pht." Dan Farmer's security assessment tool, SATAN, was described in CERT Advisory CA-1995-06.

16. Randall Schwartz provides a lot of material on his Web site regarding the Intel case, including material from his trial and links to information on other sites.

17. NIST published FIPS 181, "Automated Password Generator," in 1993.

18. Morris and Thompson described the weak password generator in their paper "Password Security: A Case History."

19. Ganesan and Davies describe an attack on FIPS 181 password generators in their paper "A New Attack on Random Pronounceable Password Generators."

20. Klein described his strategy for proactive checking in his paper "A Survey of, and Improvements to, Password Security."

21. Spafford describes OPUS in his paper "OPUS: Preventing Weak Password Choices."

22. Both Windows NT and Windows 2000 can enforce password complexity constraints as described in the Microsoft Knowledge Base article Q161990, "How to Enable Strong Password Functionality in Windows NT."

23. Comments by Gen. Eugene E. Habiger, USAF (ret.), were quoted by Vernon Loeb in the story "Energy Chief Touts Security Upgrades at Nuclear Labs."

NOTES FOR CHAPTER 4

1. Christopher Alexander's book, produced with Ishikawa and Silverstein, is titled *A Pattern Language: Towns, Buildings, Construction.* The standard collection of design patterns for object-oriented software is *Design Patterns: Elements of Reusable Object-Oriented Software* by Gamma, Helm, Johnson, and Vlissides.

2. The discussion of architectural patterns for authentication in this chapter originally appeared in the article "Authentication: Patterns of Trust" published by this author in *Information Security* magazine.

3. The privilege modes of the Ferranti Atlas are described in the papers "Manchester University Atlas Operating System" by Kilburn et al., and "The Central Control Unit of the 'Atlas' Computer" by Sumner et al. See the article "Historical Overview of Computer Architecture" by this author for a summary of the relevant features.

4. Processor privilege modes are described in typical books on computer architecture. For example, see Section 7.3 of *Computer Architecture: Concepts and Evolution* by Gerrit Blaau and Fred Brooks.

5. Attacks on BIOS passwords are described in various hacker sources and computer security books, notably the ones by Anonymous, including *Maximum Security* (see Chapter 17) and *Maximum Linux Security* (see Chapter 2).

6. See the "Report of Investigation: Improper Handling of Classified Information by John M. Deutsch," by Snider and Seikaly, paragraph 82, for the experts' concerns about an undetected physical breakin of Deutsch's household computers.

7. See the paper "Tamper Resistance—A Cautionary Note" by Ross Anderson and Markus Kuhn for examples of low-cost attacks against smart cards. Similar techniques appear to work against USB tokens, as described in the paper "Attacks on and Countermeasures for USB Hardware Token Devices" by Kingpin.

8. See the paper "Differential Power Analysis" by Kocher, Jaffe, and Jun. Anderson's *Security Engineering* describes techniques used against smart cards and other cryptographic processors.

9. The FBI used a keystroke monitor to capture PGP keys used by Nicodemo "Little Nicky" Scarfo, an alleged mob boss. See "Scarfo Case Could Test Cyber-Spying Tactic," by George Anastasia.

10. For a summary of the evolution of authentication services in Novell Netware, see Chapter 17 of the book *Network Security: PRIVATE Communication in a PUBLIC World*, by Charlie Kaufman, Radia Perlman, and Mike Speciner. Helen Custer tells the story of Microsoft networking in Chapter 9 of *Inside Windows NT* (first edition only—the second edition is by a different author and doesn't cover networking).

11. For a really good discussion on the notion of protocols, see Chapter 18 of Radia Perlman's book *Interconnections: Bridges, Routers, Switches, and Internetworking Protocols*.

NOTES FOR CHAPTER 5

1. The notion of cycles in computer history was introduced in the paper "On the Design of Display Processors" by Myer and Sutherland in 1968 and is illustrated in this author's paper "A Historical Overview of Computer Architecture."

2. Unix system design criteria are discussed in "The Unix Timesharing System: A Retrospective" by Dennis Ritchie. Windows NT design criteria are discussed in Chapter 1 of *Inside Windows NT*, First Edition, by Helen Custer.

3. Macintosh security features are summarized in the following Apple documents: "Technical Note TN1176: Mac OS 9," "Mac OS 9.1 Specification Sheet," and "Mac OS X Specification Sheet."

4. Bruce Schneier summarizes the strengths and weaknesses of both PKZIP and PGP in *Applied Cryptography*. See *PGP: Pretty Good Privacy* by Simson Garfinkel for more details on PGP. For an attack on PKZIP, see Biham and Kocher's paper "A Known Plaintext Attack on PKZIP Encryption."

5. See *A Guide to Understanding Data Remanence in Automated Information Systems* from the NCSC.

6. The $10,000 bounty may have been an urban legend. A different laptop theft bounty was described in Appendix J of the report *Cryptography's Role In Securing the Information Society (CRISIS)*, a noteworthy report on cryptographic policy by the National Research Council.

7. NIST has published the standard for DES in FIPS PUB 46-3, "Data Encryption Standard," the latest version of which calls out the use of Triple DES. See Schneier's *Applied Cryptography* for a practical description of the other algorithms.

8. William P. Crowell's testimony to Congress took place in a closed session, but a redacted transcript was released and posted on the Cryptome Web site.

9. Problems with cellular phone encryption were described in the papers "Cryptanalysis of the Cellular Message Encryption Algorithm, by Wagner, Schneier, and Kelsey, and "Real Time Cryptanalysis of A5/1 on a PC," by

Biryukov, Shamir, and Wagner. DeCSS, the software for decrypting DVDs, has been snared in legal battles with the motion picture industry, and also yielded a good deal of press coverage. DeCSS has been well covered by *2600* magazine, one of the defendants, particularly in the fall 2000 issue. That issue included the article "DeCSS in Words," attributed to an author named "CSS," that described how DVD encryption worked.

10. The FIPS for AES has not been published as of this writing, although a draft FIPS entitled "Advanced Encryption Standard" has been distributed by NIST for public comment. The paper "Report on the Development of the Advanced Encryption Standard (AES)" by Nechvatal et al. provides a good explanation of how AES was selected from among the five finalist algorithms and describes the analyses performed on those algorithms. See the article "Deciphering the Advanced Encryption Standard" by this author, for an overview of the algorithm, its selection, and its promise.

11. Susan Landau published a readable summary of DES in her article "Standing the Test of Time: The Data Encryption Standard." See Schneier's *Applied Cryptography* for the other algorithms.

12. Complementation is a well-known property of DES. It was described in Chapter 6 of Alan Konheim's textbook *Cryptography: A Primer* in 1981. In Chapter 3 of *Cryptography Theory and Practice*, Douglas Stinson presented it as an exercise to the reader, provable from the high-level description of the DES algorithm.

13. Whitfield Diffie's proposal was published in the paper "Exhaustive Cryptanalysis of the NBS Data Encryption Standard," coauthored with Martin Hellman. The history of DES cracking is well covered in the Electronic Frontier Foundation's book *Cracking DES: Secrets of Encryption Research, Wiretap Politics, and Chip Design.*

14. Gordon E. Moore first published his observations in the magazine *Electronics* in 1965. Noyce amplified on these observations in the 1977 article "Microelectronics" in *Scientific American*. Also see Chapter 2 of *Computer Engineering: A DEC View of Hardware Systems Design*, by Bell, Mudge, and MacNamara.

15. Michael J. Wiener's report was entitled "Efficient DES Key Search." See the RSA Security Web site for summaries of results of various DES cracking challenges. The report on key lengths is entitled "Minimal Key Lengths for Symmetric Ciphers to Provide Adequate Commercial Security" by Matt Blaze, Whitfield Diffie, Ron Rivest, et al. The RSA site also maintains copies of their Cryptobytes newsletter. The RSA Security article "DES-II Challenges Solved," appearing in the summer 1998 issue, describes the challenge results.

16. The *coup de grace* for DES as a strong encryption algorithm was delivered in 1998 with the publication of *Cracking DES* by the Electronic Frontier Foundation.

17. Seth Lloyd presented this approach for estimating the upper limit of computation speed in his paper "Ultimate Physical Limits to Computation."

18. NIST published the key escrow standard as FIPS 185, titled the "Escrowed Encryption Standard." The story of the Clipper chip was well covered in the press, and Steve Levy tells the story in his entertaining book *Crypto: How*

the *Code Rebels Beat the Government—Saving Privacy in the Digital Age.* See *Internet Cryptography* by this author for a high-level description of how FIPS 185 escrowed encryption was supposed to work.

19. For a survey of key escrow techniques, see "A Taxonomy of Key Recovery Encryption Systems" by Denning and Branstad.

NOTES FOR CHAPTER 6

1. See the *DOD Password Management Guideline*, produced by the NCSC.
2. See Chapter 2 of Schneiderman's *Designing the User Interface.* For a point of view more focused on usability and security, see the papers "Usability of Security: A Case Study," and "Why Johnny Can't Encrypt," by Alma Whitten and J. D. Tygar.
3. See Chapter 10 of *Designing the User Interface: Strategies for Effective Human–Computer Interaction* by Ben Shneiderman, and George Miller's article "The Magical Number Seven–Plus or Minus Two." An interesting review of memorization problems for textual passwords is provided by "The Design and Analysis of Graphical Passwords" by Jermyn, Mayer, et al.
4. In Chapter 3 of *The Design of Everyday Things*, Donald Norman talks about the problem of memory and the impracticality of techniques to improve memory.
5. Forcing functions are discussed in Chapter 5 of Norman's *Design of Everyday Things.*
6. Edward Tenner was inspired to write *Why Things Bite Back: Technology and the Revenge of Unintended Consequences* after noticing how much more paper gets used in a modern "paperless" office. Tenner summarized his taxonomy of revenge effects in Chapter 1.
7. These memorability and training experiments were reported by Yan, Blackwell, Anderson, and Grant, in their paper "Memorability and Security of Passwords—Some Empirical Results."
8. Houdini described "mind reading" techniques based on gathering personal information in Chapter 20 of his book, *A Magician Among the Spirits.* News articles about e-commerce legislation at the time reported President Clinton's password, including the article "Agencies Expect E-Sign Law to Spur E-Gov," by Christopher J. Dorobek.
9. Klein discussed this in his paper "A Survey of, and Improvements to, Password Security."
10. See "Palm OS Password Lockout Bypass" by Kingpin.
11. An example program for Palm-based systems is "Read This!" from PixIL. First reports of subverted software for Palm devices surfaced in the fall of 2000. See "Palm Virus Hits, But Don't Worry" by Michelle Delio for a published report from *Wired News.*
12. Password Safe and an introductory description stored in its help file are available from the Counterpane Web site.
13. See the Apple documents on Mac OS 9, including "Technical Note TN1176: Mac OS 9" and "Mac OS 9.1 Specification Sheet."

14. See "56 Bits?????" in the Apple Mailing List Archives for a discussion of the initial response to Mac OS 9 encryption features.

15. Al Sicherman, a newspaper columnist at the *Minneapolis Star Tribune*, has written a number of columns about his troubles with computer passwords. His column "By Any Other Name, He Probably Could Log On Somewhere" describes the classic technique of taking pairs of words from a song or poem and concatenating them to form the password.

16. Apple Computer recommended this strategy for choosing strong but memorable passwords in "Mac OS 9: File Security—Choosing a Good Password."

17. Leo Marks' *Between Silk and Cyanide* describes poem codes and their problems.

NOTES FOR CHAPTER 7

1. For further discussion of the promise of biometrics, see "Biometrics: The Future of Identification," by Pankanti, Bolle, and Jain, published in *IEEE Computer*. Ann Davis surveys biometrics in the *Wired* article "The Body as Password," and *The Economist* examined the topic in the article "Biometrics: The Measure of Man."

2. The book *Fingerprints: The Origins of Crime Detection and the Murder Case That Launched Forensic Science* by Colin Beavan describes 19th-century efforts to address the identification problem in law enforcement. Chapter 15 of *Biometrics: Personal Identification in Networked Society*, edited by Jain, Bolle, and Pankanti, talks about the problems of large-scale biometric databases.

3. Chapter 12 of Denning's *Information Warfare and Security* notes the use of biometrics in Connecticut and in other places. The article "How Biometrics Have Tamed Welfare Double Dipping" by Paul Clolery summarizes statistics from several states on cost savings. The paper "Privacy and Biometrics: An Oxymoron or Time to Take a 2nd Look?" by Ann Cavoukian identifies existing and proposed biometric systems for controlling welfare fraud, and notes their privacy policies.

4. See "Biometrics: Identifying Law and Policy Concerns" by John Woodward for a thorough review of the issues. The Cavoukian paper "Privacy and Biometrics" briefly reviews privacy issues related to biometrics from the point of view of a privacy commissioner in Canada.

5. The book *Biometrics: Personal Identification in Networked Society*, edited by Jain, Bolle, and Pankanti, provides a comprehensive survey of biometric technologies.

6. Fingerprint recognition is a well-established technique. *Fingerprints* by Beavan describes their early use. See "Practical Systems for Personal Fingerprint Identification" by Lawrence O'Gorman, "Fingerprint Biometric Devices" by Ben Rothke, and Chapter 2 of Jain et al. for information on computer-based fingerprint applications.

7. See "An Iris Biometric System for Public and Personal Use" by Negin et al. Also see Chapter 5 of *Biometrics* by Jain et al.

8. See "Face Recognition for Smart Environments" by Pentland and Choudhury for technical summary of face recognition technology. Also, see Chapter 3 of *Biometrics* by Jain et al.

9. The voice authentication feature in Apple's Mac OS 9 is summarized in the "Mac OS 9.1 Specification Sheet." Also see "Keep Your Secrets Safe with Voice-Activated Software" by Michael Himowitz, and Chapter 8 of Jain et al.

10. The lab experiments are described in the article "Six Biometric Devices Point the Finger at Security" by Willis and Lee.

11. Chapter 3 of *Internet Cryptography* by this author describes "rewrite attacks" that modify the contents of encrypted messages without having to guess the key.

12. The paper "Biometrics as a Privacy-Enhancing Technology: Friend or Foe of Privacy?" by George Tomko suggests using "biometric encryption" to control its use by institutions. The paper "Privacy and Biometrics" by Ann Cavoukian explains how the province of Ontario passed legislation that requires "biometric encryption" in any biometric systems used by social service agencies. The paper also summarizes a plan by the City of Toronto to install a biometric uniqueness validation system to control welfare fraud.

NOTES FOR CHAPTER 8

1. See a telecommunications reference, like *Technical Aspects of Data Communications* by John McNamara, for technical details about local telephone service.

2. For further information, see "Wardialing Brief" by Kingpin of @Stake. Examples of commercial wardialer programs include ModemScan by VerTTex Software and PhoneSweep by Sandstorm Enterprises.

3. This author worked for a company that was a customer of that particular modem vendor, at least until we discovered the back door.

4. Peter Neumann reported Oregon's Caller ID proposal in Chapter 6 of his book *Computer Related Risks*.

5. Penetrations of Internet service providers and telephone systems are described in Section 5.1.1 of *Computer Related Risks* by Peter Neumann. John Draper first received media attention in a 1971 article in *Esquire* magazine, and Chapter 12 of *Hackers* by Steve Levy summarizes his exploits.

6. Kevin Mitnick's activities have been chronicled by Katie Hafner and John Markoff in *Cyberpunk: Outlaws and Hackers on the Computer Frontier*, *The Fugitive Game* by Jonathan Littman, and *Takedown* by Tsutomu Shimomura with John Markoff.

7. The Phonemasters story was reported in the news article "Phone Hex" by John Simons, which was quoted in Richard Power's book *Tangled Web*.

8. See *The SAGE Air Defense System* by John F. Jacobs.

9. See BBN Report 1822, "Interface Message Processor," for a description of ARPANET addressing. Details of IMP security are based on the author's own experience working at BBN's ARPANET Network Control Center.

10. See Chapter 7 of *Interconnections* by Perlman for additional information about X.25 and ATM addressing.

11. See Chapter 2 of *Interconnections* by Perlman for more information about IEEE 802 addresses.

12. Internet addressing is briefly described in RFC 791 by Jon Postel. For further information, see Comer's *Internetworking with TCP/IP, Volume 1*, Stevens' *TCP/IP Illustrated, Volume 1*, or Perlman's *Interconnections*.

13. Perlman refers to the problem of address discovery as "autoconfiguration" and discusses it in Chapter 11 of *Interconnections*.

14. The TCP synchronization protocol is described in RFC 793 by Jon Postel. Descriptions also appear in the books by Comer, Stevens, and Perlman noted above.

15. Laurent Joncheray described a way to perform TCP splicing in his paper "Simple Active Attack Against TCP." Although papers like Joncheray's and others in the mid-1990s led to protocol stack improvements to resist such attacks, not all improvements have been effective. CERT Advisory CA-2001-09, "Statistical Weaknesses in TCP/IP Initial Sequence Numbers," summarizes these problems.

16. Mike Neumann described IP-Watcher in the paper "Monitoring and Controlling Suspicious Activity in Real-Time with IP-Watcher."

17. The SYN flood attack is described by CERT Advisory CA-1996-21.

18. The DDOS attacks were described in CERT Advisories CA-1999-17 and CA-2000-01.

19. Effects of the DDOS attacks in February 2000 were developed and reported by APB News, and reported in "CSI Special Report on DDOS: Part 1" by Richard Power.

20. RFC 2401, "Security Architecture for the Internet Protocol," by Kent and Atkinson, provides an overview of the IPSEC protocol, its security objectives, and how it works. RFC 2402, "IP Authentication Header," by Kent and Atkinson, describes how IPSEC implements authentication.

21. MD5 is described in RFC 1321 by Ron Rivest, and SHA is described in FIPS PUB 180-1, by NIST.

22. The initial version of IPSEC is described in the now obsolete RFC 1826 by Atkinson. The HMAC construction is described in "Keying Hash Functions for Message Authentication" by Bellare, Canetti, and Krawczyk, and in RFC 2104, "HMAC: Keyed-Hashing for Message Authentication," by Krawczyk et al. MAC alternatives to use with AES are described under "Modes of Operation" on NIST's AES web site.

23. The story of the attack is told in the book *Takedown* by Tsutomu Shimomura. If one struggles past the book's lurid braggadocio, one finds a well-documented example of a computer-based manhunt, comparable to *Cuckoo's Egg* by Cliff Stoll.

24. IP spoofing is described in the paper "Attack Class: Address Spoofing" by Todd Heberlein and Matt Bishop. CERT Advisory CA-1995-01 also describes IP spoofing.

25. Robert T. Morris described the problem in his report "A Weakness in the 4.2BSD Unix TCP/IP Software," and Steve Bellovin included it in his paper "Security Problems in the TCP/IP Protocol Suite."

26. See *Firewalls and Internet Security* by Bill Cheswick and Steve Bellovin for more information about RPC, NFS, and NIS vulnerabilities.

27. The weakness in the public key system was described in the paper "Computation of Discrete Logarithms in Prime Fields" by LaMacchia and Odlyzko.

28. See *Global Positioning System: Theory and Practice* by B. Hofmann-Wellenhof, H. Lichtenegger, and J. Collins for technical background on GPS.

29. GPS-based location authentication is described in the paper "Location-Based Authentication: Grounding Cyberspace for Better Security" by Dorothy Denning and Peter MacDoran. Also see the CyberLocator Web site.

30. In Chapter 7 of *Information Warfare and Security*, Dorothy Denning briefly summarizes reports of GPS jamming products and technology. While there are no reports of jammers that forge GPS signals, some observers fear that this wouldn't pose a major technological challenge.

NOTES FOR CHAPTER 9

1. The cost estimate comes from a summary of magnetic card technology entitled "Why Use Magnetic Stripe Cards?" by Larry Nickel.

2. The story of Tania Ventura, a 26-year-old cashier at Bloomingdale's, was briefly noted in Richard Power's *Tangled Web*.

3. Stories of ATM fraud abound. See "Why Cryptosystems Fail," by Ross J. Anderson. ATM fraud problems are also summarized in Section 5.6 of *Computer Related Risks* by Peter Neumann.

4. The paper "Tamper Resistance—A Cautionary Note" by Anderson and Kuhn describes low-cost experiments in penetrating smart cards. Also see "Breaking Up Is Hard to Do: Modeling Security Threats for Smart Cards" by Schneier and Shostack.

5. See "Attacks on and Countermeasures for USB Hardware Token Devices" by Kingpin.

6. This story was heavily covered by wire services and major newspapers, including the *Minneapolis Star Tribune* (19 August 1995), the *St. Petersburg (Russia) Press* (issue 141, 9 January 1995) and the *San Francisco Chronicle* (19 August 1995). Richard Power assembled a very good review of the case in Chapter 7 of *Tangled Web*.

7. Technical features of SafeWord tokens are described in the *SafeWord DES Gold Supervisor Guide*, by Secure Computing, posted on the SafeWord Web site. Also see "When Passwords Are Not Enough," by Bob Bosen. Note that some SafeWord technical material resides on its own Web site instead of the Secure Computing corporate web site. The SafeWord resynchronization procedures are described on the SafeWord product pages on the Secure Computing Web site.

8. ActivCard technical features are described in a white paper titled "ActivCard Synchronous Authentication" by PC Dynamics, that is posted on the PC Dynamics Web site.

9. See the paper "Initial Cryptanalysis of the RSA SecurID Algorithm" by Mudge and Kingpin. Although experts have occasionally identified weaknesses in parts of the overall SecurID system (which are discussed else-

where in this book), there is no evidence that SecurID has been "cracked" in the cryptographic sense. Despite the rumors that occasionally sweep the computer security community, no technical description of an efficient cracking procedure has appeared as of this writing, nor have there been reports of victims of cracked SecurID authentication.

10. The technical features of the SecurID system are summarized in a white paper by RSA Security called "Strong Enterprise User Authentication: RSA ACE/Server" that is posted on the RSA Security Web site.

11. A widely discussed set of attacks appeared in the paper "Weaknesses in SecurID" by PieterZ. The paper's attacks require more sophistication, timing, and luck than other attacks, like TCP splicing. See the rebuttal "Secur-ID White Paper—A Comment" by Vin McLellan.

12. These attacks are described in CERT Advisory CA-1995-01, and started the events described in the book *Takedown* by Tsutomu Shimomura.

13. See "The Design and Implementation of Tripwire: A File System Integrity Checker" by Kim and Spafford, or Chapter 13 of *Internet Besieged*, edited by Denning and Denning.

14. PIN implementation for ATMs is described in various standards developed by the American Bankers Association. For example, see the "PIN Security Compliance Guideline" developed by the X9 Financial Services Committee.

15. See "Probability Theory for Pickpockets—ec-PIN Guessing" by Marcus Kuhn for an example of constrained PIN guessing on EuroCheque cash cards.

16. The duress PIN is described in the "SafeWord DES Gold Supervisor Guide," by Secure Computing.

17. See the report "SafeWord e.iD Palm Authenticator PIN Extraction" by Kingpin.

NOTES FOR CHAPTER 10

1. Bob Bosen and his brother Bill recounted the story of challenge response and 80 Space Raiders in private communications with this author. Enigma Logic is now a part of Secure Computing Corporation.

2. See "Financial Institution Message Authentication (Wholesale)" (X9.9), by the X9 Financial Services Committee, and "Computer Data Authentication" (FIPS 113), of the Federal Information Processing Standards.

3. See "The S/Key One Time Password System" by Neil Haller. The original concept was published in "Password Authentication with Insecure Communication" by Leslie Lamport.

4. See Haller's paper for a discussion of S/Key usage experience, and also see "One Time Passwords in Everything (OPIE): Experiences with Building and Using Stronger Authentication" by McDonald, Atkinson, and Metz.

5. See "Technical Guideline: Managing Risk and Mitigation Planning: Withdrawal of ANSI X9.9" by the X9 Committee.

6. For some background on the cryptography community's attitudes on proprietary technology, see Bruce Schneier's article "Why Cryptography Is Harder Than It Looks" and C. Matthew Curtin's "Snake Oil FAQ."

7. The early history of Microsoft networking is outlined in Chapter 9 of *Inside Windows NT*, first edition, by Helen Custer.

8. Several books have been published describing Samba, and there is also a Samba Web site containing source code and documentation. The pwdump utility is described in its documentation note "Windows NT Password Dump Utility" by Jeremy Allison, and the software is usually made available by Samba sites.

9. The LANMAN hash format is described in several places, including the Samba documentation and in the article "Windows NT Password Security" by Eugene Schultz.

10. The attack on the LANMAN hash is described in "FAQ: NT Cryptographic Password Attacks and Defenses" by Alan Ramsbottom.

11. The TENEX password-cracking story was recounted many times while this author worked at BBN, the creators of the TENEX operating system. Anderson called this a *timing attack* in Section 3.4.1.4. of *Security Engineering*.

12. The Windows challenge response protocol is described in Microsoft Knowledge Base article Q102716: "User Authentication with Windows NT." A description also appears in the "Cryptography" chapter of *Windows NT Security Guide* by Stephen Sutton, as well as in many of the Windows references noted above.

13. The NT hash procedure is described in Ramsbottom's FAQ and in the Schultz article.

14. Ramsbottom's FAQ also describes how to attack the NT hash using the LANMAN hash.

15. Microsoft describes the System Key in the Knowledge Base article "Windows NT System Key Permits Strong Encryption of the SAM."

16. "Windows NT Security Guidelines: A Study for NSA Research," by Steve Sutton, provides recommendations on using the System Key. Russ Cooper has also published recommendations on protecting the SAM database in his report "SAM Attacks v1.1."

NOTES FOR CHAPTER 11

Regarding the chapter's opening quotation: This important folk theorem of computer science is noted briefly in the paper "Authentication in Distributed Systems: Theory and Practice" by Lampson, Abadi, Burrows, and Wobber. A footnote explains that Roger Needham attributes the statement to David Wheeler of Cambridge University.

1. This observation came from satire attributed to Lauren Weinstein and exchanged among ARPANET users around 1980. The satire consisted of an alleged typescript of a lost investigative report from the television show *60 Minutes*, entitled "ARPANET Terror." TIP security concerns were also noted by Bob Metcalfe in RFC 602: "The Stockings Were Hung by the Chimney With Care," published in 1973.

2. Craig Finseth has briefly documented the history of TACACS in RFC 1492, titled "An Access Control Protocol, Sometimes Called TACACS."

3. Dave Carrel and Lol Grant of Cisco wrote up "The TACACS+ Protocol." It isn't clear that this document exists outside of Cisco except as an expired Internet Draft.

4. The RADIUS protocol is published in RFC 2865 by Rigney et al.

5. NT pass-through authentication is described in Microsoft's Knowledge Base article Q102716: "User Authentication with Windows NT." Also see the *Windows NT Server 4 Security Handbook* by Hadfield et al., and the *Windows NT Security Guide* by Stephen Sutton.

6. Chapter 3 of *Internet Cryptography* by this author provides a further discussion of rewrite attacks.

7. Reference books on cryptography all discuss block modes; see Section 3.4 of Stinson's *Cryptography* or Chapter 9 of Schneier's *Applied Cryptography*. NIST has officially specified DES modes in FIPS PUB 81. As of this writing, AES modes are still under discussion, as noted on the AES Web site.

8. Microsoft Knowledge Base article Q183859, "Integrity Checking on Secure Channels with Domain Controllers" describes the problem and solution. Windows NT Service Pack 4 adds integrity checking to the channels.

9. Anti-replay mechanisms were incorporated in IPSec in the 1998 revision, as described in RFC 2402 "IP Authentication Header" by Kent and Atkinson.

10. Export control regulations for all products, including those containing cryptography, are posted on the Bureau of Export Administration Web site. The National Research Council report *Cryptography's Role In Securing the Information Society* (the CRISIS report) provides a thorough description of export controls, and the rationale behind them, before their phased relaxation began in the late 1990s.

11. Matt Blaze's report was entitled "Protocol Failure in the Escrowed Encryption Standard." See "Key-Experiments—How PGP Deals With Manipulated Keys" by Ralf Senderek for an example of how adding extra "recovery" keys can open a weakness in an encryption package that previously had a reputation for reasonable security.

12. Sutton's *Guide*, noted above, describes how domain controllers establish encrypted links with other computers in the domain.

13. Schneier and Mudge published the report "Cryptanalysis of Microsoft's Point-to-Point Tunneling Protocol (PPTP)" describing these vulnerabilities.

14. The NSA Web site contains detailed coverage of the Venona project, including numerous decryptions that were significant to the history of the Cold War.

15. Schneier, Mudge, and Wagner published a follow-on to the PPTP paper when Microsoft released a revised PPTP to address their concerns: "Cryptanalysis of Microsoft's PPTP Authentication Extensions (MS-CHAPv2)."

16. Russ Cooper describes security problems with the SAM in his report "SAM Attacks v1.1."

17. Shamir and van Somerin discussed these techniques in the paper "Playing Hide and Seek with Stored Keys."

18. Shamir and van Somerin note this technique. Also see *Disappearing Cryptography* by Peter Wayner.

Notes from Chapter 12

1. The ANSI X9.17 standard, titled "Financial Institution Key Management (Wholesale)," is authored by the X9 Financial Services Committee. Fr. M. Blake Greenlee describes the practical problems that drove the banking industry to X9.17 in his entertaining paper "Requirements for Key Management Protocols in the Wholesale Financial Services Industry." Dennis Branstad's pioneering approach to KDCs is described in his paper "Encryption Protection in Computer Data Communications."

2. Needham and Schroeder introduced these protocols in their paper entitled "Using Encryption for Authentication in Large Networks of Computers."

3. Denning and Sacco's concept appeared in their paper "Timestamps in Key Distribution Protocols."

4. The classic introduction to Kerberos is the paper "Kerberos: An Authentication Service for Open Network Systems" by Jennifer Steiner, Clifford Neuman, and Jeffrey Schiller. Also see "Kerberos: An Authentication Service for Computer Networks" by Clifford Neuman and Theodore Ts'o. There is also the book *Kerberos: A Network Authentication System* by Brian Tung. Bill Bryant produced a clever description of the rationale behind Kerberos in "Designing an Authentication System: a Dialogue in Four Scenes," in which two developers named "Athena" and "Euripides" discuss the design requirements for a distributed authentication system.

5. As of this writing, Kerberos V5 is a proposed Internet standard, published as RFC 1510 by John Kohl and Clifford Neuman. Theodore Ts'o et al. produced a revised version.

6. Steve Bellovin and Michael Merritt outlined the clock problem and a number of other Kerberos security problems, mostly for Version 4, in their paper "Limitations of the Kerberos Authentication System." For further discussion of timestamps in security protocols, see "A Note on the Use of Timestamps as Nonces" by Neuman and Stubblebine.

7. Microsoft has written a white paper describing their Kerberos implementation entitled "Windows 2000 Kerberos Authentication." Additional information appears in another Microsoft Web article entitled "Secure Networking Using Windows 2000 Distributed Security Services." Jalal Feghhi and Jalil Feghhi have written a book on Windows 2000 Kerberos and related security services entitled *Secure Networking with Windows 2000 and Trust Services.*

Notes from Chapter 13

1. Two of the pioneers of public key mathematics have published well-known articles describing its foundations: Martin Hellman wrote "The Mathematics of Public-Key Cryptography," and Whitfield Diffie wrote "The First Ten Years of Public Key Cryptography."

2. Rivest, Shamir, and Adelman first described the RSA algorithm themselves in their 1978 paper "A Method for Obtaining Digital Signatures and Public Key Cryptosystems." However, a brief description of their algorithm was also published by Martin Gardner several months earlier in the dramatically

mistitled *Scientific American* article "A New Kind of Cipher That Will Take Millions of Years to Break."

3. The RSA example was adapted from Diffie's paper "The First Ten Years of Public Key Cryptography."

4. Don Knuth describes some classic factorization algorithms in Chapter 4 of *Seminumerical Algorithms.*

5. Rivest's prediction appeared in the *Scientific American* article by Martin Gardner mentioned above in Note 2.

6. Atkins et al. described how they cracked the 129-digit RSA key in their article "The Magic Words Are Squeamish Ossifrage." The article's odd title is actually the text of the message that had been encrypted with the 129-digit key. Mark Uehling also reported on the crack in the *Popular Science* article "Cracking the Uncrackable Code."

7. RSA Data Security published the press release "RSA Crypto Challenge Sets New Security Benchmark" on August 26, 1999, to announce the cracking of RSA-155. In the summer of 2000, Eric Murray published his "SSL Server Security Survey," which examined the strength of cryptographic software used by secure Web sites.

8. Cryptographic texts often contain the equation to estimate the run time of factoring algorithms: see Chapter 4 of Stinson's *Cryptography.* A historical survey of factoring and the results of RSA factoring challenges appears in "A Cost-Based Security Analysis of Symmetric and Asymmetric Key Lengths" by Robert Silverman.

9. Rabin published his scheme in the report "Digital Signatures and Public-Key Functions as Intractable as Factorization." Typical cryptographic texts also cover Rabin: see Section 4.7 of Stinson's *Cryptography* or Section 19.5 of Schneier's *Applied Cryptography.*

10. Dorothy Denning described several of these attacks along with the solution in her paper "Digital Signatures with RSA and Other Public-Key Cryptosystems."

11. The practical deployment of public key technology is described in Steve Levy's book *Crypto.* For a contemporary look at the controversy surrounding the Digital Signature Standard, see the July 1992 issue of *Communications of the ACM.*

12. The "Digital Signature Standard" was published as FIPS PUB 186-2 by NIST.

13. The index calculus method is described in Chapter 5 of Stinson's *Cryptography.*

14. The Tessera Authentication Protocol was developed under Contract MDA904-92-G-0284 for the Maryland Procurement Office, and described in the contract's final report, CDRL B001, "Technical Report for the Tessera Authentication Protocol Specification Program," by Earl Boebert and Chuck Nove.

15. The standard for public key authentication was published as FIPS PUB 196 by NIST in1997.

16. Netscape's history is reasonably covered in Steve Levy's *Crypto.*

17. The protocol specification for SSL 3.0 was written up by Freier, Karlton, and Kocher in 1996. See the book *SSL and TLS: Designing and Building Secure Systems* by Eric Rescorla for an in-depth look at the protocol.
18. David Wagner and Bruce Schneier examined SSL vulnerabilities in their paper "Analysis of the SSL 3.0 Protocol."

NOTES FROM CHAPTER 14

1. Leon Kornfelder, a student of RSA co-inventor Len Adelman, proposed digital certificates in his bachelor's thesis "Towards a Practical Public-Key Cryptosystem."
2. Microsoft published a security bulletin, "Erroneous VeriSign-Issued Digital Certificate Poses Spoofing Hazard," that describes the problem.
3. The relationship between Netscape, RSA Data Security, and Verisign is briefly described in *Crypto* by Steve Levy.
4. This is described in the Microsoft security bulletin noted above.
5. Certificates are defined by ITU-T X.509. Internet use of X.509 certificates is in RFC 2459, "Internet X.509 Public Key Infrastructure Certificate and CRL Profile" by Russ Housley, Warwick Ford, Tim Polk, and Dave Solo.
6. The example certificate comes from RFC 1422, "Privacy Enhancement for Internet Electronic Mail: Part II—Certificate-Based Key Management" by Steve Kent.
7. The cost of STU III management was presented in Section 2.5.1 of the National Research Council's CRISIS report.
8. Certificate authorities like Verisign generally post their certification practices statements on their Web site.
9. The PEM certification hierarchy is also described in RFC 1422 by Kent, noted above.
10. DASS is described in the paper "SPX: Global Authentication Using Public Key Certificates" by Tardo and Alagappan. It is also described in Chapter 4 of *Authentication Systems for Secure Networks* by Rolf Oppliger.
11. PGP is thoroughly described in Simson Garfinkel's book *PGP: Pretty Good Privacy*.
12. CRLs for Internet usage are described in RFC 2459 by Housley, Ford, Polk, and Solo.
13. Microsoft's CRL patch is described in the Knowledge Base article "Update Available to Revoke Fraudulent Microsoft Certificates Issued by VeriSign."
14. One approach for on-line certificate checking has been published as a proposed Internet standard in RFC 2560: "X.509 Internet Public Key Infrastructure: Online Certificate Status Protocol—OCSP" by Myers et al.
15. Rivest describes this strategy in "Can We Eliminate Certificate Revocation Lists?"
16. PKINIT is described in "Public Key Cryptography for Initial Authentication in Kerberos" by Tung, Neumann, Hur, et al.
17. The Windows 2000 implementation is described in the Microsoft Windows 2000 white paper "Smart Card Logon."

NOTES FROM CHAPTER 15

1. Schneier presents recommendations for generating random primes in Section 11.5 of *Applied Cryptography*.

2. Rabin describes the Miller-Rabin algorithm in his paper "Probabilistic Algorithm for Testing Primality." The algorithm also appears in cryptographic texts like Schneier (Section 11.5) and Stinson's *Cryptography* (Section 4.5).

3. Garfinkel describes PGP key generation in *PGP: Pretty Good Privacy*.

4. The Lotus Notes ID file is described in Section 17.6 of *Network Security* by Kaufman, Perlman, and Speciner.

5. Mike Miller wrote the "pgpcrack" program to perform trial-and-error cracking of PGP passphrases. As of this writing, its traditional home on the Web has disappeared, but it tends to show up in other places as well. Also see Peter Gutman's note "Where do your encryption keys want to go today?"

6. Keystroke monitors can capture PGP keys. See "Scarfo Case Could Test Cyber-Spying Tactic," by George Anastasia.

7. Datakey published press releases on these applications of their smart cards, specifically "Datakey multi-purpose smart cards deployed by the FDIC for secure online communications and building access," and "Datakey smart card used by President Clinton to sign e-signature law."

8. Performance of the Datakey 330 appears on Datakey's sales materials, particularly "Technical Specifications: Datakey's Cryptographic Smart Card and Smart Key."

9. The paper "Smartcard Based Authentication" by Ratha and Bolle describes a system that uses biometrics with smart cards in which the matching is off-loaded from the card.

10. DASS is described in the paper "SPX: Global Authentication Using Public Key Certificates" by Tardo and Alagappan. It is also described in Chapter 4 of *Authentication Systems for Secure Networks* by Rolf Oppliger.

11. The Novell protocol is described in Section 17.2 of *Network Security* by Kaufman, Perlman, and Speciner. Radia Perlman and Charlie Kaufman examine additional approaches in their paper "Secure Password-Based Protocol for Downloading a Public Key."

12. Secure Computing has published a white paper entitled "SafeWord Plus Virtual Smart Card Server Solution."

13. The classic paper on the topic is "Reducing Risks from Poorly Chosen Keys" by Lomas, Gong, Saltzer, and Needham.

14. Bellovin and Merritt introduced their protocols in the paper "Encrypted Key Exchange: Password-Based Protocols Secure Against Dictionary Attacks."

15. The paper "Strong Password-Only Authenticated Key Exchange" by David Jablon provides a good overview of techniques. Recent work has been reported by Taekyoung Kwon in "Authentication and Key Agreement via Memorable Password." These authors and others have established IEEE study group "P1363a" for Password-Based Authenticated Key Exchange Methods, which has its own Web site, hosted by the IEEE.

BIBLIOGRAPHY

Important articles and papers in this field are often reprinted, and this section notes alternative sources for the article when known. However, each entry in this list is only as complete as it needs to be. When an entry contains a partial reference to another publication, look for that publication's entry here for the full citation. If the entry refers to a vendor or Web site, check the **Web and Vendor Resources** section for contact information.

Abrams, Marshall D., and Harold J. Podell, eds., *Tutorial: Computer and Network Security* (Los Angeles: IEEE Computer Society Press, 1986).

Alberts, Christopher, and Audrey Dorofee, "An Introduction to the OCTAVE Method," white paper (Pittsburgh, PA: Software Engineering Institute of Carnegie Mellon University, 30 January 2001). Posted on the CERT Web site.

Alexander, Christopher, Sara Ishikawa, and Murray Silverstein, with Max Jacobson, Ingrid Fiksdahl-King, and Shlomo Angel, *A Pattern Language: Towns, Buildings, Construction* (New York: Oxford University Press, 1977).

Allison, Jeremy, "Windows NT Password Dump Utility" software README file, March 1997. Posted on the Samba Web site.

Anastasia, George, "Scarfo Case Could Test Cyber-Spying Tactic," *Philadelphia Inquirer* (4 December 2000).

Anderson, Ross J., "Why Cryptosystems Fail," *Communications of the ACM* 37, no. 11 (November 1994). Reprinted in *Practical Cryptography for Data Internetworks*, edited by William Stallings.

———, *Security Engineering: A Guide to Building Dependable Distributed Systems* (New York: John Wiley & Sons, 2001).

———, and Markus Kuhn, "Tamper Resistance—A Cautionary Note," *Proceedings of the Second USENIX Workshop on Electronic Commerce* (Berkeley, CA: USENIX Association, 1996), pp. 1–11.

Anonymous [pseudonym], *Maximum Linux Security* (Indianapolis, IN: Sams Publishing, 2000).

————, *Maximum Security,* 2nd edition (Indianapolis, IN: Sams Publishing, 1998).

Apple, "Mac OS 9: File Security—Choosing a Good Password," Tech Info Library Article ID 60483 (Cupertino, CA: Apple, 20 October 1999). This is posted on the Apple Web site.

————, "Technical Note TN1176: Mac OS 9," (Cupertino, CA: Apple, 24 April 2000). This is posted on the Apple Web site.

————, "Mac OS 9.1 Specification Sheet," Item L12404A (Cupertino, CA: Apple, January 2001). This is posted on the Apple Web site.

————, "Mac OS X Specification Sheet," Item L13291A (Cupertino, CA: Apple, March 2001). This document is posted on the Apple Web site.

————, "56 Bits?????" by various authors, Apple Mailing List Archives, 26–27 October 1999.

Atkins, D., M. Graff, A. K. Lenstra, and P. C. Leyland, "The Magic Words Are Squeamish Ossifrage," in *Advances in Cryptology—ASIACRYPT '94 Proceedings* (Heidelberg: Springer-Verlag, 1995).

Atkinson, Randall, "IP Authentication Header," Internet RFC 1826, August 1995. Posted on the IETF Web site.

Beavan, Colin, *Fingerprints: The Origin of Crime Detection and the Murder Case That Launched Forensic Science* (New York: Hyperion, 2001).

Bell, C. Gordon, J. Craig Mudge, and John E. MacNamara, *Computer Engineering: A DEC View of Hardware Systems Design* (Maynard, MA: Digital Press, 1978).

Bellare, M., R. Canetti, and H. Krawczyk, "Keyed Hash Functions and Message Authentication," *Proceedings of Crypto'96, Lecture Notes in Computer Science* 1109, (Heidelberg: Springer-Verlag, 1996), pp. 1–15.

Bellovin, Steven, "Security Problems in the TCP/IP Protocol Suite," *Computer Communication Review* 19, no. 2, pp. 32–48 (April 1989).

————, and Michael Merritt, "Encrypted Key Exchange: Password-Based Protocols Secure Against Dictionary Attacks," *Proceedings of the 1992 IEEE Symposium or Research in Security and Privacy* (Piscataway, NJ: IEEE Press, 1992).

————, and Michael Merritt, "Limitations of the Kerberos Authentication System," *Proceedings of Winter '91 USENIX* (Berkeley, CA: USENIX Association, 1991). An earlier version appeared in *Computer Communications Review*, October 1990.

Biham, E., and P. C. Kocher, "A Known Plaintext Attack on PKZIP Encryption," in *K. U. Leuven Workshop on Cryptographic Algorithms* (Heidelberg: Springer-Verlag, 1995).

Biryukov, Alex, Adi Shamir, and David Wagner, "Real Time Cryptanalysis of A5/1 on a PC," Fast Software Encryption Workshop 2000, New York, NY, April 2000. Posted on the Cryptome Web site.

Blaauw, Gerrit A., and Frederick P. Brooks, Jr., *Computer Architecture: Concepts and Evolution* (Reading, MA: Addison-Wesley, 1997).

Blair, Bruce G., *The Logic of Accidental Nuclear War* (Washington, DC: The Brookings Institution, 1993).

Blaze, Matt, "Protocol Failure in the Escrowed Encryption Standard," research report (New Jersey: AT&T Bell Laboratories, 20 May 1994).

Blaze, Matt, W. Diffie, R. Rivest, B. Schneier, T. Shimomura, E. Thompson, and M. Weiner, "Minimal Key Lengths for Symmetric Ciphers to Provide Adequate Commercial Security," white paper, January 1996. Posted on the Counterpane Web site.

Boebert, W. Earl, and Chuck Nove, "Technical Report for the Tessera Authentication Protocol Specification Program," CDRL B001, Contract MDA904-92-C-0284 (Roseville, MN: Secure Computing Corporation, 1994).

Bolt, Beranek, and Newman, Inc., "Interface Message Processor—Specifications for the Interconnection of a Host and IMP," BBN Report 1822 (Cambridge, MA: Bolt, Beranek, and Newman, May 1978).

Bosen, Bob, "When Passwords Are Not Enough," white paper (Roseville, MN: Secure Computing Corporation, 1996). Posted on the SafeWord Web site.

Branstad, Dennis, "Encryption protection in computer data communications," *Proceedings of the 4th Data Communications Symposium* (New York: Association for Computing Machinery, 1975).

Bryant, Bill, "Designing an Authentication System: a Dialogue in Four Scenes," white paper from MIT Project Athena, 8 February 1988. Distributed on the FIRST CD-ROM.

Carlton, Steven, John Taylor, and John Wyszynski, "Alternate Authentication Mechanisms," *Proceedings of the 11th National Computer Security Conference* (Washington, DC: National Bureau of Standards, 1988).

Carrel, Dave, and Lol Grant, "TACACS+ Protocol Specification," Revision 1.78, January 1997. This has been distributed as an Internet Draft.

Carter, Ashton B., John D. Steinbruner, and Charles A. Zraket, eds., *Managing Nuclear Operations* (Washington, DC: The Brookings Institution, 1987).

Cavoukian, Ann, "Privacy and Biometrics: An Oxymoron or Time to Take a 2nd Look?" presented at Computers, Freedom and Privacy 98, Austin Texas. Posted on the Information Privacy Commissioner/Ontario Web site.

CERT, "Advisory CA-1990-03: Unisys U5000 /etc/passwd problem," issued 7 May 1990; last revised: 17 September 1997. Posted on the CERT Web Site.

———, "Advisory CA-1991-03: Unauthorized Password Change Requests Via Mail Messages," issued 4 April 1991; last revised: 18 September 1997. Posted on the CERT Web Site.

———, "Advisory CA-1992-14 Altered System Binaries Incident," issued 22 June 1992; last revised: 19 September 1997. Posted on the CERT Web Site.

———, "Advisory CA-1994-01: Ongoing Network Monitoring Attacks," issued 3 February 1994; last revised: 19 September 1997. Posted on the CERT Web Site.

———, "Advisory CA-1995-01: Spoofing Attacks and Hijacked Terminal Connections," issued 23 January 1995; last revised: 23 September 1997. Posted on the CERT Web Site.

———, "Advisory CA-1995-06: Security Administrator Tool for Analyzing Networks (SATAN)," issued 3 April 1995; last revised: 23 September 1997. Posted on the CERT Web Site.

———, "Advisory CA-1996-21: TCP SYN Flooding and IP Spoofing Attacks," issued 19 September 1996; last revised: 29 November 2000. Posted on the CERT Web Site.

———, "Advisory CA-1998-03: Vulnerability in ssh-agent," issued 22 January 1998; last revised: 2 March 1998. Posted on the CERT Web Site.

———, "Advisory CA-1999-04: Melissa Macro Virus," issued 27 March 1999; last revised: 31 March 1999. Posted on the CERT Web Site.

———, "Advisory CA-1999-17: Denial-of-Service Tools," issued 28 December 1999; last revised: 3 March 2000. Posted on the CERT Web Site.

———, "Advisory CA-2001-01: Interbase Server Contains Compiled-in Back Door Account," issued 10 January 2001; last revised: 11 January 2001. Posted on the CERT Web Site.

———, "Advisory CA-2001-09: Statistical Weaknesses in TCP/IP Initial Sequence Numbers," issued 1 May 2001. Posted on the CERT Web Site.

Cheswick, William R., and Steven M. Bellovin, *Firewalls and Internet Security: Repelling the Wily Hacker* (Reading, MA: Addison-Wesley, 1994).

Clolery, Paul, "How Biometrics Have Tamed Welfare Double Dipping," *ID World* 1, no 1 (March/April 1999).

Comer, Douglas E., *Internetworking with TCP/IP, Volume 1*, 2nd edition (Englewood Cliffs, NJ: Prentice Hall, 1991).

Cooper, Russ, "SAM Attacks v1.1," research paper, 22 July 1998. Posted on the NT Bugtraq Web site.

Corbató, F. J., "On Building Systems That Will Fail (A. M. Turing Award lecture)" *Communications of the ACM* 34, no. 9 (September 1991).

——, J. H. Saltzer, and C. T. Clingen, "Multics—The First Seven Years," *AFIPS Conference Proceedings* 40 (1972). Reprinted in the Multics Program Manual, Part I, from MIT Project MAC.

Counterpane Systems, "Password Safe," help file, 1999. Posted on the Counterpane Web site.

Crowell, William, "Testimony to the House International Relations Committee by William P. Crowell, Deputy Director, National Security Agency (NSA)," Office of Official Reporters, Office of the Clerk, U. S. House of Representatives, July 21, 1997. A redacted transcript of this closed hearing appears on the Cryptome Web site.

CSI/FBI, "Computer Crime and Security Survey," (San Francisco: Computer Security Institute, 2001).

CSS, "DeCSS in Words," *2600* 17, no. 3 (fall 2000).

Curtin, C. Matthew, "Snake Oil Warning Signs: Encryption Software to Avoid (Snake Oil FAQ)," white paper, 10 April 1998. Posted on Matt Curtin's personal Web page.

Custer, Helen, *Inside Windows NT*, 1st edition (Redmond, WA: Microsoft Press, 1993).

Datakey, "Datakey multi-purpose smart cards deployed by the FDIC for Secure online communications and building access," press release (Minneapolis, MN: Datakey, 26 October 2000). Posted on the Datakey Web site.

——, "Datakey smart card used by President Clinton to sign e-signature law," press release (Minneapolis, MN: Datakey, 26 October 2000). Posted on the Datakey Web site.

——, "Technical Specifications: Datakey's Cryptographic Smart Card and Smart Key," sales materials (Minneapolis, MN: Datakey, May 2000).

Davis, Ann, "The Body as Password," *Wired* 5, no. 7, (July 1997).

Delio, Michelle, "Palm Virus Hits, But Don't Worry," *Wired News* (22 September 2000). Posted on the Wired News Web site.

Denning, Dorothy E., and Giovanni Maria Sacco, "Timestamps in Key Distribution Protocols," *Communications of the ACM* 24, no. 8 (August 1981).

Denning, Dorothy E., "Digital Signatures with RSA and Other Public-Key Cryptosystems," *Communications of the ACM* 27, no. 4 (April 1984).

——, *Information Warfare and Security* (Reading, MA: Addison-Wesley, 1998).

————, and Dennis K. Branstad, "A Taxonomy of Key Recovery Encryption Systems," in *Internet Besieged*, edited by Denning and Denning. An earlier version was published as "A Taxonomy of Key Escrow Encryption," *Communications of the ACM* 39, no. 3 (March 1996).

————, and Peter J. Denning, eds., *Internet Besieged: Countering Cyberspace Scofflaws* (Reading, MA: Addison-Wesley, 1998).

————, and Peter MacDoran, "Location-Based Authentication: Grounding Cyberspace for Better Security" *Computer Fraud and Security* (February 1996). Reprinted in *Internet Besieged*, edited by Denning and Denning.

Denning, Peter, ed., *Computers Under Attack: Intruders, Worms, and Viruses* (Reading, MA: Addison-Wesley, 1990).

Diffie, Whitfield, "The First Ten Years of Public Key Cryptography," *Proceedings of the IEEE* 76, no. 5 (May 1988). Also appears in *Contemporary Cryptology*, edited by Gustavus Simmons.

————, and Martin Hellman, "Exhaustive Cryptanalysis of the NBS Data Encryption Standard," *IEEE Computer* 10 (1977).

Dorobek, Christopher J., "Agencies Expect E-Sign Law to Spur E-Gov," *Government Computer News* 19, no. 19 (10 July 2000).

Economist, "Biometrics, The Measure of Man," *The Economist* (9 September 2000).

Eddie the Wire, *The Complete Guide to Lock Picking* (Port Townsend, WA: Loompanics Unlimited, 1981).

Electronic Frontier Foundation, *Cracking DES: Secrets of Encryption Research, Wiretap Politics, and Chip Design* (Sebastopol, CA: O'Reilly & Associates, 1998).

Evans, Arthur, Jr., William Kantrowitz, and Edwin Weiss, "A User Authentication Scheme Not Requiring Secrecy in the Computer," *Communications of the ACM* 17, no. 8 (August 1974).

FBI (Federal Bureau of Investigation), "Financial Fraud and Failure Report" (Washington, DC: FBI, 1998). Posted on the FBI Web site.

Feghhi, Jalal, and Jalil Feghhi, *Secure Networking with Windows 2000 and Trust Services* (Boston: Addison-Wesley, 2001).

Feldmeier, David C., and Philip R. Karn, "UNIX Password Security—Ten Years Later," *Advances in Cryptology—Proceedings of Crypto '89* (Heidelberg: Springer-Verlag, 1990).

Feynman, Richard P., *"Surely You're Joking, Mr. Feynman!"* (New York: W. W. Norton, 1985).

Finseth, Craig, "An Access Control Protocol, Sometimes Called TACACS," Internet RFC 1492, July 1993. Posted on the IETF Web site.

FIRST (Forum of Incident Response and Security Teams), "Security Tools and Techniques Resource Library," CD-ROM, (Washington, DC: National Institute of Science and Technology, October 1994). Posted on the FIRST CD-ROM Web site.

Freier, Alan O., Philip Karlton, and Paul C. Kocher, "The SSL Protocol Version 3.0," 18 November 1996. Posted on the Netscape Web site.

Gamma, Erich, Richard Helm, Ralph Johnson, and John Vlissides, *Design Patterns: Elements of Reusable Object-Oriented Software* (Reading, MA: Addison-Wesley, 1995).

Ganesan, Ravi, and Chris Davies, "A New Attack on Random Pronounceable Password Generators," *Proceedings of the 17th National Computer Security Conference* (1994).

Gardner, Martin, "A New Kind of Cipher That Will Take Millions of Years to Break," *Scientific American* 237, no. 8 (August 1977).

Garfinkel, Simson, *PGP: Pretty Good Privacy* (Sebastopol, CA: O'Reilly & Associates, 1995).

Greenlee, M. Blake, "Requirements for Key Management Protocols in the Wholesale Financial Industry," in Abrams and Podell, *Tutorial: Computer and Network Security.*

Gutman, Peter, "How to Recover Private Keys from Microsoft Internet Explorer, Internet Information Server, Outlook Express, and Many Others - or - Where Do Your Encryption Keys Want to Go Today?" Research paper, posted to the Cryptography mailing list, 21 January 1999.

Hadfield, Lee, Dave Hatter, and Dave Bixler, *Windows NT Server 4 Security Handbook* (Indianapolis, IN: Que Corporation, 1997).

Hafner, Katie, and John Markoff, *Cyberpunk: Outlaws and Hackers on the Computer Frontier* (New York: Simon and Schuster, 1991).

Haller, Neil, "The S/Key One Time Password System," in *Proceedings of the Symposium on Network and Distributed Systems Security*, Internet Society, February 1994.

Heberlein, Todd, and Matt Bishop, "Attack Class: Address Spoofing" *Proceedings of the 19th National Computer Security Conference*, National Institute of Standards and Technology, October 1996. Reprinted in *Internet Besieged*, edited by Denning and Denning.

Hellman, Martin, "The Mathematics of Public-Key Cryptography," *Scientific American* (August 1979). Also appears in *Practical Cryptography*, edited by William Stallings.

Himowitz, Michael, "Keep Your Secrets Safe with Voice-Activated Software," *Fortune* (1 March 1999).

Hofmann-Wellenhof, B., H. Lichtenegger, and J. Collins, *Global Positioning System: Theory and Practice*, 4th edition (Heidelberg: Springer-Verlag, 1997).

Holzmann, Gerard J., and Björn Pehrson, *The Early History of Data Networks* (Los Alamitos, CA: IEEE Computer Society Press, 1995).

Houdini, Harry, *A Magician Among the Spirits* (New York: Harper & Brothers, 1924). Reprinted in New York by Arno Press, 1972.

Housley, Russ, Warwick Ford, Tim Polk, and Dave Solo, "Internet X.509 Public Key Infrastructure: Certificate and CRL Profile," Internet RFC 2459, January 1999.

ITU-T (formerly CCITT), "Information Technology—Open Systems Interconnection—The Directory: Authentication Framework," Recommendation X.509 ISO/IEC 9594-8.

Jablon, David, "Strong Password-Only Authenticated Key Exchange" *ACM Computer Communications Review* (October 1996). Posted on the IEEE P1363a study group Web site and on the Integrity Sciences Web site.

Jacobs, John F., *The SAGE Air Defense System: A Personal History* (Bedford, MA: MITRE Corporation, 1986).

Jain, Anil, Ruud Bolle, and Sharath Pankanti, eds., *Biometrics: Personal Identification in Networked Society* (Boston: Kluwer Academic Publishers, 1999).

Jermyn, Ian, Alain Mayer, Fabian Monrose, Michael K. Reiter, and Avi Rubin, "The Design and Analysis of Graphical Passwords," draft submitted to 8th USENIX Security Symposium, dated 8 March 1999.

Joncheray, Laurent, "Simple Active Attack Against TCP," Proceedings of the 5th *Unix Security Symposium* (Berkeley, CA: USENIX Association, 1995).

Kaplan, Ray, "Diary of a Security Incident." Usenet posting to alt.security, 22 May 1992.

Kaufman, Charlie, Radia Perlman, and Mike Speciner, *Network Security: PRIVATE Communication in a PUBLIC World* (Englewood Cliffs, NJ: Prentice Hall, 1995).

Kent, Stephen, "Privacy Enhancement for Internet Electronic Mail: Part II—Certificate-Based Key Management," Internet RFC 1422, February 1993. Posted on the IETF Web site.

———, and Randall Atkinson, "IP Authentication Header," Internet RFC 2402, November 1998. Posted on the IETF Web site.

———, and Randall Atkinson, "Security Architecture for the Internet Protocol," Internet RFC 2401, November 1998. Posted on the IETF Web site.

Kilburn, T., D. J. Howarth, R. B. Payne, and F. H. Sumner, "The Manchester University Atlas Operating System, Part 1: Internal Organization," *Comp. J.* 4 (October 1961), pp. 222–225.

Kim, Gene H., and Eugene H. Spafford, "The design and implementation of Tripwire: A file system integrity checker," *Proceedings of the 1994 ACM Conference on Communications and Computer Security* (New York: ACM Press, 1994).

Kingpin, "Attacks and Countermeasures for USB Hardware Token Devices," research paper, file date: 17 October 2000. Posted on the @stake Web site.

———, "Palm OS Password Lockout Bypass," @stake Security Advisory, 3 March 2001. Posted on the @stake Web site.

———, "SafeWord e.iD Palm Authenticator PIN Extraction," @stake Security Advisory, 14 December 2000. Posted on the @stake Web site.

———, "Wardialing Brief," white paper, file date: 1 August 2000. Posted on the @stake Web site.

Klein, Daniel V., "A Survey of, and Improvements to, Password Security," *Unix Security Workshop II* (Berkeley, CA: USENIX Association, 1990).

Knuth, Donald E., *Seminumerical Algorithms: The Art of Computer Programming, Volume 2* (Reading, MA: Addison-Wesley, 1969).

Kocher, Paul, Joshua Jaffe, and Benjamin Jun, "Differential Power Analysis," *Proceedings of Crypto '99.* Posted on the Cryptography Research, Inc., Web site.

Kohl, John, and Clifford Neuman, "The Kerberos Network Authentication Service (V5)," Internet RFC 1510, September 1993. Posted on the IETF Web site.

Konheim, Alan G., *Cryptography: A Primer* (New York: John Wiley, 1981).

Kornfelder, Leon, "Towards a Practical Public-Key Cryptosystem," B.S. thesis, Massachusetts Institute of Technology, May 1978.

Krawczyk, H., M. Bellare, and R. Canetti, "HMAC: Keyed-Hashing for Message Authentication," Internet RFC 2104, February 1997. Posted on the IETF Web site.

Kuhn, Marcus G., "Probability Theory for Pickpockets—ec-PIN Guessing," COAST working paper (West Lafayette, IN: Purdue University, 1997). Posted on the COAST Web site.

Kwon, Taekyoung, and J. Song, "Authentication and Key Agreement via Memorable Password," Cryptology ePrint Archive Report 2000/026, 20 August 2000. Posted on the IACR Eprint Web site.

L0pht, "L0phtCrack 2.5 FAQ," Web page, 16 March 2001. Posted on the Security Software Technologies Web site.

La Macchia, B. A., and A. M. Odlyzko, "Computation of Discrete Logarithms in Prime Fields," *Designs, Codes, and Cryptography* 1, pp. 47–62 (1991).

Lamport, Leslie, "Password Authentication with Insecure Communication," *Communications of the ACM* 24, no. 11 (November 1981).

Lampson, Butler, Martín Abadi, Michael Burrows, and Edward Wobber, "Authentication in Distributed Systems: Theory and Practice," *ACM Transactions on Computer Systems* 10, no. 4 (November 1992). Also appears in *Practical Cryptography*, edited by William Stallings. A preliminary version appeared in the *Proceedings of the 13th ACM Symposium on Operating System Principles*.

Landau, Susan, "Standing the Test of Time: The Data Encryption Standard," *Notices of the AMS* 47, no. 3 (March 2000).

Levy, Matthys, and Mario Salvadori, *Why Buildings Fall Down* (New York: W. W. Norton & Co., 1992).

Levy, Steven, *Crypto: How the Code Rebels Beat the Government—Saving Privacy in the Digital Age* (New York: Viking, 2001).

———, *Hackers: Heroes of the Computer Revolution* (New York: Dell Publishing, 1984).

Lions, J., "A Commentary on the Unix Operating System," Department of Computer Science, University of New South Wales, 1977.

———, "Unix Operating System Source Code Level Six," Department of Computer Science, University of New South Wales, 1977.

Littman, Jonathan, *The Fugitive Game: Online with Kevin Mitnick* (Boston: Little, Brown & Co., 1996).

Lloyd, Seth, "Ultimate Physical Limits to Computation," *Nature* 406 (August 2000).

Loeb, Vernon, "Energy Chief Touts Security Upgrades at Nuclear Labs," *Washington Post* (January 26, 2000), p. A13.

Lomas, T. M. A., L. Gong, J. I. Saltzer, and R. M. Needham, "Reducing Risks from Poorly Chosen Keys," *Proceedings of the Twelfth ACM Symposium on Operating Systems Principles* (December 1989), pp. 14–18.

Marks, Leo, *Between Silk and Cyanide: A Codemaker's War 1941–1945* (New York: The Free Press, 1998).

Maxwell, Scott, *Linux Core Kernel Commentary* (Scottsdale, AZ: The Coriolis Group, 1999).

McCarthy, Michael J., "Thinking Out Loud," *Wall Street Journal* 105, no. 47 (March 7, 2000).

McDonald, Daniel L., Randall J. Atkinson, and Craig Metz, "One Time Passwords in Everything (OPIE): Experiences with Building and Using Stronger Authentication," *Proceedings of the 5th Unix Security Symposium* (Berkeley CA: USENIX Association, 1995).

McLellan, Vin, "SecurID White Paper—A Comment," posted to best-of-security mailing list, 10 September 1996.

McNamara, John E., *Technical Aspects of Data Communication* (Maynard, MA: Digital Press, 1978).

Meinel, Carolyn P., *The Happy Hacker*, 2nd edition (Show Low, AZ: American Eagle Publications, 1998).

Metcalfe, Bob, "The Stockings Were Hung by the Chimney with Care," Internet RFC 602, December 1973. Posted on the IETF Web site.

Microsoft, "Erroneous VeriSign-Issued Digital Certificates Pose Spoofing Hazard," Microsoft Security Bulletin MS01-017, 22 March 2001. Posted on the Microsoft Web site.

———, "How to Enable Strong Password Functionality in Windows NT," Knowledge Base Article Q161990, revised 18 December 2000. Posted on the Microsoft Web site.

———, "Integrity Checking on Secure Channels with Domain Controllers," Knowledge Base Article Q183859, revised 10 April 1999. Posted on the Microsoft Web site.

———, "Secure Networking Using Windows 2000 Distributed Security Services." Microsoft TechNet article network/distsec.asp, 19 January 2000. Posted on the Microsoft Web site.

———, "Smart Card Logon," Windows 2000 white paper, 1999. Posted on the Microsoft Web site.

———, "Windows NT System Key Permits Strong Encryption of the SAM." Microsoft TechNet article Q143475, 17 February 2001. Posted on the Microsoft Web site.

———, "Windows 2000 Kerberos Authentication," Windows 2000 white paper, 1999. Posted on the Microsoft Web site.

———, "Update Available to Revoke Fraudulent Microsoft Certificates Issued by VeriSign," Microsoft TechNet article Q293811, 29 March 2001. Posted on the Microsoft Web site.

———, "User Authentication with Windows NT," Knowledge Base Article Q102716, revised 5 October 2000. Posted on the Microsoft Web site.

Miller, George A. "The Magical Number Seven—Plus or Minus Two: Some Limits on Our Capacity for Processing Information," *Psychological Science* 63 (1956), pp. 81–97.

Miller, Mike, "Pgpcrack README," software documentation.

MIT Project MAC, "Multiplexed Information and Computing Service: Programmers' Manual—Part I: Introduction to Multics," Revision 14 (Cambridge, MA: Massachusetts Institute of Technology, 30 September 1973).

———, "Project MAC Progress Report III: July 1965 to July 1966," Report MAC-PR-3 (Cambridge, MA: Massachusetts Institute of Technology, 1966).

Moore, Gordon E., *Electronics* 38, no. 11, (1965), pp. 114–117.

Morris, Robert, and Ken Thompson, "Password Security: A Case History," *Communications of the ACM* 22, no. 8 (November 1979).

Morris, Robert T., "A Weakness in the 4.2BSD Unix TCP/IP Software," Computing Science Technical Report No. 117 (Murray Hill, NJ: AT&T Bell Laboratories, 1985).

Moynihan, Daniel Patrick, *Secrecy: The American Experience* (New London, CT: Yale University Press, 1998).

Mudge and Kingpin, "Initial Cryptanalysis of the RSA SecurID Algorithm" research paper, January 2001. Posted on the @stake Web site.

Murray, Eric, "SSL Server Security Survey" research paper, 21 July 2000. Posted on Eric Murray's personal Web site.

Myer, T. H., and I. E. Sutherland, "On the Design of Display Processors," *Communications of the ACM* 11, no. 6 (June 1968).

Myers, M., R. Ankney, A. Malpani, S. Galperin, and C. Adams, "X.509 Internet Public Key Infrastructure: Online Certificate Status Protocol—OCSP," Internet RFC 2560, June 1999.

NBS (National Bureau of Standards), "Computer Security Guidelines for Implementing the Privacy Act of 1974," FIPS Publication 41 (Washington, DC: NBS, 30 May 1975). The standard was withdrawn on 18 November 1998.

———, "Guideline for Automatic Data Processing Risk Analysis," FIPS Publication 65 (Washington, DC: NBS, 1 August 1979). The standard was withdrawn on 25 August 1995.

NCSC (National Computer Security Center), "Department of Defense Password Management Guideline," CSC-STD-002-85 (Fort Meade, MD: National Computer Security Center, 12 April 1985).

———, "A Guide to Understanding Audit in Trusted Systems," NCSC-TG-001 Version 2 (Fort Meade, MD: NCSC, 1 June 1988).

———, "A Guide to Understanding Data Remanence in Automated Information Systems," NCSC-TG-025, Version 2 (Fort Meade, MD: NCSC, September 1991).

———, "Department of Defense Trusted Computer System Evaluation Criteria," DOD 5200.28-STD (Fort Meade, MD: NCSC, 26 December 1985).

NIST (National Institute for Standards and Technology), "Advanced Encryption Standard (AES)," Draft FIPS (Washington, DC: NIST, 2001). Posted on the NIST Web site.

———, "Automated Password Generator," FIPS Publication 181 (Washington, DC: NIST, 5 October 1993). Posted on the NIST Web site.

———, "Data Encryption Standard (DES)," FIPS Publication 46-3 (Washington, DC: NIST, 25 October 1999). Posted on the NIST Web site.

———, "DES Modes of Operation," FIPS Publication 81 (Washington, DC: NIST, 2 December 1980). Posted on the NIST Web site.

———, "Digital Signature Standard," FIPS Publication 186-2 (Washington, DC: NIST, 27 January 2000). Posted on the NIST Web site.

———, "Entity Authentication Using Public Key Cryptography," FIPS Publication 196 (Washington, DC: NIST, 18 February 1997). Posted on the NIST Web site.

———, "Escrowed Encryption Standard," FIPS Publication 185 (Washington, DC: NIST, 9 February 1994). Posted on the NIST Web site.

———, "Secure Hash Standard," FIPS Publication 180-1 (Washington, DC: NIST, April 1995). Posted on the NIST Web site.

National Research Council, *Cryptography's Role In Securing the Information Society: CRISIS* (Washington, DC: National Academy Press, 1996).

Nechvatal, James, Elaine Barker, Lawrence Bassham, William Burr, Morris Dworkin, James Foti, and Edward Roback, "Report on the Development of the Advanced Encryption Standard (AES)" (Washington, DC: NIST, 2 October 2000).

Needham, Roger M., and Michael D. Schroeder, "Using Encryption for Authentication in Large Networks of Computers," *Communications of the ACM* 21, no. 12 (December 1978).

Negin, Michael, Thomas Chmielewski, Jr., Marcos Salganicoff, Theodore A. Camus, Ulf M. Cahn von Seelen, Péter L. Venetianer, Guanghua. G. Zhang, "An Iris Biometric System for Public and Personal Use," *IEEE Computer* 33, no. 2 (February 2000).

Neuman, B. Clifford, and S. Stubblebine, "A Note on the Use of Timestamps as Nonces," *Operating Systems Review* (April 1993).

Neuman, B. Clifford, and Theodore Ts'o, "Kerberos: An Authentication Service for Computer Networks," *IEEE Communications Magazine* 32, no. 9 (September 1994). Also appears in *Practical Cryptography for Data Internetworks*, edited by Stallings.

Neuman, Michael, "Monitoring and Controlling Suspicious Activity in Real-time With IP-Watcher," *Proceedings of the 11th Annual Computer Security Applications Conference*, December 1995.

Neumann, Peter, *Computer Related Risks* (Reading, MA: Addison-Wesley, 1996).

Nickel, Larry, "Why Use Magnetic Stripe Cards?" Web page file "why-use.htm," 1998. Posted on the Mercury Security Web site.

Norman, Donald, *The Design of Everyday Things* (New York: Doubleday Currency, 1988).

Noyce, R. N., "Microelectronics," *Scientific American* 237, no. 3 (September 1977), pp. 62–69.

O'Gorman, Lawrence, "Practical Systems for Personal Fingerprint Identification," *IEEE Computer* 33, no. 2 (February 2000).

Oppliger, Rolf, *Authentication Systems for Secure Networks* (Boston: Artech House, 1996).

Pankanti, Sharath, Ruud M. Bolle, and Anil Jain, "Biometrics: The Future of Identification," *IEEE Computer* 33, no. 4 (February 2000).

Parker, Donn, *Crime by Computer: Startling New Kinds of Million-Dollar Fraud, Theft, Larceny, & Embezzlement* (New York: Charles Scribner's Sons, 1976).

———, *Fighting Computer Crime: A New Framework for Protecting Information* (New York: John Wiley & Sons, 1998).

PC Dynamics, "ActivCard Synchronous Authentication," Report ALL/TU.90.001/En, (San Francisco: PC Dynamics, 1997). Posted on the PC Dynamics Web site.

Peltier, Tom, *Information Security Risk Analysis* (Boca Raton, FL: Auerbach, 2001).

Pentland, Alex (Sandy), and Tanzeem Choudhury, "Face Recognition for Smart Environments" *IEEE Computer* 33, no. 2 (February 2000).

Perlman, Radia, and Charlie Kaufman, "Secure Password-Based Protocol for Downloading a Public Key," *Proceedings of the 1999 Network and Distributed System Security Symposium* (Reston, VA: Internet Society, 1999).

Perlman, Radia, *Interconnections: Bridges, Routers, Switches, and Internetworking Protocols*, 2nd edition (Reading, MA: Addison-Wesley, 2000).

PixIL, "Read This! User Manual," Version 2.62, 2 October 1999. Posted on the PixIL Web site.

Postel, Jonathan, "Internet Protocol—DARPA Internet Program Protocol Specification," Internet RFC 791, 1 September, 1981. Posted on the IETF Web site.

———, "Transmission Control Protocol—DARPA Internet Program Protocol Specification," Internet RFC 793, 1 September, 1981. Posted on the IETF Web site.

Power, Richard, "CSI Special Report on DDOS: Part 1. Diary of a Debacle," *Computer Security Alert* 205 (April 2000).

———, *Tangled Web: Tales of Digital Crime from the Shadows of Cyberspace* (Indianapolis, IN: Que, 2000).

Rabin, M. O., "Digital Signatures and Public-Key Functions as Intractable as Factorization," MIT Laboratory for Computer Science, Report MIT/LCS/TR-212, January 1979.

———, "Probabilistic Algorithm for Testing Primality," *Journal of Number Theory* 12, no. 1 (February 1980).

Raleigh, T. M., and R. W. Underwood, "CRACK: A Distributed Password Advisor," *Proceedings of the USENIX UNIX Security Workshop* (Berkeley, CA: USENIX Association, 1988).

Ramsbottom, Alan, "FAQ: NT Cryptographic Password Attacks and Defenses," 17 July 1997. Posted on the NT Bugtraq Web site.

Ratha, Nalini K., and Ruud Bolle, "Smartcard Based Authentication," Chapter 18 of Jain, Bolle, and Pankanti, eds., *Biometrics: Personal Identification in Networked Society*.

Reeds, J. A., and B. J. Weinberger, "File Security and the Unix Crypt Command," *AT&T Technical Journal* 63, no. 8 (October 1984).

Rescorla, Eric, *SSL and TLS: Designing and Building Secure Systems* (Boston: Addison-Wesley, 2001).

Rigney, C., S. Willens, A. Rubens, and W. Simpson, "Remote Authentication Dial In User Service (RADIUS)," Internet RFC 2865, June 2000.

Ritchie, D. M., "The Unix Time-Sharing System: A Retrospective," *Bell System Technical Journal* 57, no. 6, part 2 (July–August 1978).

Rivest, Ron, "Can We Eliminate Certificate Revocation Lists?" *Proceedings of Financial Cryptography 1998*.

———, "MD5 Digest Algorithm," Internet RFC 1321, April 1992. Posted on the IETF Web site.

———, A. Shamir, and L. Adelman, "A Method for Obtaining Digital Signatures and Public Key Cryptosystems," *Communications of the ACM* 21, no. 2 (February 1978).

Rochlis, Jon, and Mark Eichin, "With Microscope and Tweezers: The Worm from MIT's Perspective," *Communications of the ACM* 32, no. 6 (June 1989), pp. 689–698. Also in *Computers Under Attack*, edited by Denning.

Roper, C. A., and Bill Phillips, *The Complete Book of Locks and Locksmithing*, 3rd edition (Blue Ridge Summit, PA: Tab Books, 1991).

Rothke, Ben, "Fingerprint Biometric Devices: How They Work and How to Choose Them," *Computer Security Journal* 14, no. 4 (fall 1998).

RSA Security, "DES-II Challenges Solved," *Cryptobytes* (summer 1998). Posted on the RSA Security Web site.

———, "RSA Crypto Challenge Sets New Security Benchmark," press release, 26 August 1999. Posted on the RSA Security Web site.

———, "Strong Enterprise User Authentication: RSA ACE/Server" (Bedford, MA: RSA Security, 1999). Posted on the RSA Security Web site.

Salus, Peter H., *A Quarter Century of Unix* (Reading, MA: Addison-Wesley, 1994).

Schneier, Bruce, *Applied Cryptography: Protocols, Algorithms, and Source Code in C* (New York: John Wiley & Sons, 1996).

———, "Why Cryptography Is Harder Than It Looks," white paper (Minneapolis, MN: Counterpane, 1997). Posted on the Counterpane Web site.

———, and Adam Shostack, "Breaking Up Is Hard to Do: Modeling Security Threats for Smart Cards," *Proceedings of the USENIX Workshop on Smart Card Technology* (Berkeley, CA: USENIX Association, 1999), pp. 175–185. Posted on the Counterpane Web site.

———, and Mudge, "Cryptanalysis of Microsoft's Point-to-Point Tunneling Protocol (PPTP)," *Proceedings of the 5th ACM Conference on Communications and Computer Security* (New York: ACM Press, 1998).

———, Mudge, and David Wagner, "Cryptanalysis of Microsoft's PPTP Authentication Extensions (MS-CHAPv2)," *CQRE '99* (Heidelberg: Springer-Verlag, 1999), pp. 192–203.

Senderek, Ralf, "Key-Experiments—How PGP Deals with Manipulated Keys," Web page security/key-experiments.html, August 2000. Posted on Ralf Senderek's personal Web site.

Shoch, John, and Jon Hupp, "The 'Worm' Programs—Early Experiences with a Distributed Computation." *Communications of the ACM* 25, no. 3 (March 1982), pp. 172-180. Also in *Computers Under Attack*, edited by Denning. An earlier version, dated September 1980, was distributed as Internet Working Group (INWG) Note 242 and presented at the *ACM SIGOPS/SIGPLAN Workshop on Fundamental Issues in Distributed Computing* in December 1980.

Schultz, E. Eugene, and Thomas Longstaff, "Internet Sniffer Attacks," *Proceedings of the 18th National Information Systems Security Conference*, National Institute of Standards and Technology, October 1995, pp. 534–542. Also in *Internet Besieged*, edited by Denning and Denning.

Schultz, Eugene, "Windows NT Password Security" *Computer Security Journal* 15, no. 2 (spring 1999).

Schwartau, Winn, *Information Warfare: Chaos on the Electronic Superhighway*, 2nd edition (New York: Thunder's Mouth Press, 1996).

Secure Computing, "SafeWord DES Gold Supervisor Guide" (Roseville, MN: Secure Computing Corporation, 1996). Posted on the Secure Computing Web site.

———, "SafeWord Plus Virtual Smart Card Server Solution," white paper (San Jose, CA: Secure Computing Corporation, July 2000). Posted on the Secure Computing Web site.

Shamir, Adi, and Nicko van Somerin, "Playing Hide and Seek with Stored Keys," research paper, 22 September 1998.

Shimomura, Tsutomu, with John Markoff, *Takedown: The Pursuit and Capture of Kevin Mitnick, America's Most Wanted Computer Outlaw—By the Man Who Did It* (New York: Hyperion, 1996).

Shneiderman, Ben, *Designing the User Interface: Strategies for Effective Human–Computer Interaction,* 3rd edition (Reading, MA: Addison-Wesley, 1998).

Sicherman, Al, "By Any Other Name, He Probably Could Log On Somewhere," *Minneapolis Star Tribune* (23 November 1998), p. E4.

Silverman, Robert, "A Cost-Based Security Analysis of Symmetric and Asymmetric Key Lengths," Bulletin 13, RSA Laboratories, April 2000. Posted on the RSA Security Web site.

Simmons, Gustavus J., ed., *Contemporary Cryptology: The Science of Information Integrity* (New York: IEEE Press, 1992).

Simons, John, "Phone Hex," *Wall Street Journal* (1 October 1999).

Smith, Richard, "Deciphering the Advanced Encryption Standard," *Network Magazine* 16, no. 3 (March 2001), pp. 96–101.

———, "Authentication: Patterns Of Trust" *Information Security* 3 (August 2000).

———, "Historical Overview of Computer Architecture," *Annals of the History of Computing* 10, no. 4 (1989).

———, *Internet Cryptography* (Reading, MA: Addison-Wesley, 1997).

———, "Mandatory Protection for Internet Server Software," *Proceedings of the 12th Annual Computer Security Applications Conference,* December 1996, San Diego, CA.

Snider, L. Britt, and Daniel S. Seikaly, "Report of Investigation: Improper Handling of Classified Information by John M. Deutsch," Report 1998-0028-IG, (Washington, DC: Central Intelligence Agency, 18 February 2000). Posted on the Federation of American Scientists Web site.

Spafford, Eugene H., "Crisis and Aftermath" *Communications of the ACM* 32, no. 6 (June 1989), pp. 678–687. Also in *Computers Under Attack,* edited by Denning.

———, "Observing Reusable Password Choices" Purdue Technical Report CSD-TR-92-049, (West Lafayette, IN: Purdue University, 1992). Also appeared in *Proceedings of the 3rd USENIX Security Symposium* (Berkeley, CA: USENIX Association, 1992). Posted on the COAST Web site.

———, "OPUS: Preventing Weak Password Choices," Purdue Technical Report CSD-TR-92-028, (West Lafayette, IN: Purdue University, 1991). A version of this paper also appeared in *Proceedings of the 14th National Computer Security Conference* (Washington, DC: NIST, 1991). Posted on the COAST Web site.

Stallings, William, *Practical Cryptography for Data Internetworks* (Los Alamitos, CA: IEEE Computer Society Press, 1996).

Standage, Tom, *The Victorian Internet* (New York: Berkley Books, 1998).

Steiner, Jennifer G., Clifford Neuman, and Jeffrey I. Schiller, "Kerberos: An Authentication Service for Open Network Systems," *Proceedings of the 1988 USENIX Winter Conference* (Berkeley, CA: USENIX Association, 1988).

Stevens, W. Richard, *TCP/IP Illustrated, Volume 1* (Reading, MA: Addison-Wesley, 1994).

Stinson, Douglas, *Cryptography Theory and Practice* (Boca Raton, FL: CRC Press, 1995).

Stoll, Clifford, *The Cuckoo's Egg* (Garden City, NY: Doubleday, 1989).

Sumner, F. H., G. Haley, and E. C. Y. Chen, "The Central Control Unit of the 'Atlas' Computer," *Proceedings of the IFIP Congress* (1962), pp. 657–662.

Sutton, Stephen, *Windows NT Security Guide* (Reading, MA: Addison-Wesley, 1997).

———, "Windows NT Security Guidelines: A Study for NSA Research" (Urbana, IL: Trusted Systems Services, 1998).

Tardo, J., and K. Alagappan, "SPX: Global Authentication Using Public Key Certificates," *Proceedings of the IEEE Symposium on Security and Privacy* (Los Alamitos, CA: IEEE Computer Society Press, 1991).

Tenner, Edward, *Why Things Bite Back* (New York: Alfred A. Knopf, 1996).

Tomko, George, "Biometrics as a Privacy-Enhancing Technology: Friend or Foe of Privacy?" from the *9th Privacy Commissioners'/Data Protection Authorities Workshop*, 15 September 1998. Posted on the Information Privacy Commissioner/Ontario Web site.

Ts'o, Theodore, Clifford Neuman, George Kohl, Tom Yu, and Kenneth Raeburn, "The Kerberos Network Authentication Service (V5)," 7 March 2001. This has been distributed as an Internet Draft.

Tung, Brian, *Kerberos: A Network Authentication System* (Reading, MA: Addison-Wesley, 1999).

———, Clifford Neuman, Matthew Hur, Ari Medvinsky, Sasha Medvinsky, John Wray, and Jonathan Trostle, "Public Key Cryptography for Initial Authentication in Kerberos," 15 July 2000. This has been distributed as an Internet Draft.

Uehling, Mark, "Cracking the Uncrackable Code," *Popular Science* (September 1994). Also appears in *Practical Cryptography*, edited by William Stallings.

van Eck, Wim, "Electromagnetic Radiation from Video Display Units: An Eavesdropping Risk?" (Leidschendam, The Netherlands: PTT Dr. Neher Laboratories, 16 April 1985).

Van Vleck, Tom, "The IBM 7094 and CTSS," Web page thvv/7094.html, 18 December 1997. Posted on the Multicians Web site.

———, "Multics: Security," Web page security.html, 15 February 1995. Posted on the Multicians Web site.

Wagner, David, and Bruce Schneier, "Analysis of the SSL 3.0 Protocol," *Proceedings of the Second USENIX Workshop on Electronic Commerce* (Berkeley, CA: USENIX Association, 1996) pp. 29–40.

———, Bruce Schneier, and John Kelsey, "Cryptanalysis of the Cellular Message Encryption Algorithm," (Minneapolis, MN: Counterpane Labs, 20 March 1997). Posted on the Counterpane Labs Web site.

Wayner, Peter, *Disappearing Cryptography* (San Francisco: Morgan Kaufmann, 1996).

Weinstein, Lauren (lauren@UCLA-SECURITY), "60 Minutes Parody," text file, circa 1980. Probably first distributed via the "Human-Nets" e-mail distribution list.

Weizenbaum, Joseph, *Computer Power and Human Reason: From Judgement to Calculation* (San Francisco: W. H. Freeman and Co., 1976).

Whitten, Alma, and J. D. Tygar, "Usability of Security: A Case Study," Report CMU-CS-98-155, (Pittsburgh, Pennsylvania: Carnegie Mellon University Computer Science Department, 18 December 1998).

———, "Why Johnny Can't Encrypt: A Usability Evaluation of PGP 5.0," *Proceedings of the 8th USENIX Security Symposium* (Berkeley, CA: USENIX Association, 1999).

Wiener, Michael J., "Efficient DES Key Search." Technical Report TR-244, School of Computer Science (Canada: Carlton University, May 1994). Also appears in *Practical Cryptography*, edited by Stallings.

Wilkes, Maurice, *Timesharing Computer Systems* (London: Macdonald, 1968).

Willis, David, and Mike Lee, "Six Biometric Devices Point the Finger at Security," *Network Computing* (1 June 1998).

Woodward, John D., "Biometrics: Identifying Law and Policy Concerns," in *Biometrics: Personal Identification in Networked Society*, edited by Jain, Bolle, and Pankanti. The article is based on the paper "Biometrics: Privacy's Friend or Foe?" *Proceedings of the IEEE* (September 1997).

X9 Financial Services Committee, "Financial Institution Key Management (Wholesale)," Standard X9.17, (Washington, DC: American Bankers Association, 1985). Posted on the X9 Online Web site.

————, "Managing Risk and Mitigation Planning: Withdrawal of ANSI X9.9," Report X9/TG-24-1999 (Washington, DC: American Bankers Association, 1999). Posted on the X9 Online Web site.

————, "PIN Security Compliance Guideline," Report X9/TG-3 (Washington, DC: American Bankers Association, 1997). Posted on the X9 Online Web site.

Yan, Jianxin, Alan Blackwell, Ross Anderson, and Alasdair Grant, "Memorability and Security of Passwords—Some Empirical Results," research paper (Cambridge, UK: Cambridge University Computer Laboratory, 2001).

Yeager, Wayne B., *Techniques of Safecracking* (Port Townsend, WA: Loompanics Unlimited, 1990).

Zipes, Jack, ed., *The Arabian Nights: The Marvels and Wonders of the Thousand and One Nights* (New York: Signet Classic, 1991).

WEB AND VENDOR RESOURCES

This section contains all URLs for referenced information on the World Wide Web and all vendor contact information. The book centralizes this information here because the information is likely to change. Consult the author's Web site for updates to this information. Entries are alphabetical based on the site name, vendor name, or an individual's last name.

@Stake security Web site
    Topic: technical reports on computer security vulnerabilities
    Product: computer security consulting
    http://www.atstake.com

    196 Broadway
    Cambridge, MA 02139-1902
    617-621-3500
    Fax: 617-621-1738

Advanced Encryption System Web site
    Topics: Advanced Encryption System, U.S. encryption standards
    http://csrc.nist.gov/encryption/aes/index.html

American Biometric Company
    Products: BioMouse, BioMouse II fingerprint scanners and software
    http://www.biomouse.com

    DEW Engineering & Development Ltd.
    3429 Hawthorne Rd.
    Ottawa K1G 4G2 Canada

Apple Computer
    Product: Macintosh systems, voice authentication
    http://www.apple.com

    1 Infinite Loop
    Cupertino, CA 95014

AuthenTec Inc.
   Product: FingerLoc fingerprint authentication system
   http://www.authentec.com

   P.O. Box 2719
   Melbourne, FL 32902-2719
   321-308-1300
   Fax: 321-308-1340

Biometric Access Corporation
   Product: SecureTouch 98 fingerprint reader
   http://www.biometricaccess.com

   2555 N. IH 35
   Round Rock, TX 78664
   512-246-3760 x119
   Fax: 512-246-3760

Bureau of Export Administration Encryption Web site
   Topics: commercial encryption, export controls
   http://www.bxa.doc.gov/Encryption/Default.htm

   800-888-8242
   Fax: 650-802-7777

CERT (Computer Emergency Response Team) Web site
   Topics: computer security, vulnerabilities, incident reports
   http://www.cert.org

CIAC (Computer Incident Advisory Capability) Web site
   Topics: computer security, vulnerabilities, incident reports
   http://www.ciac.org/ciac/

COAST (Computer Operations, Audit, and Security Technology) Web site
   Topic: computer security
   http://www.cs.purdue.edu/coast/

Communication Intelligence Corporation (CIC)
   Product: InkTools—biometric authentication toolkit using handwritten
   signature verification
   http://www.cic.com

   275 Shoreline Dr., Suite 500
   Redwood Shores, CA 94065

Compaq Corporation
   Product: fingerprint scanners
   http://www.compaq.com

Computer Security Institute (CSI) Web site
   Topics: computer security, CSI/FBI crime survey
   http://www.gocsi.com

Counterpane Internet Security Web site
    Topics: cryptography, computer security
    http://www.counterpane.com

    19050 Pruneridge Ave.
    Cupertino, CA 95014
    408-777-3600
    Fax: 408-777-3601

Cross Match Technologies
    Products: ID 100, MV5, Verifier 200, Verifier 250 fingerprint scanners
    http://www.crossmatch.net

    777 S. Flager Dr., Suite 1200, East Tower
    West Palm Beach, FL 33401
    561-802-3442
    Fax: 561-802-3117

CryptoCard
    Products: CryptoCard RB-1 one-time password tokens and related
    server software
    http://www.cryptocard.com

    300 March Rd., Suite 304
    Kanata, Ontario K2K 2E2
    613-599-2441
    Fax: 613-599-2442

Cryptography Research Web site
    Topics: cryptography, differential power analysis, DES cracking, SSL
    http://www.cryptography.com

Cryptome Web site
    Topics: cryptography, NSA, surveillance
    http://cryptome.org

Curtin, Matt, personal Web site
    Topics: Snake Oil FAQ, other security-related information
    http://www.interhack.net/people/cmcurtin/

CyberLocator
    Product: location-based authentication using GPS signals
    http://www.cyberlocator.com

    2465 Central Ave., #110
    Boulder, CO 80301
    303-447-0300

Cyber SIGN
Product: Cyber SIGN Developers Workshop—biometric authentication toolkit using handwritten signature verification
http://www.cybersign.com

2635 N. First St., Suite 103
San Jose, CA 95134
408-324-1001
Fax: 408-324-1057

Dallas Semiconductor Corp.
Products: iButton, Java Ring
http://www.dalsemi.com

4401 South Beltwood Pkwy.
Dallas, TX 75244
972-371-4000
Fax: 972-371-3715

DigitalPersona, Inc.
Product: U.are.U Pro Fingerprint Security System
http://www.digitalpersona.com

805 Veterans Blvd., Suite 301
Redwood City, CA 94067
877-378-2738 or 650-261-6070
Fax: 650-261-6079

Enigma Logic, Inc.
See Secure Computing Corporation

Ensure Technologies
Product: XyLoc—token-based proximity sensing system used for authentication
http://www.ensuretech.com

2610 W. Liberty Rd., Suite C
Ann Arbor, MI 48103
734-668-8800
Fax: 734-668-1242

FIRST (Forum of Incident Response and Security Teams) CD-ROM Web site
Topic: computer security
http://www.alw.nih.gov/Security/first-papers.html

IACR (International Association of Cryptographic Research) EPrint Web site
Topics: cryptography, computer security
http://eprint.iacr.org

Identix
>   Products: TouchSAFE Personal and TouchNet III fingerprint verification
>   devices
>   http://www.identix.com
>
>   510 N. Pastoria Ave.
>   Sunnyvale, CA 94086
>   408-731-2000
>   Fax: 408-739-3308

IEEE P1363a Study Group on Password-Based Authenticated-Key-
Exchange Methods Web site
>   Topic: strong, password-based protocols for authentication and key
>   exchange
>   http://grouper.ieee.org/groups/1363/StudyGroup/Passwd.html

Information Privacy Commissioner/Ontario Web site
>   Topics: privacy, legal issues, Ontario
>   http://www.ipc.on.ca/

Informer Systems, Ltd.
>   Product: SentriNET fingerprint authentication software
>   http://www.informer.co.uk
>
>   Grosvenor House
>   Market Street, Bromsgrove
>   B61 8DA Worcestershire, UK

Integrity Sciences Web site
>   Topics: encrypted key exchange, SPEKE, password-only authentication
>   http://www.integritysciences.com
>
>   c/o Phoenix Technologies Ltd.
>   411 East Plumeria Dr.
>   San Jose, CA 95134
>   800-452-8603 or 408-570-1000
>   Fax: 408-5700 -1001

IriScan, Inc.
>   Products: PC Iris—biometric authentication based on iris recognition
>   http://www.iriscan.com
>
>   9 E. Stow Rd., Suite E
>   Marlton, NJ 08053
>   877-IRISCAN or 856-797-6890
>   Fax: 856-797-6877

Keyware Technologies, Inc.
   Products: Voice Guardian, Layered Biometric Verification Server—biometric authentication based on speaker recognition
   http://www.keyware.com

   500 W. Cummings Park, Suite 3600
   Woburn, MA 01801
   800-KEYWARE or 781-933-1311
   Fax: 781-933-1554

Mercury Security Web site
   Topic: magnetic stripe cards
   www.mercury-security.com

Miros, Inc.
   Products: TrueFace Web, TrueFace Network—biometric authentication based on face recognition
   http://www.miros.com

   572 Washington St., Suite 18
   Wellesley, MA 02482
   888-367-6476 or 781-235-0330
   Fax: 781-235-0720

Mytec Technologies, Inc.
   Products: Touchstone Pro, Mytec Gateway—fingerprint recognition using encrypted patterns stored on personally carried tokens
   http://www.mytec.com

   1220 Sheppard Ave. E., Suite 200
   Toronto M2K 2S5 Canada
   416-467-6000
   Fax: 416-467-9631

National Security Agency (NSA)
   Topics: information security, cryptography, evaluations, cryptographic history
   http://www.nsa.gov:8080

NIST Computer Security Resource Center
   Topics: computer security, federal standards, cryptography
   http://csrc.nist.gov/

NT Bugtraq Web site
   Topic: Microsoft Windows NT security
   http://www.ntbugtraq.com

PC Dynamics, Inc.
> Products: ActivCard authentication tokens and servers
> http://www.pcdynamics.com
>
> 31332 Via Colinas, Suite 102
> Westlake Village, CA 91362 USA
> 800-888-1741
> Fax: 818-889-1014

PixIL Web site
> Topics: Read This! and other encryption software
> http://members.nbci.com/pixil/index.htm

Recognition Systems, Inc.
> Products: ID3D-R HandKey, HandKey II—biometrics based on hand
> geometry
> http://www.handreader.com
>
> 1520 Dell Ave.
> Campbell, CA 95008
> 408-364-6960
> Fax: 408-370-3679

RSA Security, Inc.
> Products: SecurID authentication tokens and servers (formerly Security
> Dynamics). Other products include the BSAFE cryptographic libraries
> that provide RSA (Rivest Shamir Adelman) public key ciphers, Rivest's
> symmetric ciphers (RC2, RC4), and "message digest" hash algorithms
> (MD4, MD5).
> http://www.rsasecurity.com
>
> 123 Concord Ave.
> Bedford, MA 123455
> 877-RSA-4900 or 781-301-5000
> Fax: 781-301-5170

SafeWord Web site
> Topics: SafeWord password tokens and authentication server software
> Also see the Secure Computing Web site
> http://www.safeword.com/

Samba Web site
> Topics: file server software to provide Microsoft SMB protocols to Unix
> and other platforms
> http://www.samba.org/

Sandstorm Enterprises
> Product: PhoneSweep phone scanner/wardialer
> http://www.sandstorm.net/

Schwartz, Randall, personal Web site
> Topics: Perl, Intel v. Schwartz legal case
> http://www.stonehenge.com/merlyn/

Secure Computing Corporation
Products: Safeword authentication tokens, E.id authentication tokens, and Safeword authentication servers (formerly Enigma Logic)
Other security products include Sidewinder firewalls.
Also see the SafeWord Web site.
http://www.securecomputing.com

4810 Harwood Rd.
San Jose, CA 95124-5206
800-692-5625 or 408-979-6100
Fax: 408-979-6501

Security Dynamics, Inc.
See RSA Security, Inc.

Security Software Technologies
Topics: security software tools, notably l0phtcrack
http://www.securitysoftwaretech.com/

Senderek, Ralf, personal Web site
Topics: computer security, cryptography, PGP
http:/senderek.de/

Sensar, Inc.
Product: Sensar...SecureCam—biometric authentication based on iris recognition
http://www.sensar.com

121 Whittendale Dr., Bldg. 2
Moorestown, NJ 08057
856-222-9090 or 888-4-SENSAR
Fax: 856-222-9020

Smith, Rick, personal Web site
Topics: authentication, cryptography, computer security
http://www.visi.com/crypto/

T-NETIX Inc.
Products: SpeakEZ Voice Print, VeriNet WEB, VoicEntry II—biometric authentication based on voice recognition
http://www.T-netix.com

67 Inverness Dr. E.
Englewood, CO 80112
800-352-8628 or 303-790-9111
Fax: 303-790-9540

Tri-Sage

    Products: Sage-ID—token-based proximity sensing system used for authentication
    http://www.tri-sage.com

    1333 Butterfield Rd., Suite 300
    Downers Grove, IL 60515
    630-241-0500
    Fax: 630-241-3835

Verisign

    Products: public key certification authority, cryptographic software
    http://corporate.verisign.com/index.html

Veritel

    Product: Caller Verification System (CVS)—biometric authentication based on voice recognition
    http://www.veritelcorp.com

    70 W. Madison, Suite 710
    Chicago, IL 60602
    312-803-5000 x2009
    Fax: 312-803-3311

VerTTex Software

    Product: ModemScan telephone number scanner/wardialer
    http://www.verttex.com

Visionics Corporation

    Products: FaceIt face-recognition software
    http://www.visionics.com

    1 Exchange Pl., 8th fl.
    Jersey City, NJ 07302
    201-332-9213
    Fax: 201-332-9313

Wired News Web site

    Topic: technology news
    http://www.wired.com/news/

X9 Online Web site

    Topics: American Bankers Association standards, security, encryption
    http://www.x9.org

GLOSSARY

For the most part, this book uses standard terms and jargon according to their generally accepted usage in the field. However, some terms have several common interpretations. In such cases, the definition will usually begin with the phrase "In this book" and describe how the text of this book uses that term. Alternative definitions may be provided, but a term will have only one meaning in this book.

Abstract Syntax Notation #1 (ASN.1) - A notation for specifying the syntax of computer data items. It is widely used in certain communications protocols and related standards, including public key certificates (X.509), network management, and the X.400 and X.500 e-mail standards.

access control - In this book, a mechanism or process that grants or denies access based on predefined rules. Often, the rules depend on the user's identity as established by the authentication mechanism.

   This is how the computer security community typically uses this term. In more general use, however, the term may include the authentication mechanism.

Active Directory - A facility in Microsoft's Windows 2000 that stores security and other configuration information about users, services, and other facilities at a site.

application program interface (API) - A standard specification for how one program can use the facilities of another program.

ARPANET - A pioneering computer network established by the Advanced Research Projects Agency (ARPA) of the Department of Defense (DOD). The ARPANET evolved into the backbone of the Internet.

asymmetric encryption - A cryptographic algorithm that uses different keys for encryption and decryption. Public key cryptography is the most common example of this.

asynchronous password - A one-time password mechanism that requires input data to generate a new one-time password. Usually, the input data is a random challenge or nonce.

attack prevalence - In this book, a relative estimate of how likely a particular attack might be used by an attacker.

authentication - A mechanism or process that associates a particular person's identity with a statement, action, or event. In a computer system it verifies that an internal user identification is correctly associated with its owner.

authentication factors - A classification of authentication techniques into one of three possible categories: something you know, something you have, or something you are.

back door - A mechanism built into a program that bypasses conventional protection mechanisms. A typical example would be a program that accepts a secret command or password to grant access without checking the conventional user password database.

base secret - A piece of secret information that is associated with a particular user. An authentication mechanism that uses a base secret will not be able to authenticate a user unless the user has access to the corresponding base secret.

biometric - A measurement of a unique physical or behavioral feature that is used to uniquely identify an individual.

bit space - In this book, the number of bits of binary storage required to store a particular numeric value. For example, the number 16 million has a bit space of 24.

buffer - A storage area in RAM, typically used to temporarily store data as it is moved between different components of the system.

buffer overrun - A problem that can arise if a software procedure fails to keep track of the amount of data being placed into a buffer. If the procedure does not enforce a limit on the amount of data being stored in a buffer, it runs the risk of overflowing the buffer and storing the data atop other, unrelated data items. The results can be unpredictable; in some cases a buffer overrun can enable a security breach.

Caller ID - A feature by which the telephone company transmits the number of the telephone originating a call to the station receiving a call. A more precise technical term for this feature is "Calling Number Identification," since it identifies the telephone, not the person making the call.

central processing unit (CPU) - The computer circuitry that performs computations and executes programs stored in RAM.

certificate - A data item that reliably identifies the owner of a particular public key pair. The certificate contains a digital signature that is used to authenticate the certificate's contents.

certificate authority - A device that creates a public key certificate by placing its digital signature on the certificate's contents. The authority may be the system's proprietor or it may be a third party hired by the proprietor. In some cases, individuals may act as authorities.

certificate chain - A series of public key certificates in which one certificate's digital signature was produced by the public key pair identified in the next certificate. The last certificate in the chain must be authenticated by a trustworthy public key. We use the series of public keys to authenticate the certificates' signatures.

certificate revocation list - A list of certificates that have been declared invalid before they have reached their expiration dates.

challenge - In one-time passwords, it is random data that the person must use to compute the correct password for that particular authentication attempt. A challenge may also be called a nonce.

challenge response - An authentication process in which the server demanding authentication issues a random challenge to the user being authenticated, and the user must transform the challenge into the correct response and send it back.

chosen message attack - An attack against a public key signature operation in which the attacker constructs a message with a particular mathematical structure and asks the victim to sign it. The signed message can then be mathematically processed to yield the desired signature.

computationally secure - A common property of cryptographic algorithms that indicates it may be theoretically possible to attack the algorithm, usually through trial and error, but the attack is not technically feasible, usually because of the time and resources required to succeed.

connection hijacking - An attack that takes over one end of an established connection between two host computers, so that the attacker can masquerade as the host that was cut off.

cracker - A person who attacks communication systems. Also called phreaks.

cryptographic algorithm - A computational procedure for protecting data: usually either an encryption algorithm, a hashing algorithm, or some combination of them.

cryptography, cryptographic techniques, crypto - A set of techniques for protecting information by applying computations that are hard to reverse. The computations usually involve secret information that is known only to authorized or trusted people or procedures.

daemon - A service process running on a computer without a particular person associated with it. Network server processes are usually daemons.

decryption (noun), decrypt (verb) - The process of transforming encrypted data back into readable plaintext using an encryption algorithm.

defensive measure - One of the six general measures used to reduce the risk of attack: prevention, deterrence, indications, detection, preparation, recovery.

Digital Signature Standard (DSS) - The FIPS standard public key algorithm for digital signatures. The algorithm is based on the discrete logarithm problem.

direct authentication - A design pattern for an authentication system in which servers authenticate remote users based on a database of user records stored on each server.

discrete logarithm problem - A hard mathematical problem that is used as the basis for some public key cryptographic algorithms. The problem is that it is easy to exponentiate a secret number and take its modulus relative to a prime, but it's difficult to reverse the process and derive the secret number (that is, find the logarithm of the computed modulus).

distinguished name - The format of a full name in an X.509 public key certificate. The name generally contains a series of hierarchically defined components, often corresponding to organizational subdivisions of the enterprise issuing a certificate.

distinguishing characteristic - Data that the authentication mechanism uniquely associates with a particular user. A distinguishing characteristic is often a base secret.

domain controller - In the context of authentication for Microsoft Windows NT, a server that maintains authentication information for a group of users within a particular network.

downgrade attack - An attack in which the attacker induces the system to use an older, less secure protocol that can be attacked, when it should be using a newer protocol that would resist the attack.

duress signal - A signal sent by a victim to indicate that an attacker is forcing the victim to perform the authentication process.

Encrypted Key Exchange (EKE) - A protocol that uses a memorized secret password with relatively low entropy to exchange a randomly generated public key pair that contains significantly higher entropy.

encryption (noun), encrypt (verb) - The process of transforming plaintext data into unreadable, encrypted data using an encryption algorithm.

encryption algorithm - A computational procedure for encrypting data.

enrollment - The process of entering a new user name into an authentication system. This includes the process of entering the necessary information (password, PIN, biometric readings, etc.) to authenticate the correct person when logging on with that user name.

external password - A password that travels across an untrustworthy external network.

factoring problem - The problem of taking a number and determining all of its prime factors, that is, all of the prime numbers that must be multiplied together to produce that number.

factors - In classic arithmetic, it refers to the inputs to a multiplication operation.

In authentication systems, it refers to a classification of authentication techniques into one of three possible categories: something you know, something you have, or something you are.

false acceptance - An error in which the system should have answered "no" but answered "yes" instead. A false acceptance error is generally a security problem in an authentication system since it may grant access to a person when it should have denied access.

false rejection - An error in which the system should have answered "yes" but answered "no" instead. A false rejection error is generally a reliability problem since the system may then fail to provide services when it should have.

Federal Information Processing Standard (FIPS) - A computing systems standard established by NIST, a U.S. government agency, for use by government agencies. FIPS standards for security are often used by private industry on the assumption that the U.S. government would not approve a weak standard for its own use.

finger - An Internet service that retrieves identification and status about users at a particular host. Hosts that provide this service must run the finger daemon.

firewall - A network device that tries to reduce the risk of attacks on a network by restricting the message traffic that passes through it. A site's proprietor generally places the firewall between the site's local network and an external, untrusted network like the Internet.

forwardable ticket - A Kerberos TGT that can be used to issue another TGT that the owner forwards to a server for use on the owner's behalf.

Global Positioning System (GPS) - A system of satellites built by the DOD to provide highly accurate information about geographical position anywhere on Earth.

hard drive - The random access disk drive used in a computer system to store permanent data, like the operating system and application programs that it routinely runs.

hash (verb) - To perform a hash function, with the verb's object being the input to the hash function. For example: "We hash the passphrase to generate the secret key."

hash (noun), hash value - The numeric result generated by a hash function.

hash function (noun) - A function that takes an arbitrary amount of input data and computes a fixed-size result. A *one-way hash function* is an important special case that plays an essential role in many authentication systems.

honey pot - A computer system that has been configured to look like an interesting and worthwhile target to an attacker, but whose real purpose is to capture and maintain an attacker's interest while the proprietor investigates the attack.

ID file - The file used in Lotus Notes to keep user-specific security information, including the user's private key. The file is encrypted with the user's secret password.

indirect authentication - A design pattern for an authentication system in which servers authenticate remote users by using a separate server that maintains the database of user records.

interface message processor (IMP) - A device that allowed host computers to connect to the ARPANET. IMPs served a similar role to routers on the Internet.

internal password - A memorized password used in an environment where it is unlikely to be subjected to sniffing or other interception attacks.

Joe account - a user account whose password is the same as its user name.

Kerberos - In this book, Kerberos is a cryptographic protocol used for authentication and cryptographic key exchange via a KDC.

The name *Kerberos* refers to the three-headed dog that defends the entrance to Hades in Greek mythology. In Roman mythology, the dog's name is Cerberus.

Kerberized - A software package that has been adapted to use the Kerberos protocol for authentication and/or key exchange.

key distribution center (KDC) - A server that provides session keys to its population users, servers, and other entities.

least privilege - A security engineering principle in which the proprietor grants each user or other entity exactly as many privileges and permissions the entity requires, no more and no less.

local authentication - A design pattern for an authentication system in which a device authenticates its current user through a direct, hands-on interaction.

login, logon, log on - The process by which a person provides identification and authentication to a computer system in order to be granted access to its services.

main memory - The internal memory used by a computer's central processing unit, more often called random access memory (RAM).

man in the middle (MIM) - A style of attack in which an attacker intercepts messages traveling between two victims, often making it appear to one or both of the victims as if the messages are traveling safely when in fact they have been disclosed to and/or modified by the attacker.

masquerade - An attack in a system is tricked into associating the wrong user name with a person.

master key - A shared secret key that is never used to encrypt actual data messages, but only to encrypt temporary session keys that in turn are used to encrypt data messages.

Microsoft Challenge/Reply Handshake Protocol (MS-CHAP) - A challenge response authentication protocol used by Microsoft in most of its network products. The protocol appears in older ("v1") and newer ("v2") versions.

modulus (mod) - In arithmetic, an operation that returns the integer remainder result when dividing an integer by some base integer.

Moore's Law - Summarizes improvements in computer technology by estimating that computers improve yearly by a factor of two in price, size, and speed.

National Bureau of Standards (NBS) - The U.S. government agency responsible for national standards. It has been renamed the National Institute of Standards and Technology (NIST).

National Computer Security Center (NCSC) - The U.S. government organization, part of the NSA, that was originally given the task of developing and promoting standards for computer system security. Originally called the DOD Computer Security Center when established in 1981, it was renamed the NCSC in 1985.

National Institute of Standards and Technology (NIST) - The U.S. government agency responsible for national standards.

network access server (NAS) - A device that accepts dial-in connections to an internal network.

nonce - Data used in an authentication or key exchange protocol to prevent replay attacks. Most, but not all, protocols require that nonces are seldom repeated. Some, but not all, protocols require that nonces be unpredictable.

off-line authentication - A design pattern for an authentication system in which a device authenticates a remote entity (a user, server, or something else) without having to contact a separate authentication server or maintain a collection of base secrets. Off-line authentication generally uses public key cryptography.

one-way function - A function for which it is not practical to determine the input value that yielded a particular result.

one-way hash function - A one-way function that takes a block of data of arbitrary size and computes a fixed-sized result. Whenever a change is made to the input, even a minor one, there will be changes in the result. There should be no simple way to associate changes in the function's result to changes in its input.

open standard - Indicates that the technical details are open for inspection by other members of the community, and usually means that competing vendors can use the standard to construct interoperable products.

passphrase - A memorized base secret constructed of text that may include embedded blanks. Passphrases are typically allowed to be much longer than passwords, and may extend for dozens of characters. It is usually assumed that a passphrase consists of a piece of readable text that the owner finds memorable.

password - A memorized base secret that is constructed from keystrokes. Traditionally, passwords consisted of letters without special characters or embedded blanks, but many modern systems have relaxed these restrictions. Many systems restrict the length of passwords to 10 or 20 characters, or even less.

password equivalent - A transformed version of a password that is used to protect the plaintext version of the password from sniffing. A hashed password is a password equivalent.

pass-through authentication - A term used by Microsoft to refer to indirect authentication in Windows network domain environments.

phreaks (noun), phreaking (verb) - People who attack telephone systems, or the activity of attacking telephone systems.

plaintext - Data that is in a readable, unencrypted form, as opposed to ciphertext.

premaster key - A random secret generated by a client in the SSL protocol and shared with the server using public key encryption. This random secret provides the secret entropy for generating SSL session keys.

private key - The part of a public key pair that must be kept secret to avoid compromising security. The private key is generated from random, secret information.

protocol - A definition of how two computers (or, sometimes, a computer and a person) must exchange information in order to achieve some result, like authentication. The protocol defines the messages that must be exchanged, their content, and the sequence in which they should be exchanged.

protocol stack - The software implementing a layered network protocol, like the Internet protocol suite.

proxiable ticket - A Kerberos TGT that can be used to request tickets that are bound to a different network address from the one appearing in the TGT. This allows the TGT's owner to issue tickets for use by servers to access other services on the TGT owner's behalf.

proxy ticket - A Kerberos ticket issued for use by a server to use a different server on a user's behalf. The user requests the ticket and forwards it to the server along with a copy of the associated session key.

public key - The part of a public key pair that can be shared with others without compromising security. The public key's value is computed from its corresponding private key.

public key pair - A pair of keys used in a public key cryptographic algorithm. The keys in the pair are called the private key and the public key. The private key is generated randomly, and the public key is derived from the private key.

public key cryptography, public key algorithms - A cryptographic technique that performs asymmetric encryption with a public key pair.

random access memory (RAM) - The main memory area within a computing system from which the central processing unit (CPU) extracts instructions and data when running a program.

Registry - A storage area on the hard drive of a Microsoft Windows system that contains administrative data

rekey - The process of changing one cryptographic key for a different one.

remote authentication - A term occasionally used in Microsoft documentation to refer to indirect authentication.

Remote Authentication Dial In User Protocol (RADIUS) - A protocol used for indirect authentication, often with NASes and firewalls.

replay attack - An attack in which an attacker simply transmits a previously intercepted message to try to trick the recipient into processing the message a second time and performing some related action, like crediting an account.

reputation capital - The qualitative value of a person's reputation within an Internet discussion group as established by the person's activities within that group. Reputation capital is usually established entirely by activities within the group, unaffected by a person's role or status in the rest of the world.

request authenticator - A 128-bit random number, or nonce, used to detect replay attacks in the RADIUS protocol.

response authenticator - A 128-bit keyed hash used to detect forged or modified messages in the RADIUS protocol.

rewrite attack - An attack in which an attacker intercepts an encrypted message and modifies selected ciphertext bits in order to systematically change the contents of the message that recipient reads after decrypting the message.

roaming user - A person authorized to use the system from unpredictable locations.

rubber hose cryptanalysis, rubber hose disclosure - A situation in which the attacker uses threats and/or physical force to compel a victim to disclose a secret, like a password or secret encryption key.

secret key - In this book, a secret key is a block of secret, hard-to-guess data used in a cryptographic algorithm to protect other data. The secret key must be shared by both the creator and the recipient of the protected data. The secret key can protect the data as long as an attacker can't guess it or somehow retrieve a copy of it.

While this is a reasonably common use of this term, some writers also use this term to refer to the private key of a public key pair.

secure attention - A reserved keystroke or other interactive signal that is always intercepted by trusted software in the system and that cannot be intercepted by Trojan horse software.

security accounts manager (SAM) - In Microsoft Windows NT and 2000, the database within the Registry that stores user identification and authentication information, including hashed passwords.

self-signed certificate - A public key certificate that has been signed by the key it contains. People can verify the certificate by checking its digital signature with its own key.

separation of duty - A security principle in which a security critical activity cannot be performed by a single person, but instead requires separate steps performed by separate people. In some cases, this can be achieved by establishing the right procedures, though it may often require technical measures.

server message block (SMB) - A network protocol developed by Intel and Microsoft to facilitate resource sharing (files, printers, etc.).

session key - A secret key that is temporarily established between two parties for authentication or to cryptographically protect messages they exchange.

shadow password file - In Unix systems, this refers to an arrangement in which a copy of the system's password file is made visible to the user population, but the password hash values are left blank. The hashes appear in a separate file, called the "shadow" file, that users can't read.

shoulder surfing - An attempt to retrieve a person's password or PIN by standing nearby as the password or PIN is typed.

single sign-on - A feature that minimizes either the number of times people must authenticate themselves when using a system or the number of different characteristics they must use (that is, different passwords), or both.

sniffing, password sniffing - The process of intercepting a password that has been entered into a computer, either while it is being typed or while it is being transmitted in a plaintext across a network.

social engineering - Attacks on security systems in which the attacker convinces an insider to unwittingly help the attack succeed. The point is that the insider is not intentionally supporting the attack. Typically, the attacker convinces the insider to provide help on a technical problem by disclosing or changing a secret password.

soft PIN - A PIN whose value is explicitly included as part of an external password. For example, the user may need to type the legal password by first typing six digits displayed by a password token, followed by typing the four digits of the PIN.

steganography - A technique for hiding information by spreading it among other information in a way that is reversible but hard to detect.

strong authentication - In this book, an authentication mechanism that incorporates at least two authentication factors.

symmetric encryption, symmetric key - A cryptographic algorithm that uses the same key for both encryption and decryption. This generally involves secret keys as opposed to the public key pairs used with asymmetric encryption.

system key (SYSKEY) - A secret key used by Windows NT to encrypt the SAM database.

TCP splicing - An attack in which the attacker redirects an authenticated TCP connection so that it communicates with the attacker's session instead of the victim's session.

terminal access controller access control system (TACACS) - A protocol developed for indirect authentication on the ARPANET. Variants are still used, often with NASes and firewalls.

terminal IMP (TIP) - A device that allowed users to connect remotely to the ARPANET using a simple computer terminal.

ticket - An encrypted data item created for a particular party that contains a shared secret key for temporary use. The ticket usually contains other information to ensure its validity, like the name of the other party sharing the temporary key.

timesharing - A mechanism by which several computer users can use the same computer interactively at the same time.

time stamp - A data item indicating the time at which a particular message was constructed. The recipient can look at the time stamp and determine whether the message was recently produced. This can help the recipient detect replayed messages.

token - A physical item that a person must possess in order to perform an authentication operation.

transitive trust - A situation in which any person or entity in a group that trusts one another may independently add other members to that group, and new members can in turn add new members themselves. Secret keys are shared secrets that produce transitive trust.

Transmission Control Protocol (TCP) - The protocol used on the Internet for reliably sending data so that the recipient sees the data in the order it was sent.

trial and error - An attack strategy that makes a systematic series of guesses in order to uncover a base secret.

Trusted Computer Systems Evaluation Criteria (TCSEC) - A set of criteria published in the 1980s by the U.S. government for evaluating the level of security provided by different computer systems. The TCSEC defines a range of increasingly sophisticated requirements so that systems may be judged as providing relatively stronger or weaker security.

trusted path - A mechanism to ensure that when someone types some security-critical input, the input goes to the appropriate program on the computer. This mechanism is required in high-security systems as defined by the TCSEC.

tunneling protocol - A way of "nesting" a stream of data inside a communications protocol so that it can travel over a network that can't handle that particular form of data directly. Sometimes tunneling is used to reformat data for encryption and other forms of cryptographic protection. Sometimes tunneling is used by irresponsible users to circumvent security-related filtering of particular data formats.

user - A single entity whose behavior is uniquely identified within a computer system. Individual users typically correspond to individual people, but they may also represent particular system services or resources.

User Datagram Protocol (UDP) - The basic Internet protocol for sending simple, low-overhead data messages with no sequencing, flow control, or retransmission. Appropriate for application protocols that implement their own loss detection and flow control. Other applications tend to use TCP.

user name - A unique identifier assigned by a system to a particular user. User names are often constructed of text so that people can easily remember and type in their user names during logon. Some systems, like Unix, assign more than one user name wherein one is textual and another is an integer.

user record - A data structure maintained by an authentication system that contains the data necessary to authenticate a particular user. At a minimum the record contains the user name and the user's distinguishing characteristic.

van Eck radiation - The electromagnetic radiation produced by video monitors, which can be captured by a receiver that can then display the same information that appears on the monitor that generated the radiation.

verifier - A data item transmitted from a user and used to authenticate that user. Here are examples of verifiers used by various authentication strategies: distinguishing characteristics, base secrets, biometric patterns, and one-time passwords.

virus - A computer program, possibly malicious, that reproduces itself by embedding itself in an application program or its data files. Whenever the infected file is used, the virus searches for other files to infect and copies itself into those files.

wardialer - A computer program that finds the telephone numbers of all computers connected to phone lines within a given range of telephone numbers. The program uses a modem to call all telephone numbers within the range in order to detect the modem answer tone that indicates a computer is connected to the phone line.

web of trust - A set of certificates signed by individuals who vouch for the certificates' authenticity. People can authenticate chains of certificates within the web of trust.

worm - A computer program, possibly malicious, that uses a computer network to copy itself from one host or victim to the next.

INDEX

A

Abstract Syntax Notation #1 (ASN.1), 410, 411

Access control, 3–6
  authentication versus, 5, 412
  design patterns and, 104
  limitations of, 5–6, 135–136
  mechanisms, 3, 4, 120
    disabling through operating system substitution, 109, 130, 131
    network-based, 136
    policies, 6, 76, 79
      public key certificates and, 412
    smart cards and, 438–442
      using biometrics, 439–442
      using PINs, 438–439, 442
    user-based, 135–136

ActivCard, 268–269, 271, 286, 288

Active Directory facility, 363

Active tokens, 256, 258–261. *See also* Tokens

Addresses. *See also* Authentication, by address; Telephone numbers
  arbitrary, 223
  hard wired, 224–225
  Internet protocol, 232–234
  LAN, using 802 standard, 232
  network enforced, 225, 230–234
  "soft," 233

Adelman, Len, 373. *See also* RSA public key algorithm

Administrative requirements. *See* Authentication systems, administrative requirements

Administrators, 74, 76–78, 80, 117
  access to user encryption keys, 151

access to user passwords, 20
passwords for, guidelines, 167, 175–178
physical security systems, 106, 107
system abuse by, 77, 100, 101, 279–280, 283, 284, 310

Advanced Encryption Standard (AES), 131, 144, 146, 242, 293

AFIS (automated fingerprint identification system), 196, 197, 219

Air Force, 16, 230

Alexander, Christopher, 103

Algorithms
  Blowfish, 144, 146
  CAST, 144, 146
  ciphers
    block, 143–144, 329, 330–331, 346
    stream, 143, 144–145, 329, 334–335, 329–330, 345
  Diffie-Hellman, 381, 427, 431, 438
  homegrown encryption, vulnerability of, 145, 153, 154
  International Data Encryption Algorithm (IDEA), 144, 146, 148
  open review of encryption, 146, 154
  RSA public key, 373–380. *See also* RSA public key algorithm
  Secure Hash Algorithm (SHA), 241, 385

AltaVista, 52

American Bankers Association, 288

Analysis
  of costs and benefits, 8–9, 31, 218
  of risk, 8–9, 31

Andressen, Mark, 389

ANSI X9.9 standard, 242, 288–289, 292
  trial-and-error attack on, 293, 311, 312

ANSI X9.17 standard, 341, 344

Arbitrary addresses, 224

X